Other People's Kids

The Search Institute Series on Developmentally Attentive Community and Society

Series Editor
Peter L. Benson, *Search Institute, Minneapolis, Minnesota*

Series Mission
To advance interdisciplinary inquiry into the individual, system, community, and societal dynamics that promote developmental strengths; and the processes for mobilizing these dynamics on behalf of children and adolescents.

DEVELOPMENTAL ASSETS AND ASSET-BUILDING COMMUNITIES:
Implications for Research, Policy, and Practice
Edited by Richard M. Lerner and Peter L. Benson

OTHER PEOPLE'S KIDS:
Social Expectations and American Adults' Involvement with Children and Adolescents
Peter C. Scales with Peter L. Benson, Marc Mannes, Nicole R. Hintz, Eugene C. Roehlkepartain, and Theresa K. Sullivan

A Continuation Order Plan is available for this series. A continuation order will bring delivery of each new volume immediately upon publication. Volumes are billed only upon actual shipment. For further information please contact the publisher.

Other People's Kids

Social Expectations and American Adults'
Involvement with Children and
Adolescents

Peter C. Scales
Search Institute
Minneapolis, Minnesota

with

Peter L. Benson, Marc Mannes, Nicole R. Hintz,
Eugene C. Roehlkepartain, and Theresa K. Sullivan

Kluwer Academic / Plenum Publishers
New York, Boston, Dordrecht, London, Moscow

Library of Congress Cataloging-in-Publication Data

Scales, Peter, 1949–
    Other people's kids : social expectations and American adults' involvement with children and
adolescents/by Peter C. Scales ; with Peter L. Benson . . . [et al].
        p.   cm. — (The Search Institute series on developementally attentive community and society)
    Includes bibliographical references and index.
    ISBN 0-306-47734-3
    1. Children and adults—United States.   2. Child development—United States.
    3. Social change—United States   4. Parenting—United States.   I. Title   II. Series
HQ792.U5S33   2003
305.23–dc21
                                                                                              2003044644

ISBN   0-306-47734-3

© 2003 Kluwer Academic/Plenum Publishers, New York
233 Spring Street, New York, New York 10013

http://www.wkap.nl

10 9 8 7 6 5 4 3 2 1

Permission for books published in Europe: permissions@wkap.nl
Permission for books published in the United States of America: permissions@wkap.com

Printed on acid-free paper.

Printed in the United States of America.

This book is dedicated to my wife, Martha, who nurtures and guides other people's kids every day, and to the young people outside our own family who have enriched our lives so much over the past few years.

Foreword

Most of us know of instances in which a caring relationship with a nonparent adult has positively influenced the course and quality of a young person's life. Such stories converge with the research literature, which suggests that supportive older adults—such as teachers, neighbors, extended family members, and volunteers—can attenuate risk and contribute to positive developmental outcomes among children and adolescents. Unfortunately, many youth do not readily find supportive adults beyond the boundaries of their household. Shifting marital and maternal employment patterns, overcrowded schools, and a loss of community cohesiveness have dramatically reduced the availability of caring adults and restricted opportunities for informal intergenerational contact.

The social fabric is stretched particularly thin in urban centers, which are largely bereft of the middle-class adults who once served as respected authority figures in the community. Sadly, far fewer American adults who remain in cities, and even those who have left, are willing or able to offer support and guidance to youth outside their families. An influential national survey of adult–youth relationships, conducted through Search Institute and Lutheran Brotherhood, revealed that, although many adults recognize the importance of close, one-to-one relationships with youth, far fewer are willing to act to develop such relationships. The problem they face is a lack of time and, perhaps, will. According to the poll, 75% of adults reported that it is "very important" to have meaningful conversations with children and youth, whereas fewer than 35% reported actually having such conversations.

Peter Scales's stimulating book, *Other People's Kids: Social Expectations and American Adults' Involvement with Children and Adolescents* delves into the very basis of this disconnection between values and action. At the heart of Scales's analysis is the national survey of adult–youth relationships, the findings of which reveal the roles that adults could take in relating to, supporting, and guiding young people. Yet, this book goes beyond the survey to illuminate the psychological basis for the relative neglect of our nation's youth and map out a thoughtful means for redressing it. As Scales suggests, the diminishing availability of caring adults is caused not only by changing communities, schools, and families, but also by a deep cultural ambivalence that has emerged regarding what it means to connect with other people's kids. In Western societies, parents have come to be considered solely responsible for their children, so the involvement of other adults is often met with suspicion and discomfort. Moreover, words like *clergy, uncles,* and even *neighbors* no longer simply conjure images of front-porch warmth and goodwill; they also evoke confusion and concerns about boundaries, trust, and safety.

The norms that are imparted to children regarding adults outside the family reflect this ambivalence. Crime and other dangerous conditions have led many parents to sequester their children in their homes, greatly reducing opportunities for contact with caring adults in the community. Additionally, media coverage of high-profile kidnappings and sexual abuse scandals have become frequent triggers of parental anxiety and warnings about strangers. Such admonishments, however, are intermixed with parental encouragement to connect with other adults who, by virtue of their position and/or familiarity, have gained parental sanction.

Yet, even sanctioned adults are finding it increasingly difficult to engage with the children of others. Close and confiding student–teacher relationships, for example, are rapidly becoming more the exception than the rule. The same teachers who, in the past, provided more personalized support are being saddled with additional obligations. A growing emphasis on high-stakes standardized testing has given rise to dense curricular demands that have constrained teachers and left little room for the sorts of conversations and activities that typically draw them closer to their students. Sadly, many adults who were initially attracted to teaching and youth service professions out of the desire to establish meaningful connections with children and adolescents have become increasingly disillusioned by the structural and cultural impediments to such ties. Scales points to findings that suggest that most adults are reluctant to give *any* advice to children or adolescents out of fear of negative repercussions from parents.

In essence, the high value modern society attaches to family privacy and the growing fears of child abuse accusation have begun to extinguish our basic human desire to be helpful to children and youth. Scales points to other cultural assumptions that have fed this trend, including a focus on youth deviance as opposed to strengths and normal development; a youth culture that distances and devalues adults; and an overall absence of social pressure to play a caring role. As a result, he argues, "Americans are neither sure of the importance of adults outside the family to children's and youth's development, nor even debating how best that influence might be exerted to promote positive, optimal development for all children and youth."

This book opens that debate, and in doing so offers the most unique and helpful explanation and critique to date of the norms that have conspired to make *really caring* about another person's child increasingly difficult. The reader is left with a better understanding not only of how our attitudes toward other people's kids have been shaped, but also of how they can change. In essence, if our current neglectful standards of behavior are influenced and sanctioned by cultural norms, then the solution lies in changing those norms. Rather than anticipating negative consequences, Scales argues, we must determine how people can come to feel "collective permission and social expectations" to engage with youth in ways that promote positive developmental outcomes. The challenge, as he sees it, is to nudge our cultural expectations and incentives toward "reasonable responsibility" for getting involved with other people's children without offending parents or other caregivers. I fully agree with this analysis and believe that if norms of reasonable responsibility were adopted in our country, more young people would have caring adults in their lives, leading in turn to the enrichment of adult lives and the positive development of all citizens.

Jean E. Rhodes
University of Massachusetts, Boston

Acknowledgments

This book is the product of three years' intensive work by a team of social scientists and advocates for young people. This study on which the book is based was conducted through a partnership between Search Institute and Lutheran Brotherhood. The national poll of American adults was conducted for Search Institute and Lutheran Brotherhood (now Thrivent Financial for Lutherans) by the Gallup Organization, under the capable leadership of Dr. Harry Cotugno.

Many individuals contributed to the development of this study.

Members of the Steering Committee: Rebecca Grothe, convener, formerly with Search Institute; Ellen Albee, Lutheran Brotherhood; Peter L. Benson, Ph.D., Search Institute; Pam Desnick, Lutheran Brotherhood; Kathleen Janasz, Shandwick International; David Rustad, APR, Lutheran Brotherhood; Peter C. Scales, Ph.D., Search Institute; Terri Swanson, Search Institute.

Members of the Research Subcommittee: Peter C. Scales, Ph.D., chair, Search Institute; Peter L. Benson, Ph.D., Search Institute; Nancy Garrett, Ph.D., formerly with Lutheran Brotherhood; Rebecca Grothe, formerly with Search Institute; Nicole R. Hintz, Search Institute; Marc Mannes, Ph.D., Search Institute; Janet Mickish, Ph.D., formerly with Search Institute; Kevin Olsen, Lutheran Brotherhood; Terri Sullivan, formerly with Search Institute.

Members of the Communications Subcommittee: David Rustad, chair, Lutheran Brotherhood; Rebecca Grothe, formerly with Search Institute; Kathleen Janasz, Shandwick International; Barbara Stemson, Lutheran Brotherhood; Terri Swanson, Search Institute.

All of these people helped shape the study, as did consultation with Dr. William Damon, Stanford University, and Dr. Francis Ianni, professor emeritus at Columbia University. The thoughtful commentary of those two consultants helped us redesign the study and create a better frame of reference for interpreting the findings.

I am especially indebted to Nicole Hintz and Karen Bartig of Search Institute. As senior research assistant, Nicole skillfully shepherded the work of all the committees and kept the enterprise moving smoothly forward. Every step of the way, she helped shape the study and the publications that came from it. Karen kept a sharp eye on all the details and kept her sense of humor intact as she conducted the innumerable analyses required, including the numerous recodings and reanalyses of data we conducted to confirm initial results.

My deep appreciation also goes to Brent Bolstrom and Sandy Longfellow, research assistant and information resource center director, respectively, at Search Institute. They enabled me to acquire the numerous articles and books needed to construct the scholarly context within which the study and its findings could be meaningfully presented.

All the coauthors made important contributions. Their ongoing immersion in the study and its findings was reflected in countless insightful suggestions that materially strengthened this book. To a person, they judged their contributions to be modest, but the book would not exist without them. I can see their contributions on every page, whether in their exact words or implicitly in the way certain passages were revised. The imprint of those colleagues may be subtle, but it is pervasive, reflecting a true team effort.

A special thanks goes to two external reviewers, Steve Farkas of Public Agenda, and Dr. Dale Blyth of the 4-H Center for Youth Development, University of Minnesota. They pored over the manuscript with relentless vigor, raising numerous thorny questions, making many suggestions for improvement, and offering articulate and candid critiques that prompted extensive revisions. Their involvement significantly elevated the quality of the book, and I am grateful to them.

Finally, my thanks go to Gene Roehlkepartain and Mary Byers for their editorial leadership. They kept the manuscript development process on track, expertly managed the review process, and made both large and small suggestions for tightening and clarifying the manuscript.

The errors and weaknesses that remain in this book are mine, whether they are ones of omission or commission. The strengths and assets of this book belong to all of us, and I am grateful for having had the chance to work with such exceptional colleagues.

Peter C. Scales, Ph.D.
Manchester, Missouri

Contents

Tables, Figures, and Sidebars

Tables

Figures

Sidebars

Other People's Kids

Introduction

Public opinion polls reveal that American adults are concerned about young people. They are concerned about what the media depict, with varying degrees of accuracy, as high rates of problems among the young, ranging from school failure to alcohol and other drug abuse to adolescent pregnancy. Adults are concerned with what they see as a lack of positive values among young people, including too little respect shown to adults and too little commitment to hard work. And they think that preparing young people for the future should be the nation's number one priority.

But whom do adults hold responsible for reducing problems among young people and preparing them for the future? For the most part, they hold parents and professionals responsible. In this book, we propose a different, broader option: Young people need all adults to recognize their own capacity for and role in nurturing the next generation, and then to take action to connect with young people in meaningful, sustained relationships.

Adults need to define a reasonable responsibility for themselves to help care for other people's kids. This responsibility would lie somewhere between the primary role of parents and the current standard, which is hardly any responsibility at all except for adults who are temporarily taking care of young people in formal settings such as schools and child-care centers.

Part of defining this reasonable responsibility is to effect a sea change in social expectations or norms regarding adult engagement with young people. As we detail in this book, today there is little social reward for getting involved with other people's kids, and little social consequence for failing to do so. It simply is not normal for most adults to be deeply engaged with young people outside their own families.

In this book, we discuss why that is the case, and based on the findings from a nationally representative study of U.S. adults we conducted in 2000, we suggest what might be done to change these norms. We begin by describing why deeper relationships with multiple adults are important to all young people, not only those who are at risk of or already experiencing problems. We explore the differing roles of parents and other adults, and show how relationships with adults outside the family can be a key source of "developmental assets" or building blocks of success for young people (Search Institute's framework of developmental assets is discussed more fully in Chapter 1). We also discuss studies that show most young people are not experiencing those kinds of assets that caring relationships with adults outside the family can provide for them. We use the framework of developmental assets to introduce 19 positive actions adults can take to promote healthy development in children and youth. Examining the degree to which adults think those actions are important, and the extent to which the people adults know actually do these things with young people, was at the heart of our national study.

1

We provide an extensive look at the concept of social norms or expectations as unwritten rules for people's behavior, and examine how cultural forces in the United States have worked together to define a norm of nonengagement with other people's kids. We show how the American tradition of ambivalence between tolerance and responsibility for others, negative media depictions of the young, a focus on the negative even in research on children and youth, and other influences render it unusual for most adults to play an active positive role in the nurture of children and youth outside their families.

In later chapters, we present the results of our national study of adults. We draw out two themes in the data that reflect that great American ambivalence. We discuss the considerable consensus adults have regarding the actions that are most important for all adults, not just parents, to take in relationship with young people. But we also elaborate on the significant variation in how adults view their responsibility as a function of gender, race/ethnicity, parental status, and other variables. We also note the pervasive discrepancy between what most adults believe is important and what they see most adults actually doing when it comes to engagement with young people. Finally, we consider how various personal and collective strategies may help individuals, neighborhoods, and communities promote a new norm of adult engagement with the young.

Our hope is to conduct similar nationally representative polls over the first decade of the 21st century. Our 2000 data underscore how important most adults think it is for all of us to share in nurturing the coming generations, and yet how far the great majority of adults are from acting on that conviction. Future national studies will help demonstrate whether our caring about other people's kids remains largely rhetorical or whether we as a nation will have succeeded in mobilizing the vast positive developmental influence that resides in each one of us to make a difference in young people's lives.

1 Adults' *Real* Relationships with Young People

Most young people are not bereft of positive interactions with their parents and other adults in the extended family, or with adults such as teachers, after-school program leaders, and youth workers in religious congregations. Obviously, all these adults, to varying degrees, can and do play positive roles in young people's development, and playing these roles is the job of these adults. It is clearly codified in law, regulations, and social expectations that families and adults in the formal institutions that kids frequent—schools, youth programs, congregations—have a measure, usually a high degree, of responsibility for the well-being of those young people in their charge. More recently, the role of one-on-one mentor to a young person has emerged as a possibility for many adults. As welcome as those mentoring relationships are, however, they too are usually formal ones, offered within the structure of a program or organization. They also tend to be provided mainly to young people perceived as being at risk, not those basically doing "OK" but who could benefit from more sustained adult relationships.

But what about neighbors or the other adults young people meet in informal settings in the community, who do not have any legally or institutionally sanctioned responsibility for them? What is their role, if any, in the nurturance and guiding of young people? In exploring this question here, we discuss what a national study of American adults suggests about how Americans view their responsibility for other people's kids, and what can be done to increase the degree to which it becomes normal to become engaged with young people outside one's own family.

At heart, this book is about what all adults can do to support the positive development of young people. Child and youth development occurs "in" several major settings or contexts: socializing systems such as schools, families, and religious institutions; youth programs, child-care centers or youth organizations such as the YMCA or YWCA, or Boys and Girls Clubs (most often the focus of

3

those who work with youth); and the "community" at large (Benson & Saito, 2001). Community is the most difficult to define and includes influences ranging from neighbors to law enforcement, the media, and everything in between. It can be conceptualized as both the terrain where all the other developmental contexts intersect, and as the place where "social norms, resources, relationships, and informal settings . . . can dramatically inform human development, both directly and indirectly" (p. 127).

A "developmentally attentive community" marshals a wide range of aware-nesses, capacities, and energies to build developmental strengths among young people. Residents (adults, youth, and children), as well as community "sectors" (families, congregations, neighborhoods, schools, youth organizations, places of work), work together, supported by policy, financial resources, and "social norms that promote adult engagement with the young," to reach three targets: (1) to help young people experience many developmental strengths, (2) to help them experience such assets across multiple life contexts (family, school, peers, community), and (3) to ensure that all young people are included, not only those judged to be "at risk" (Benson, Scales, & Mannes, 2003).

Small and Supple (2001), in their treatment of communities as systems, presented a useful scheme for thinking about the multiple issues we discuss in this book, including developmental attentiveness, the socialization roles of adults in general, and social norms. They viewed "first order" community effects as the direct results of the aggregate of those settings and institutions in which individuals live. Such effects as they apply to child and youth development include parental socialization, peer influences, and the role modeling of other adults. "Second order" community effects occur from the interaction or linkages among the settings in children's worlds. For example, consistency of values, boundaries, and expectations across family, school, peer group, and community, or young people experiencing the influence of other caring adults in multiple settings, are examples of second-order community effects. Finally, "third order" community effects are not merely the sum of the first and the second order, although they grow out of them. Third-order effects represent the whole that is more than the sum of its parts. Examples of third-order effects include the degree of closeness felt among community members (social trust); their ability to act collectively to achieve goals (collective efficacy); and the presence of values, expectations, and norms that most people in the community are perceived to share (social norms) and that are "at the core of what the community represents and what it desires for its members" (p.171). In a developmentally attentive community, all young people experience the positive benefits of all three kinds of community effects.

In this book, we suggest that at none of those three levels is the poten-tial positive contribution of informal community settings to child and youth development being tapped in most American communities. In other words, beyond the influence of parents and other adults in their own families, most young people do not enjoy the kinds of supportive, caring relationships with other adults—first-order community effects—that could significantly improve their well-being. Nor are there enough linkages among the adults in young people's lives (second-order effects) or sufficient collective social expectations (third-order effects) to make it normal for adults to have deeper relationships with young people and connections with the other adults in young people's lives.

In short, millions of adults could do more for America's kids. For some, undoubtedly, lack of time is the culprit. But for the majority of Americans, limited time may be more of a perceived than a real obstacle. After all, time is, as Farkas and Johnson (1997) described it, an "elastic" concept in that people who want to find the time for their interests, including being involved with kids, will find it, no matter how busy they are. For millions of Americans, other factors than time keep them from getting to know young people more, and therefore keep them from creating those first-, second-, and third-order effects that reflect an attentive community in which children and youth can develop in positive and healthy ways.

If it is not really a matter of time, is it because adults don't care about other people's kids? Data we cite later showing the high priority Americans place on preparing young people for the future and the consistent ranking of education as a top priority argue against such a cynical view. So, what other factors keep adults from being more engaged with young people outside their own families?

Our sense is that a host of underlying cultural assumptions and active social norms are at work that collectively inhibit even caring adults from helping nurture and guide other people's children and adolescents. For example, adults might consider some ways they could relate to kids more important than others, and therefore more acceptable to do. An example might be feeling it more acceptable to praise someone else's child for doing well at school than to admonish him or her for doing poorly. Some adults might be in social networks in which connecting with young people is expected, that is, the norm, and so feel more social support for doing so. Many more adults might feel that it is simply not their place to get involved with other people's kids. In other words, superordinate third-order community effects in the form of norms discouraging adult engagement with kids could depress the possibility of second- and first-order effects that more directly influence positive child and youth development.

In this book, we describe the light that existing research seems to shed on those issues. We also describe a national study of American adults we conducted that shows how Americans think all adults could contribute to the socialization of young people and the kinds of social support and expectations they currently experience for such engagement. Broadly, the study was an examination of the role of social expectations or norms in influencing whether and how adults get involved with other people's children in positive relationships in informal, everyday settings. We examined beliefs and actions, and the gap between them, regarding obligations, responsibilities, and expectations for nurturing and guiding children and adolescents. Lutheran Brotherhood (now Thrivent Financial for Lutherans), a member-owned financial services corporation for Lutherans, and Search Institute, a private, not-for-profit organization that since 1958 has conducted practical research to benefit children and adolescents, partnered in January 1999 to conceptualize the study, and later contracted with the Gallup

Organization to conduct the national survey (details on the survey instrument and study methodology are found in Chapter 5 and Appendix A).

We wanted to get beneath the surface of attitudes to better understand what has been called the underlying "mental operating software" (conversation with David Walsh, National Institute on Media and the Family, January 3, 2000)—the unwritten rules of behavior that people are often unaware of, but that powerfully shape how adults think about and relate with young people. For many adults, these social norms may play the same role in structuring relationships with young people as the "unquestioned presuppositions" identified by Kuhn (1962) do in structuring scientific understandings. For example, all of the following relatively unquestioned presuppositions have significantly affected people's behavior at the time they were current: The sun revolves around the earth; only white men can own property and vote; children are just miniature adults and so can be treated as adults; the biological family is always the best place in which to grow up.

Norms about adult interaction with children and youth might well be operating in contemporary society as unquestioned presuppositions that likely shape those relationships. Such norms today might include (1) only parents have the right to tell their children what to do, as long as they're not breaking a law (e.g., engaging in child abuse or neglect), and (2) in this society we mind our own business. Such beliefs may seem benign enough to most Americans, rooted as they are in democratic and capitalist notions of privacy, freedom, and individualism. Their effect, however, may be to allow those positive values of tolerance and respect for the privacy of others (which promote parental responsibility in raising children) to slide almost imperceptibly into relative indifference to ensuring the well-being of the next generation.

If Kids Are Basically OK, Why Do They Need More Adults?

Why should other adults be involved with young people, anyway? Despite the drumbeat of negative press about young people, the data show that most young people are not failing at school, not depressed or suicidal, not involved in adolescent pregnancies, not abusing alcohol or other drugs, and not engaging in violent or other criminal behavior (Scales, 2001). If this is so, then can't we conclude that most young people are getting the adult guidance they need from their parents, extended family, and the other adults who have formal roles in their lives?

For many children and youth, of course, the answer is yes. They enjoy an abundance of formal and informal adult caring, support, boundary setting, role modeling, and positive influence. Their parents may be doing a better job than the majority of adults in public opinion surveys give them credit for. Since primary caregivers are clearly the most important resources in a child's life, especially in the early years, that may be sufficient for many young people to do "OK." In addition, research has consistently shown that a caring and supportive relationship with even one adult—not necessarily a parent—makes a considerable contribution to a young person's well-being and resilience (see review in Scales & Leffert, 1999). For many young people, deep and meaningful relationships with a *multitude* of adults may not be necessary for adequate functioning. For those children, additional caring and positive relationships with other adults certainly can't hurt them, but they also don't seem necessary, to make up for deficits.

But there is still a cost to individuals and society for adults' lack of engagement with young people. That cost is reflected most obviously in the numerous studies that show how such relationships can help prevent problems such as substance abuse among the young, as well as promote thriving, such as success at school (reviewed in Scales & Leffert, 1999). For many young people, it is precisely that positive, compensatory influence that relationships with other adults seem to provide (see review in Scales & Gibbons, 1996). For example, it has been estimated that roughly 25% of adolescents experience serious problems such as school failure, delinquency, substance abuse, or adolescent pregnancy (Dryfoos, 1990). Similarly, a recent Census Bureau study showed that 46% of school-age children ages 5–17 have at least one of seven other kinds of individual or familial risk "conditions," such as disability, grade retention in school, either or both parents absent from the household, or low family income. That study found that 18% of U.S. children have more than one such risk factor (Kominski, Jamieson, & Martinez, 2001). For those young people, having adults other than immediate and/or extended family involved in their lives may provide extra opportunities for support and mentoring, as well as a consistency of socialization, that together are necessary for them to be resilient in the face of those challenges. Adults who care about and get engaged with those kids may help them function at a basic acceptable level of developmental adequacy.

But it is not just young people who already are experiencing risks who can benefit from more adult engagement. Young people's developmental pathways are not always predictable: Children and youth who are doing "OK" one day may the next day experience adversities or tragedies that at least temporarily knock them off a positive trajectory, ranging from purely personal crises (such as unhappiness over their appearance, rejection by a friend, or failure to achieve a desired goal) to deeply collective moments of uncertainty and transformation they share with peers and adults (such as reactions to faraway school shootings or to national events such as the September 2001 terrorist attacks). In fact, setbacks are common for most young people (Eccles, Roeser, Wigfield, & Freedman-Doan, 1999). Deeper engagement with all young people by a broader range of adults may help to buffer such influences and promote developmental well-being.

Such broader assumption of reasonable informal involvement on the part of more adults represents additional support to the parents, teachers, youth workers, and counselors who are formally charged with responsibility for young people. They may be more effective in their formal caregiving roles when the broader social context calls for all adults to be greater resources to all young people. Such reasoning is lent support by a study of parenting networks of mothers of 1st through 4th graders in ethnically diverse Boston neighborhoods (Marshall, Noonan, McCartney, Marx, & Keefe, 2001). In that study, it was reported that parents' social networks indirectly benefit children, through improving parenting. Specifically, the more emotional support they got from their networks, and the more their social networks involved nonrelatives, the warmer and more responsive parents were, the more cognitive stimulation they offered their children, and the more effective parents felt they were as parents. Their children, in turn, were more socially competent, mentally healthy, and adjusted to school than the children of parents whose social networks offered less support and/or comprised mainly family members.

The cost that limited adult engagement brings in potentially higher levels of risk behaviors may be felt especially by particularly vulnerable children and youth. There is still another cost of limited engagement, or of engagement mostly with "at-risk" young people, and that is a lost opportunity for thriving that is borne by all young people and by society. Low levels of risk behaviors and social problems among children or youth may signify adequate functioning, but they do not imply optimal levels of functioning. There is no exact answer to the question of how much of young people's full potential is lost to them and to society because they have only limited relationships with most adults in their lives. But the lost opportunities for growth can be significant. Yes, most young people are doing "OK," but is that what we want to or are willing to settle for? How much better might they be doing if they had more adults in their lives who cared for and about them, and who guided and nurtured them in the ways we examined for this study?

The limited engagement with other people's kids that adults reported in the current national study, and the limited engagement youth themselves report in the studies we later cite, probably are not as consequential for developmental adequacy as they are for optimal development or thriving. For example, Masten (2001) has argued that the "great surprise" of resilience research is how ordinary an occurrence resilience is, reflecting the robustnesss of human development (p. 227). So long as major adaptational systems such as intellectual functioning and parenting are not impaired, even severe adversity does not seem to greatly disrupt normal development.

So, even under great stress and challenge, many and perhaps most kids probably will do "OK," and even be described as "competent," regardless of whether they have meaningful relationships with adults outside their own families. And yet, there is a critical difference between adequate development, which is usually what is meant by the term "competence" when it is applied to children and adolescents, and optimal development to the fullest of one's capabilities, reflected in the term "thriving." A young person who stays in school and achieves at average levels, stays off drugs, is not chronically depressed, and doesn't get involved in an adolescent pregnancy would likely be described in the developmental jargon as "competent." But is that young person fully developing his or her talents and becoming prepared to be a socially responsible and contributing citizen, a productive worker, a loving partner in a long-term relationship, a nurturing parent, a discriminating consumer, an ethical human being with a sense of purpose? To raise the question is to answer it. Most of us hope that young people are far more than adequate. Relationships with adults outside their own families may especially help promote young people's optimal development.

A final and perhaps less noticeable cost of limited adult engagement is the price paid in lost opportunity to help rebuild, through those intergenerational relationships, a sense of community that, according to social commentators and social scientists alike, has faded and even disappeared from many American neighborhoods, towns, and cities. For example, Robert Putnam (2000) presented a wealth of large- and small-scale data to show that the past several decades have seen a "striking diminution of regular contacts with our friends and neighbors." He concluded that "we spend less time in conversation over meals, we exchange visits less often, we engage less often in leisure activities that encourage casual social interaction. We spend more time watching . . . and less time doing. We know our neighbors less well, and we see our old friends less often" (p. 115). In short, Americans are less engaged in civic activities than in previous generations, but we are also less engaged in connecting informally. Parents in a given neighborhood may be adequately taking care of their own children, but if they live in a neighborhood or community that Putnam describes as common, in which most adults are not engaged with each other, then it is hardly likely that adults are deeply engaged with youth outside their own families.

How can we describe a neighborhood in which parents only take care of their own kids but don't engage much with other people's kids, and in which adults without children don't connect much with young people? It may be a setting where social isolation and independence from one another, much of it guarded in the name of tolerance and privacy, can all too readily grow, and where nurturance and caring can slowly wither, eroding the bonds that all too tenuously connect us in community. Putnam amassed considerable evidence that such circumstances can lead to greater levels of mistrust and a lessened ability of residents to work together to solve common problems and advance the welfare of all. In this way, when adults don't attend much to other people's kids, they may be putting their entire neighborhood or community "at risk."

Adults' Contributions to Young People's Social Capital

"Connectedness" with caring others is a fundamental experience in that it helps individuals meet "basic requirements of human development" (Barber & Olsen, 1997, p. 228). Connectedness experienced at an individual level is a by-product of the broader ecological concept of social capital, which refers to resources inherent in the relationships among people that help promote desired social outcomes (Parcel & Dufur, 2001). In Small and Supple's framework outlined above (2001), social capital is seen as an aggregate second-order community effect arising out of the connections across family, school, peers, and community. But social capital can just as readily be seen as domain specific, more plentiful in some settings than in others. Children's social capital in the family, for example, reflects the time and care that parents put into raising their children, from promoting values to monitoring children's behavior and teaching them social conventions and skills. Similarly, children's social capital in the community reflects the number and quality of nurturing, guiding relationships with adults such as teachers, neighbors, members of religious congregations, and youth workers, as well as the relationships children's parents have with those resources. It also includes the opportunities young people are provided to develop effective skills and self-perceptions.

Putnam (2000) constructed the Social Capital Index (SCI) to compare states on 14 measures ranging from membership in local organizations to the extent of volunteerism, engagement in public affairs, informal socializing, and the presence or absence of social trust. He found that states high on the SCI strongly tended to be states where children did better on measures of risk that comprise the Kids Count Index, including school dropout, teen parenthood, and juvenile crime rates. The reported correlation coefficient of .80 between the two indexes is unusually high in social science research. Social capital was especially important in helping reduce states' rates of babies with low birth weights, school dropout, and adolescent parenthood. Additionally, the informal kinds of social capital measured, such as social trust and informal socializing, were more strongly related to young people's academic achievement than the formal types, such as club membership or participation in civic affairs.

Parcel and Dufur (2001) studied more than 1,800 young people ages 14–21 from the National Longitudinal Survey of Youth, and investigated how family and school social capital may affect children's behavior. Using the Behavior Problems Index (BPI) as the dependent variable, they reported that family social capital (such as the number of children's friends parents know by name, how often they know children's whereabouts, or the frequency the child attends church) explained more of the variance in the BPI than did school social capital (such as whether teachers are seen as caring for the student, and parental involvement in school). However, children with high levels of both family and school social capital had the fewest behavioral problems. Moreover, the interaction effects of family and school social capital operating together significantly increased the explained variance in behavior problems. These results led the researchers to conclude that *combinations* of investment in the child from home and school are important for children's social adjustment.

Bowen and Richman (1997) linked the concept of social capital to the ecological model of development articulated by Bronfenbrenner (1979), proposing that a key attribute of social capital was the connection of parents with other adults in the child's world. Through those relationships, children may experience greater consistency of socialization across settings. Bowen and Richman identified eight sources of social capital: neighborhood, neighbor–parent connections, school, family, parent, parent–friend connections, parent–school connections, and receiving help from others. They analyzed more than 600 students from the Communities in Schools program (students "at risk" of school failure), compared with a national middle and high school sample of about 2,000 students. The researchers found that for students in both samples, increases in social capital were associated with increases in school performance and social adjustment. Moreover, as social capital increased, the number of risk factors in students' lives, in both samples, decreased significantly. Finally, Bowen and Richman reported that only about 25% of each sample had 12–15 of the 15 social capital indicators, suggesting that all students, not only those at educational disadvantage, are "suffering from depleted social relationships" (p. 14).

The potential impact of social capital is further illustrated by a study of 160 African American high school students living in a low-income, inner-city environment (Stevenson, 1998). Social capital was measured by asking the adolescents such questions as whether neighbors watched what they or other children in the neighborhood did, or whether adult neighbors kept up with the their accomplishments and activities at school. Higher levels of social capital were associated with lower levels of depression. The ecological nature of the connection among these variables is underscored by the finding that the association of higher social capital with lower depression was especially strong for youth reporting low kinship social support. That is, when family support was lower, experiencing caring neighborhood relationships was especially protective against depression. The power of neighborhood social capital to limit depression also was especially pronounced for girls and for young people living in particularly high risk neighborhoods (where "negative or unsafe activities" at least "sometimes" happened on their block).

As suggested already, it is not only connection of adults with young people that can be a positive influence in young people's lives. The connections among the adults in children's worlds can be as important in affecting children's development through their effects on ecological health, as the connections between adults and young people can profoundly affect development through more proximal effects. These connections are promoted in part by the presence of social norms or expectations about how people should behave, a concept we focus on in this book.

For example, in more than 300 Chicago neighborhoods, Sampson, Raudenbush, and Earls (1997) studied the relationship of "collective efficacy" to violence. They hypothesized that the observed relationship between violence and neighborhood economic disadvantage should be explained by differences among neighborhoods in the degree to which residents had higher levels of mutual trust and a willingness to intervene for the common good. That is, neighborhoods in which there were stronger norms or expectations that individuals act to protect shared values and exercise informal social control should be safer, regardless of their poverty levels.

Their findings were striking. Collective efficacy was strongly and negatively associated not only with people's perceptions of neighborhood violence but also with their self-reports of victimization, and with actual homicides. The researchers estimated that a two-standard-deviation increase in collective efficacy was associated with a 30% reduction in the victimization rate and a 40% reduction in the expected homicide rate. Moreover, although collective efficacy was, as expected, positively correlated with friendship and kinship ties, participation in organizations, and the number of neighborhood services available, collective efficacy remained "by far" the largest predictor of the violent crime rate when those other factors were controlled. This suggested that variations in rates of violence were more directly explained by mutual trust and norms supporting individuals' willingness to intervene for the common good—collective efficacy—than by these other variables. In a comprehensive review of the literature, Leventhal and Brooks-Gunn (2000) also concluded that, although the research base overall does not allow firm conclusions about the pathways through which neighborhoods affect children and youth, the strongest support among three possible pathways (institutional resources, parental characteristics and support, and norms/collective efficacy) exists for the role that social norms play. In short, the more adults in the neighborhood watch out for, supervise, monitor, and support young people, the better the outcomes will be for young people.

Clearly, a developmentally attentive community, state, and nation must enable families to have fundamental supports that ensure a basic adequacy of development for their children. Jobs for parents that pay a decent living wage, affordable, accessible, high-quality child care for those who want it, health-care coverage for all family members, affordable and safe housing, challenging and inviting schools, safe and affordable places for young people to live and play—all these are among the sources of social capital families, children, and youth need, and that most Americans across political persuasions would consider essential, even though we often disagree vigorously about how to bring all this about.

We are not suggesting that an expression of social capital on which we focus here, engagement of adults with kids outside their families, can make up for a serious societal abnegation of responsibility in these fundamental areas of ensuring opportunity and family support. Adults becoming more deeply connected with young people is no substitute for compassionate government that invests in the health of its physical infrastructure, its economy, and the well-being of all its residents. But for all the reasons we have noted above, the engagement of kids with adults outside their families—and the connection of adults to each other as they share the responsibility for such nurturing and guidance—helps strengthen and nourish young people, adults, and communities well beyond their "basic" levels of need, and likely beyond our current ability to quantify its value.

The Current Study

In this book, we expand on these themes and present data from a nationally representative study of American adults we conducted that sheds light on the unwritten social rules and expectations that shape how adults engage with children and youth outside their own families, or choose not to. We describe how social norms governing adults' relationships with young people can either promote or inhibit young people's healthy development. This aspect of social capital is reflected in young people's experience of a variety of "developmental assets" or building blocks of success that are rooted in relationships with family, peers, and other adults (Benson, 1997). We discuss the importance that American adults attribute to specific actions all adults, not just parents, should take in order to help young people build developmental assets and grow up healthy, productive, and responsible, from encouraging them to do well in school to talking about personal values with them. We look too at how much Americans think the adults they know actually are engaged with kids in these ways, how much they are surrounded by others whose connections with kids suggest that this is a normal, expected thing to do. Finally, based on previous research, and new data from our national study, we offer suggestions for making it culturally more acceptable and normal in American society for adults to get more involved with other people's children, as friends, teachers, coaches, mentors, and role models.

We have written about this research in a briefer report titled *Grading Grown-Ups: American Adults Report on their Real Relationships with Kids* (Scales, Benson, & Roehlkepartain, 2001). That title reflects the study's broad purposes to:

- Advance knowledge and awareness about the relatively unexamined territory of the influence of social norms on adults' relationships with children and youth;
- Inform community-based efforts, as well as formal program practice and service delivery, in hundreds of settings nationwide that are intentionally mobilizing to improve the developmental attentiveness of all adults to children and youth (Healthy Communities · Healthy Youth, a nationwide initiative promoted and supported by Search Institute); and
- Suggest actions that could positively change the informal ways Americans think about and act toward children and youth, not just in programs and policies, but in their everyday lives and personal relationships.

These purposes led to the articulation of two broad goals for the study:

- **Research goal**—Identify the values and norms among American adults that seem both to inhibit and to promote the active involvement of adults in the healthy development of the next generation, and with repeated polling over a number of years (similar national studies are planned for 2002 and beyond); document whether change seems to occur in those values and norms; and
- **Mobilization goal**—Disseminate information in order to affect public opinion in support of adults getting more positively engaged with children and youth; inform strategies for changing norms that inhibit this involvement and reinforcing norms that promote it.

Two implications in the title of the brief report on this study deserve mention. First, adults themselves shared their perspectives on how important and widespread they believed various adult interactions with children and youth to be. Based on those responses, we drew conclusions about the degree to which there is a normative sense among American adults of shared responsibility for the next generation's well-being. Were we in fact assigning grades based on those responses, most Americans would get a C or D, a large minority would get a B for trying, and a handful would get A's or fail. To the extent that normative sense of responsibility is lacking, young people are deprived of potentially positive influences. Even in applying a metaphor as crude as "grade," we can draw a clear conclusion: American adults have considerable room to improve their grade when it comes to nurturing all children and adolescents to be and become healthy, responsible, caring, productive, and happy.

Second, the report title referred to adults' "real" relationships with children and adolescents, implying that what was previously understood about those relationships was based on limited and perhaps distorted information. There has been great interest in recent years in understanding how American adults perceive children and adolescents, and what can and should be done to advance their health and well-being (we review much of this research later in this book). Most of these studies tend, however, to emphasize traditional influences on development, such as parents, policies, and programs. In contrast, our study specifically looked at the role *all adults* can play in socialization, not just the roles of parents, policy makers, or those who work with young people. This study was unique in asking a national sample of adults extensively and in-depth about their beliefs and what they perceive as the actions of the adults around them in getting engaged with young people. In so doing, we tried to tease out an implicit framework of social rules that might be operating, often without their awareness, to lead all adults toward or away from greater involvement with other people's children and youth. This study offered a richer and more focused glimpse into American adults' perceptions and actions: How important are specific types of involvement with kids? To what degree do adults perceive their peers to be involved with young people in these ways? And, by inference, to what extent do adults' personal attitudes and social networks provide support and even expectations for making it normal to be engaged with young people? That is, how strong are adults' personal and social motivations for engaging with young people outside their own families?

"Real" has another meaning as well. We suspected, and found (see especially, Chapters 7 and 8), that there are huge gaps between what adults say is important in relating to kids, and what they report the adults they know actually do in their everyday lives. Adults' ideal relationships with other people's children, expressed in their attitudes about what adults should do, represent one dimension of reality. But how adults *really* interact with young people—or don't—presents a very different and more troubling dimension that we examine in depth in this book.

The American Psychological Association has aptly designated the period from 2000 to 2010 as the "Decade of Behavior." Considerable research attention, of course, has been paid to how the behavior of parents and the behavior of peers affect children and adolescents, both positively and negatively. The research we have already discussed, and will subsequently, is evidence that positive relationships with unrelated adults can have significant effects on young people's developmental pathways (see also reviews in Scales & Gibbons, 1996; Scales & Leffert, 1999). Yet relatively little research has been conducted on many of those relationships, save for research on mentoring and on teacher-student interactions as a contributor to school success. Thus, a vast gold mine of information about healthy developmental influence has been left largely untapped from a scientific standpoint. Consequently, we know too little about the factors that limit such relationships among adults and other people's kids, and the factors that promote those relationships, to be able to deeply inform efforts to effect sweeping normative change across the country.

The ultimate purpose of conducting the current study and replications over the first decade of the 21st century is to add to this scientific foundation and document possible national trends in how Americans relate to and with other people's kids. In so doing, our hope is that this research might suggest personal, organizational, and community actions that collectively can encourage the seeding and maturation of new norms that promote deeper relationships among adults and young people as a central way of advancing positive human and community development.

2 Parents, Other Adults, and Responsibility for Positive Child and Youth Development

The Primary Role of Parents

As summarized by the National Research Council and the Institute of Medicine (2000), a "vast store" of research has shown that parents are "the most influential adults" in children's lives, even when children spend most of their waking hours in child care. The key feature of "parenting" is not necessarily who provides that nurture and guidance, but that those primary caregivers are "not interchangeable with others" (p. 226). They are the people who should care the most about and for the child, and who should be the most available to a child. Everyone else, no matter how loving their relationship is with a child, no matter how valuable their impact, plays a supplemental role.

Given those scientific realities, it is not surprising that the public and public policy hold parents, for the most part, responsible for the well-being of their children (Duffett, Johnson, & Farkas, 1999). In a poll of American adults by the group America's Promise, 96% said parents are the ones responsible for "helping America's youth," compared to 66% who thought teachers were responsible, 53% who said churches were, and just 26% who said community nonprofit organizations were responsible (America's Promise, 2000). Seven in 10 adults in a national *New York Times* poll said parents should be held responsible in some way if their child did something unlawful (Smiley, 2000). And the U.S. Supreme Court ruled in a case involving grandparent visitation rights that parents, not others, had a "fundamental right . . . to make decisions concerning the care, custody, and control of their children" (Walsh, 2000). Among the consequences of such norms, Sylvester (2000) observed that obtaining public funding for child care and early childhood initiatives, among other child well-being efforts, has been difficult "in the face of widespread belief that parents bear primary responsibility for children" (p. 3), especially in, but not limited to, the preschool years. She further noted that although Americans are quite concerned with young people, their concern tends to center "primarily on moral and character issues" (p. 6), which fundamentally are seen as family responsibilities.

Indeed, perceptions about parents' responsibility for their kids may be the single greatest reason other adults don't get more involved in helping other people's children develop positively. Susan Nall Bales (2001) concluded that studies reveal an emphasis in American culture on parents' rights, parent involvement, and a strong "sense of ownership" (p. 67) of practically sole responsibility for child well-being. Such a frame of reference, she argued, can make it difficult for other adults to see a meaningful role for themselves in child and adolescent development.

Given the strength of this cultural sensibility, what role do adults other than parents have for guiding and nurturing the next generation, especially adults who are not in the child's extended family? The difficulty of defining a nurturing and socializing role for other adults also derives from the observation that most parents and most young people seem to be doing OK. Yes, there are approximately one million substantiated or "indicated" (i.e., sufficient evidence to suspect but not prove) victims of child maltreatment annually (*Trends in the well-being of America's children and youth,* 1998), a shameful figure by any reckoning. But there also is ample evidence, from both carefully done studies and less scientific, popular reports, that most Americans care deeply about their *own* offspring and that most young people feel cared for by their parents.

For example, the National Commission on Children surveyed both children and parents and concluded that most children are "growing up in families that tend diligently and lovingly to their physical, social, and emotional needs" (1991, p. 28); about 60% of the parents surveyed said they wanted to spend more time with their families. In a study of nearly 100,000 6th–12th graders, Search Institute found that nearly two-thirds of the adolescents said they experienced love and support from their families (Benson, Scales, Leffert, & Roehlkepartain, 1999). And although teenagers don't confide in their fathers nearly as much as they do in their mothers, about 90% of both boys and girls say their parents really care for them and that they respect their parents (Horatio Alger Association, 1998). An unscientific survey of 84,000 6th–12th graders done for *USA Weekend* in 2000 found that half of adolescents gave their parents a grade of "A" in raising them. Eighty percent said one of their parents had expressed love for them recently, and 75% thought their parents understood the problems they faced very well or somewhat well (Damon, 2001).

The ethic of parental responsibility, and the apparent adequacy of family life for most kids, work to discourage the involvement of other, especially unrelated, adults with young people, apart from adults who have formal roles with children such as teachers, youth program workers, or clergy. As a result, most adults remain unsure about their responsibility for other people's children and about the possible benefits of their engagement for young people, other adults, and the community.

For example, a Public Agenda survey of American adults found that 43% think most parents resent unsolicited advice about their children (Duffett,

Johnson, & Farkas, 1999). Only 33% of the adults in that study said they would be "very comfortable" telling a neighbor if their child had been "getting into mischief." Only a few more (39% vs. 33%) said they would tell children to stop misbehaving.

The African proverb "It takes a village to raise a child" became common-place in the mass media in the 1990s, but a Child Welfare League of America survey found that most Americans don't intervene even when they see what they suspect is child maltreatment. Their inaction stems primarily from fear of being held accountable for any resulting negative consequences that may occur to the child or the child's parent(s) (Child Welfare League of America, 1999). This view itself grows out of the perceptions Bales noted about exclusive parent responsibility. If only parents are responsible for their children, then others get involved at their own risk.

Journalist Jeffrey Rosen described the broader U.S. social context that in-forms these concerns, not simply as one in which lawsuits are justifiably feared as they have proliferated. He concluded that our social-cultural landscape has become insidiously defined by "legalisms" that affect "even the most fleeting in-teractions" (2001, p. 46). In the absence of a social consensus on how we should behave toward each other, the "vocabulary of law and legalisms is the only shared language we have left for regulating behavior" (p. 48). Instead of bring-ing people together, however, such reliance on legalisms to inform our social norms has led to increased social division as people become more and more reluctant to risk meaningfully relating to each other outside of tightly scripted and regulated situations.

Other Adults' Roles in Young People's Positive Development

And yet, there are data that also suggest adults may at least theoretically see more of a role for themselves in nurturing and guiding the young. To begin with, Americans are sympathetic to the difficulties of being a parent: More than 70% believe it is harder to be a parent today than in earlier eras (Duffett et al., 1999). This finding does not directly suggest that people think parents could use help and support in raising kids. The increased difficulty of parenting as perceived by so many Americans suggests, however, that most adults might be receptive to considering more explicitly the role they could play in supporting parents to raise healthy, responsible, caring, and productive kids.

Second, even most parents don't feel prepared for parenthood. For example, a national study of 3,000 parents of children under age six found that two-thirds felt either unprepared or only somewhat prepared to be a parent (*What grown-ups understand about child development*, 2000). Parents' anxieties and feelings of inad-equacy may make them less willing to have their shortcomings noted, but this sense of unpreparedness could also signify that parents would welcome help-ful suggestions or resources. And on specific issues, parents overwhelmingly indicate that others have a role to play. For example, the debate regarding the supposedly controversial subject matter of sexuality education often centers on whether schools are usurping parents' rights when they teach about sexuality. But public opinion polls consistently show that 90% of parents want such instruction for their children, with the great majority also favoring the schools teaching young people about contraception (How do adults view sex ed?, 1999).

Finally, Americans also believe in general that raising successful young people should be a top priority. A national study found that the public considers the effective raising of the next generations even more important than preventing crime and creating more jobs (Farkas & Johnson, 1997). Similar results came from a more recent Gallup poll taken in the fall of 2000. In that research, twice as many Americans thought "preparing young people for the future" should be the nation's *highest* priority as thought that strongly about improving health care, keeping the economy strong, reducing crime, or protecting the environment (America's Promise, 2001). One can argue, of course, that all these issues are interrelated and therefore that such polls on "priorities" are meaningless in practical terms. But Americans still could have ranked the reduction of crime first, or a strong economy. Instead, they ranked kids first as a priority for the entire country.

These data suggest that the challenges and inadequacies many adults, including parents, note about parenting in contemporary America, and the importance of well preparing young people, create the potential for clarifying and broadening the role and contributions of other adults to child and adolescent well-being.

Young People's Developmental Assets

We have talked in general terms about the role that adults both in and outside the family can play in promoting young people's positive development, but what specifically does that positive role imply adults should do? Connell and Kubisch (2001), in a synthesis of influential youth development frameworks, noted that research suggests there is a "short list of key experiences" young people need to develop into people who can be economically self-sufficient, healthy, have good family and social relationships, and contribute to their communities: adequate nutrition, health care, and shelter; multiple supportive relationships with adults and peers; challenging and engaging activities and learning experiences; meaningful opportunities for involvement and membership; and physical and emotional safety. They call the advantageous role played by multiple positive experiences of support with the people in one's environment "perhaps the most consistent and robust finding" in research on human development (p. 191).

One of the youth development frameworks included in their synthesis was Search Institute's developmental assets. This framework structured the current study and our thinking about how adults should be engaged with kids. Through survey research with more than one million 6th–12th graders in more than 1,000 U.S. communities since the early 1990s, Search Institute has identified

40 developmental assets or building blocks of success (see Table 1) that young people need to be healthy, caring, responsible, and productive (Benson, 1997; Benson et al., 1999). (The collective Search Institute database is large and reasonably diverse, but is not a nationally representative sample of young people. The surveys largely are completed anonymously by youth in public and alternative schools that self-select to have the surveys administered. More details on the sampling and survey are found in Benson, Leffert, Scales, and Blyth [1998] and Leffert et al. [1998].)

These 40 assets are not all young people need in their lives, but the research foundation for their importance in promoting healthy development is comprehensive and compelling (Scales & Leffert, 1999). Parents and family clearly are the exclusive providers of some of the assets (e.g., family support) and the primary sources of others (e.g., the positive values). It is clear, however, that whether young people experience most of the assets also depends directly or indirectly on the quantity and quality of their relationships with adults outside their own families.

Although Search Institute is just beginning to collect comparable data for children in grades 4 and 5, there is reason to believe that similar, age-appropriate trends would be found for children from infancy through middle childhood as have been found among young and older adolescents. The research clearly suggests that younger children require similar developmental experiences for positive growth. Although parents and family play an even greater role in the positive development of these younger children than they do adolescents, adults outside the family play increasingly important roles as children grow (Leffert, Benson, & Roehlkepartain, 1997).

The 20 "external" assets are grouped into four categories: Support, Empowerment, Boundaries and Expectations, and Constructive Use of Time. These refer to relationships and opportunities that are provided for young people, including such assets as a caring neighborhood, support from nonparental adults, opportunities to contribute service to others, receiving high expectations from teachers, and opportunities to spend time in constructive after-school activities and in religious communities. The 20 "internal" assets are values, self-perceptions, and skills young people develop to guide themselves, and are grouped into the four categories of Commitment to Learning, Positive Values, Social Competencies, and Positive Identity. These include assets such as emotionally bonding to school, the values of caring and responsibility, the ability to resolve conflicts nonviolently, and a sense of one's personal power (Benson, 1997).

Research has shown that the more of these assets youth report in their lives, the less they engage in various kinds of high-risk behaviors (Leffert et al., 1998). In addition, the greater the number of assets, the more young people show evidence of developmental thriving, such as doing well in school, valuing racial diversity, helping others, and overcoming adversity (Scales, Benson, Leffert, & Blyth, 2000).

Clearly, interactions with adults (as well as with peers) are implicated in the experience of practically all the developmental assets. Thus, both common sense and social research indicate that young people need adults to be involved with them—not just their own parents and other family members, but adults

Table 1. 40 Developmental Assets for Middle and High School Youth

Search Institute has identified the following building blocks of healthy development that help young people grow up healthy, caring, and responsible. Search
Institute has surveyed more than 1.5 million 6th through 12th graders in more
than 1,000 cities and towns across the country to measure their asset levels.

Asset type	Asset name and definition
Support	1. **Family support**—Family life provides high levels of love and support.
	2. **Positive family communication**—Young person and her or his parent(s) communicate positively, and young person is willing to seek parent(s), advice and counsel.
	3. **Other adult relationships**—Young person receives support from three or more nonparent adults.
	4. **Caring neighborhood**—Young person experiences caring neighbors.
	5. **Caring school climate**—School provides a caring, encouraging environment.
	6. **Parent involvement in schooling**—Parent(s) are actively involved in helping young person succeed in school.
Empowerment	7. **Community values youth**—Young person perceives that adults in the community value youth.
	8. **Youth as resources**—Young people are given useful roles in the community.
	9. **Service to others**—Young person serves in the community one hour or more per week.
	10. **Safety**—Young person feels safe at home, at school, and in the neighborhood.
Boundaries and Expectations	11. **Family boundaries**—Family has clear rules and consequences, and monitors the young person's whereabouts.
	12. **School boundaries**—School provides clear rules and consequences.
	13. **Neighborhood boundaries**—Neighbors take responsibility for monitoring young people's behavior.
	14. **Adult role models**—Parent(s) and other adults model positive, responsible behavior.
	15. **Positive peer influence**—Young person's best friends model responsible behavior.
	16. **High expectations**—Both parent(s) and teachers encourage the young person to do well.
Constructive Use of Time	17. **Creative activities**—Young person spends three or more hours per week in lessons or practice in music, theater, or other arts.
	18. **Youth programs**—Young person spends three or more hours per week in sports, clubs, or organizations at school and/or in community organizations.
	19. **Religious community**—Young person spends one or more hours per week in activities in a religious institution.
	20. **Time at home**—Young person is out with friends "with nothing special to do," two or fewer nights per week.
Commitment to Learning	21. **Achievement motivation**—Young person is motivated to do well in school.
	22. **School engagement**—Young person is actively engaged in learning.
	23. **Homework**—Young person reports doing at least one hour of homework every school day.
	24. **Bonding to school**—Young person cares about her or his school.

Table 1. 40 Developmental Assets for Middle and High School Youth (Continued)

Asset type	Asset name and definition
	25. **Reading for pleasure**—Young person reads for pleasure three or more hours per week.
Positive Values	26. **Caring**—Young person places high value on helping other people.
	27. **Equality and social justice**—Young person places high value on promoting equality and reducing hunger and poverty.
	28. **Integrity**—Young person acts on convictions and stands up for her or his beliefs.
	29. **Honesty**—Young person "tells the truth even when it is not easy."
	30. **Responsibility**—Young person accepts and takes personal responsibility.
	31. **Restraint**—Young person believes it is important not to be sexually active or to use alcohol or other drugs.
Social Competencies	32. **Planning and decision making**—Young person knows how to plan ahead and make choices.
	33. **Interpersonal competence**—Young person has empathy, sensitivity, and friendship skills.
	34. **Cultural competence**—Young person has knowledge of and comfort with people of different cultural/racial/ethnic backgrounds.
	35. **Resistance skills**—Young person can resist negative peer pressure and dangerous situations.
	36. **Peaceful conflict resolution**—Young person seeks to resolve conflict nonviolently.
Positive Identity	37. **Personal power**—Young person feels he or she has control over "things that happen to me."
	38. **Self-esteem**—Young person reports having a high self-esteem.
	39. **Sense of purpose**—Young person reports that "my life has a purpose."
	40. **Positive view of personal future**—Young person is optimistic about her or his personal future.

next door, in their neighborhoods, their schools, and the organizations they join. Hopefully the majority of American adults do not necessarily see parents and other adults as competing sources of socialization. But it is an open question whether they are likely to recognize the importance to child and youth development of the *connections* among these varied sources of socialization. The ecological perspective on human development (Bronfenbrenner, 1979) holds that those influences interact with each other and with the characteristics of individual children to produce a socialization experience in which various influences are not merely additive, but interactive and synergistic (Collins, Maccoby, Steinberg, Heatherington, & Bornstein, 2000), more of a bouillabaisse than a mere buffet of influences.

Indeed, Vandell (2000) concluded that research overwhelmingly supports a multiple socialization model of development, rather than favoring either parents or, as some have speculated, peer groups (Harris, 1995) as predominant influences. Vandell further pointed out that in complex systems, such as a child's "world," no single influence typically accounts for a large amount of variance in an outcome of interest. In fact, computer simulations built to account fully for behavior having multiple determinants report that most simple correlation coefficients between predictors and the behavior in question are moderate, only in the .30s. It is the aggregate of those determinants and the interactions among them that more strongly predict outcomes. Given such ecological perspectives, we would expect the socialization influences of unrelated adults to make a similar significant and moderate contribution to child and adolescent development outcomes on their own, and to be an important part of an aggregate of influences.

Consistent with that reasoning, research strongly confirms that the supportive involvement of adults other than parents with young people contributes to positive child and adolescent development. For example, a synthesis of more than 800 research studies concluded that adult connections with and caring for children and youth, including connections with unrelated adults, are consistently associated with positive outcomes, including: higher self-esteem, greater engagement with school and higher academic achievement, lessened delinquency, lessened substance abuse, better mental health, and better social skills (Scales & Leffert, 1999). The literature on resilience also consistently concludes that "connections with competent, prosocial adults in the wider community" (Luthar, Cicchetti, & Becker, 2000, p. 545) is one of three recurring thematic correlates of resilience (the other two correlates are close primary—i.e., parents or other main caregivers—relationships with supportive adults, and effective schools).

Farver, Ghosh, and Garcia (2000) observed that children, more so than adults, are the "primary consumers of neighborhoods" as places where they "encounter contrasting role models for societal conventions, rules, morality, notions of justice and fairness, and conflict resolution" (p. 142). Although most of the research on neighborhood influences has been concerned with effects on adolescents more than younger children, that body of work also suggests that neighborhoods have modest influences (in nonexperimental studies) and larger effects (in experimental designs) on young people's development. This research generally has supported the framework of social organization theory, which emphasizes shared values and role modeling as critical behavioral influences on young people (National Research Council and Institute of Medicine, 2000). In other words, research with young people has shown that values and norms shared and redundantly reinforced by adults in the community have important developmental impacts on the young. Similarly, our current study was based on the hypothesis that current social norms, shared and redundantly reinforced by the adults around them, essentially undermine adults' ability to engage with young people. These social messages and shared understandings limit how much adults outside the family can build the developmental assets that are so strongly related to young people's success.

Should All Adults Be Engaged with Kids?

In general, young people with more plentiful and high-quality relationships with adults do better than children and adolescents who lack them. Thus, in our study, we asked Americans what they thought about actions "all adults, not just parents" could take to influence young people in the positive ways reflected in the developmental assets framework. The phrase "all adults" underscores the notion that many other adults can play important socialization roles beyond parents, adults in the extended family, and adults whose jobs formally charge them with caring for young people.

Of course, not "all" adults are good for kids. Not all adults—even in some families, much less in neighborhoods—are safe, responsible, or knowledgeable enough to be positive influences, and not all kinds of adult "engagement" are salutary. Adults outside the family can serve as forces for both healthy and unhealthy development.

Apart from obvious examples such as child abuse, adult–child connections can sometimes contribute to undesirable outcomes through more indirect pathways of role modeling and social learning. For example, Shurnow, Vandell, and Posner (1999) reported that the frequency of 5th graders' contact with neighbors in high-risk neighborhoods was negatively associated with academic performance. The lower the average household income and adult educational levels in the neighborhood, and the greater the proportion of female-headed households and number of violent crimes, the more neighborhood contact weakened academic performance. That these relations held for 5th graders, but not for the same children when they were in 3rd grade, led the researchers to conclude that children increasingly are exposed to the social fabric of the neighborhood during those upper elementary school years. As such, the socialization potential of the neighborhood context becomes increasingly important. If children are overexposed to the role modeling of adults who have not achieved broader social markers of well-being, including stable marriage, sufficient education, and adequate income, then the impact on children is likely to be negative.

Most parents try to exert control over their children's social networks based on such considerations. For example, a number of studies have shown that parents who perceive their neighborhoods as being dangerous and filled with unsavory, untrustworthy, or unpredictable adults are more restrictive than parents in more desirable neighborhoods. In unsafe neighborhoods, parents tighten the reins on how much they allow their children to play outside and in the level of association with neighborhood adults that they encourage (e.g., Cochran, Larner, Riley, Gunnarsson, & Henderson, 1990; Furstenberg, 1993).

Clearly, contact with adults probably is not by itself a beneficial influence, but specific forms of adult engagement with children and their families likely are. Thus, when we discuss the study's focus on the role "all" adults can play, we do not literally mean that every adult should engage with every child. We mean instead that most adults who have no formal relationship with a child but who are themselves responsible, law-abiding, caring, productive people, and who are quite capable of having a positive influence on young people, should intentionally try to do so more frequently than seems to be the case today.

That is, for *most adults*, increased engagement with young people can make a positive contribution. Participants in a Seattle focus group discussing this issue, for example, noted that most children already have some sort of relationship with a number of adults outside the family, such as neighbors, parents of the child's friends, teachers, coaches, and church and youth group leaders. They felt that recognizing, encouraging, and supporting those adults who already are in children's worlds to get more involved was a message that would feel safe to parents and doable to those adults (Lee, 2001).

So, in practical terms, when we refer to "all adults," we really mean "most adults." But in addition, we mean to suggest more than just the desirability of encouraging those individual adults to be more engaged with young people. We also use "all adults" to suggest that the collective adult community, not just a few adults with formal roles, has a responsibility to work together to create the healthiest environment possible in which the next generations can develop. Part of that effort should be for adults to name the kinds of things "other" nonfamily adults in the community are expected to do with and for all kids, that is, to create a norm about how adults in this community are *supposed* to be engaged with young people (see Chapter 9 for a more extended treatment of these issues).

Ultimately, argued Takanishi, Mortimer, and McGourthy (1997), by the time young people are adolescents, the primary criterion for judging whether they are developing positively is whether they have cultivated the social competencies necessary for adult roles and responsibilities. Positive adolescent development, of course, builds upon the positive development of infants, toddlers, preschoolers, and elementary-age children. If parents and others have done a good job with children throughout all these periods of development, then by adolescence the following would indicate that young people are living positively:

- Education and work indicators—graduation (with a high level of literacy) from high school, critical thinking and problem-solving skills for a technology-oriented, global economy, postsecondary educational aspirations and expectations, perceptions of opportunity regarding future adult social and economic status;
- Indicators of health—the health-enhancing behaviors of exercise, adequate sleep, use of seat belts, a healthy diet, accessing appropriate medical treatment, preventive health exams, dental hygiene, positive mental health (skills to cope with stress and to engage in personally meaningful activities); and
- Indicators of preparation for the adult roles of parenthood and citizenship—knowledge of infant, child, and adolescent development, skills to support children with developmentally appropriate guidance, knowledge of and access to family planning and contraception, motivation to be a good parent, knowledge of civics, involvement in community service, and registering to vote at age 18.

All of these indicators of well-being, just as do the 40 developmental assets, recognize the influence of adults, not just adults in the family and those with formal care-giving roles, but the adults kids interact with every day.

The Relation of "Other Adult" Developmental Assets to Youth Thriving and Risk Behaviors

Although adults are directly or indirectly relevant to young people's experience of all the developmental assets, adults outside the family may be most clearly involved in helping young people build a smaller number of assets. As part of the current study, we used a large Search Institute database (unpublished at the time of this writing) to further test the hypothesis that the presence of such "other adult" assets in kids' lives has an important relationship to their well-being.

We created an aggregate sample of more than 229,000 6th–12th graders surveyed in the 1999–2000 school year, using the same screening procedures as were employed to create the 1996–1997 sample that is the basis for most of Search Institute's analyses to date (Benson et al., 1999). Additionally, and unlike the earlier sample, the 2000 sample was weighted by race/ethnicity and urbanicity to align better with 1990 census figures, the most recent available at the time of sample creation.

We then identified 12 of the 40 developmental assets that, according to their definitions (see Table 1), appeared to most explicitly tap the influence of adults other than parents: Other adult relationships, Caring neighborhood, Caring school climate, Community values youth, Youth as resources, Service to others, School boundaries, Neighborhood boundaries, Adult role models, High expectations, Youth programs, and Religious community. In all of these, adults outside the family are either mentioned directly in the definition (e.g., caring neighborhood) or are potentially present if young people experience the asset (e.g., youth programs). Treated together as a broad measure of asset-building engagement with adults outside the family, this scale had an acceptable alpha (internal consistency) reliability of .73.

The 229,000 youth were divided into quartiles. Those who said they experienced 9–12 of these "other adult" assets were considered adult-rich. Students with 6–8 of these assets were considered above average in other-adult assets. Those with 3–5 of the assets were termed average in their engagement with adults. And young people with 0–2 of these assets were called adult poor. We then examined how differences in young people's reported experience of other-adult assets affected their reported experience of eight thriving indicators (such as helping others, overcoming adversity, or exhibiting leadership) and an overall index of thriving. In addition, we looked at the relationship of those assets to their reported experience of 10 risk behavior patterns (such as alcohol or other drug abuse, delinquency, or school failure) and an overall index of risk.

The results were significant and parallel the results of other studies we have discussed that report on the overall relationship of developmental assets to well-being. As Table 2 shows, *each increase in the level of other-adult assets was related to a significant increase in the proportion of students' saying they were thriving, and a significant decrease in the proportion who said they engaged in patterns of high-risk behavior.* Adult-rich young people thrived more and took fewer risks than young people who were above average, average, or adult poor. Young people above average in their other-adult assets thrived more and took fewer risks than those with only average other-adult assets or who were adult poor. And even those students with just average levels of other-adult assets thrived more and reported taking fewer risks than young people who were adult poor. We observed these relations for each separate thriving indicator and risk behavior pattern, as well as for the thriving and risk behavior indexes.

Table 2. Relation of Other-Adult Assets to Thriving and Risk Behavior Patterns among 6th- to 12th-Grade Youth: Proportion of Youth with Each Thriving Indicator or Risk Behavior Pattern (N = 229,970)

	9–12 Assets	6–8 Assets	3–5 Assets	0–2 Assets	F
THRIVING INDICATORS					
Resists danger	36%	27%	21%	16%	1509.77*
Values diversity	81%	70%	59%	47%	3682.05*
Maintains physical health	82%	65%	49%	33%	7471.67*
Delays gratification	63%	50%	42%	35%	2204.35*
Helps others	96%	89%	81%	63%	5829.52*
Exhibits leadership	85%	77%	66%	48%	5059.56*
Overcomes adversity	81%	75%	69%	62%	1241.82*
Succeeds in school	36%	27%	19%	12%	2494.57*
RISK BEHAVIOR PATTERNS					
Alcohol use	8%	16%	25%	38%	3883.58*
Antisocial behavior	6%	13%	21%	35%	4178.03*
Driving and alcohol	6%	12%	18%	28%	2485.79*
Depression/suicide	9%	17%	26%	36%	3117.34*
Illicit drug use	3%	9%	17%	32%	4903.63*
Gambling	9%	14%	18%	23%	996.25*
School problems	8%	14%	23%	36%	3728.46*
Sexual intercourse	7%	13%	19%	29%	2583.66*
Tobacco use	3%	6%	12%	25%	3870.37*
Violence	16%	26%	36%	46%	3071.53*

Note: Search Institute, unpublished data, 1999–2000 school year aggregate sample.
* = Significant at $p \leq .0001$.

We can imagine the assets might be highly correlated with the thriving behaviors in particular. If that is so, then these findings would be rendered highly predictable. However, a previous analysis of a similar sample of nearly 100,000 youth (Scales, Benson, et al., 2000) showed that 90% of the correlations between the assets and the thriving indicators were .30 or below, and that 80% of the variance inflation factors and tolerances showed similarly low to mild interrelationships. Thus, the assets can be viewed as statistically independent predictors of the thriving outcomes, further supporting the strong relationship we found between young people's experience of engagement from "other" adults and their well-being.

The Disconnection among Adults and Young People outside Their Own Families

That young people can benefit from relationships with unrelated adults may seem self-evident, and the research we have discussed to this point shows it is also well founded. And yet the available evidence suggests that most American adults are not very engaged with children and youth outside their families.

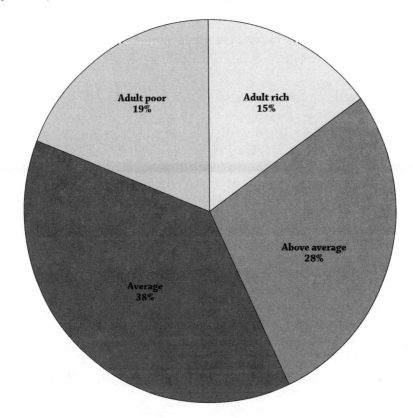

Figure 1. 6th–12th Graders' Experience of Other-Adult Assets

For example, in the aggregate sample of 229,000 students from the year 2000 just discussed, we found that only 15% of young people were "rich" in their reported experiencing of the "other adult" assets (i.e., they reported experiencing 9–12 of those assets). Nearly one in five young people was "adult poor" (i.e., reported experiencing just 0–2 of those assets), as Figure 1 depicts.

Other studies corroborate these findings. A Yankelovich survey of 1,000 adults in 1998 found that only a little more than one-third of adults (36%) said they currently participated in any activity or volunteer setting in which they interacted with young people outside their own families (Youth involvement, 1998). The drive to increase adults' connection with youth through volunteerism has been given heightened visibility since 1997 by America's Promise—The Alliance for Youth, the movement headed by retired General Colin L. Powell until he became secretary of state in 2001. There is little doubt that effort has served as a rallying point and a catalyst, but there is also little agreement about whether it has actually met its goal of connecting adults more deeply to young people (Archer, 2000). Despite a great push in the ensuing years toward increasing such volunteerism, a Gallup poll in 2000 found little change, with just 38% of adults in 2000 saying they volunteered to help children and youth in their community (America's Promise, 2001). Apart from formal volunteering, a Public Agenda survey (Duffett et al., 1999) reported that only a minority of adults—35%—said they spent a lot of time with young people.

The most basic level of connectedness, which falls well short of having developmentally meaningful relationships with young people, is simply seeing children as a part of one's world. In this respect, the average adult statistically has less chance of even encountering a child or adolescent today than in earlier eras. Children make up just 26% of the current U.S. population, compared with 36% in 1960 (*Trends in the well-being of America's children and adolescents, 1998*). Moreover, the proportion of American households with children 18 or younger has declined significantly over the past 40 years, from 57% in 1960 to just 36% in 2000 (*Profiles of general demographic characteristics, 2000*, 2001).

From a series of focus groups in Seattle, it was concluded that parents interact with young people many times a day in a wide variety of settings, largely encountering other kids through their own children's activities. For nonparents, or parents of grown children, however, interactions with kids seemed to be more isolated to the neighborhood, occasional family gatherings, or retail stores, with little of that interaction meaningful (It's About Time for Kids, 2001). Indeed, a nationwide sample of teenagers gave adults an average "grade" of just C+ across 20 subject areas such as spending quality time with their families, being a lot of fun, and stopping young people from drinking. But perhaps the most telling grade was a C− for "really listening to and understanding young people," a subject that young people "consistently" rate as the most essential for having quality relationships with adults (*What teens are saying*, 2001).

Yet the limited real involvement of adults with children outside their own families or work responsibilities seems too pervasive to be solely or even mostly a function of demographic trends. Few Americans would disagree with the assertion that children are, as one state's report on its young people in the 1980s was titled, "our greatest natural resource" (Alaska Governor's Interim Commission on Children and Youth, 1988). But the majority of adults do not seem to devote much effort to actively helping other people's children develop positively and thrive. Journalist Anna Quindlen has put it this way: "This is a nation that loves the notion of children but doesn't really like the reality of kids" (Anna Quindlen says . . . , 2000). And although many adults who choose to be "child free" volunteer in programs for kids and certainly do not want children out of their lives, many others do. For them, even the notion of children is unappealing. The idea that they should, and should *want* to, contribute to children's healthy development is seen as an infringement on their rights as purposely childless people (Belkin, 2000).

Unfortunately, Search Institute data from a 1996–1997 school year sample of nearly 100,000 6th–12th graders suggest that too few young people experience positive relationships with adults other than their parents. As we have noted, those relationships can help build the developmental assets young people need for healthy development, and so their relative absence is especially worrisome:

- Only about 40% of young people say they experience a caring neighborhood or supportive relationships with adults other than parents;
- Only about one-quarter say they have good adult role models in their lives or feel cared for at school;
- Only one-fifth report feeling valued by the community (Benson et al., 1999).

A study conducted among a racially and ethnically diverse sample of more than 5,000 adolescents in Colorado Springs reported similar findings. Just 22% of the young people said that they regularly experienced positive relationships with adults outside the family. Among the questions youth were asked were whether they had conversations with adults that lasted more than five minutes, whether adults made extra efforts to try to get to know them, and whether young people were provided help or advice by adults outside their families (Scales, Leffert, & Vraa, 2003).

In statewide polls of Colorado adults and youth (Scales, Lucero, & Halvorson, 1998), more than 4 in 10 young people said adults do not spend enough time with them. Ironically, nearly 70% of adults said they themselves spent adequate time with youth who are not related to them, but they thought that just 25% of other adults were comparably involved with young people. That the youths' estimates on the same question fell squarely between these figures suggests that adults give themselves too much credit for getting involved with young people, and give other adults too little credit. Research that has used beeper-prompted diary sampling of young people's daily experiences and mapped how they spend their time comes to the startling conclusion that the typical adolescent spends only about a half an hour per day even with his or her mother. Yet that slim connection seems enormous in comparison to the average five minutes per day adolescents spend with their fathers, and the less than five minutes they typically spend in "one-on-one interaction" with a teacher or other adult (Larson & Richards, 1989; Csikszentmihalyi, 2000). (A recent national study indicated that children ages 3–12 spent more time with their parents in 1997 than in 1981 [Time with mothers and fathers, 2001; Hofferth & Sandberg, 2001], but the criterion was weekly hours children were "engaged or accessible." With the advent of cell phones and e-mail, among other communications advances in the period between studies, many children and their parents certainly are more "accessible" to each other these days, but that may have only marginal implications for how emotionally connected and effectively communicating they really are.)

Journalist Patricia Hersch spent several years chronicling the lives of a half-dozen youth, getting an in-depth glimpse few adults are fortunate to experience. More qualitatively and intimately than the research cited earlier, she ended up describing today's teenagers as "a tribe apart," bereft of much adult interaction outside their own families and the typically limited, formal relationships they have with adults at school (Hersch, 1998). Adults' disconnection from children and youth got so extreme in one retirement community outside Orlando that residents refused to pay school impact fees to the school district of which they were a part. When the Florida Supreme Court ruled in their favor, the school superintendent observed that the ruling "allows a community of adults, basically, not to have anything to do with children. That's potentially disastrous in this democratic society" (Florida court frees retirement community, 2000, p. A10).

The White House Conference on Teenagers, held May 2000, drew attention to the role of parent involvement in the lives of American adolescents, but said little about what *other* adults can and should be doing. During the conference, a report was released based on a secondary analysis of data from the National Longitudinal Study of Adolescent Health. The report showed that teenagers who eat dinner five nights a week or more with their parents are much less likely to engage in smoking, alcohol use, and other high-risk behaviors, and more likely to get better grades (President's Council of Economic Advisors, 2000). However, as important as parents' involvement is in the lives of their own children, it is only part of the picture. Neither the report nor the conference drew significant attention to the critical influence other adults can have on young people, and to the absence of adequate involvement by adults other than parents in most young people's lives.

If adult engagement is unusual for most young people, it is even less likely for older adolescents than for younger children. For example, high school students in a Colorado study (Scales, Leffert, et al., 2003) reported significantly fewer positive relationships with adults both in and outside their families than did middle school students. This age difference is consistent with both the Search Institute data aggregated over hundreds of communities (Benson et al., 1999) and the public opinion research described later (Farkas & Johnson, 1997; Duffett et al., 1999) about negative adult images of young people. Across all those studies, adults think more negatively of older teenagers than they do younger children, and spend less time with them.

A small longitudinal study suggested that the decrease in adult networks may begin even earlier than high school (Feiring & Lewis, 1991). For both boys and girls, the number of adults in their lives decreased between middle childhood (age 9) and early adolescence (age 13). The lower reported levels of adult contact among older youth also are consistent with numerous other studies, most of which used cross-sectional samples but some of which did employ longitudinal designs (see review in Scales & Gibbons, 1996).

Of course, what makes such declines in adult contact so distressing is that the number and depth of developmental assets youth experience matter and adults provide so many of the opportunities for young people to build those assets. As young people grow older and enter adolescence, their exposure to opportunities for risk taking increases, and their potentially protective engagement with adults decreases, adding to their vulnerability instead of limiting it and enhancing their capabilities. In our study, as we report in later chapters, we looked in particular at differences in how important adults thought it was to be engaged with younger children, compared to what they thought about adolescents. We also examined differences in their reports of how the adults they know actually seem to relate to kids of different ages.

The Need to Define "Reasonable Responsibility" for Other People's Kids

We have seen how the assumption that parents are solely responsible for raising children can inhibit the involvement of other, especially unrelated, adults. We have also seen that such broad adult engagement with kids—beyond the caregiving of parents—can have a wide array of positive benefits for child and youth development. Finally, we have noted that the American public, while holding parents primarily responsible, is not uncomfortable with the idea that other adults have a stake in helping nurture and guide the next generations. The conundrum for those who are committed to developing healthier communities for children and youth is this: Adult relationships can be powerful positive influences in young people's lives, but what stops most adults from relating to children and especially to youth outside their family and playing the positive socialization roles in their lives?

There appear to be two fundamental sources of barriers to adult engagement with kids. One is a set of cultural norms and assumptions that together seem to limit the implicit and explicit permission adults perceive for such engage-ment. (We treat additional inhibiting norms and assumptions in more depth in Chapter 4.) The other major contributor to adults' limited connection with other people's kids grows in part out of the first. If it is only or primarily parents who are supposed to see to young people's requirements, then it is neither necessary nor appropriate to suggest or specify what role other adults might play, other than the ambiguous cultural edict to "support" parents and families. If other adults have no responsibility, or only quite limited responsibility, then it is not necessary to make clear the basis on which adults could or even should hold themselves and each other accountable for the healthy development of children and youth who are not their own.

We as a society have assumed that parents have the primary role. In doing so, we have left undefined the supplemental role and contribution of other adults, especially adults outside the family. Instead, a vacuum has been created in place of social-cultural agreement about the role of other adults. Of course, some adults do not want to be involved with young people, regardless of the social-cultural norms. But the majority of adults may be more open to increasing their involvement with kids. For this group, it is not only the cultural norms about parents' responsibility for raising kids that can hold them back. In addition, there are relatively few clear guidelines about which ways of adults engaging with kids are important and expected. This gap leaves many caring adults either indifferent to the young or, perhaps more typically, uncertain about how they are *supposed* to relate to other people's kids.

In this study, we examined a number of actions adults can take in relating to the young to learn which actions appeared both significant and acceptable to

Table 3. *Adult Engagement Actions Studied, by Category of Developmental Assets*

Category of developmental assets	Adult actions studied
Support	• Have meaningful conversations with young people • Know young people's names • Give advice to young people
Empowerment	• Tell parents when young people do something good • Feel responsibility for ensuring well-being of neighborhood kids • Provide opportunities for young people to serve others • Seek young people's opinions
Boundaries and Expectations	• Expect young people to respect adults • Expect parents to set clear boundaries for kids • Tell parents when young people do something wrong • Believe parents alone should discipline their kids* • Be a role model for volunteering and charitable giving
Commitment to Learning	• Encourage kids to succeed in school
Positive Values	• Teach young people widely shared values • Discuss own personal values with young people • Discuss personal religious or spiritual beliefs with young people**
Social Competencies	• Teach young people to respect cultural differences • Guide young people in making decisions • Give young people financial guidance
Positive Identity	• Teach young people to preserve and pass down their cultural traditions

*This action was reverse-scored, as it was considered inconsistent with the premise that nurturing and guiding children should be a responsibility widely shared among many adults, not just parents.
**While religion is clearly related to important values people hold, the framework of developmental assets does not include specific religious values or beliefs as part of the framework.

the majority of Americans, including parents. If the clear results on this question were disseminated, perhaps more discussion would begin occurring among adults about how each of us could nurture and guide a greater number of young people. Ultimately, more adults would feel comfortable getting involved with kids outside their own families, thereby helping to build the assets that can be such positive dimensions of young people's development.

We used the framework of developmental assets to define a variety of possible actions adults could take in relationships with children and youth (see Table 3). For each of the categories of the developmental assets framework except Constructive Use of Time (which as currently operationalized is more about formal programs than the informal relationships of interest in the current study), we posed at least one way adults could be engaged with kids and help build the developmental assets in that category (the rationale for including each action in the study is provided in depth in Chapter 5).

We then asked our national sample of adults to tell us how important they considered it for all adults—not just parents—to do these things with young people. We also asked how many of the adults they knew actually related to kids in these ways (i.e., the degree to which engaging with other people's kids was the norm in their social networks).

Our hope was that the results of this study (detailed in Chapters 6–8) would begin to help define a territory of "reasonable responsibility" for other adults' roles in socialization and positive development. In practical terms, that new cultural expectation would fall somewhere between the notion of exclusive parental responsibility and the idea that all adults are equally important in and responsible for young people's lives. Parents do have primary responsibility, after all, and so it is not reasonable to expect other adults to play the same nurturing and guiding roles as parents do, no matter how valuable those relationships with other people's kids can be. Our results begin the process of defining what in American society is a *reasonable responsibility to expect most other adults to assume.*

But before we consider these actions in more depth, we need to return to the notion of social expectations or norms. In the next three chapters, we expand on the argument that it is the very lack of such clear positive expectations, and the presence of strong inhibiting ones, that limit adult engagement with the young. In so doing, we set the stage for our presentation of results in Chapters 6–8, and for our discussion in Chapter 9 of strategies that might be effective in changing those norms so that they encourage adults' connections with other people's kids.

What about the Extended Family?

Clearly, although not the focus of this study, adults in the extended family—grandparents, aunts, uncles, cousins—are indeed the primary "other"—nonparental—adults in some children's lives. For example, Cochran et al. (1990) used mothers' reports to study the social networks of 225 families with 6-year-olds in Syracuse, New York. They reported that the other adults in the social networks of children from single-parent Black families were much more likely to be relatives than was the case for Black children from two-parent families, or for white children. Although there is some evidence that girls, younger children, and young people of color spend more time than boys, adolescents, and white children with other adults in their extended families (see review in Scales & Gibbons, 1996), even that contact is not substantial for most. In one of the largest studies of its kind, for example, Blyth, Hill, and Thiel (1982) found that the majority of the 7th through 10th graders in their sample had telephone contact or visits with extended family adults just once a month or even less frequently. The number of children living with their grandparents has increased 76% since 1970, owing to parental drug use, divorce, mental illness, child maltreatment, and incarceration, representing nearly four million children, or 5.5% of those under 18 (Casper & Bryson, 1998). But the effects on children of those living arrangements do not seem positive: Smaller studies have found significant health problems among children being raised by grandparents, and Casper and Bryson's national Census Bureau study found those children significantly more likely to be raised in poverty than children raised by their parents.

A study of more than 900 adolescents done for the National Commission on Children (Moore, 1992) found that nearly half said a grandparent, aunt, uncle, or cousin was a "special adult" in their life. Grandparents and other relatives, however, were named by only about 22% of parents as sources of help to go to if the parents had a concern about their child. Even more would go to a clergyperson or adult at school, and almost as many would go to a friend or neighbor as would go to a relative for help.

In part because of increasing longevity, and cycles of divorce-remarriage-stepfamily formation, Bengston (2001) suggested that multigenerational bonds, including extended family and stepkin networks, may become more important in the 21st century than they have been over the past few decades. But even in the context of describing their value, he hypothesized that they likely will function as "latent" kin networks that may be "inactive and unacknowledged for long periods of time" (p. 12), and accessible mostly in times of crisis. Considering three-generation families, he reported that about two-thirds say they have close affectional ties. However, at least one-third of American families' intergenerational relationships are distant in terms of physical proximity and contact. For another 40% of families, either extended family members give little help or help is given, but with little emotional attachment. Thus, even though the majority of families *say* they are emotionally close across generations, geographic distance keeps some of them from being much of an influence, and the emotional distance of others limits them to a sporadic socialization, nurturing, and guiding role for children.

Finally, the mobility of modern families plays a role in changing the social networks of both parents and children. Duncan and Raudenbush (1999), for example, used data from the national Panel Study of Income Dynamics to calculate that more than 80% of children move at least once by the age of 15, about 33% move more than three times, and about 17% move more than five times by midadolescence. Even extended family members who once were close by may not remain so for long for substantial proportions of American children, and thus the degree of mobility places a premium on both parents' and children's abilities to regularly construct new social networks.

3 The Nature and Operation of Social Norms

The available evidence suggests that cultural assumptions and social norms about the appropriate roles of parents and unrelated adults may be a significant force that keeps many adults from contributing more positively to the development of the young people around them. In other words, the ambivalence American adults seem to have about their relationships with children and youth other than their own may stem from a lack of clarity and consensus about how they are expected to behave, and about the perceived consequences, both positive and negative, for behaving one way or another.

In this chapter, we examine more closely the territory of expectations and perceived consequences for behavior, which together constitute the most salient elements in the concept of social norms. We discuss the psychological and sociological context that defines what social norms are, how they form, and how they may change, and relate this general discussion to the specific issue of how various norms may collectively work to inhibit adult engagement with young people outside their own families.

What Are Social Norms?

What exactly do we mean by a "norm" and, especially, a "social norm"? A standard sociological definition of a norm is a "cultural rule that associates people's behavior or appearance with rewards or punishments . . . norms create social consequences" (Johnson, 1995, p. 190). Less formally, Rosen (1997, p. 2) defined social norms as "the informal standards of behavior that people obey rather than risk ostracism or humiliation." Forsyth (1999) wrote that norms "prescribe the socially appropriate way to respond in the situation (the 'normal' course of action) as well as proscribing actions to avoid if at all possible." More simply, a norm is a "standard or rule that is accepted by members of the group" (Eagly & Chaiken, 1993, p. 631).

All those definitions imply that norms are units of cultural transmission. They are replicated through imitation or cultural transmission (e.g., schooling, advertising, entertainment, parenting). All societies exhibit some degree of social norms that directly or indirectly guide people's behavior. Indeed, Elster (1989) argued that there are two principal problems of social order—coordinating expectations and achieving cooperation—and that social norms are especially important for coordinating the expectations of society. Anthropologists have argued that the main effect of norms is to "stabilize social expectations and thus establish commitments to particular ways of acting in common social situations" (Ensminger & Knight, 1997, p. 2). The unique feature of social norms is that deviations from social norms bring the "sanctioning of deviant behavior" (p. 3). It is not simply the reaction of powerful others to enforce the norm that brings obedience, but, as Florini (1996) observed, a "sense of 'oughtness'" that reflects the norm's status as a "legitimate behavioral claim" (pp. 364, 365).

Saam and Harrer (1999) described four different ways norms have been conceptualized. There are statistical norms (whatever the majority of people do) and sociological norms (institutionalized role expectations that have sanctions if they are violated). There also are ethnographic norms (no general norms operate, only expectations for behavior that are situation specific) and ethical norms (one conforms to norms perceived through the lens of one's level of moral development).

In terms of adults' relationships with young people, the statistical and sociological norms that currently exist seem to define the social expectation that most adults will not be deeply engaged with young people. Statistically, as we reported in Chapter 2, adults and youth alike report that most adults don't relate to young people outside their families very much. Sociologically, the most institutionalized norm of all seems to be for adults to keep their distance from kids outside their own families. Ethnographic and ethical norms could also inhibit adult relationships with the young, depending on the situation and the moral values that adults bring to bear on them. But those also seem to be the kinds of norms that could promote engagement. That is, based on one's moral worldview, and the particulars of the situation one is in, circumstances might be favorable to getting involved with a young person. Absent those special circumstances, though, the statistical and sociological norms seem more operative in America. That is, since most adults don't get very involved with other people's children, the lack of involvement is statistically normal. In addition, there is both little negative consequence for avoiding involvement and little reward for being engaged. On the other hand, there is a considerable amount of anticipated negative consequence to getting involved where one shouldn't.

The Influence of Social Norms on Behavior

Studies have demonstrated the powerful role that social norms play in regulating people's behavior across countless situations, including prejudice and discrimination (e.g., Jetten, Spears, & Manstead, 1996), the development of property rights (e.g., Young, 1998), the expression of aggression (e.g., Cohen, Vandello, Puente, & Rantilla, 1999), international standards of secrecy or transparency regarding military capabilities (e.g., Florini, 1996), and even who gets to play pickup basketball (e.g., Jimerson, 1999).

Among adolescents, inaccurately believing that smoking or having sexual intercourse is the norm among their peers is associated with greater engagement in those behaviors (Urberg, Shyu, & Liang, 1990; Romer et al., 1994). The same effect of normative beliefs has been reported concerning college students and binge drinking. Students who overestimate actual levels of binge drinking are more likely themselves to report being binge drinkers. A focused public information campaign helped students understand that fewer students were binge drinkers than most students imagined. In changing the perceived norm, actual levels of reported binge drinking also declined (Haines & Spear, 1996). Young people's perception of parents' norms about the acceptability of young adolescents drinking alcohol also have been found to influence 10- to 12-year-old children's actual drinking behavior two years later, through their effects on children's own norms about drinking (Brody, Ge, Katz, & Arias, 2000).

In the face of research showing it was ineffective, the widely implemented DARE drug abuse prevention program used in 75% of U.S. school districts has adopted a new curriculum designed to change students' social norms about drug use (DARE to revamp its anti-drug strategy, 2001). In addition, research has shown that people's perceptions of a normative obligation to do certain behaviors "rather consistently" add significantly to the prediction of intention to do those behaviors, and ultimately to the actual behaviors, including donation of blood, committing driving violations, and volunteering for nonprofit organizations (Manstead, 2000).

However, the impact of norms on behavior is not always consistent and may vary with the issue under consideration. For example, a study of more than 200 white women ages 18 to 27 found that perceived sun-protection and sunbathing norms predicted intentions to protect oneself during sun exposure, but not actual protective behavior. The young women's perceived susceptibility to sun damage, and the perceived advantages of tanning, were stronger predictors of both behavioral intentions and actual behavior than were norms favoring protection (Jackson & Aiken, 2000). This study suggests another element of the norms landscape: At any given time, there usually are competing and even contradictory norms operating. To protect against skin cancers, we are supposed to protect ourselves from the sun, but there is also high value placed in American society on a well-tanned look that suggests one is both youthful and vigorous as well as financially able to afford time in the sun.

Social Norms and Adults' Engagement with Young People

Perceptions of norms may influence adult relationships with the young in two ways. First, perceptions about norms among young people may lead adults to evaluate young people either positively or negatively, attracting or distancing

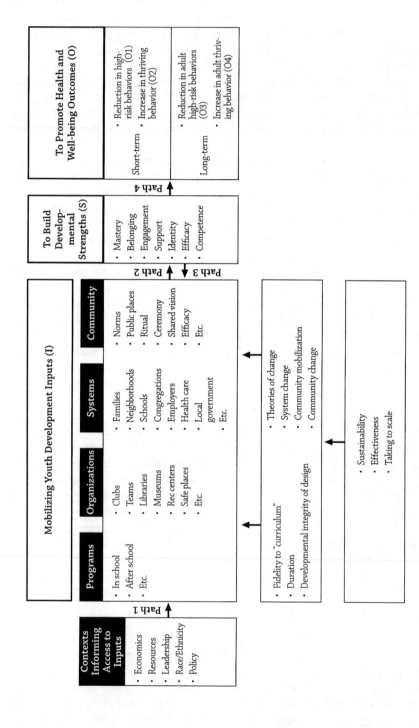

Figure 2. Conceptual Framework for Youth Development Theory and Research
(*Source:* Benson & Saito, 2001)

adults from relationships. For example, if adults feel it is a norm among young people to disrespect adults, then adults are less likely to want to engage with them. Second, adults' perceptions about norms for behavior *toward* the young— when they are supposed to engage and when not, and how—can either promote or inhibit those relationships.

Norms that define the kinds of behavior expected and appropriate among children and adolescents affect how adults think about young people. In some communities, for example, graduating from college is a high expectation well understood by young people, whereas in other communities, equal pressures may be felt to graduate from high school and begin working. Adults who perceive young people living up to their community's norms will likely evaluate those young people more favorably than they would young people whom they perceive to be violating or disrespecting the norms. Elster (1989) described a number of categories of common social norms that adults other than parents may play a role in reinforcing: consumption norms (table manners, types of movies seen), norms of fairness (do unto others, don't take advantage of those weaker than yourself), norms against behavior "contrary to nature" (incest), money-related norms (earn it, don't show it off, donate part of it), norms of reciprocity (returning favors), norms related to medical ethics (the most serious cases get treated first), codes of honor, norms of retribution (who is liable for harm), work norms (appropriate effort, sexual harassment), and norms of distribution (norms of equality, particularly strong in democratic societies).

Social norms about expected adult behavior, especially unacceptable behavior, also can mobilize or inhibit adult relationships with and action on behalf of children and adolescents. For example, because of legitimate concerns about child sexual abuse, there are strong norms in many communities about adults not being alone with a young person who is not related to them. In that normative climate, most adults will avoid relating to kids without others around, to avoid even the possibility of being misinterpreted. Although this norm protects children, it also lessens opportunities for adult-child relationships, socialization, and nurturing.

As depicted by Benson and Saito (2001) in Figure 2, both the norms adults think young people hold, and the norms adults perceive govern their potential engagement with the young and with other adults, can be seen as "youth development inputs." Those inputs contribute to (and are influenced by) young people's own developmental strengths, which in turn are linked to a variety of outcomes related to health and well-being. In this way, norms can materially affect the quality and path of a young person's development.

What Features Do Social Norms Have?

Social norms have a number of features we discuss throughout this chapter and the remainder of the book.

There often are competing and even contradictory norms operating in a given situation (e.g., protect yourself from the sun, but have a well-tanned look; give plentiful quality time to your kids, but stay as long at work as your company requires; respect parents' right to raise their kids as they see fit, but report suspected abuse or neglect to the authorities).

Some norms are transitory and some are long-standing. Some change as historical eras go by (e.g., during World War II, it was expected that most women would work outside the home, but after the war they were expected to return to being housewives), and some are long-standing, often rooted in religious texts (e.g., the Ten Commandments, the Golden Rule). Social norms are not static over time. They can and do change, certainly over generations. For example, bottle-feeding babies was the accepted norm in the 1950s, whereas in contemporary America, the "right" thing to do is breast-feeding. Norms also may change more rapidly within a brief historical period. For example, the September 2001 terrorist attacks prompted a groundswell of patriotism, a coming together of residents in grief and anger, and an increased sense of common cause. They stimulated or resurrected norms supporting stringent safety precautions and demonstrations of patriotism. One of the immediate impacts of those attacks was to make people feel closer to each other. It is plausible that an additional normative by-product of such a catastrophic event could be an alteration of social norms about adults' shared sense of responsibility for the protection and care of all the children in their various worlds.

Norms not only change from one historical period to another, they also operate situationally in a given time period. Both expectations for behavior and enforcement/consequences for abiding by or violating a norm may differ depending on the situation. For example, whether an adult has a meaningful conversation about personal values with a young person probably depends on a host of situational and contextual considerations: the age and gender of the child, the setting where the conversation might occur, how well the adult knows the child and his or her parents, whether an event or incident has prompted the possibility for such a conversation, how capable the adult feels guiding without being preachy, whether the adult is in a hurry, how interested the child seems to be, and so on. The same person may respond differently to a given norm, depending on his or her perceptions about the immediate situation and about what other norms may be operating in concert or conflict at that moment. Adherence to particular norms may also be a function of how they reinforce personal and group identity as much as it is a consequence of social pressure. Indeed, Williams (1968b) argued that norms are about "what should or should not be done by particular types of actors in given circumstances," whereas values express desirable standards less tied to specific situations (p. 284).

Norms discouraging undesirable behaviors are more common and powerful than norms promoting desirable behaviors (e.g., there are strong norms against all adults hurting children, but not so much for all adults to help children). In addition to inhibiting negative behaviors, norms also can promote prosocial behaviors. Illustrations of this effect are more difficult to come by, however. For example, failing to send a thank-you note after receiving a gift may carry more negative social consequences than sending only a perfunctory one. On the other hand, sending a highly personalized and eloquent thank-you note may accrue to the sender the positive reputational and self identity value of being thought to be unusually considerate and gracious, qualities most people would wish to have attributed to them. Tipping a waiter or hairstylist might be a second example. Tipping is not legally required, but it is expected, and those who would be repeat patrons fail to tip at their own peril. They might be quite unhappy with their service on their return visit. Another example might be the expectation that younger persons should give up their seat to an elderly person when the bus or train is full. Stares and even disapproving comments might befall a person who violates that norm, but they might not too. In other words, the consequences are uncertain. Similarly, in most religious traditions, members are expected to give money to their congregation; in many traditions, they are also expected to donate to other charities. But since most giving is done privately, it is uncertain what kinds of consequences accrue to those who do not measure up to those expectations.

Even fewer examples of this kind of social encouragement of positive behaviors come to mind when considering the forces that might shape what adults do to engage with young people. It is not uncommon for people to be recognized for a formal mentoring role they have played for a young person, such as a teacher, coach, or volunteer. But overt rewards for simply being informally engaged with young people on a daily basis, such as knowing their names or having meaningful conversations with them, seem far less common. And it is not immediately obvious what any negative consequences would be to an adult for not volunteering or not knowing young people's names in the neighborhood.

The multiplicity of roles we each have in modern society makes the application of general norms difficult. In a given situation, does one act as a man is expected to act, as a father or son, as a friend, as an African American, as a coworker, as a Christian, as an expert in some aspect of history or science, as an American? What does each of those roles mean for expected behavior in a given situation? For example, Phinney (1996) pointed out that cultural norms and values help account for the psychological importance of one's sense of ethnicity. But the very labels people use to self-identify ethnically may contribute to differences in what a person perceives to be the norms operating in given situations, as when the same individual refers to himself in different circumstances as a Latino, Chicano, or Hispanic. One could argue that such an example mixes ethnicity issues with how norms shape one's behavior in a given situation. After all, people "have" their specific ethnic background, regardless of what they choose to call themselves. But although the differing labels do not literally affect the facts of one's ethnicity, and although there are many cultural attitudes and norms common across those self-labels, each also implies a unique set of cultural and political orientations and expectations for how one is supposed to behave. There are many such circumstances and considerations that affect which norms may be salient for any given person at any given moment. Some cultural norms even have legal consequences for the cultural groups to whom they apply. For example, although its application is typically limited to Orthodox communities, and is rare even then, Jewish religious law allows for the intentional shunning of those whose conduct is judged to weaken the cohesiveness of the traditional Jewish community (Broyde, 2000). Shunning includes not speaking to the shunned, not hosting them in one's home, and not even visiting them if they are ill. The intent of shunning is to "serve notice to the members of the community that this conduct is unacceptable" (p. 47) and to create "a climate where religious behavior is the social norm" (p. 50).

Norms are about perception. Except for norms codified into law, which have an "objective" reality and require us to behave in certain ways, most social norms exist outside a legal framework, simply because people *think and feel* that they exist and ought to be paid attention to. Their power derives from the more subtle influence of social expectations and consequences, positive or negative, rather than from enforcement by government or other officials.

Norms are about social expectations, but they function as internalized rules. As individuals encounter various life situations, they engage in a modicum of social calculus, in which the costs and benefits of particular actions are, however fleetingly and imperceptibly, sifted before one acts. When people encounter similar situations repeatedly, of course, little conscious deliberation is involved. They "know" what to do much as an experienced musician or athlete, after thousands of hours of practice, does not "think" about what to do next in the flow of performance. Instead, they simply "know" and act as best they can at that moment in the ways colleague performers, athletes, and spectators (i.e., key reference groups) expect them to act in a given competitive or creative situation. Eventually, such norms for behavior become internalized rules that the individual obeys *even in the apparent absence of external pressure to do so.* In part, it is thought that this effect occurs because the very idea of disobeying an internalized norm triggers feelings of anxiety, embarrassment, and guilt. This "emotional aspect of norms is a more fundamental feature than the more frequently cited cognitive aspects," and is an important source of the ability of social norms to coordinate behavioral expectations (Elster, 1989, p. 100). In fact, as McKenzie-Mohr (2000) observed, many mass media behavior-change campaigns are based on the implicit assumption that humans make behavior decisions solely on the basis of rational considerations; neglecting the emotional and normative issues involved leads most such information-based campaigns to be less effective than they could be.

Social norms have two important features: They are shared or mutually agreed to, and they have consequences. A "rule" for behavior is only a norm if it is shared by enough members of an individual's primary reference groups (or by enough members with the power to reward and punish) that the individual initially feels some external expectation to comply or not comply with that rule. In this sense, norms are a form of peer pressure, positive or negative, from culturally relevant reference groups. There may be little more reward for abiding by a norm than social indifference to one's behavior (i.e., the reward of indifference is that one at least is not being criticized for one's behavior), but a genuine norm requires that there be a perceived consequence for abiding by or violating the norm. If one perceives that a social norm can be violated without penalty, then it is more of a social *value* that can be applied or not in a given situation. It is not a shared rule that prescribes or proscribes behavior, but merely a common preference that might influence behavior. This distinction will become especially important in Chapters 6–8 when we examine the findings from our study. For example, Good Samaritan laws protect helpers from being sued for any unintended negative consequences of the assistance they provide. Such laws may encourage more people to help strangers. But coming to the aid of others does not carry the status of a norm unless those who refuse to help incur consequences for their indifference, and such punishments for remaining a bystander are rare. Minnesota, Vermont, and Wisconsin have required strangers to help those in distress, but the laws were written narrowly, rarely implemented, and carried only small penalties in any case (Few "good Samaritan" laws in America, 1997). Similarly, an organization's charter might be revised to allow youth to become voting board members. But what if adults can, without social consequence, reject all attempts to take seriously the nomination of youths for such roles, or effectively ignore youth who manage to get seated? In those cases, a *value* of youth involvement and leadership may or may not be present, but no genuine *norm* of youth leadership or of necessary adult active promotion of youth leadership exists.

Social Norms, Laws, and Consequences

In saying that, for a true "norm" to exist, there need to be "consequences," "punishments," and "penalties" for violations, we do not intend to suggest, for example, that people ought to be fined for not getting involved with other people's kids. The consequences for not being connected with kids can and arguably should be as informal as recognizing that others whose opinions one values are disappointed by one's lack of engagement.

True, some social norms are backed up by legal sanctions. But others are supported by more subtle expressions of social approval or disapproval, and it is this latter class of "consequences" that we think pertinent to the discussion about adults engaging with young people. We do not argue for the Puritan response of publicly punishing and ridiculing people who did not obey various behavioral dictates. Neither do we argue, however, for continuing the current situation regarding adults' engagement with young people, which might best be described as laissez-faire, in which there is little public reward for engaging and even less consequence for not doing so. Somewhere between Puritanism and laissez-faire, there lies an appropriate expression of informal public will concerning adults' engagement with young people that can help define for all what is expected of them. That expectation would be backed up, not with law, but with the informal yet considerable power of people's informal social bonds, needs for belonging, and quests for satisfying personal identities (see Chapters 8 and 9 for more on these issues).

Some common values and beliefs are indeed codified in law and formal social policy. The rule they reflect is clear, and penalties for violating them are specified. They clearly represent social norms. Child abuse laws and laws governing ages at which driving or drinking alcohol are permitted are examples of norms that have been institutionalized into formal social policy.

Smoking is another example of a behavior governed by social norms that have both legal and informal foundations. In this case, the predominant mechanism for a change in norms about smoking may have been fear of both personal (health) and social (ostracism) consequences, but there also has developed a legal foundation supporting and reinforcing antismoking sentiments. Although smoking is not generally illegal for adults in the United States, it is illegal in specific locations (e.g., most restaurants have no-smoking sections and smoking is often entirely prohibited in public buildings) and for minors. Yet, quite apart from the medical and legal impacts, the social consequences of smoking have encouraged many to quit. Those consequences include being unwelcome in many businesses, having to go outside instead of being able to smoke in the workplace, or even losing romantic attachments because of one's partner's distaste for the habit. Smoking may be a case where medical information created an initial impetus for many to quit. But laws then followed that began to protect the rights of nonsmokers not to be subjected to what science had shown was a deadly poison. The combined force of medical knowledge and legal support for not smoking made it easier and more socially acceptable not only for people to stop smoking but also to prohibit visitors from smoking in one's home, a policy that would have been an unthinkable social affront in the 1950s and early 1960s.

There also are laws, of course, that may reflect values shared by significant proportions of people but whose violation carries little if any consequence, primarily because most people ignore them, as do the authorities who are supposed to enforce them. For example, jaywalking in urban areas is, for the most part, illegal but largely tolerated. Similarly, walking across the street against a red light technically is illegal everywhere in the United States. However, whether one can cross penalty-free against a red light, as long as no traffic is coming, varies so much that it is understood that strangers to a town or city should observe what the locals do and then do the same. They should not assume that the social norm in their community is the same as the norm elsewhere. The consequences for violating such a norm may be small indeed, such as receiving disapproving stares. Experiencing a few hard looks, though, may be enough eventually to keep newcomers from crossing against red lights. Unlike the abuse of children, where a single transgression of the norm can (but does not always) bring severe consequences, a single violation of a weak norm such as jaywalking would rarely result in material consequences.

In this book, we are concerned mostly with other kinds of norms, those that might not be codified into public policy but that are better understood as examples of social expectations. For example, until quite recently, in many rural areas and small towns it was not unusual for people to leave their homes unlocked, a practice that most urban and suburban residents abandoned years ago in the face of actual and perceived increases in crime rates. The shared expectations differ in differing types of communities. Yet the penalties for "violating" the norm also differ. In an area where the norm is to lock one's home, leaving doors unlocked when one is not at home carries the consequence (other than it being easier to be robbed) only of perhaps being thought foolish or naive by one's friends and neighbors. In an area where unlocked homes are the shared expectation, a locked home might be considered an insult to one's neighbors, implying a lack of trust, with a much more serious potential effect on the quality of one's social network.

Early Developmental Influences on Later Engagement with the Young

Of course, attitudes and norms about altruism and helping behavior do not simply emerge out of thin air. Adults do not arrive at a moment of possible involvement with other people's kids as a tabula rasa, but rather as the product of all their interactions with and shaping of their environment up to that moment. A considerable body of research exists describing how children develop in a social world of multiple, interconnecting ecologies. In this "nested" world, they are influenced not only through the distinct experiences lived in their families, schools, communities, and peer groups, but as well through the interactions among those developmental contexts. Longitudinal studies also have shown the importance not only of connections across developmental contexts in one time period but also of the linkages between assets or protective factors in one stage of development and resiliency in subsequent periods of individual growth (Bronfenbrenner, 1979; Lerner, 1992; Jessor, 1993).

For example, in Werner and Smith's (1992) classic 30-year study of children on the Hawaiian island of Kauai, infants who were cuddly and affectionate had greater numbers of supportive and caring adults in their lives during their school-age years. Those networks of social support in middle childhood were in turn related to greater school success during their subsequent teenage years, and to greater resilience and mental health as adults in their 20s and 30s.

Those early experiences with parents, neighbors, and the wider community all contribute to the attitudes and values, the specific expectations and perceptions of norms, that individuals will carry with them decades later as adults (Benson et al., 1998). In the same way that early experiences play a role in predicting current behaviors among young people, so early experiences may also differentiate among *adults* who are more and less likely to engage in specific prosocial behaviors that promote positive involvement with young people outside their own families.

Researchers have found that the development of prosocial values begins very early in a person's life. For example, secure attachment to parents is related to having prosocial values, empathy, social conscience, altruism, and other dimensions of moral development later in life (Berkowitz & Grych, 1998). Prosocial values, empathy, social conscience, and altruism all are personal qualities that are expressed in social relationships and connections with others. It is reasonable to suspect that people for whom these kinds of social connections are normal also are likely to be more socially connected to young people as well as age peers and older adults.

It is not only identification with parents' values that contributes to a child's evolving value formation, but also how warm and "democratic" (child-centered) mothers are in their child-rearing practices that is important. For example, Kasser, Ryan, Zax, and Sameroff (1995) reported research with 140 youth 18 years old and their mothers from the Rochester Longitudinal Study. More nurturant mothers (less cold and controlling) had adolescents who rated financial aspirations lower in importance than self-acceptance, affiliation, and "community feeling" values.

A study of university students suggests that parents' child-rearing styles also may be related to the differential development of shame or guilt, which in turn seem to have substantial differing effects on behavior and conformity to norms (Abell & Gecas, 1997). Parents' use of child-rearing practices such as reasoning and explaining the rationale for parental decisions and behaviors, within a context of warmth and demandingness, seems to connect children to normative obligations and responsibilities, and induces guilt when those norms are violated. Guilt seems to promote a desire to make amends and protects children from inappropriately denigrating themselves for unintended norm violations; that is, it contributes to more positive mental health and socially adaptive functioning. Guilty kids, in short, try to do better next time, but are more accepting of themselves as fallible human beings who do make mistakes but who still are morally good. Those young people who are able to feel guilt instead of shame may carry such emotional responses into adulthood, where they affect how adults respond to exhortations to get involved with kids. Adults who can feel guilty about being less engaged, instead of ashamed, may be more likely to do something about it when suggestions are made to them about how they might get more engaged.

In contrast, when parents employ child-rearing styles that involve withdrawing love and warmth, children still learn about norms in the sense of expectations. But in these cases, they respond more to norm violations with feelings of shame, distress, hostility, withdrawal, self-rejection, and general psychological maladjustment, rather than "other-oriented, empathetic responsiveness" (Abell & Gecas, 1997, p. 119). Instead of encouraging children to accept mistakes as a normal part of life, such parental reaction to children's transgressions teaches children to think of themselves as morally unfit.

Thus, shame and guilt may both be behavior-motivating emotions triggered by the actual or even anticipated violation of norms, but they are not the same and have differing sequelae. Abell and Gecas (1997) described shame as focused on perceived personal deficiencies and incompetence, whereas guilt was seen as arising from violating one's sense of interpersonal connections and relationships. In their view, guilt can be behaviorally motivating, whereas shame is more likely to contribute to behavioral paralysis.

How Social Norms about Engagement of Adults and Young People May Change

We have pointed out that adults could help build young people's developmental assets and more meaningfully promote positive development not just within but beyond their own families if doing so were the norm or social expectation. Such a norm can be thought of as a specific example of a broader class of norms about doing good deeds that benefit others. Spending time with children and youth outside one's own family, communicating more than casually with them, and being supportive and providing guidance to them may be considered prosocial behaviors, actions that are good for society. In the following pages, we consider why people engage in such prosocial behaviors, and how social norms might work to promote that behavior. How can such norms spread among people who are not already culturally connected to each other? How can such norms break out from being solely individual (i.e., an ethical norm, in Saam and Harrer's language) social values, or held by just a subgroup (i.e., an ethnographic norm) to being more universal (i.e., a statistical and ultimately a sociological norm for the majority of people)? In the following discussion, we illustrate some broad anthropological and sociological principles that may help create norms and shape their evolution. This discussion may deepen understanding of how the strategies we later suggest in Chapter 9 might promote norm changes regarding adult engagement with young people.

Batson (1994) described four motives for acting for the public good: (1) egoism, in which the ultimate goal is to increase one's own welfare, even if it is just to boost feelings of self-worth; (2) collectivism, whose ultimate goal is to increase the welfare of a group in which one sees oneself as a member; (3) altruism, that is, increasing the welfare of other individuals, even at a cost to oneself; and (4) principalism, in which the ultimate goal of behavior is to uphold a moral tenet. This last motive is most closely aligned with Saam and Harrer's (1999) description of "ethical" norms. Although Batson thought principalism might be a subtle form of egoism rather than a distinct motive, a person committed to nurturing the young might reflect more advanced (postconventional, or principled) levels of moral development. In looking at all four motives, Batson concluded that there is considerable research support that an individual's empathy for others can lead to genuinely altruistic helping; in other words, altruism is not just a form of egoism simply because, in helping others, a person might also feel good or simply avoid punishment.

Simmons (1991) argued that empathy and prosocial norms are connected, in that empathy influences altruism at the individual level, and norms influence altruism at the societal level. In her view, individuals typically seek a balance between doing what is considered "right" (e.g., obeying norms to help others) and what is pleasurable (e.g., serving egoistic purposes). She agreed with Batson that much research on altruism trivializes the behavior by concluding it inevitably reduces to "egoistic" motives, instead of accepting the reality that in everyday life, it is a mixture of motives for behavior that usually predominates.

For example, "individuals are motivated [toward altruistic behavior] by the need to feel that they matter—that they count in this world" (p. 10).[1] Simmons did not mean this as a purely egoistic "mattering," but rather that people both want to see a good larger than their own self-interest happen (a more altruistic motive) and want to feel they personally have contributed to making that good occur (a more egoistic motive).

Allison (1992) described norm evolution as analogous to biological evolution. However, he went beyond the biological aspects of kinship theory, which claims that we will be altruistic only to those who share our genes, and then only in direct proportion to the percentage of genes they share with us. This line of thinking does not help us understand altruistic behavior toward nonkin, especially when they have no chance to reciprocate the kindness. Allison proposed that for "beneficent" acts to become norms, it is important to do the good act for or with people who are most likely to "carry" the cultural "gene" for that act. So, if we want to promote adult engagement that builds young people's developmental assets, we should be engaged with and building the assets of those who themselves, whether adults or young people, are most likely to be engaged with others.

Who are these people? Simply, they are people who are already "like us" in some important ways. According to Allison, they are our cultural ancestors (our teachers), descendants (those we teach), our cultural relatives (those who share a similar exposure to the literature, myths, and symbols of "our" culture), our physical neighbors, and all those who act as we do. This framework, however, only explains how norms might spread among people who *already* are like each other. Allison acknowledged this problem when he noted that even though some traditions call for universal altruism, it is "incontrovertible that people are much more willing to sacrifice their own interests for those who are similar to them, who live near them, who share the same social position, etc." (1992, p. 297).

Selznick (2000) also noted that most people feel the most obligated toward those closest to them—family, friends, and those with whom we have a sense of "shared allegiance," such as with fellow citizens more than noncitizens, or those who share our religion, race, or ethnicity. These affiliations give us a sense of our "anchored identity" (p. 59) that feels rooted and authentic.

---

[1] Clary and Snyder (1993) studied attributes associated with volunteering and described prosocial attitudes, values, and actions (e.g., humanitarian concerns, community service, altruism) as satisfying several psychological functions: understanding/learning, career experience, values expressive, social approval/disapproval, protection against guilt/escape from personal problems, and esteem. Their research suggested that the values-expressive function was the strongest motivator for people volunteering, followed by the understanding/learning and esteem functions. But, even though values may be the strongest motivators for volunteering, a direct appeal to humanitarian values was found to be the least effective advertising means of recruiting volunteers, although it was judged more effective in retaining existing volunteers. The finding that social approval/disapproval was not the strongest motivator for volunteering may seem to contradict our reasoning about the importance of social norms to such behaviors. However, social norms most often operate beneath the surface of everyday awareness; it is not surprising that most people would not ascribe their motives for helping others, an overtly altruistic action, to such apparently selfish reasons as the desire for approval or the fear of disapproval.

Sometimes we may feel a degree of allegiance to those who share our local space, our community or neighborhood. However, as we describe in Chapters 4 and 5, modern society is fragmented socially and filled with a multiplicity of competing values. In that cultural context, it is quite challenging to broaden our sense of anchored identity to include connection with others beyond family, friends, and those in our immediate social circles. When anchored identity does expand to include strangers, this blurs the "line between personal and collective responsibility" (Selznick, 2000, p. 60). For too many American adults, then, it would seem that the boundaries of their "anchored identity" are relatively narrow and firm, discouraging them from getting too involved with other people's'kids.

In discussing the adherence to and violation of norms of military restraint, Legro (1997) provided some additional clues to how norms may spread, change, or be resistant to change. He described several components of norm strength or robustness: *specificity* (how simply and clearly normative guidelines are defined and understood), *durability* (how long the rules have been in effect, and how successful violations of them get punished), and *concordance* (how widely endorsed the rules are). The greater a norm's robustness according to these three criteria, the fewer violations of that norm should be observed. Not coincidentally, such a robust norm would also be more resistant to change.

An example of a robust norm might be adults' expectation that young people act respectfully toward them. It is clear, has been reasonably durable, and appears to be widely endorsed and monitored by adults. Whether young people in fact do treat adults with respect is another matter, and one of which adults and youth have differing perceptions. For example, in statewide studies of Colorado adults and youth, 68% of adults thought young people did not treat them with respect, compared to 46% of youth who said youth were disrespectful to adults (Scales et al., 1998). It is important to underscore here that the "robust" norm in this example is adults' *expectation* that they should be treated with respect, not necessarily that young people *are* treating them with respect. There appear to be few such robust norms that promote positive engagement among adults and other people's kids. In contrast, the norm of adults not engaging very deeply seems robust and resistant to change.

Norms promoting adult engagement with young people might become established through emulation of engaged adults by others, largely because most adults are linked to others through the various social groups they are a part of and the various roles they play. For example, initially, it is those who already are engaged with young people who might make such actions the norm within their primary reference groups. Most adults are "members" of numerous reference groups (our families, work settings, religious organizations, neighborhoods, clubs, etc.). Gradually, other adults in differing reference groups engaged adults belong to may become aware that those engaged adults are experiencing rewards at both personal and public levels (e.g., senses of satisfaction and/or belonging, recognition, pride). As they perceive more and more others doing this action, those other adults may begin to find it easier to emulate the action until it becomes a norm in a subsequent reference group, with the process repeated endlessly.

Is this scenario likely, however? The key to its plausibility is the clarity with which others perceive that there are rewards for getting involved with kids, and consequences, however subtle, for being unconnected. The perceived rewards have to be considerable enough to overcome the more easily imagined risks of getting involved. We would argue that neither the rewards for getting involved nor the consequences for not being engaged are sufficiently strong to change the existing norm that governs most adult interaction with the young: Parents have the overwhelming responsibility for their kids, people in formal roles with young people have some responsibilities that are, to some extent, legally stipulated, and the rest of us don't have much expectation at all to be that involved.

Ensminger and Knight (1997) used anthropological data to conclude that changes in social norms such as those inhibiting adult engagement with young people seem to occur through three broad processes: coordination on focal points, competitive selection among contracts, and, especially, bargaining.

"Coordination of focal points" refers to the observation that human beings seem to prefer order and predictability. This implies that we will try to coordinate our behaviors with those of others whenever possible, in order to avoid chaos and inefficiency. The rules behind the coordination of players' "moves" provide the foundation for game theory, for example. Norms help us determine how to respond to, and seem to arise as solutions for, "recurrent problems" (Williams, 1968a, p. 204). They are an efficient social mechanism for knowing what to do without having to think through and/or renegotiate social expectations and consequences each time a frequent dilemma occurs. Norms for driving, "rules of the road," are examples of the coordination-of-focal-points approach. We do not need to think about what to do if we wish to drive at the speed limit and others wish to drive faster, because the rule in the United States is that slower drivers use the right-hand lane. Table 4 shows that, with regard to children, a legally enshrined example of this type of norm might be laws requiring all children to receive formal education at least until age 16. An example of a more informal

Table 4. Types of Norms Changes Related to Children and Youth

Type of norm change	Example(s)
Coordination	• Laws requiring children to receive formal education at least their midteens • Children expected to respect adults
Contractual	• Decisions about what curriculum content will be allowed in schools (e.g., debates over sex education, "appropriate" literature, evolution) • Whether adults report possible child maltreatment (each situation depends on whether adult is legally required and other circumstantial elements)
Bargaining	• Changing of child labor laws to regulate children's work participation • Minor children being able to make some of their own health care decisions (e.g., diagnosis and treatment of sexually transmitted diseases), but parents having control over most others

social norm is the expectation of adults that young people should show them respect. Adults don't have to wonder each time they interact with a child whether they should be treated respectfully (although they may be quite uncertain as to whether they *will* be treated with respect).

"Competitive selection among contracts" treats each interpersonal exchange as if it were a negotiated contract. If competitive selection among contracts dictated how we drive, there would chaos on the roads because each driver would be negotiating with every other driver how best to share the road. In this contractual approach, until an overriding norm emerges, people will mutually agree on how to behave in a given situation in order to derive mutual benefit. Competition among norms will tend to drive out norms that fail to yield a collective benefit, that is, are too disadvantageous to one party or the other. The evolution of property rights is an example of this kind of norm emergence. In Table 4, we note too that decisions about school curriculum, and whether adults report suspected child maltreatment, are other examples. In most districts, curriculum content negotiations come and go with regularity, with changes in school district and parental leadership virtually assuring that what was done before is not necessarily how things will always be handled. Then too, even though adults such as teachers and child-care providers are supposed to report suspected child maltreatment, whether they do depends on numerous considerations, including their interpretation of the law and how serious they think the maltreatment is. Adults not covered by such laws determine even more situationally what they will do if they suspect child maltreatment.

Finally, norms arise from "bargaining" in which some people or institutions simply have more resources at their disposal, more bargaining power, and so can influence social expectations such that they retain or increase their advantages. In Ensminger and Knight's (1997) anthropological studies, bargaining was most often the process by which norms came into existence. In essence, the "victors" in struggles over values and priorities in society (the process of "bargaining") institutionalize their norms. In the ongoing debate (and sometimes upheavals) over what kind of a society we shall have, victors change, and so do the norms they "impose" on the rest of us.

Whites in the pre–civil rights era American South, for example, were able, through power, intimidation, and violence, to maintain social norms, including those legally codified, that promoted racial segregation. Politicians passed discriminatory laws, and the Ku Klux Klan and other private citizens committed acts of harassment and violence, largely without consequences, on both African Americans and whites who favored civil rights. When Rosa Parks refused to give up her bus seat to a white person, she "violated" a powerful social norm that had functioned essentially as an unquestioned presupposition for as long as most Southerners could remember. In that one act of resistance, she not merely challenged a law, which would have been far-reaching in itself, but shook the entire *edifice of expectations* that governed "normal" social order among whites and blacks, not just in the American South but throughout the country.

Another, less inspiring example of norm bargaining is the legal notion of "liability rights" (Cooter, 1997). For example, if they compensate victims in predetermined ways, companies may have legal permission to do things that violate what would otherwise be considered norms of proper corporate behavior, such as not polluting rivers with industrial waste. If the level of compensation is "perfect" in a legal sense, it simply restores the victim to her or his earlier state as if no injury had occurred. Thus, the compensation is not a "punishment." Companies are then free to determine whether they will violate the norm, simply because they have the resources to build the "perfect" compensation into their business plans.

An example that pertains more directly to children and youth is the evolution of child labor laws to restrict the hours that children may work, the types of work they can do, and other conditions under which they work. Another example is the granting through case law and state legislation to even minor children the right to make some health-care decisions for themselves, such as seeking treatment for sexually transmitted diseases or obtaining contraception without parents' permission. In each case, these norms emerged through at times bitter "bargaining" between groups with often competing interests, including child welfare agencies, parents, religious groups, child advocates, businesspeople, and the medical community, with differing coalitions among those groups formed to battle on different issues. Like the monumental struggles to enforce civil rights for all Americans, today's norms concerning these child and youth issues involved confrontations of all sorts, including struggles among various powerful groups, and between the powerless and the powerful.

One has to wonder if certain kinds of norm changes that would promote greater adult engagement with children and youth may well involve changes in established power structures, not only grassroots mobilization. Those trying to mobilize communities around building developmental assets for children and youth, including changing norms about adults' relationships with young people, might note the conclusions of Oliver (1984) and Prilleltensky (1999). They imply that getting more Americans to accept personal and collective responsibility, and even accountability, for the well-being of young people, and to believe in their own capacity to make a difference for kids, goes beyond changing adults' thoughts and feelings about their roles and responsibilities. Changing the normative landscape may also need to include strategies for dealing with the tension of leadership in maturing movements, and with the skills and attributes needed (e.g., emotional fortitude, persistence, comfort engaging with powerful people) to confront prevailing customs.

For example, Folbre (1998), in applying feminist theory to economics, argues that the explanation that "rational" or neoclassical economists give for the development of economic norms fails to recognize the "distributional struggle" between stronger and weaker groups. In her view, another way of seeing the evolution of norms is that the norms that survive do so, not because they are "efficient" (i.e., on balance, those norms are best for the entire society even if they cause negative consequences to some), but because norm development is "part of a process of collective action and *collective struggle*" (p. 50, emphasis added).

Folbre went on to argue that the rational economic view has so influenced social thinking that it has literally devalued the nurturing of children. Those who "do caring work" are underpaid because the benefits they produce—healthy children, for example—are a "public good," the diffuse benefits of which are over and above what the people who pay for child care, education, and other child-nurturing services are actually "contracting" for. Because the benefits are so diffuse, many people want them, but few want to put out the effort to attain those goods, since their efforts will personally gain them very little. Ironically, since nurturing children is a public good, "well-nurtured children will be underproduced" (Folbre, 1998, pp. 52–53).

Sometimes, a norm that develops out of a long process of cultural bargaining seems, years later, to be much more an example of coordination of focal points. We do not see the power struggle so much as we see an agreement to make a potentially contentious situation more orderly for everyone's benefit. The emergence in late 1800s and early 1900s America of the idea of universal and compulsory schooling until midadolescence, and the concomitant "invention" of adolescence (Kett, 1993), provide an example of a truly "bargained" norm eventually feeling more like one attained through coordination of focal points. Before the Industrial Revolution, most children worked at a young age, and few Americans had even a high school education. But collectively, the struggle of competing interests, their willing or unwilling "bargaining," created a number of social forces that caused a change in the norm, including increased immigration and competition for jobs in the new economy; the emergence of what are now thought of as "youth" organizations such as the YMCA and YWCA; the growing movement for women's voting rights; new public health focuses on disease prevention, family planning, and child development; and the popularization of developmental theories from figures such as Sigmund Freud and G. Stanley Hall. Today, the "bargaining" is not over whether children should have schooling until a certain age but over related issues: whether home schooling should be as allowable as institutional schooling, how tax dollars should be used to support public and/or private schools, what young people ought to be learning, and how best to document whether they are learning. We're not debating the importance of schooling, only how it should happen. In contrast, in this book we argue that Americans are neither sure of the importance of adults outside the family to children's and youth's development, nor even debating how best that influence might be exerted to promote positive, optimal development for all children and youth.

The preceding discussion implies that norm change is typically gradual and slowly evolving. But a final kind of norm change occurs suddenly. Florini's concept of norm "coherence" refers to the fact that new norms, new expectations for behavior, enter a cultural arena already filled with existing norms. To have a chance at cultural survival of the fittest, new norms must either "make the case that they are logical extensions" of the existing "web of shared normative understandings" or "necessary changes to it" (Florini, 1996, pp. 376–377). In Florini's view, norm "reproduction" can take place vertically, through successive generations of leaders (as in genetic reproduction), or horizontally, through sudden changes in the norm within the same generation or epoch.

In this light, rapid social change is usually a case of horizontal reproduction, and is most likely under these conditions: There is a large-scale turnover of decision makers; the prevailing norms are seen as failing to deal with emergent realities, so that it becomes "virtually impossible" to continue with the old ways of doing things; and new issues emerge for which the relevance of old norms is uncertain, and for responding to which new norms have not yet taken hold. For example, the September 2001 terrorist attacks on the United States fulfill both of the latter conditions. Showing one's patriotism became a norm overnight, as did the acceptance of heightened security measures and lengthy airport delays, while at the same time cultural changes occurred, such as movies with terrorist themes being shelved. What had been socially acceptable suddenly became un-acceptable. What a day earlier would not have been socially expected suddenly was. Similar sudden normative changes can take place on a personal level with the occurrence of life-threatening illness or injury. Breast cancer survivors, for example, learn not to wait for a return to "normal," but instead learn to define a "new" normal.

How Norms Interact with Attitudes, Behavioral Intentions, and Actions

Azjen's (1988) theory of planned behavior deepens the conceptual founda-tion for understanding how social norms may operate to encourage some adults to get more involved than others with children and especially older youth, and how that proportion of involved adults might be increased. In this section, we discuss the theory explaining how attitudes influence behavior, and how norms can influence attitudes and intentions to act in particular ways, dynamics that have implications for adults' decisions about engaging positively with other people's children.

Three components of the theory of planned behavior are an individual's attitude toward the behavior in question, the perceived social norms concerning that behavior, and the perceived control that a person has over doing the behav-ior. Together, the first two components can offer a strong base for predicting a person's intention to do a behavior, which itself is a strong predictor of actual behavior.

Attitudes about a behavior depend on beliefs about the outcomes of doing that behavior, as well as attitudes about the "attitude object," which, in terms of adults' engaging with other people's kids, is young people. Favorable attitudes are a function of believing that the outcomes of a behavior will be mostly positive. For example, people will be more likely to get involved with other people's kids if they think it will help the young people, be enjoyable for themselves, and if they're comfortable with and like those kids.

As we have described, social norms involve beliefs about whether specific groups of people important to the individual will approve or disapprove of the individual doing the behavior. Will the young person and/or his or her parents welcome the involvement or be upset? Will neighbors or coworkers think well or badly of an adult, for example, for telling parents whose child he or she saw doing something wrong?

Perceived behavioral control addresses the fact that not all behaviors are entirely voluntary or believed to be under one's own influence. A person may lack the information or skills to do a behavior, not experience the opportunity to do so, be dependent upon others to do the behavior, or even be prevented by various strong emotions, stress, or compulsions from doing a behavior in which he or she otherwise might well engage. If people feel incapable of exercising control over an action, their thought processes, motivational patterns, and emotions all may be affected, with the result that they think they will fail. They will be less likely even to want to try. And they will feel anxious (Bandura, 1989). For example, even if there were norms supporting adults' greater involvement with young people, many adults might feel inadequate to the task, unsure of how to relate to children and especially youth outside their own families. They might feel that the children or adolescents themselves didn't want the adult getting involved with them, or feel they had no time to do so. As we discuss at other points in this book, a focus in the media on youth problems might leave many adults feeling powerless to contribute much positive in the face of such overwhelming odds. Feeling limited self-efficacy, they would try to avoid the situations as much as possible.

In addition to their perceptions of risks and benefits to themselves, individuals may weigh the risks and benefits of their actions to larger groups, such as the community. For example, Tyson and Coulter (1999) studied small-area landowners' intentions to be environmentally responsible. They reported that the landowners' environmental behavior was explained more when they considered both community risks and benefits as well as risks and benefits to themselves, than when they considered only the personal risks and benefits of their actions. Thus, an adult might consider it personally or socially "risky" (i.e., awkward, embarrassing, open to rejection) to engage with young people in particular ways, such as saying hello to and striking up a conversation with a youth with whom one has not previously communicated. That adult still might engage if at some level he or she feels the community would benefit ("my spending time with this young person will help keep them healthy, and that is good for all of us"). But it is far from clear what circumstances would lead an adult to place more weight on those positive community benefits in contrast to the perceived personal discomforts or risks.

In general, research shows that people may well be more likely to take an action under several conditions: "If their personal evaluations of it are favorable, if they think that important others would approve of it, and if they believe that the requisite resources and opportunities will be available" (Azjen, 1988, p. 144). Thus, it is reasonable to suspect that adults will be more likely to engage positively with young people if they think that:

- Doing so is important, in that it will lead to positive outcomes, instead of thinking it will make no difference or even hurt young people or the community (they have a positive attitude about it);
- Most of the important people in their lives, including young people themselves, will approve of and even expect them to be positively involved

with children and youth (they perceive a supportive norm for that action); and

- They have the skills, resources, and opportunities to engage in positive ways with children and adolescents, including belief in their self-efficacy to do so (they have the capacity).[2]

Those hypotheses reinforce the importance of adults' perception of norms as factors in whether and how they interact with young people.[3] In this study, we focused on collecting new data about the first two elements that affect behavioral intention, attitudes and norms, and on reviewing other research to indirectly deepen our understanding of the third element, capacity or self-efficacy. Thus, in the current study, we asked two basic questions of our national sample of U.S. adults: How important do adults consider various ways of their relating to young people? And, how much support do adults perceive in their social networks for engaging with young people outside their families?

Norms and Personal/Group Identity

One of the most powerful ways norms may operate is to reinforce one's sense of identity, which reflects the different reference groups to which one belongs. The true power of norms occurs when individuals do not simply respond

---

[2] A study of 400 British adults' health-screening behavior found that the theory of planned behavior successfully explained initial and subsequent attendance at health screenings; however, it could not reliably distinguish between those who attended consistently, delayed attendees, and those who started out attending but then failed to continue (Sheeran, Conner, & Norman, 2001). Thus, just because an adult is more likely to be engaged with kids if they evaluate such actions favorably and feel important others will as well, that is no guarantee they will do so sooner rather than later, or that they will continue being deeply engaged.

[3] It is also nevertheless true that some attitudes may change only after behavior has changed. For example, prejudicial attitudes toward people of particular race/ethnicity, religion, sexual orientation, gender, or physical capabilities sometimes change after laws requiring nondiscrimination have become common. Rosen (2000) also reported in a meta-analysis of 47 cross-sectional studies of health behavior change that the sequence of processes people used to change varied with the type of behavior studied. For successful smoking cessation, for example, people used cognitive strategies earlier than they used behavioral ones. However, for successful exercise adoption and diet change, doing behavior changes and cognitive restructuring tended to occur together throughout all stages of the change process. Fishbein (1966) observed that a "change in behavior implies a new set of relationships between the individual and the attitude object" (p. 210). The fact that one has performed a behavior and experienced positive or negative consequences informs one's attitudes about the behavior, as well as perceived control over doing that behavior. The attitude toward a behavior may change based on perceived "punishment" for that behavior, which may be enough to change the behavior without an accompanying attitude change (Bem, 1967). However, this kind of behavior "change" may hold up only in settings where a person can get caught doing the unacceptable behavior. Changing both the perceived consequences and the attitudes toward a behavior are usually more effective than just enforcing sanctions in changing the behavior in both public and private settings. Nevertheless, this discussion suggests that it should not be assumed that adults' attitudes toward specific ways of engaging positively with children and youth necessarily need to change before they can engage.

with what Forsyth (1999) called "compliance" (doing the expected behavior publicly but rejecting the legitimacy of the norm privately), but with "conversion" (changing one's private feeling about the norm to match the reference group's position). In this process, some norms become shapers of behavior not merely so that individuals can avoid negative results, but because obeying them contributes to their unique sense of *personal identity*, in part through allowing them to establish or maintain a sense of belonging to groups they value. Obeying those norms allows individuals "to fulfill their own expectations about proper behavior" (Forsyth, 1999, p. 4), to behave as the people they feel themselves to'be.

Wood, Christensen, Hebl, and Rothgerber (1997) made the same case in studying sex-typed norms, showing that, if traditional sex role norms were personally relevant to their research participants, then adhering to those norms had a positive effect on self-concept, such that there was greater similarity between one's actual self-concept and one's ideal. Given that research shows a powerful tendency for people to want to think well of themselves (Gibbons & Walker, 1996), norms that provide the opportunity to feel closer to one's ideal self should have special strength and stability. They should provide the chance to feel good about oneself because of ego reinforcement (this is the kind of person I am). In addition, they should be effective because of group identity reinforcement—strengthening a perceived connection to others who hold the prevailing norm one is adhering to and further buttressing one's favorable self-impressions (these admirable people like and accept me; therefore, I too am admirable).

Indeed, social influence researchers consider the aim of maintaining a coherent and favorable self-image to be one of the three fundamental motives for attitude change (the other two motives are to ensure satisfactory relationships with others and to understand the issue in question better and act more effectively around it; Wood, 2001). Perhaps this is why studies have suggested that telling people they already hold certain attributes broadly accepted as positive may make them more likely to act in ways that "live up to" that assessment.

Freedman and Fraser (1966) conducted classic experiments that illustrate this principle. In the first study, they found that people who had agreed to a small request (i.e., answering an eight-question survey on household cleaning products) were more likely subsequently to agree to a much larger and intrusive request (i.e., a half-dozen men visiting their homes to find and classify the products actually in the home). In a second experiment, they found that people who had agreed to put up a small yard sign about either driving carefully or keeping California beautiful were much more likely to agree subsequently to put up a very large sign. This was true even if the second sign advocated the *other* issue posted on the first sign. In other words, people who posted a small sign about keeping California beautiful were more likely to put up a large sign about either keeping California beautiful *or* driving carefully than were people who did not agree to any small sign initially. Controls were asked only to put the large sign up, without the small sign first, and were much less likely to agree to the request.

The researchers concluded that when a person agrees to a small request, subsequent agreement to a larger request is more likely. In part, this occurs because the request for a larger commitment implicitly communicates to the individual that he or she is already the kind of person who does this (after all, they've agreed to a much smaller, similar request). In the researchers' words, "he may become, in his own eyes, the kind of person who does this sort of thing, who agrees to requests made by strangers, who takes action on things he believes in, who cooperates with good causes" (Freedman & Fraser, 1966, p. 201).

For our discussion, let us assume that most adults feel that they care about kids and want to see young people grow up healthy, and also think of themselves generally as responsible people who are good neighbors. Public communication messages might then reinforce that this description of caring and responsible people accurately portrays who adults already are. The messages might then encourage adults to do just a little bit more for kids, say, by talking for five minutes with one young person unrelated to them this week (instead of just waving hello to them or ignoring them).

Such a campaign has two powerful advantages. First, affirming for people that they already are doing some of these desirable things (being energy-conscious, being nurturing with kids) has the effect of making any request to do additional similar behaviors seem less overwhelming than if they had to change their behavior significantly to meet that request. Second, it taps into the power that compliance with perceived norms can have to affirm favorable aspects of one's personal and group identities. This approach might be quite effective in encouraging increased adult engagement with the young, as we further describe in Chapter 9.

This approach to behavior change—telling people that they already are "the kind of person who does this sort of thing" and then asking them to do a bit more—also has been found to be more effective than traditional persuasive appeals in getting adults to be more energy-conscious(Allen, 1982). It also has been more successful than simple persuasion in encouraging children to be more careful about not littering (Miller, Brickman, & Bolen, 1975). In each case, in television appeals to the adults, and interpersonal comments to 5th graders, the most effective messages were those that asserted that these were adults who *already* cared about conserving energy, and that these were children who *already* were ecology-minded, especially about littering.

Recall, too, our earlier discussion of the research on norm-based campaigns to discourage binge drinking by students. If membership in a desired group is also part of one's personal identity, then knowing that most students do not binge drink, and behaving according to that norm so as to be part of that group, is of course a reinforcement of needs for belonging. It also reinforces one's self-image as being a person who already is a responsible drinker or some similar positive self-description. Thus, the role that conformity to perceived norms plays in reinforcing one's sense of personal and group identities should not be overlooked as a mechanism that can promote desired social and community changes that turn shared values into actual social norms.

In contrast, one-on-one or public communications that try to encourage adult engagement with the young by labeling less engaged adults as uncaring or irresponsible likely promote feelings of shame, a dubious way to motivate behavior (Abell & Gecas, 1997). Instead, messages that reinforce self-perceptions that one is already caring toward young people, and a responsible person, but has a lot on one's plate and a lot of choices to make, may tap into a milder feeling of guilt. Because a principal way people "fix" feelings of guilt is through interpersonal connections, that process may be more likely eventually to produce the desired behavior—in this case, adults getting more engaged with kids.

Of course, positive identity reinforcement can promote both behavior change and resistance to change. For example, research has found that a significant reason why many smokers do not quit smoking, even in the face of normative pressure to do so, is that they are strongly identified with membership in the group "smokers." Many smokers, in the face of public health campaigns that try to stigmatize their identity, are instead moved to defend it by hardening their intention to smoke and building their solidarity or benefiting from their solidarity with other smokers. As a minority group visibly acting in opposition to the dominant norm, smokers clearly experience an in- and out-group division, and a particular identity as a member of a visible "out" group. The defensive reaction to antismoking campaigns seems especially to be the case if an antismoking message is presented from a "high status" source such as an expert, as contrasted with a "regular" person. This is because the expert's antismoking claims are usually seen as particularly valid, and therefore even more threatening to a smoker's identity (Falomir, Mugny, & Perez, 2000).

In contrast, people who are more or less engaged with other people's kids are not divided into clearly visible groups, one dominant and the other obviously stigmatized. Only an extreme minority of Americans, it can be assumed, strongly desire to be thought of as unconnected with kids and not wanting to help out in their development. Even adults who are committed to not having their own children aren't necessarily uninterested in other people's kids, in being their friends, mentors, and guides. Moreover, unlike smoking, which is seen as a negative behavior by the majority of Americans, and therefore has the power to unite those who do it, most people do not consider failing to engage with young people to be a "bad" action. Thus, there is little for those who are unengaged with young people to unite against.

Therefore, appeals to the relatively less engaged to engage more with young people could well be met with far less resistance to change than trying to change a behavior like smoking, which carries such strong identity ramifications. There is no particular "identity" called "not engaged with young people" for adults to have a special need to hang on to. Thus, they should be more open to a variety of behavior change strategies to promote this form of altruism and helping behavior than a group such as smokers can be successfully invited to change their smoking behavior. Then too, the strategy we described earlier is applicable. A campaign could communicate that they already care about kids and want to do their part to help them grow up healthy, responsible, and productive. That strategy simply cannot be used in the case of smoking, for to do so would mean assuming that smokers already are and want to be nonsmokers, an assumption that flies in the face of both logic (smokers cannot "already" be nonsmokers) and identity research.

To this point, we have discussed how norms operate in a broad sociological sense, and how early developmental experiences and psychological processes such as personal and group identity formation may later affect one's disposition as an adult to being engaged with young people. The differing cumulative personal experiences different people have from infancy through adolescence promote differing probabilities and styles of connectedness with others when they are adults. But there also are broader cultural influences that affect adults' likelihood of being engaged with young people. Before presenting our results in Chapters 6–8, we examine in Chapters 4 and 5 some of those broader cultural influences in more detail.

4 How Context and Culture Influence Adults' Sense of Reasonable Responsibility for Young People

Cultural Trends Working against Shared Norms for Adult Engagement

An increasing body of research points both to the important role that community influences, apart from demographic factors, play in the healthy development of young people, and also to "features of the cultural context that signal rupture in key community dynamics" (Benson et al., 1998, p. 140). The apartness of children and especially of youth from adults is a challenge to the well-being of society. Price, Ciocci, Penner, and Trautlein (1993) observed that young people need to be surrounded by positive "webs of influence" for healthy development. Not only do family, school, and community influences need to be consistent in promoting norms and opportunities. As we described in Chapter 1, there also need to be abundant connections among the family, school, and community resources in young people's lives for effective socialization consistency and for young people to experience an abundance of social capital. Among those cultural themes that have worked in concert to keep Americans from placing children and adolescents at the center of civic life are the isolation of families, civic disengagement, the professionalization of care, the loss of socialization consistency, and the marginalization of youth (elaborated in Benson et al., 1998).

Family Isolation

Furstenberg (1993) wrote that the privatization of families—the expectation that the family has sole or dominant responsibility for the care of children—is a radical departure from historical social norms. Those formerly pervasive norms held parents to be representatives of the larger society: "Other adults in the community are no longer relied upon to supervise and sponsor children" (p. 253).

Coupled with increasing mobility, longer work hours and a high proportion of working parents, and increased disconnection from religious and other membership organizations, these trends have left families more isolated than in previous eras. Disconnection of families from other adults has also reduced the likelihood that adults will speak in a consistent voice when transmitting values and standards, providing support, and promoting empowerment, among other core developmental processes.

Civic Disengagement

The isolation of families and increased reliance on professionals may also have contributed to a depletion of civic engagement in America (Putnam, 1996). A recent Public Agenda study, for example, found that the majority of Americans would like to see more community involvement with their schools (especially among those who rate their schools only as fair or poor). However, the majority of Americans also are comfortable leaving decisions in the hands of professionals, and few participate in the school board elections and meetings that can influence school policies (Farkas, Foley, Duffett, Foleno, & Johnson, 2001).

Expanding Professionalization of Care

Paralleling those trends has been the increasing professionalization of all aspects of contemporary society, and the focus in America on naming and solving problems among young people rather than promoting positive development. This has been connected to an increased reliance on trained professionals to provide the primary developmental supports historically supplied by a community's residents (McKnight, 1995; Benson et al., 1998). The professionalization of society further depletes a community's indigenous sources of strength and capacity to meet its challenges, including caring for its young.

Marginalization of Youth

Finally, young people themselves, especially adolescents, have become marginalized through the prolonged education that characterizes industrialized societies. Young people in general have few useful roles available to them other than as students and family members. There are occasional exceptions involving relatively small numbers of youth (such as the expansion over the 1990s in opportunities for youth community service and service-learning programs [Schine, 1997]). But in general, young people are not well integrated into society. This marginalization can result in lost opportunities to build young people's capacities and a negative impression of young people in the minds of adults. For example, Bales (2001) conducted focus groups with adults and concluded that perceptions adults have of young people's lack of core values about hard work, productivity, and responsibility are a significant element in the overall negativity adults feel toward youth in general.

Cultural Fragmentation and Ambiguity about Norms

Some of these trends may have affected not only how adults relate to children and youth, but also other broad indicators of social health and happiness: Whether the data are gathered by liberal- or conservative-leaning groups, whether the focus is on social and economic indicators such as welfare, charitable giving, and AIDS, or those characterized as moral and cultural indicators, such as divorce, community participation, and levels of trust or mistrust in government, measurements of Americans' well-being tend to show that we are richer but less happy than we were 30 years ago (Stille, 2000). And as we discussed in the preceding chapter, the malleability of many social norms in contemporary society—their inconsistency over time and circumstances (Fukuyama, 1999)—may have contributed to the divergence between trends in wealth and happiness. Social commentators have noted that the evolution of contemporary American society has contributed mightily to a drift away from a prevailing set of broad-based social norms—expectations with real consequences—to competing clusters of values based on personal or subgroup preferences (Fukuyama, 1999; Putnam, 2000). One result of these social trends has been a loss of socialization consistency for young people, as the adults in their lives have become less clear and united about how young people should be reared.

This is not to say that there are no values, norms, or trends that operate to unite Americans. The values accorded to work and tolerance for others certainly are widespread and hold us together. In a sense, Americans are becoming more homogeneous in some ways, for example, as consumers. Similar shopping malls dotted with identical chain stores offering identical merchandise are a shared feature of American consumer demography from Alaska to Florida, as are the fast-food eateries that boast of "billions" of identical products served. Similarly, the print and electronic news Americans consume is increasingly standardized as fewer owners control more newspapers and TV and radio stations. Such trends may help make regional and subcultural distinctions less common and some aspects of consumerism more standardized. But these examples of a more standardized culture seem fewer in number and importance than the diversity of values and norms that define American life today.

American society today is arguably more diverse than ever in some of the foundational experiences that help build culture, including marriage and childbearing patterns, religion, race and ethnicity, and language. People define themselves (as does public policy in many cases) as never before by their membership in particular groups, such as by sexual orientation, by physical or mental disability, as the parent of a child with special needs, as a cancer survivor, and so on. Carried with those subcultural identities are sets of social norms for what the members of that group should believe and how they should behave. In addition, the gap between the wealthiest Americans and even the comfortably middle class has mushroomed in a generation, with the working class and the poor left very far behind indeed (Teachman, Tedrow, & Crowder, 2000), creating strikingly different saving and spending patterns that both contribute to and reflect underlying norms tied to socioeconomic status. Culturally fragmenting us still further has been the explosion of media and entertainment choices, from hundreds of cable television stations to thousands of magazines to millions of Web sites on the Internet (Turow, 1997), defining increasingly narrow niches of interests and lifestyles.

Although we do not suggest that there was ever a "golden age" when all Americans shared the same values and norms, the beginning of the 21st century does seem very much unlike earlier eras. Just 50 years ago, an eye blink in human history, broad cultural values in the United States seemed less fragmented. The Pledge of Allegiance typically started the day for most schoolchildren. Divorce was far less common, immigrants were expected to learn English, children grew up in closer contact with larger extended families in closer proximity, and there were fewer media isolating us into smaller and smaller consumer niches. There were fewer choices to make about one's role in life; less opportunity to leave one's community of origin for college, travel, or employment; and fewer choices generally, especially for women and people of color. Since the 1960s, it could be argued that cultural change, although contributing to far-reaching improvements in the openness, opportunities, choices, and democracy afforded in American society, also has helped to fractionalize what once was a more shared ethos regarding how to raise the next generation.

The practice of "targeted marketing" supports that plethora of media and also can be seen as shifting the balance away from "society-making media" to "segment-making media" that move the nation from "overarching connectedness" to a greater degree of separateness (Turow, 1997, p. 51). Customized media and messages can strengthen feelings of union with groups with which a consumer already holds similar values or engages in similar clusters of lifestyle pursuits. But they also can "reinforce suspicion, lack of empathy, and alienation across groups," with the result that, much like living in gated communities, people can remain isolated from "people and issues they don't care about and don't want to be bothered with" (p. 54). Given these diverse media and marketing influences contributing to a splintering of truly "mass" culture, it is probably remarkable that the majority of Americans ever agree on anything, but it is also understandable why they may disagree on so much.

Cultural fragmentation has led to a burgeoning number of often conflicting norms about almost every aspect of American life, including social expectations about how we relate to work, family, and community. Ambiguity surrounding how adults are supposed to relate to young people is connected both to these broader cultural changes as well as to a historical ambivalence Americans have demonstrated between tolerance and responsibility for others (see the following section). The evidence seems to be that as older patterns of connectedness have frayed, we as a society have not established many genuine new norms encouraging individual adults to promote the positive development of children and youth. This is a critical gap in developmental attentiveness to kids, because to the extent clear norms for engagement with young people are lacking, so is adult involvement likely to be lacking. Research has shown, for example, that when the norms for expected performance of a task are either weak, or only weakly related to a person's perception of identity (recall our discussion of norms and identity in Chapter 3), then one's personal sense of responsibility for and engagement in that task also will tend to be weak (Britt, 1999).

A *New York Times* poll of more than 1,000 adults in March 2000 concluded that the dawn of the 21st century represents an "age of autonomy" in which social institutions no longer provide as much certainty about the critical values we all should espouse. In many respects, we appear to be living in an era when "everyone seems to have an opinion on truths that were once considered self-evident" (Wolfe, 2000). Among the guiding principles people seem to be rethinking are what ought to be public concerns of everyone and what ought to stay in the private, personal realm. Indeed, nearly 4 in 10 (37%) American adults say that a lot of what is really important to them, they would rather keep to themselves and not talk about with anyone (Powers, 2000). One might ask, if 4 in 10 American adults don't want to talk about the things that are really important to them, doesn't that already limit the role they can play in positively socializing the young? Few overarching norms unify our expectations for behavior, and a solid proportion of us doesn't appear to want to reveal to others what they think is important, making the task of establishing a consensus on social expectations for behavior all the more difficult.

The Ambivalence between Tolerance versus Responsibility

Our study allowed us to examine the extent to which there is a national core of social norms promoting adults' positive engagement with the young, or whether normative and cultural fragmentation around these issues is more characteristic, as our discussion thus far indicates. What we found, however, was no either-or result. Our results (Chapters 6–8) reflect both a core consensus and significant differences among various groups of Americans in their attitudes and the normative climate they experience for getting involved with children and youth outside their families.

Perhaps this duality of our results, showing both solid consensus and striking differences among Americans, should not be surprising. A *New York Times* survey showed that Americans strongly identify with what has been called utilitarian individualism and expressive individualism: Three of the four top values of adults (out of 15) reflected these orientations (being responsible for your own actions, being able to stand up for yourself, and being able to communicate your feelings) (Cherlin, 1999). Well down the list—ranked 13th out of 15 values—was being involved in one's community, which only 35% of adults thought was very important. Youth too may be learning to place community connections at a low level of priority: Similar to adults, only 32% of 13- to 17-year-olds in a *New York Times/CBS News* poll said it was very important to be active in their community (Goldberg & Connelly, 1999).

Sociologist Andrew Cherlin (1999) noted that Americans have not forsaken community involvement (membership in service clubs has dropped, but participation in shorter-term, more focused service projects is up). He concluded, however, that it is nevertheless "clear that the fabric of public life has frayed" (p. 6). Adult ambivalence and uncertainty about how they are supposed to relate with children and youth are hardly surprising. The larger social context is one in which the "most fundamental quality of the American sense of self" is neither individualism nor commitment, but "rather our continuing ambivalence as we steer a life course between them" (p. 6).

Expressing it another way, there seems to be a continuing balancing act being played out between two fundamental American values, tolerance and responsibility. A live-and-let-live philosophy is rooted in the conviction that we all have the right to do as we please within the limits of the law. That value bumps up repeatedly in American life against an alternative ethos that we are responsible for each other and for doing what is ethically and morally right, such as providing for the "less fortunate." Today, the live-and-let-live approach appears to be culturally more influential. The challenge for promoting developmentally attentive communities is how to reignite the norm for adults to feel a "reasonable responsibility" for getting involved with others, and especially kids, without offending parents or other caregivers. By "reasonable," we mean a heightened sense of recognition of the value and importance of our social and cultural interconnectedness, but tempered to accommodate the strong strain of individualism inherent in the American character and reflected in the increased busyness of contemporary life.

The Knight Foundation's national Community Indicators Survey (*Community Indicators Survey—National*, 1999) also illustrated this ambivalence. It appears as if Americans see lack of community involvement and limited adult connection with young people as problems, but expect or hope that others will do something about it. This reliance on "someone else" to address and take care of social challenges may also be one of the negative outgrowths of the expanding professionalization of American life we described earlier.

For example, nearly 3 in 10 adults (28%) said that "too many unsupervised children and teenagers" were a "big problem" in their community, a higher proportion than said crime and drugs were big problems. Tied for second place with crime and drugs as a perceived problem was people not getting "involved in efforts to improve the community." And yet, just 26%–29% said they personally had volunteered in the past 12 months in after-school programs or "youth development" programs such as "a day care center, scouts, or little league." Similarly, adults seem to view young people negatively and, although sympathetic to parents, feel that raising kids is mostly the parents' problem to solve, rather than personally feeling some degree of responsibility for the positive development of young people.

Additional Assumptions and Norms That Inhibit Adult Contact with Kids

Within the broad cultural tug between tolerance and responsibility, other kinds of ambivalence play out regarding how adults should relate to young people. We have described the primary ambivalence as being between Americans

Table 5. Key Cultural Norms and Assumptions That Limit Adult Engagement with Young People

Assumption or norm	Likely effect
• It is overwhelmingly the responsibility of parents to nurture and guide kids	• Except for adults in formal/legal care-giving roles, leaves impression that other adults have little or no clear responsibility—no mandate to be engaged
• Conflict between tolerance and responsibility, as a general rule, not just as applied to young people	• Adult uncertainty as to which value—tolerance or assumption of responsibility—should prevail in a given situation
• Negative images of young people	• Promotes desire to keep distance • Repels adults from relationships with young people
• Typical focus on the negative in research and services for kids	• Reinforces negative media images of young people • Creates sense that only professionals can deal with young people • Creates sense of powerlessness for individual community residents to do anything on a personal, everyday level
• Limited adult knowledge of normal child development	• Creates mismatch between what kids really need from adults and what adults think they ought to provide • Reinforces negative media images of kids
• Young people don't initiate deeper engagement with other adults	• Reinforces adult sense that kids don't really want to be involved with them
• Weak neighborhood ties and sense of community	• Promotes social mistrust and suspicion, or at best, ignorance • Reinforces adults' sense that they do not have permission from parents to get more involved
• Adult fears about being accused of child abuse	• Possibility that parents, children, and other adults could misinterpret adult interest in a child or youth keeps many adults from getting too close
• Lack of shared expectations for getting involved	• Creates gray areas where responsibility and what to do are uncertain • Creates absence of both rewards for getting engaged with kids, as well as negative consequences for staying distant

thinking preparing youth for the future is our number one national priority (suggesting that everyone has a stake in helping out) and the assumption that guiding the next generation is really their parents' responsibility. Today, the norm about leaving the nurturing and guiding of young people to parents (and the adult professionals kids come into contact with) seems to hold greater sway than the norm of everyone taking responsibility for preparing young people.

But as Table 5 indicates, there are other norms and cultural assumptions of considerable significance inhibiting adult engagement with the young, including negative images of children and adolescents; a focus in broader society on naming and trying to fix problems more than on promoting positives; limited adult knowledge of normal child development; lack of relationship initiation by young people themselves (and the consequent belief of adults that young people don't really want to connect with them); declining community involvement and weakened neighborhood connections (i.e., the norms of valuing privacy and of "minding one's own business"); adult fears of child abuse accusations; and lack of social pressure or normative expectation to get involved with young people (Scales, Benson, & Roehlkepartain, 2001).

Negative Images Adults Have of Young People

Superficially, attention to the positive development of young people seems to have increased. Since the 1997 Presidents' Summit urging adults to get involved with young people, campaign, television, and print ads have regularly urged Americans to volunteer to help youth, and especially to become mentors. Election years often see heightened rhetoric on behalf of families and children, and 2000 was no exception in that regard.

But deeper evidence is less reassuring. Two-thirds of American adults, according to the Public Agenda surveys in 1997 and 1999, already think of teenagers in negative terms, describing them spontaneously as irresponsible, wild, and rude (more than half used negative adjectives even to describe younger children). Only a little more than 10% of adults offered positive comments about young people (Farkas & Johnson, 1997; Duffett et al., 1999). Bostrom (1999) also asked adults in focus groups to name the first word that enters their mind in thinking about children and teenagers. She concluded that children are considered "innocent and precious," whereas teenagers are "feared" (p. 31), so much so that she advised children's advocates not even to use the word "teenager" in their communications.

Steinberg (2001) noted that there is a "dramatic disjunction" between the more positive view of adolescents that has become the normative perspective among academics, and the view presented to parents and other adults through the popular media. In advice books, he commented, adolescents continue to be portrayed as "puzzling, troublesome, angry, and ungrateful" (p. 4). Such images hardly would seem to motivate adults to get closer to young people. On the contrary, widespread negative images and perceptions of young people interfere with adults' interest in and desire to form meaningful relationships with them. This reasoning is lent support by a study of Colorado adults. Adults who were more connected with young people thought media images of them were too negative (Scales et al., 1998). In other words, the more they know young people, the less likely adults are to think negative depictions are true.

An ad from the Partnership for a Drug-Free America in the *New York Times* (March 4, 2000, p. A12) illustrated a common presentation of images about adolescents. It was headlined "Smelly. Lethargic. Incoherent. It's hard to detect inhalant abuse in the average teenager." The focus of the ad, drug-abuse prevention, is of course a laudable cause, and the statement about detecting inhalant abuse may literally be true—it may be hard to do. But the underlying message sent to millions of readers was that the average teenager is smelly, lethargic, and incoherent. Such "knowledge" about kids, communicated explicitly or reflected implicitly countless times in advertisements and entertainment programming, or in news programs covering "our troubled youth," is hardly conducive to encouraging adults to volunteer in child and youth programs or to spend more time with young people (Scales, 2001).

Focus on the Negative in Research and Helping Relationships with Children and Youth

The focus on the negative also characterizes most research about children and youth. In an article introducing the emerging science of "positive psychology," Seligman and Csikszentmihalyi (2000) wrote that the entire field of psychology has devoted "almost exclusive attention to pathology" (p. 5). Ironically, they also concluded that the largest gains in our understanding of how to prevent major social, emotional, and mental health problems have come "from a perspective focused on systematically building competencies, not on correcting weaknesses" (p. 7). Nevertheless, Furstenberg's (2000) review of the leading journals on adolescence indicated that the "vast majority" of articles and studies on youth focus on problem behavior rather than on successful development. He concluded that the emphasis on the negative was even more prevalent in the research on early adolescence. Such a focus effectively consigns successful young people, Furstenberg wrote, to the image of "escape artists who manage to dodge the hazards of growing up" (p. 900). In a similar way, Bales (2001) concluded that when media portray young people in a positive light, it is mostly for doing extraordinary deeds, making positive behavior, which is actually typical among young people, appear to be highly unusual.

This orientation toward the negative is not limited to older children. From their extensive review of the science of early childhood development, the National Research Council and Institute of Medicine (2000) also concluded that there is much more known about deprivation than enrichment in the early years of life, more about developmental dangers than developmental opportunities, resilience, and thriving. The consequence of this emphasis is not merely distortion in the scientific bases for understanding child development, but the reinforcement of public pessimism about what individual and local efforts can accomplish. The media drumbeat emphasizing the extent of various child and youth problems can leave the typical community resident with a feeling of despair over what he or she can do to help resolve these seemingly widespread and intractable issues (Farkas & Johnson, 1997). This focus on the negative may also make it harder for adults to consider as deeply their role in promoting positive development among kids who seem basically to be doing OK. In effect, adults may assume that intervening to prevent negative development is crucial, but that positive development is more likely to take care of itself.

It is not that adults don't appreciate the value of a positive, growth-centered approach. For example, a Gallup poll in early 2001 found that 45% of American adults think the secret to a successful life is to know and build on their strengths, compared to 52% who prefer to know and improve their weaknesses (Buckingham, 2001). So only a small plurality of adults seems to focus more on the negative in their lives than on the positive. But it seems reasonable to suspect that adults use a different, more positively oriented frame of reference to determine what is helpful for their own development than they do for that of young people. In young people's negative media images, adults may more easily see weaknesses needing correction, the traditional frame of reference in thinking about children and adolescents.

Getting involved to build *positive* qualities of life for and with the young is made more difficult because it apparently is not at all certain that most adults will get involved even when they think something terrible is happening to a child. For example, a study by the Child Welfare League of America (1999) reported that 54% of adults had witnessed what they considered to be "child abuse" in public (the study defined "child abuse" as including anything from slapping a child to yelling at or calling the child names). However, half of those adults—53%—did nothing at all, a little more than 10% got passively involved (making eye contact or staring in ways that showed disapproval), and only 35% got actively involved (26% mostly by talking with the parent). This level of reported intervention in child maltreatment of various kinds is consistent with what other studies have reported. When adults are asked to predict their willingness to intervene when they see children publicly misbehaving (Duffett et al., 1999), or see youth hanging out and obviously cutting school (Scales et al., 1998; Sampson, 1997), only about 25%–33% of adults say they would get involved.

We seem to have difficulty defining "reasonable responsibility" for child well-being even for an issue most adults think they understand: Child abuse obviously is bad for kids, and everyone should do what he or she can to prevent or stop it. But adults have widely differing views even on the definition of child abuse. Although 75% in the Child Welfare League study said "extreme" child abuse was indicated by adult behaviors such as sexually fondling a child, others were not sure. About half thought it was extreme abuse to rarely hug a child, not enforce curfew on those under age 16, or use a hand to spank a child, with substantial proportions not sure it was. And although half to two-thirds said that rarely talking to children at home, calling them names, or not knowing their whereabouts constituted extreme abuse, one-third to one-half were not sure that it did. Obviously, we are grouping what child welfare practitioners technically define as "abuse" (e.g., the sexual touching of a child) with actions that are more properly defined as "neglect" (e.g., rarely hugging a child or not knowing her or his whereabouts). The point is that Americans find it difficult to come to a shared definition of what constitutes adult behavior that *hurts* children and adolescents. If that is the case, then one might imagine it would be even more difficult to achieve a shared definition—and its implied social expectations—for what constitutes necessary adult behavior that, instead, *helps* kids and promotes child and youth well-being.

After all, it has been more difficult for adults to agree on what constitutes evidence of success or "thriving" among young people than to agree on what constitutes failure or problem behavior (Scales, Benson, et al., 2000). It is relatively rare for adults to talk about positive behavior among young people, relative to the attention given to youths' problem behaviors. But as rare as it is, much more of this societal conversation has been about what is desirable behavior on the part of young people than what is desirable behavior for adults in their roles of nurturing and guiding children and adolescents. Much of this lack of definition for a reasonable responsibility in young people's positive development may be due to a predominant societal focus on the negative. In addition, there may be a widespread sense that we should intervene to prevent or stop negative behavior, but that positive development more or less happens on its own.

Limited Adult Knowledge of Normal Child Development

The knowledge many adults, including parents, have of child and adolescent development is of uneven accuracy, and so can reinforce both negative media images and a sense of helplessnesss and powerlessness in dealing with young people. Inaccurate knowledge of what young people need at different developmental stages also could lead to adults, including parents and other family members, failing to encourage the experiences, opportunities, and relationships that could provide children and adolescents with much of what they need for healthy development. For example, in a study by the group Zero to Three, it was reported that 69% of parents of young children know that children's capacity for learning is not set at birth. The study also reported, however, that about 25% of parents "know" that a 3-year-old should be able to sit quietly for an hour and that exposure to violence will not have long-term negative effects on children. Research shows that both of these statements are inaccurate (Jacobson, 2000; *What grown-ups understand about child development*, 2000).

Similarly, Scales (1997) reported in a national study of family support programs that while most family support professionals, who often work with middle and high school–age youth, had adequate levels of basic knowledge about adolescent development, between 16% and 45% misunderstood key developmental concepts. For example, 45% incorrectly thought adolescence was "usually a stormy period marked by outright rebellion," and 39% inaccurately thought that young adolescents or middle school youth "need a lot of independence from adults" (p. 621). If even professionals who work with youth think that adolescents normally are in turmoil, in conflict with adults, and need a lot of separation from adults, how much more likely are those erroneous assessments among people who have no professional responsibility or training for connecting with youth? Moreover, if many professionals don't have accurate knowledge about adolescent development, what does this signify about the value for child and adolescent development of the expanding professionalization of care for the young that we described earlier?

Combined, such faulty knowledge about child and adolescent development, and the negative images of young people prevalent in the media (another
kind of "knowledge" adults acquire), can contribute to too many adults perceiving young people only as problems to be fixed rather than as positive contributors to society (Scales, 2001). Indeed, Bales (2001) reported that 60% of television
news coverage of adolescents concerns violence or risky adolescent behavior;
in print coverage, studies have shown that youth violence appears as often as
stories about schools. In each medium, the result is a gross distortion of reality
and a false perceptual basis for the formation of norms about who young people
are and how adults ought to relate to them. The negativity about young people
even permeates the professions: A widely known postulate in the economics of
the family is called the "rotten-kid theorem" (Bruce & Waldman, 1990).

Thus, today's young people are considered less mature than their peers from
earlier eras. A Gallup poll of American adults found that far fewer adults in 2000
than 50 years earlier thought young people are levelheaded and have common
sense. Just 19% of adults said young people have those positive qualities, and
66% said they do not. Those negative evaluations cut across all demographic
groups. In contrast, the same question asked in 1949 revealed that more than
twice as many adults—42%—thought young people were more levelheaded
than in years past, whereas only 28% disagreed (Carlson, 2000). So pronounced
are these negative frames of reference that Bales (2001) found that even when
adults were presented with evidence that most American youth are not irresponsible, lacking values, or criminal, they rejected the facts, not their preconceived
negative frames of reference.

Young People's Own Choices about Involvement with Adults

Children also are not merely observers but active participants and even
initiators in aspects of their interactions with adults outside the family.
Developmental systems theory, through its transactional-ecological framework
(Lerner, Lerner, De Stefanis, & Apfel, 2001), posits that children are not recepta-
cles to be influenced by external events. Instead, children themselves, through
their own personalities and behaviors, help construct their environments and
relationships, with older children doing so more intentionally. For example, in
their longitudinal study of children on Kauai, Werner and Smith (1992) reported
that the children who years later demonstrated the most successful developmental outcomes and resiliency were those who, as infants, had been cuddly
and affectionate and able to elicit smiles from their caregivers. Infants are not
aware that they are "constructing" their environments, but as children get older,
the influence they exert on their environment indeed becomes more intentional.
Developmentally, even before they could be aware of it, they helped create the
network of adults they had caring for them.

Like adults, as children get older, they also make choices, about which
adults they like, whom they trust, and with whom they want to share meaningful conversation or activities. In fact, Stattin and Kerr (2000) reported in a study

of Swedish 14-year-olds that what parents know about their children's where-abouts is more often due to what children decide to tell them, rather than mainly being the result of parents' monitoring of them.

The formation of social norms about young people is a reciprocal process. The environment is not simply "out there" to act on young people (National Research Council and Institute of Medicine, 2000): *Children and adolescents help construct the norms that govern adults' interactions with them.* Children whose neigh-borhoods are characterized by plentiful interaction with multiple adults outside their families live in a different environment of relationships and socialization than children who see adults around but rarely interact on more than a super-ficial level with them. In each case, it is not just the neighborhood's adults who develop expectations about their behavior. Children too develop their own ex-pectations about how adults and young people are supposed to relate, and so can reinforce or challenge adults' sense about what is appropriate.

We can imagine that children in neighborhoods with high levels of posi-tive adult engagement may also initiate such interactions with adults more. In contrast, in low-engagement neighborhoods, children may be more reluctant to approach unrelated adults, just as the adults in those neighborhoods may be more reluctant to engage with young people. If true, such dynamics would help to solidify a shared understanding among residents young and older alike that "this is a place where adults and kids don't talk to each other." In short, children's own reactions to adults' lack of engagement "contribute over time to the 'psychological' climate of the community and define the *expected* character-istics of the neighborhood environment" (Farver et al., 2000, p. 142, emphasis in original).

Children are influenced by and contribute to the nature and degree of adult-child relationships. They already are making choices about becoming closer with some but not other adults. In addition, many adults may have concerns about parents' possible negative reactions to involvement with their children. In combination, these realities of the social ecology may account for a significant amount of the lack of adult engagement with young people.

Weak Neighborhood Ties and Sense of Community

In large measure, how neighbors would predict parents might feel about their relating to their son or daughter is a function of how well those neigh-bors know or think they know those parents and their values. But the Knight Foundation's national Community Indicators Study of American adults found that nearly two-thirds of adults (63%) said they either knew only *some* of the names of the "neighbors who live close to you," or knew *none* of their closest neighbors' names (*Community Indicators Survey—National*, 1999). The national Social Capital Community Benchmarks Survey (Saguaro Seminar, 2001) found that the dynamic of not being close to one's neighbors may be even more preva-lent among African Americans and Hispanics: Fifty-six percent of whites said they trusted people in their neighborhoods, versus 21% for blacks and 19% for

Hispanic respondents, and only 6% of whites said they never talked with their neighbors, versus 16% of African Americans and 26% of Hispanics. If knowledge of even the most basic information about one's nearest neighbors—their names—is lacking for the majority of American adults, and if substantial portions of Americans do not trust or feel close to their neighbors, how much more difficult might it be for a neighbor to accurately understand those parents' values and norms concerning relating to their children? It is hardly surprising that most adults keep that involvement fairly limited.

Adult Fears about Being Accused of Child Abuse

The prevalence of messages to both kids and adults about "stranger danger" and child abuse prevention, although clearly valuable and intended to protect children, may also have a negative impact in making many adults fearful that their interest in a child will be misinterpreted. One of the respondents to Search Institute's 2000 survey of Healthy Communities Healthy Youth initiatives, for example, wrote that fears of children being abused or of adults being accused of abuse have helped create a "non-emotional society where many, even with good intentions, do not get involved because it is too strenuous or the rules are too ambiguous."

In many, and arguably most, communities today, there is a strong wariness of touching children, such as hugging to offer comfort or to celebrate a child's accomplishment, because it could be misconstrued as child abuse. Media reports of clergy, teachers, and child-care providers being accused of child abuse, some substantiated and some not, communicate to the public at large that they walk through a minefield if they choose to get close to children who are not their own. For example, in a recent study, Public Agenda reported that more than 6 in 10 parents are very concerned about abuse and neglect occurring in child-care centers, expressing "almost paralyzing fears" about that possibility (Farkas, Duffett, Johnson, Foleno, & Foley, 2000). It is obviously critical to protect children from harm, and important for the public to know about the nature and extent of threats to children's well-being. And yet, it is easy to understand how these dynamics of concern for children's safety, and the media, law enforcement, and educational attention they get, dampen many adults' enthusiasm for getting engaged with other people's kids. Vigilance and awareness about children's safety should not be compromised, of course. But this example does illustrate how ambiguity and uncertainty are principal framers and shapers of how adults engage with young people.

Lack of Shared Expectations for Getting Involved

Today, a majority of American adults perceive that giving advice to children or youth who are not their own will bring resentment and perhaps anger from the parents of those children or youth (Farkas & Johnson, 1997). Many adults might give lip service to the African proverb "it takes a village to raise a child," but they do not seem to feel the social permission and expectation more commonly experienced in a true village to actually help "raise" the next generation.

Villages in developing societies are usually small and culturally homogeneous. The residents have a relative lack of exposure to competing values through media or personal contact with different others, and depend on each other for survival as well as companionship. Those attributes allow for more certain knowledge of what is acceptable or unacceptable behavior in that village, and, where uncertainty exists, allow also for an adult to more confidently assume there will be a similarity of expectations and therefore less risk of misjudgment among neighbors. Together, these attributes promote the social trust and sense of community that we described earlier as often lacking in contemporary developed societies, especially in urban and most suburban areas.

A stronger norm for helping behavior, for example, may exist in relatively smaller communities. Bridges and Coady (1996) reported on a "lost letter" study in Florida, in which letters, prestamped and with local addresses, were dropped in larger cities, as well as smaller cities and towns. Some addresses were neutral, and some were phrased to be "deviant," such as "Supporters of Legalized Prostitution" or "Communist Party." The findings showed that helping behavior (the mailing of the found letters) was generally greater in the smaller communities, *especially* when the addressees were "deviant." This result was surprising, because smaller communities might be presumed to have less tolerance for deviance from local norms. However, an even stronger norm of doing the right thing by mailing an obviously lost letter apparently operated at the same time, allowing residents of smaller communities to feel a social expectation to help even those who might have been perceived to be quite different from themselves.

In many communities and neighborhoods today, however, the relative absence of the qualities characteristic of villages promotes uncertainty of expectations, and a lack of trust and confidence in making assumptions about how one is to get involved with young people. For example, most parents certainly would want neighbors to step in to prevent their child from being hit by a car, or to call 911 and give CPR if the neighbor found their child not breathing. Most adults also would feel an obvious implicit permission—indeed, a requirement—to aid a child in those circumstances.

But how might those parents feel if the neighbor, knowing that the parents and older sibling of a 10-year-old smoke, happens to be in a situation with that 10-year-old where talking about the dangers of smoking feels like the "right" thing to do? It is now a social norm (among the great majority but not all Americans) that smoking is frowned upon, and certainly considerable social support would be available to adults who reinforced that children and adolescents should not smoke. But would most neighbors feel it permissible, much less expected (i.e., a rule, a norm), for them to talk with the 10-year-old about how bad smoking is? Would that conversation encourage the child to feel less respect for or simply more worry about his or her parents, and if so, could that not cause the parents to be irritated with the neighbor? If neighbors considered what to do, they might not sense much social gain from providing support to the child for abstaining from smoking, but weigh negatively the possible charge from that child's parents that they were interfering in the parents' business.

The Gray Areas Resulting from Lack of Shared Expectations

The preceding example illustrates what Elster (1989) called the "penumbra" around a main norm, a "gray area" that defines legitimate exceptions to a norm based on circumstances, situation, and individual judgment. Felmlee (1999) also noted that standards for behavior are affected most powerfully by the "local context" or situation in which the actions take place: Characteristics of the situation, the behavior in question, and the interaction between the two account for "substantial" proportions of the variance in whether people judge behaviors in a given situation to be appropriate.

A variety of considerations may enter into how norms operate. Imagine that an adult is talking more than just casually to a youth (itself apparently a behavior among only a minority of adults, according to Search Institute's research; Benson et al., 1999), and the young person says she doesn't like school. What is the adult supposed to do next? Is it acceptable to ask why? Is it not only acceptable but expected by the parents of the student, and other neighbors, that the adult will try to help the student identify reasons to like school instead? Perhaps the adult knows that this student's parents do not place much value on doing well in school. Does the adult still try to encourage liking and doing well in school? Perhaps the cultural norms of the youth's parents are to elevate family privacy above mere problem solving. Perhaps the adult knows the parents put too *much* pressure on the child to do well in school. Then what does the adult say? That school isn't everything in life?

The interaction also probably depends on a variety of other factors, such as how well the adult and youth already know each other, as well as where this conversation is taking place. Is the expectation for the adult's response different if the student is an adolescent or a younger child? How do the genders of adult and young person affect the range of normative options the adult may feel he or she has? What happens if other people are overhearing this conversation, as contrasted with it occurring in private? In the absence of an adult's prior meaningful knowledge of the likely answers to such questions, he or she must hazard a guess, rapidly, in order to seize the opportunity for interaction with a child or adolescent, or let that moment slip away. In the instantaneous calculus of the moment, it is understandable that many adults are reluctant to get involved, for they are dealing with many gray areas and uncertainties about what is expected of them and how people will react.

Lack of Expectations Connected to Lack of Consequences

Perhaps most fundamental for this discussion of how prevailing social norms influence adults to get involved with kids, or not, is the consideration of whether it even matters to others what the adult does in this situation. If adults do nothing but acknowledge the youth's dislike of school, do they pay any social price for their inaction? If they intervene more actively, do they pay a price for interfering in other people's (i.e., parents') "business," or do they experience any positive reinforcement or reward for assuming "reasonable" responsibility?

In 2000, for example, the Child Welfare League of America worked with the Digital Software Development Association to promote community-wide involvement in preventing child abuse and neglect, with the slogan "Protecting America's Children: It's Everybody's Business" (Software industry unites for kids, 2000). No data are yet available on the effectiveness of this campaign, but clearly, this message was meant to directly counter an existing norm that involvement in the lives of children and youth is not everybody's business. And yet, we must repeat a question we have raised a number of times already: Do any real consequences fall to adults who hear this message and do nothing about it? And do substantial rewards accrue to those who do get involved? The answer of course, is that neither rewards nor consequences are very likely. Indeed, one commentator described American society as one that "does not impose duties on people to go out and intervene in other people's behavior" (Lewin, 2001, p. A14). If this is true in general, it is especially so when the assumption of parental responsibility, and the other cultural assumptions and norms discussed in this chapter, are added to the situational dynamics.

If adult involvement with young people is so limited, as the research we have cited in Chapter 2 and elsewhere seems to suggest, what becomes of the neighborhood or community's intergenerational capacity to define the common good? A sense of shared commitments is "the glue that unites neighbors in purpose and action," and often is intimately connected to the "welfare of the neighborhood children" (Benson & Saito, 2000, p. 132). As we have described, adult engagement with young people is good for the young people themselves. But beyond that effect, perhaps a relative absence of social norms that support, encourage, and reward getting involved with young people is evidence that our sense of the common good, and our energy to work for it, is weak. Perhaps the limited engagement of adults with other people's kids is a signal that it is not just the quality of life for children and adolescents that is at stake here, but ultimately the quality of life for all of us.

We have ascribed the limited engagement adults currently have with young people to two main sources: The presence of a number of cultural norms and assumptions about young people and who is responsible for them, and cultural ambiguity and uncertainty about expected adult behavior caused both by cultural fragmentation and a vacuum in explicitly defining what is a reasonable responsibility for most unrelated adults to assume in helping nurture and guide other people's kids. We have also briefly introduced in Chapter 2 the adult actions we studied. In the next chapter, we define more precisely those adult actions that may begin to mark the territory of reasonable responsibility each of us could have for promoting the well-being of all kids.

Voices from the Field: Some Assumptions and Norms That Healthy Communities • Healthy Youth Initiative Leaders Say Limit Adult Engagement with Kids in Their Communities

Another indication of cultural assumptions and norms operating to prevent positive relationships among adults and the young comes from responses of 52 Healthy Communities • Healthy Youth initiatives to a survey Search Institute mailed to nearly 600 initiative leaders in 2000. These community leaders were asked to "describe or list some of your community norms or values (negative and positive) that affect adults' capacity, responsibility, and motivation for contributing to young people's healthy development." Although the roughly 10% response rate precludes any generalizing of these responses to other communities, the themes are remarkably similar to those we have touched on in this chapter:

- Those who have energy and ideas for engaging with kids are already involved in many other committees/activities/groups.
- People have a hard time committing to an ongoing role instead of a one-time event.
- Wherever more than one youth is gathered, that constitutes a "gang" and a threat in some way.
- People will judge parents negatively if they admit they need help in raising their kids.
- People are more comfortable with younger children who don't question their authority as much as teenagers do.
- Many adults believe they already are communicating with young people when in fact they are not.
- Elderly, retired citizens have raised their children and now just want to pay school taxes and that's enough: "kids are not my responsibility anymore."
- People are afraid to engage with kids from lower socioeconomic levels.
- The community norm is disengagement: Let them alone and let them leave me alone.
- Too much liability in engaging with kids, especially if there are no other adults around.
- Lack of support from parents if you do try to get involved; they see it as undermining their authority.

5 Personal and Collective Action to Raise Healthy, Caring, Competent Young People: Defining Reasonable Responsibilities and Expectations for All Adults

Multiple and contradictory cultural norms and assumptions about the young and about adults' relationships with young people build a perceptual bias and create a frame of reference within which adults make decisions about personal and collective actions to benefit young people. We have alluded to adults' various fears of negative consequences for getting involved as significant barriers to engagement with young people, and we will expand on that theme later. But a genuine norm about behavior operates only if there also are consequences for failing to do that behavior and/or palpable rewards for doing it. From this perspective, there is little predictable negative result most adults would experience for staying unconnected with kids, and little anticipated positive benefit from getting engaged. Public opinion polls suggest that the majority of American adults do support norms such as "paying one's fair share or assuming the obligation to help those who have helped you" (Wolfe, 2000, p. 54). But how fully do such general norms of shared responsibility for others translate to expectations for adult behavior toward the young?

When it comes to engaging with young people in ways that help build the 40 developmental assets young people need, are most adults likely to feel a sense of reasonable responsibility to play a role? In this chapter, we consider these issues more fully, and we conclude by describing the adult actions we studied that we believe begin to define a sphere of reasonable responsibility for all adults in nurturing and guiding young people. We do so to bring clarity to the ambiguity and ambivalence that characterize how adults are supposed to engage with young people.

To place in proper perspective the relative absence of true norms about the engagement of all adults with kids, we need first briefly to consider how social norms—expectations and consequences—apply to parents. We have described most parents, and most youth, as doing okay. But the degree to which parents are expected to have a practically exclusive right to raise their children as they see fit affects where and to what degree society should intervene when parents are not doing okay, such as when they fail to protect their children or to provide basic needs such as food and shelter. This uncertainty about responsibility and consequences is even greater when it comes to a parent's responsibility to nurture, set boundaries and high expectations, and provide opportunities children and youth need to succeed.

We do not suggest that society should impose significant consequences on parents who fail to nurture their children by adequately building their developmental assets. Rather, there is a disparity between the general belief that parents are responsible for their children and the consequences society imposes for ignoring that social expectation. Moreover, neither public policy nor public opinion has much to say about parents whose children are essentially safe but unchallenged, or who are provided basic necessities but not nurtured to develop their capabilities.

For example, parents are supposed to ensure that their children go to school, do not engage in vandalism, and in other ways keep out of trouble. But it was only in the 1990s that about half the states began passing laws holding parents responsible for their children's misbehavior, and even now, such laws are rarely enforced and they are considered to have had little impact (Lewin, 2001). Florida legislators had "second thoughts" about a law passed in 2000 that charged parents of juvenile offenders up to $50 per day of detention and dropped the daily charge to $5 while questioning the wisdom of trying to legally establish parental control (Krueger, 2001). The Chicago public schools took an unusual step in fall 2000 by assessing and reporting back to parents what parents themselves were doing to support their children's education, in an effort to underscore parental accountability. But there has also been considerable argument over how appropriate those parent "report cards" are (Galley, 2000). In addition, violent tragedies at the hands of children and teenagers, including the Columbine High School shootings in 1999 and Santana High shootings in 2001, have led to heated debate about parents' accountability for their children's violence. Many hold parents responsible, whereas many others argue that parents ultimately can have little control over such deeply disturbed behavior.

Short of technically defined child abuse and neglect, even parent behavior that clearly has an adverse impact on young people does not necessarily bring negative consequence for parents. For example, analysis of data from the National Health Interview Study (Zill, 1999) showed that 3 in 10 mothers and 4 in 10 fathers engage in at least one of several risk behavior patterns (smoking, heavy drinking, sedentary lifestyle, being overweight, and driving after drinking) that put themselves at risk of poor health, increased family stress, lowered ability to care for their children and to set positive examples for children's own behavior, and becoming a tax burden on other citizens. Fines, driver's license suspension, and even jail time are possible penalties for driving after drinking, but there would appear to be few other legal or social consequences associated with parents engaging in those other risk behavior patterns, despite the terrible costs to their children and the public.

If consequences to parents for doing even the minimum are not necessarily consistent or significant, then consequences are all but absent if parents take care of those basics (keep their kids safe and out of trouble, get them to school, etc.) but do not necessarily help their children thrive. For example, most people would expect parents to ensure some sort of adult supervision for an 8-year-old after school, and habitual failure to provide that child care might be an element in a charge of chronic neglect. But do public policy or neighbors reflect any expectation for that 8-year-old to be in a developmentally rich after-school program that provides numerous opportunities to build social skills, strengthen positive values, and enrich academic abilities?

Moreover, the consequences, if any, whether positive or negative, to parents for raising kids who are perceived to be "good" or "bad" may accrue quite slowly rather than immediately or profoundly. Ultimately, despite widespread belief in parental responsibility, how a young person turns out may also be seen as only partly under the control of parents. There seems to be little support or condemnation for the actions parents might take, or fail to take, to "stack the deck" on behalf of their children's positive development.

To the extent children and youth do not exhibit certain assets, their parents may be thought less of by neighbors, teachers, and other adults. It is not at all certain, however, that these other adults would even communicate their displeasure or concern to parents, much less that parents would feel a serious consequence in terms of social ostracism or loss of self-esteem. This is not to suggest that most parents are unaware of whether neighbors or other adults whose opinion they value think they are good parents. Most parents obviously care about their children's well-being, do the best they can, and likely have a pretty good sense of whether others think they are doing a good job. But our sense is that the great majority of such awareness is mined or intuited by parents through whatever subtle, behind-the-back, or mostly silent hints their neighbors give. Until laws have been or may be about to be broken, by parents or their children, there do not seem to be social norms operating in America that give those neighbors permission to be explicit about their concerns.

Consider another example. In a 1998 survey of 14- to 18-year-olds done by the Horatio Alger Association, 15% of respondents said they did not have rules at home about drinking alcohol. Further, close to 20% didn't have rules about completing schoolwork, smoking, or curfews, and almost 40% had no have rules about attending religious services or dating (Horatio Alger Association, 1998). Most Americans likely would believe that such rules were at least desirable and perhaps even necessary. And yet, how likely is it that the parents who fail to set and enforce such boundaries and expectations are subject to any social consequences by their friends, neighbors, or coworkers? How likely is it that people outside the family are even aware of the absence of such rules in particular households? And how likely is it that parents are socially rewarded for having such rules? Isn't that just what ought to be expected of them?

Similarly, if children are not caring, honest, and principled (i.e., not exhibiting the Positive-Values assets), parents might be thought of as not doing their job, or at worst, be thought of as uncaring, dishonest, or prejudiced. But only if people share what they think with parents, and only if parents care what those people think of them, can such judgments reinforce a social norm that says parents not only should have those positive values but also should impart them to their children. In general, research has shown that Americans are dissatisfied with the job parents are doing, holding them responsible for what, in the public mind, is seen as a population of young people who honor too few of such basic values. But few adults seem willing to share such views directly with parents (Farkas & Johnson, 1997).

Expectations and Consequences for Other Adults

Expectations and consequences are not well aligned for parents, even for protecting children from adverse influences. And there seem to be few strong social expectations for parents to ensure that their children thrive, as long as they stay out of trouble. The situation is even murkier for other adults, especially unrelated adults and those not dealing with kids in formal programs. Meaningful consequences seem relatively rare for adults who do not get very engaged with young people. Even where there are real consequences, such as occur if adults fail to ensure the safety of children and youth from abuse or neglect, the consequences fall largely on parents, not unrelated adults.

Of course, there are some clear guidelines for how adults are *not* supposed to behave with young people, as expressed in laws against, for example, sexual abuse and selling tobacco products or alcohol to minors. More positively, many adults outside a child's family also might feel comfortable reinforcing with young people such relatively noncontroversial customs as table manners, the importance of saying thank you, of returning favors, or of exerting effort at school or work. It is hardly clear, however, that those adults are expected to play such a role, or rewarded if they do.

Where expectations are more involved than table manners and encouraging children to obey the law, the role of other adults may fairly be described as quite limited and not well understood. More specific to the discussion of child and adolescent development, Table 6 shows the degree to which expectations for adult behavior may be operating that help adults build or inhibit them from building the 40 developmental assets of young people as identified by Search Institute. (Much of the content in Table 6 is speculative rather than based on exhaustive research. Especially speculative are what norms support adults building a particular asset through their relationships with young people, and the social consequences that may accompany a failure to build that asset [or, rarely, the social rewards that might accrue to an adult who did try to build a particular asset]. For example, variation in those columns may be particularly great across different cultural groups in American society. Nevertheless, the table does suggest how infrequently adults other than parents probably experience any legal or even social consequences for not being positively engaged with the young, much less experience rewards for being involved.)

A review of Table 6 suggests that many of these expectations regarding adults' roles in promoting positive child and adolescent development may function more as values or beliefs than as genuine norms. This is because there seem to be relatively few cases in which there is a substantive consequence if adults fail to engage with young people to promote the assets, or much meaningful social reward for adult behavior that helps build those assets. As we have discussed, without real legal or social consequences or rewards, there may be strong habits or customs for relating to children and youth, but there are few genuine norms.

The greatest emphasis on real consequences appears to be in the empowerment asset of safety, where adults such as teachers and child-care providers clearly are held responsible and accountable for reporting suspected maltreatment. Overall, however, it is largely parents and guardians who would experience legal or social effects of either promoting or failing to promote the assets. The absence of punishment for failure to get involved with other people's children, and the presence only of limited extrinsic rewards for doing so, suggest that adults often may perceive the possible negative social consequences of getting involved with children and youth to be stronger than any reward. These perceptions may then discourage greater engagement.

For example, although there might well be social disapproval leveled at a neighbor who speaks meanly to children on a regular basis, there is unlikely to be any sanction for more common adult passivity. Simply ignoring children or youth, failing to smile and wave hello when one sees children and youth in the neighborhood, failing to encourage youth decision making or community service, or their liking of school, are adult omissions hardly likely to generate feelings of guilt and anxiety in those adults. But such feelings, Elster (1989) argued, are the internalized emotional guardians of true social norms and may be the root source of the power of norms to shape behavior.

Indeed, Azjen's (2001) review of recent research on attitudes suggests that when beliefs and feelings conflict, it is feelings that are more motivating. Thus, an adult might believe getting involved with other people's kids is highly important. But, if he or she also feels uncomfortable or hesitant about doing so, it is those latter feelings that will tend to influence behavior most. The result will be the relative lack of engagement reported in previous studies, and that we found in our study as well (see Chapters 6–8).

There might be differences among various groups of adults in how much they feel expected to build such assets in young people. For example, the list of developmental assets reflects "conventional" values that were perhaps more widely held and/or simply discussed in earlier eras (respecting and connecting with elders, working hard in school, being honest, having an optimistic outlook on life). Moreover, most of the assets imply the kinds of closer relationships youth used to have with adults. Thus, we might speculate that older adults would identify more of the assets as desirable for young people, and might do more to try to build those assets than would younger adults. In fact, as we describe in Chapters 7 and especially 8, we did find that adults 35 and older rated

Table 6. Norms and Consequences Reflected in the Developmental Assets Framework

Asset category/asset	Existing "norms"	Legal impact	Social impact
SUPPORT			
Family support	Norms mainly regarding what is not OK (abuse, neglect). Support is mainly a parent's job; financial support is the most important support; parents should work hard to give children what they "need" (although some cultural groups may expect more from children, e.g., children working to provide income for the family)	*Parents and guardians only*—Child abuse and neglect laws; child support enforcement, but covers only financial, not emotional support; Family and Medical Leave Act allowing (but not requiring) employment leave, but that is not limited to support of children	Possible social isolation, disapproval/rejection by other adults; feelings of guilt, shame
Positive family communication	Is a good thing	Possible, *parents and guardians only*—Child abuse and neglect laws	Possible social isolation, disapproval/rejection by other adults; feelings of guilt, shame
Other adult relationships	Be friendly and helpful, but don't get too close	Only if abuse child	None, absent abuse
Caring neighborhood	Be friendly and helpful, but mind your own business	Only if abuse child	None, absent abuse
Caring school climate	Tough academics and high standards are more important	None	*Disapproval of school adults* by parents if child feels lack of caring
Parent involvement in schooling	Parents should be involved (home support, meetings)	Slight chance of *parents* violating child neglect laws	*Disapproval of parents* by school adults
EMPOWERMENT			
Community values youth	Community does *not* value youth; e.g., case law that limits student expression in school newspapers—*Tinker v. Des Moines* superseded by *Hazelwood* decision	None	None
Youth as resources	Conflict: some believe youth need to be treated as resources; others believe young people don't have enough experience/wisdom to contribute much	None	None

Service to others	It's good to volunteer, but it shouldn't be required	Some students *required* to do community service, but no consequences to nonschool adults	None
Safety	Children and youth should be safe in their homes, schools, and neighborhoods	Child abuse and neglect laws, laws against sex with minors, selling alcohol and tobacco products to minors, background checks on school, child-care staff (some of this may work against support, e.g., adult fear of consequences for nonsexual touching, hugs)	Definite social isolation, disapproval/rejection of *adults* by other adults; possible guilt, shame
BOUNDARIES AND EXPECTATIONS			
Family boundaries	Parents are the only ones who should set boundaries	*Parents and guardians only*—Possible police or social services involvement	Possible social isolation, disapproval/rejection by other adults; possible guilt, shame
School boundaries	Schools should have and enforce rules ensuring safety, drug-free climate, behavior disruptions, cheating	*School adults and parents* for not enforcing compulsory schooling ages and truancy laws, laws against weapons and drugs on school property	Disapproval, rejection by other adults
Neighborhood boundaries	You shouldn't break the law	Little for adults unless they help youth violate laws: curfew laws; disturbing-the-peace laws; vandalism laws; laws on access to alcohol and other drugs, on sexual experiences (e.g., age of consent, statutory rape)	Neighborhood mistrust, suspicion, loneliness, loss of social capital and collective efficacy
Adult role models	Kids need them, but who are role models? Parents? Athletes, music and movie stars?	None	None
Positive peer influence	Friends don't let friends drive drunk	None	Disapproval/rejection of *parents* if seen as allowing children to be in a "bad crowd" (but possible sympathy from other adults too, if seen as out of parents' legitimate control)

(Continued)

Table 6. Norms and Consequences Reflected in the Developmental Assets Framework (Continued)

Asset category/asset	Existing "norms"	Legal impact	Social impact
High expectations	We should expect children to achieve at high levels	None	Slight *teacher/administrator* job threat, *parent* social isolation, rejection by other adults
CONSTRUCTIVE USE OF TIME			
Creative activities	Not good for kids to just hang out ("idle hands are the devil's workshop")	Curfew laws, not specific to any asset, loitering laws	Slight chance of disapproval of *parents* if seen as pushing child into activities child doesn't like
Youth programs	None	None	Slight chance of disapproval of *parents* if seen as pushing child into activities child doesn't like
	Varies: generally a good thing; in some circles, kids should participate in *numerous* activities		Some chance of disapproval of *parents* if most of friends are religiously active
Religious community	Children should be exposed to a religion	None	
Time at home	Varies: young adolescents shouldn't be out; expect high school-age youth to exert more independence	None, except to parents if child violates other laws	Disapproval of parents, but only if neighbors see child creating disturbance, "hanging out" at wrong times, with wrong people, etc.
COMMITMENT TO LEARNING			
Achievement motivation	A good education leads to earning power and a better life	None	*Positive:* Parental "bragging rights" ("my child is on the honor roll"); shame and *disapproval of parents* if child does poorly
School engagement	Go to school and pay attention	*Parents and guardians* only for allowing child to violate truancy laws	Occasional *positive* rewards to students and *parents* for staying and achieving (e.g., I Have a Dream scholarships)

Homework	"Is your homework done?" (before watching TV, going out)	None	Disapproval of *parents* by school adults
Bonding to school	Varies—for young children: "so do you like school/your teacher?"; older assumed not to like school as much	None	None
Reading for pleasure	Reading is for doing well in school and getting ahead	*Parents and guardians only*—slight chance of neglect accusations if child is illiterate, but no consequences for child not reading for fun, per se	None
POSITIVE VALUES			
Caring	Do unto others	*Adults*—Good Samaritan laws that protect people from liability when they offer emergency help to strangers (not specific to teaching caring to children and youth, though)	Possible disapproval of *parents* if child seen as mean
Equality and social justice	Foundational national value: racism is bad; sexism is often bad; discriminating against handicapped is bad	*Adults*—antidiscrimination laws (but no legal penalty for failing to proactively promote equality)	Disapproval, rejection of *adults* who model discrimination, are racist in front of kids, etc., and of *parents* whose children discriminate or are racist
Integrity	Stand up for what you believe in (but don't rock the boat)	*Adults*—violation of contract laws	Little for adults other than parents unless children are aware of the violation and other adults know this
Honesty	Tell the truth, but lie if you have to in order to keep someone you love from being hurt	*Adults*—Laws against cheating on taxes (infrequently punished), lying under oath, fraud and misrepresentation	Little for adults other than parents unless children are aware of the violation and other adults know this
Responsibility	Take responsibility for your actions	None	Disapproval of *parents* if child seen as always blaming others for own behavior

(Continued)

Table 6. Norms and Consequences Reflected in the Developmental Assets Framework (Continued)

Asset category/asset	Existing "norms"	Legal impact	Social impact
Restraint	Even though against the law, it is OK for high school–age teenagers to have sex and drink alcohol, but don't spread disease, get pregnant, or be promiscuous, and, if drinking, "know when to say when"	*Mostly parents & guardians*—Other adults only if aid minors in violating laws, e.g., against minors having sex, buying and using alcohol, against abortion without parental consent	Shame and disapproval if child (especially daughter) is perceived as promiscuous; shame, disapproval of parent if children abuse alcohol, use other drugs (but some parents allow drinking parties, etc., so disapproval may have little effect)
SOCIAL COMPETENCIES			
Planning and decision making	Conflict: some believe kids shouldn't make own decisions about meaningful issues	None	Little for any social competencies— *parents and guardians* only
Interpersonal competence	Be friendly, polite	None	Some possible disapproval of *parents* if children have poor social skills
Cultural competence	At least tolerate people different from you, but you don't have to like them	None	None
Resistance skills	Know "when to say when"; "just say no"	None	*See Restraint*
Peaceful conflict resolution	Varies: avoiding violence is good, but for males, also pressure to not be a "sissy" or allow self or friends to be disrespected	None	Little—*parents and guardians* only
POSITIVE IDENTITY			
Self-esteem	Norms in conflict: to some, critical to feel good about yourself; for others, today's kids have too much self-esteem already	None	None
Personal power	Conflict: "be all you can be" versus "God's plan"	None	None
Sense of purpose	"What do you want to be when you grow up?"	None	Some disapproval of *parents* if child seen as aimless, lacking goals, ambition
Positive view of personal future	Be optimistic	None	None

Note: Shading indicates assets accompanied by greatest emphasis on real consequences.

a variety of ways of getting involved with young people to be more important than young adults did. And Americans ages 55 and older were actually more engaged with young people than were younger adults.

For most Americans, though, the challenge of deepening connections between adults and young people is difficult. Even relatively simple acts of adult engagement may be less common than imagined. For example, it should be easier, theoretically, for many adults to provide high expectations for school achievement or to reinforce rules of appropriate adolescent behavior such as not vandalizing property, because these would seem to be well-articulated and presumably widely shared expectations among adults. Those adult actions may be seen as supporting traditional social institutions and values, the mark of being a good citizen. Presumably this is an element of their own identity that most adults would wish to reinforce; that is, they are already good citizens who contribute to the preservation of "our way of life." In fact, when asked who should take special responsibility for getting involved in school issues, nonparents are even more likely than parents (by 62% to 48%) to say that all taxpayers should, whether or not they have children, "since the schools belong to everyone" (Farkas et al., 2001).

In contrast, it should theoretically be more difficult for many adults to provide nurturance and support to adolescents, to show they care. How to do so is far less well articulated, and consensus on what is appropriate adult nurturing behavior is far less well defined than encouraging young people to succeed at school. The social gains for adults are also then less well defined when it comes to providing most kinds of nurturance and support than for reinforcing "boundary" rules against vandalism or encouraging school success.

Although this makes sense theoretically, the data from previous research present a more mixed picture. The asset of "neighborhood boundaries" is indeed reported by more youth than are the nurturing or support assets of "other adult relationships" and "a caring neighborhood," according to Search Institute's research. This supports the notion that adults do a better job of telling young people what not to do than they do of providing supports and opportunities for positive growth. But as few youth report getting "high expectations" from parents and teachers, a theoretically easy action for adults to take, as report that several adults other than parents care about them ("other adult relationships"). The latter is a support asset theoretically more difficult to provide than "high expectations," which we would imagine to be a widely endorsed value. Moreover, the range of youth reporting that they experience neighborhood boundaries or high expectations is just 40%–46%, suggesting that *most young people do not experience even the assets theoretically easiest for most adults to help build through their engagement with kids* (Benson et al., 1999).

Consequences to Other Adults for Getting Involved

The absence of consequences for being relatively unconnected with kids certainly helps maintain adult inertia and lack of engagement. However, even stronger forces inhibiting engagement may be operating if the imagined positive consequences of getting involved with young people are less clear or powerful than the imagined negative ones. Norm activation theory (Schwartz, 1970) states that complying with a norm is more likely if it is clear that noncompliance will result in negative consequences, and if individuals ascribe personal responsibility for those consequences to themselves.

In other words, it is not currently a norm for adults to get more involved with children and youth, in part because the territory of their "reasonable responsibility" for child well-being has not been explicitly defined. In this study, we try to help define that territory more clearly. In part, engagement does not take place because the consequences for failing to be involved with kids are not obvious. If an adult fails to volunteer in programs for youth, or just doesn't wave hello to teenagers when driving by, it seems unlikely that in most American communities any social disapproval would accrue to that adult.

Adults may not perceive clear consequences for failing to get involved, but they seem to perceive negative consequences if they do get involved, particularly when the involvement might be because of issues considered particularly sensitive. Thus, adults are often inhibited even more sharply about discussing such issues with children and youth outside their families. For example, studies routinely show that parents, usually considered in public opinion surveys to be the primary (but not the exclusive) sexuality educators of their own children, tend not to fulfill that role very well (Miller, Kotchick, Dorsey, Forehand, & Ham, 1998; Jaccard, Dittus, & Gordon, 2000). Moreover, for decades public opinion polls have shown that sexuality education in middle and high schools is supported by 80%–93% of American adults, with 70%–80% even favoring school personnel's referring sexually active students to providers of family planning and treatment of sexually transmitted disease (How do adults view sex ed?, 1999). These data clearly indicate that adults do not believe parents have the sole responsibility for providing their children with guidance about sexuality.

But what consequences would accrue to neighbors outside a formal teaching or religious setting who talked with a neighborhood 12-year-old about sex? Despite the social approval given to formal school courses in sexuality education, could a similar implied permission be experienced in informal settings? That hardly seems likely. Studies (e.g., Miller et al., 1998; Jaccard et al., 2000) also have found that parents report having more conversations with their adolescent children about sexuality than their children report having such conversations with their parents. What if the discrepancies in these perceptions contribute to parents' feeling they are doing their job and that their child certainly doesn't need additional conversations with a neighbor about sexuality, while at the same time the adolescent feels that such conversation and guidance from another adult would be welcome?

We can imagine an even more likely scenario, in which a conversation with a 12-year-old turns not to sex per se but to boyfriends, girlfriends, friendship, and love. Does a neighbor have any reasonable responsibility to help the 12-year-old deal with questions such as the difference between mature and immature love, how we can tell if we're really in love, and what the signs of a healthy relationship are? Since guiding young people on these issues would mean helping them understand that mature love involves, among other things, respect, responsibility, patience, and kindness, all widely endorsed values (Gordon, 2001), wouldn't adults feel greater permission to deal with it? In the current climate of expectations and consequences, we think not.

Almost regardless of the topic, we suspect that in those neighborhood settings, parents may be far more concerned that an unrelated adult might share values that are at odds with the values parents want to pass on to their children, than they are about what is taught in school. In years past, perhaps an uncle or aunt who had both wisdom and emotional distance could play a welcome part, but the capacity of extended family to play those roles today is uncertain. For example, in a particularly comprehensive study of the social networks of adults and children, it was found that, in single-parent African American families, for whom much has been written about the supportive role of extended family, the majority of children's extended family contacts were not with adults but with other *children* (Cochran et al., 1990).

So, we might ask, what is the appropriate role, if any, for unrelated adults in such situations? Parents would hardly want just anyone talking with their child about sex or similar "difficult" issues, but they might be grateful for the supportive role that could be played by a neighbor they really know and trust. This discussion highlights the need for adults to get to know each other more in neighborhoods and the other domains of their lives, including talking explicitly about their values and their expectations for how most adults ought to be engaged with young people most of the time. In such a climate of increasing social trust, it may become easier for parents and unrelated adults to provide and seek permission for increased engagement with young people.

Perhaps most people would not be willing to talk with young people about values and decisions related to sexuality, or even love and relationships, but what about other important issues? Even for these, we can imagine that the decision to become more involved with other people's kids may indeed be accompanied by anxiety that inhibits deeper relationships among young people and unrelated adults.

For example, parents may be seen by most people as the primary educators, although not the exclusive ones, of their children concerning money matters. More than 90% of children and youth want to be able to get financial advice from their parents, but just 31% say parents "often" have talked with them about setting financial goals, and only 28% about savings and investing. More than 60% of youth have access to a course in school on money, but only 20% take it, so the question may be raised, if parents aren't doing the job, and school isn't either, then who is (Teaching financial values . . . , 1999; *Youth and money . . . ,* 1999)? (A related question may be, do such courses have the reputation of being for the less academically able? If so, then the "norm" among young people may be not to take them in order to preserve one's self-image.)

This is not merely a theoretical discussion; it affects the future economic health of young people and the nation. For example, in a survey of the nation's high school seniors, it was reported that only about 52% were "financially literate," a decrease of 10% from the level found in a similar 1997 survey. Furthermore, nearly 75% thought savings bonds or savings accounts offer the highest potential for growth, and only about 25% correctly answered that, over the long run, stocks offer the highest return (Mandell, 1998; Missing the basics, 2000). Helping young people become more financially literate would seem to be in everyone's best interests, not just parents'.

And yet, if money matters come up in a conversation with a child or adolescent, how much should a neighbor venture into that arena? Should he or she hesitate to share knowledge and values because of fear of intruding upon an area of parental responsibility, even though plenty of schools also assume responsibility by offering such courses? Many adults are likely to resist getting more involved until their anxiety over *not* playing this role (i.e., their motivation to avoid being seen as not caring about the next generation) exceeds their anxiety over the possible consequences of being so involved (i.e., their motivation to avoid being thought a busybody). This is especially true if an adult can clearly envision the immediate possible negative social consequences of involvement with children and youth, but can less readily imagine the negative social consequences of inaction.

If adults perceive weak or inconsistent support from parents to play more involved roles with children and youth, they may communicate fairly ambiguously and weakly with those children and youth. In turn, research has found that school-age children pay less attention to adults who seem low in power or who communicate in ambiguous ways (Bugental, Lyon, Lin, McGrath, & Bimbela, 1999). Thus, even if adults are willing to play these roles, confused signals from parents around normative expectations for other adult involvement with their children could produce ineffective adult-child communication. Such communication might fail to engage children and thereby miss the opportunity to positively influence their development.

Ultimately too, people "partly determine the nature of their environment and are influenced by it" (Bandura, 1989, p. 1182). Because of this bidirectional dynamic, adults who experience too many negative consequences from engaging with children and youth may construct their thinking and behavior to minimize the opportunity even to be in a situation where they have to make that choice about getting involved. Their sense that there is normative support for doing those behaviors, and their perceived self-efficacy in doing them, may become so compromised that they simply withdraw from situations where they could connect with other people's kids.

Changing the Calculus of Social Expectation by Defining Reasonable Responsibility

The preceding discussion illustrates a critical principle: Adults seem most likely to experience the powerful emotional feelings of social norms that *inhibit* their connection to children and youth, and least likely to experience powerful emotional rewards (and, less desirably, negative consequences) that *encourage* it. In other words, adult indifference to children and youth is predictable given the vacuum in defining the reasonable responsibility all adults should share for child well-being, and adult indifference is resistant to change because it is often implicitly rewarded and certainly not "punished."

Thus, one of the strategies for increasing adult engagement with young people is to stand this equation on its head. Instead of anticipating negative consequences, what can be done to get people to feel *collective permission and social expectations* to engage with children and youth in ways that promote their positive development, as well as to know the settings in which this involvement would be welcomed or not?

In Chapter 9, we discuss a variety of strategies that the results of our study suggest. But the foundation for all the strategies is for adults, whether in a neighborhood or a community, to understand the kinds of adult engagement with kids adults already expect from each other, however implicit that expectation may be, and then to begin making those expectations more explicit, intentional, and consequential.

We therefore designed the heart of our study to yield a description of the terrain of reasonable responsibility. Drawing on the developmental assets framework, we asked questions about a number of ways adults could relate to, nurture, and guide young people, actions that for the most part should help young people build those important developmental assets. We presented these actions briefly in Chapter 2 (see Table 3), but detail now the rationale for including each.

The actions that adults said were both highly important and done by the majority of adults they know may be considered to function as genuine social norms—they are among the key unwritten expectations or rules for how American adults should relate with children and youth. Moreover, actions that a great majority of adults thought were important for all adults to do, not just parents, can also be considered part of the landscape that defines the reasonable responsibility most adults should assume for the well-being of the young. The actual survey questions are presented in Appendix B.

Together these actions provided data on the degree to which American adults feel it is important to teach or model various behaviors, interact more than casually with children and adolescents who are not in their family, and feel responsible for the well-being of those children and youth. The actions also were meant to reveal the degree to which adults perceive that other adults in their lives actually teach, model, and get involved with children and youth in these ways.

Four of the actions dealt with adults' supporting children and youth to become giving, helping people financially as well as through service. Those prosocial values and behaviors are important contributors to young people's overall well-being (reviewed in Scales & Leffert, 1999 [for example, pp. 53–54 and 152–153]; Chaskin & Hawley, 1994).

In addition, consistency of values and expectations across the pieces of young people's lives has been found to be a meaningful contributor to positive outcomes such as succeeding in school and being mentally healthy (reviewed in Scales & Leffert, 1999 [for example, pp. 41, 88, and 137]; Sanders, 1998). Thus, a number of actions concerned values and expectations. One item asked about the consistency with which different adults in children and youth's lives are believed to teach the "same core values such as equality, honesty, and responsibility."

Additional actions concerning values and expectations included: How important is it for adults openly to share their own values, and their religious or spiritual beliefs in general, with children and youth? Further, two statements allowed a glimpse into adults' thoughts about diversity and cultural values. One asked how important it is for adults to teach young people the importance of respecting people of differing races or cultures, "even when the values and beliefs of those people conflict with adults' own values and beliefs." The other asked how important it is for adults to teach children and youth to "protect, preserve, and pass down" the traditions and values of their own ethnic or religious culture. The ratings adults gave about the legitimacy of and perceived conformity of adults to those normative expectations can illuminate a particularly difficult challenge of democratic societies, how to help residents honor their own ethnic and religious values while simultaneously respecting the differing values of others.

Two related items about boundaries and expectations were derived from the study of Sampson et al. (1997), in which it was reported that adults' collective efficacy—working together to promote and protect shared values and norms such as the inappropriateness of youth skipping school—was related to lower levels of both perceived and actual crime in those neighborhoods. Therefore, in the present study, adults were asked if it was important to tell parents if they saw children or adolescents doing something wrong. In addition, study participants were asked the less traditional twist on that question, one that reflects more of an asset-building orientation to normative expectations: How important is it for adults to tell parents when they see a child or youth doing something right? Such an action reinforces for both neighbors and parents (as well as for children and adolescents) that this is a child who already is the kind of person we wish him or her to be, a powerful motivator for desired behavior (discussed in both Chapters 3 and 9).

Because American adults consistently rate the quality of children's education as one of the nation's top priorities (*All for all ...*, 2000), it ought to be important and acceptable for most adults to reinforce with children and youth the value of school. Thus, another question asked how important it is for adults to encourage children and youth to "take school seriously and do well at school."

Because the research presented earlier suggests that adults' interactions with young people are generally limited, several items inquired about the following adult asset-building actions: How important it is for adults to know the names of many children or youth in their neighborhood? To have conversations with them that allow each to "really get to know" the other? To help children or youth "think through" the possible consequences of decisions? To ask children and youth for their opinions on decisions that affect them? And, to give advice to children or youth who are not members of their own family? Together, these may be considered a description of how acceptable and common adults feel it is for them to connect with, support, empower, and guide children and adolescents—or, in contrast, to be essentially ignorant of and uninvolved with young people outside their own families.

Finally, the developmental assets framework, and the philosophy of building those assets in young people, is constructed explicitly on the premise that "all kids are our kids" (Benson, 1997). What if that fundamental premise of shared responsibility is contradicted by most adults in everyday life, and most adults really don't feel a personal responsibility for all kids? Then, it is difficult to imagine how many of the other adult actions asked about in the rest of the study could become normative. Thus, we asked a direct question about how important it is for all adults to "feel a responsibility to help ensure the health and well-being" of children and youth "in their neighborhood."

We also used the referent of "neighborhood" in several questions for two reasons. First, many of the children and adolescents geographically closest to adults will, because of their proximity, be among the people those adults see and observe the most (and about whose parents adults may also know something). If adults do not feel such a responsibility for those nearby children and youth, then it is difficult to imagine them feeling greater responsibility for children and youth who are even more unknown to them and whose parents also are more unknown to them. Second, the geographical neighborhood may for many people be the social unit that comes closest to Picker's (1997) notion (discussed further in Chapter 9) of a "payoff neighborhood." This unit of experience is the relatively small number of people in relatively closer association with oneself who, depending on the issue at hand, serve as a key normative reference group to illuminate what are acceptable and expected, as well as unacceptable and prohibited, behaviors.

We conducted the telephone survey with a nationally representative sample of 1,425 Americans ages 18 or older. African Americans and Hispanics were oversampled to allow us to analyze the data by race/ethnicity. All data were weighted to account for any differences between a group's percentage in the U.S. population and its percentage in our sample. Percentages reported for the entire sample have a margin of error of +/− 4 percentage points; percentages reported when comparing subgroups have larger margins of error (Appendixes A and D provide details on the sampling, margins of error, and analysis procedures we used).

In the next three chapters (6–8), we present and discuss the results of our study. Those results help define what Americans already believe, albeit implicitly, is a reasonable responsibility all adults could assume for young people. The results suggest a number of strategies for turning that definitional sense of responsibility into a more explicit social expectation for greater adult engagement with kids, strategies we will detail in Chapter 9.

6 Engagement with Kids: An American Consensus on Core Adult Actions

Cultural observers of America, from Alexis de Tocqueville to Francis Fukuyama, have feared that tolerance for individual differences can be overweighted as a value, to the detriment of agreement on fundamental common principles of social order. Tocqueville (1835/2000), for example, worried in the 19th century that as democratic equality increases, dependence of each individual on others decreases, such that "the bond of human affection is extended, but it is relaxed... [and] the interest of man is confined to those in close propinquity to himself" (p. 621). Fukuyama wrote that the tendency of liberal democracies at the end of the 20th century was to "fall prey to excessive individualism" in which "tolerance would become the cardinal virtue... in place of moral consensus" (1999, p. 58). With regard to adults' engagement with young people, perhaps the "default norm" is to "tolerate" noninvolvement in the absence of consensus about how adults are expected to be engaged.

Do our results confirm or contradict these sentiments? We asked adults to rate how important 19 adult actions were, on a scale from 1 (least important) to 5 (most important). If we consider the proportion who rated the actions as either a 4 or 5, the equivalent of reasonably to highly important, then three-fourths or more of the adults surveyed thought *all* of the actions were at least reasonably important. The only exception was it being okay for neighbors to give advice to young people, which only 33% thought was at least reasonably important. Table 7 presents the means and standard deviations for all the actions.

At first glance, practically all of these actions seem to have considerably broad support. However, people are more likely to act on attitudes or beliefs they hold intensely rather than loosely. Therefore, this depiction is somewhat misleading, and it becomes important to disentangle the top two ratings of importance to see which actions are considered the most highly important of all. When we examine more closely the *intensity* of these results, a different picture emerges.

Table 7. Means and Standard Deviations of Importance and Conformity Items

	Importance		Conformity	
	Mean	SD	Mean	SD
Top-Rated Actions				
Encourage school success	4.87	0.82	3.95	1.88
Expect respect for adults	4.51	1.46	3.89	1.99
Expect parents to set boundaries	4.76	1.08	3.27	2.13
Teach shared values	4.69	1.27	3.32	2.17
Teach respect for cultural differences	4.65	1.33	3.04	2.18
Guide decision making	4.66	1.28	3.18	2.15
Have meaningful conversations	4.65	1.18	3.07	2.11
Give financial guidance	4.62	1.33	3.05	2.23
Discuss personal values	4.58	1.40	3.10	2.14
Actions with Majority Support				
Report positive behavior	4.42	1.61	2.41	2.33
Ensure well-being of neighborhood kids	4.46	1.44	2.96	2.32
Report misbehavior	4.40	1.60	2.87	2.40
Discuss religious beliefs	4.30	1.81	2.99	2.32
Pass down traditions	4.34	1.59	3.12	2.17
Parents be sole discipliners	4.27	1.66	3.62	2.12
Know names	4.23	1.65	2.90	2.40
Actions with Less than Majority Support				
Provide service opportunities	4.18	1.71	2.16	2.09
Seek opinions	4.15	1.79	2.76	2.16
Model giving and serving	4.14	1.75	2.31	2.12
Give advice	3.06	2.06	2.38	2.21
Overall Importance-Conformity Scales	**4.27**	**0.71**	**2.89**	**1.11**

Figure 3 shows that, of the 19 actions, 15 were rated a "5"—the most important rating possible—by 50% or more of American adults. However, only eight were rated this important by 70% or more of adults. Those eight, plus one more that fell within the margin of error (+/−4 percentage points), might be considered to reflect core ways of engaging with children and adolescents on which the great majority of Americans have consensus. If that is so, then two important implications are suggested.

First, when it comes to the role all adults play in raising the next generation, there really may be truths we as a people hold to be self-evident, that is, that are highly important to vast majorities of people. There are core ways of adults' engaging with the young that Americans consider it highly important for all adults to do, not just parents. These nine actions have such a high degree of consensus that they may then be considered to begin to define the reasonable responsibility all adults might assume for the upbringing of the young.

Two of these actions may represent what Legro (1997) called "robust" norms that are strong and resistant to change (encouraging young people to take school seriously, and expecting them to respect adult authority). They are simple and clear, enduring, and considered highly important by 7 out of 10 American adults.

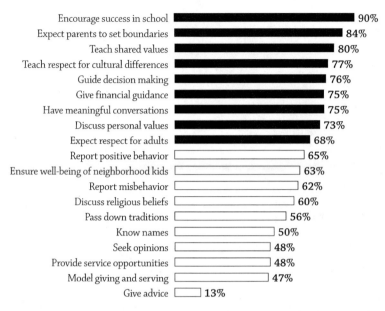

Figure 3. Proportion of American Adults Ranking Each Action as "Most Important"
Note: Shading indicates actions about whose importance there is a broad consensus; i.e., 70% or more of Americans agree they are highly important (including +/− 4% margin of error). Lack of shading indicates actions about whose importance there is not a consensus.

And although not part of Legro's definition of "robust" norms, they also are reportedly practiced by a majority of adults. In contrast, knowing the names of many neighborhood children and youth seems to be a clear, but not necessarily a simple, expectation (how many is "many"?; what are the boundaries of the "neighborhood"?). Only half of adults think this is highly important to do, and only one-third actually know the names of many neighborhood kids (see Table 8).

These results suggest that the great majority of Americans consider it highly important for all adults to teach and reinforce a core of beliefs and behavioral expectations to the young. Those expectations reinforce the passing on of such traditional values as taking school seriously and doing well, respecting adult authority, being honest and responsible, abiding by rules, and respecting people whose values and traditions differ from one's own. These results do not suggest that cultural diversity, pluralism, and tolerance have undermined consensus. Rather, the great majority of Americans across a variety of backgrounds seem to have defined a core set of actions around how adults ought to relate to the next generation, including passing down core values and respecting differences in values.

A second implication of these results is that such core agreement means there is more social permission to engage with young people in these ways than most people may have thought. Because there is a set of core understandings and values about adults' relationships with children and adolescents, the majority of adults in America ought to be able to actually live up to these normative

Table 8. Gap between Importance and Involvement, in Descending Order of Gap (in %)

	Importance	Engagement	Gap
Top-Rated Actions			
Encourage success in school	90	69	21
Expect respect for adults	68	67	1
Expect parents to set boundaries	84	42	42
Teach shared values	80	45	35
Teach respect for cultural differences	77	36	41
Guide decision making	76	41	35
Have meaningful conversations	75	34	41
Give financial guidance	75	36	39
Discuss personal values	73	37	36
Actions with Majority Support			
Report positive behavior	65	22	43
Ensure well-being of neighborhood kids	63	35	28
Report misbehavior	62	33	29
Discuss religious beliefs	60	35	25
Pass down traditions	56	38	18
Parents be sole discipliners	55	38	17
Know names	50	34	16
Actions with Less Than Majority Support			
Provide service opportunities	48	13	35
Seek opinions	48	25	23
Model giving and serving	47	16	31
Give advice	13	17	−4

expectations with less fear of negative consequences than they might have imagined.

According to the results shown in Table 8, 70% or more of Americans consider it highly important (i.e., expected) for adults to:

- Encourage children and youth to take school seriously and do well in school;
- Expect children and youth to respect adults as authority figures;
- Expect parents to set and enforce clear and consistent rules and boundaries;
- Teach children and youth the same shared values as other adults do, such as equality, honesty, and responsibility;[4]
- Teach children and youth to respect the values and traditions of different cultures, even when those values conflict with adults' own values;

---

[4] The Gallup Organization noted that the question about adults all teaching the same core values to young people "was confusing to some respondents" and that "some may have answered without their fully understanding the item" (Gallup Organization, 2000, p. 10). Although an exact tally was not recorded, estimates are that no more than 1%–2% of respondents expressed such confusion, or a total of no more than 14–28 respondents out of 1,425 (e-mail from Harry Cotugno, Gallup Organization, to Peter C. Scales, Search Institute, July 19, 2000). Given the large proportions rating this item among the most important norms, it is extremely unlikely that such small numbers of responses could affect the conclusions drawn here.

- Help children and youth think through the possible good and bad consequences of their decisions;
- Have more than casual conversations with neighborhood children and youth;
- Give guidance to children and youth on saving, sharing, and spending money; and
- Openly discuss their *own* values with children and youth.

The differences among Americans on those top-rated nine actions, while of interest, seem less meaningful than the very great consensus that exists across these groups. Figure 4 shows that, across subgroups formed by adults of different races/ethnic backgrounds, frequency of attendance at religious services, annual income, and educational background, the mean percentages of those rating the core nine actions as highly important were well within the sampling tolerances (i.e., the +/− margins of error) when comparing subgroups. (See Appendix D for the tables of sampling tolerances.) For example, on average, 73% of those with less than a high school education rated the core nine actions highly important, but so did 75% of college graduates. Among African Americans, an average 81% rated the core nine as highly important, but so did 75% of Hispanics and 77% of whites. People who never attended religious services, and those who say they attended daily, were hardly different, with 76% and 77%, respectively, rating the core nine actions highly important. And regardless of income level, 75%–80% of Americans rated the core nine highly important. There are some differences within groups on how important each of the separate actions was considered, as we discuss in Chapters 7 and especially 8, but the differences on those core nine actions are less striking than the relative similarity of responses among them. Gender was the only demographic category in which there was a significant average difference in importance ratings for the core nine actions, with 73% of men and 82% of women rating those core nine highly important (not shown in Figure 4).

A central message of this study is that, for the nine actions rated the most important, even though some groups were more supportive of them than others, support for their importance cuts across traditional differences in race, religiosity, income, and education. In other words, these actions reflect relative consensus and uniting of diverse Americans around a common agenda of expectations for adult behavior toward kids, which is remarkable given the cultural fragmentation of modern society. White, African American, and Hispanic adults, people of varying commitment to religion, wealthy, middle income, working class, and poor Americans all consider this group of nine actions around relating to other people's kids to be highly important.

The high consensus on the importance of these nine actions is both reassuring and, for some of the actions, somewhat surprising. For example, it certainly is not a controversial issue to encourage children and youth to take school seriously and do well in school, nor to expect parents to enforce rules for the behavior of their children, nor for adults to expect children and youth to respect them as authority figures. But for the remaining six core actions, the degree of importance Americans assign to them, across differences of race, religiosity, income, and

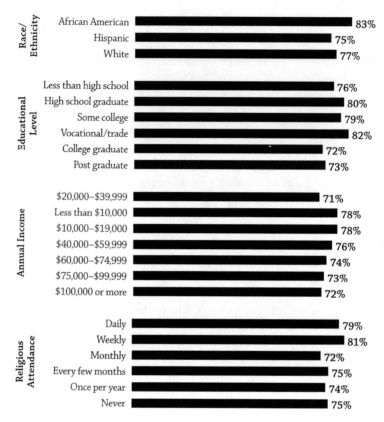

Figure 4. Mean Percentage of American Adults Rating the Top Nine Actions "Most Important," by Selected Variables

education, is unexpected. Given the often contentious debate between liberals and conservatives over values and the extent to which young people should be making decisions, in contrast to doing what they are told, we expected to see less agreement, as we detail below.

The Gap between Beliefs and Actions

The identification of a core group of apparently agreed on social norms and social values about how adults should relate to other people's kids is an important finding of this study. Nevertheless, beneath the surface, several cautions and conflicts also are apparent.

The literature we reviewed earlier suggests that it is not only the worthiness or legitimacy of a potential norm that affects its strength in shaping behavior, but also the degree to which social support and even pressure are felt for living out that expectation. Recall that we asked adults to tell us, for each action, whether they perceived that almost all, the great majority, about half, some, or very few

Table 9. Gaps between Beliefs and Actions (in %)

	Importance	Engagement	Gap
Expect parents to set boundaries	84	42	42
Teach respect for cultural differences	77	36	41
Have meaningful conversations	75	34	41
Give financial guidance	75	36	39
Discuss personal values	73	37	36
Teach shared values	80	45	35
Guide decision making	76	41	35
Encourage success in school	90	69	21
Expect respect for adults	68	67	1
Report positive behavior	65	22	43
Report misbehavior	62	33	29
Ensure well-being of neighborhood kids	63	35	28
Discuss religious beliefs	60	35	25
Pass down traditions	56	38	18
Know names	50	34	16
Provide service opportunities	48	13	35
Model giving and serving	47	16	31
Seek opinions	48	25	23
Give advice	13	17	−4

of the adults in their own lives lived each of the actions. This tells us to what degree the action is perceived to be a norm. The more people see an action as common (or "normal") among the great majority of the adults around them, the more those adults live in a social world that models, supports, and perhaps even exerts pressure on them to also do the action. In effect, doing the action has become, for those adults, "just what normal people do," a social expectation or norm that is part of their daily lives.

When we look at the results beyond the simple ratings of importance, to adults' reports of how many other adults in their lives actually relate to kids in these ways, a less rosy picture emerges.

Table 9 displays those results. It shows that the majority of Americans consider most of these actions highly important in theory, but most report that the majority of adults they know don't actually do these things.

Table 10 displays this information in a somewhat different way. It shows that the majority of the adult actions regarding relationships with children and adolescents, despite being thought at least reasonably important by large majorities of Americans, actually function more as social values than as social norms.

Only two of the nine actions that have widespread importance (i.e., 70% or more consider them highly important) also are perceived as being lived by a majority of the other adults Americans know: encouraging young people to take school seriously and do well, and expecting young people to respect adults as authority figures. These may be considered to function as genuine social norms, at least in the statistical sense (in terms of being what most people do).

Table 10. Actions by Intersection of Importance and Adults Reported to Do

	70% or > Importance	50%–70%	< 50% Importance
Most adults reported to do the action	• Encourage school success • Expect respect for adults		
Most adults reported *not* to do the action	• Expect parents to set boundaries • Teach shared values • Teach respect for cultural differences • Guide decision making • Have meaningful conversations • Give financial guidance • Discuss personal values	• Report positive behavior • Ensure well-being of neighborhood kids • Report misbehavior • Discuss religious beliefs • Pass down traditions • Parents be sole discipliners • Know names	• Provide service opportunities • Seek opinions • Model giving and serving • Give advice

A majority considers the remaining seven of the top-rated nine actions, and seven additional actions, to be very important, but people report that only a minority of adults around them live those actions. There does not appear to be a great amount of social support or pressure to reflect these actions in daily living, although the values they represent receive majority agreement; that is, between 50% and 70% consider them highly important actions. These might more accurately be called *social values* than genuine norms: parents' enforcing boundaries; adults' teaching equality, honesty, and responsibility; teaching kids to respect different cultures; helping them think through decisions; having meaningful conversations with young people; providing guidance on money matters; discussing values; telling parents about children's good behavior; adults' feeling responsible for the well-being of all kids; telling parents about wrongful behavior; discussing religious beliefs with kids; teaching them to preserve their own culture; parents' having a right to discipline without interference; and knowing many neighborhood kids' names.

The remaining four actions are neither considered important nor lived by the majority. Statements that fell into that category might best be called *personal preferences*: providing young people opportunities to make the community better; seeking kids' opinions; volunteering/donating money monthly; and neighbors' giving advice to kids.

The Relationship between Importance Beliefs and Being Surrounded by Engaged Adults

Another way of looking at the apparently weak relationship between whether adults believe an action is important, and whether they report that the adults around them do the action, is to look at the correlation between those

Table 11. The Relationship of Personal Importance Beliefs and Being Surrounded by Other Adults Who Do the Action

	Correlation coefficient between belief and surrounding adults doing the action
Top-Rated Actions	
Encourage school success	.21
Expect respect for adults	.17
Expect parents to set boundaries	.14
Teach shared values	.27
Teach respect for cultural differences	.19
Guide decision making	.24
Have meaningful conversations	.21
Give financial guidance	.17
Discuss personal values	.26
Category average coefficient	**.21**
Actions with Majority Support	
Report positive behavior	.19
Ensure well-being of neighborhood kids	.28
Report misbehavior	.24
Discuss religious beliefs	.31
Pass down traditions	.25
Parents be sole discipliners	.30
Know names	.34
Category average coefficient	**.27**
Actions with Less than Majority Support	
Provide service opportunities	.29
Seek opinions	.19
Model giving and serving	.27
Give advice	.12
Category average coefficient	**.22**
Overall Importance—Conformity Scales	**.22**

Note: N = 1,384–1,418 for item correlation; 1,307 for overall scale correlation.

two dimensions overall, and for each of the 20 actions individually. Table 11 shows that, on average, the more highly an adult rates an action's importance, the more likely he or she is to say that other adults do this action.

But the relationship is relatively modest. Most of the correlation coefficients between pairs of belief and reported adult action items are in the .20s, and none is higher than the .30s. The correlation coefficient between the importance and conformity scales, .22, suggests that, on average, knowing what a person's belief is about the importance of an action would explain only 4% (.22 squared × 100) of how much he or she reports that other adults do the action.

Another perspective on how little personal attitudes may affect what a person perceives other adults around him or her actually do is to examine the correlation coefficients by how highly rated an action is. The mean correlation coefficient (.21) for the nine most highly rated actions is little different from that for the actions without even majority support (.22), and the actions with majority support but not the broadest consensus support have the highest mean of all (.27). No doubt, had we asked whether adults themselves did these actions, we would have seen a somewhat higher correlation between beliefs and action. But these data do suggest that even adults who are personally supportive of engaging with kids in these ways don't perceive most of the adults around them doing these things. Therefore, in all likelihood they do not experience a strong social support for doing the actions themselves, despite their personal beliefs about the importance of the actions. The lack of social support may be especially critical, since a review of attitude research over the last half of the 1990s (Azjen, 2001) suggests that negative feelings around getting engaged with other people's kids (such as discomfort, fear, or embarrassment) are likely to outweigh positive beliefs about getting engaged.

The differences in support for each of the actions do offer insights, however, into adults' recognition of their possible roles in contributing to the positive development of young people. As shown in Table 12, support for actions varies by different categories of developmental assets.

When we look at the actions related to each category of developmental assets, some intriguing patterns emerge:

- The Support-related actions receive mixed ratings, with adults rating one highly, but giving two less support. This finding may reflect an inaccurate belief that these actions are not that important or are not high priorities, particularly with respect to unrelated adults. Of course, as Table 8 showed, just one-third of adults reported that the adults around them did even the highly rated support action of having meaningful conversations with young people.
- None of the actions related to Empowerment reach the level of consensus among adults, and at best, only about one-third of adults say the adults around them actually do any of these things.
- The two actions related to the Boundaries-and-Expectations assets that received broad consensus focus on what parents and young people need to do. The actions that focus on unrelated adults intervening and being role models do not garner as much support. Only one action was reportedly done by most adults—expecting young people to respect adults. No more than about 40% of adults said most of the adults around them did any of the remaining Boundaries-and-Expectations actions. These findings reinforce the perception of parents having primary, if not exclusive, responsibility for boundary setting and discipline.
- There is a consensus about the only action included in the study related to the Commitment-to-Learning assets, encouraging young people to do well in school. This action was one of the genuine norms, in that the majority of adults also said most of the adults they knew did this action.
- Two out of the three actions related to Positive Values are supported by a consensus of Americans. This finding suggests that there are some core values that we share across our religious, political, cultural, and socioeconomic differences. Nevertheless, fewer than half of Americans say the

Table 12. Asset-Building Actions by Asset Category: Consensus versus No Consensus

Related asset category	Adult asset-building actions explored in this study
Support	• **Have meaningful conversations**—Have conversations with young people that help adults and young people "really get to know one another." • **Know names**—Know the names of many children and teenagers in the neighborhood. • **Give advice**—Give advice to young people who are not members of the family.
Empowerment	• **Report positive behavior**—Tell parent(s) if they see a child or teenager doing something right. • **Ensure well-being of neighborhood kids**—Feel responsible to help ensure the well-being of young people in their neighborhood. • **Provide service opportunities**—Give young people lots of opportunities to make their communities better places. • **Seek opinions**—Seek young people's opinions when making decisions that affect them.
Boundaries and Expectations	• **Expect respect for adults**—Expect children and teenagers to respect adults and elders as authority figures. • **Expect parents to set boundaries**—Expect parents to enforce clear and consistent rules and boundaries. • **Report misbehavior**—Tell parent(s) if they see the child or teenager doing something wrong. • **Model giving and serving**—Volunteer time or donate money to show young people the importance of helping others.
Commitment to Learning	• **Encourage success in school**—Encourage children and teenagers to take school seriously and do well in school.
Positive Values	• **Teach shared values**—Teach children and teenagers the same core values as other adults do, such as equality, honesty, and responsibility. • **Discuss personal values**—Openly discuss their own values with children and teenagers. • **Discuss religious beliefs**—Openly discuss their own religious or spiritual beliefs with children and teenagers.
Social Competencies	• **Teach respect for cultural differences**—Teach children and teenagers to respect the values and beliefs of different races and cultures, even when those values and beliefs conflict with their own. • **Guide decision making**—Help children and teenagers think through the possible good and bad consequences of their decisions. • **Give financial guidance**—Offer young people guidance on responsibly saving, sharing, and spending money.
Positive Identity	• **Pass down traditions**—Actively teach young people to preserve, protect, and pass down the traditions and values of their ethnic and/or religious culture.

Note: Shading indicates actions about whose importance there is a broad consensus. Lack of shading indicates actions about whose importance there is not a consensus.

adults around them teach even those highly important, consensus values to young people.

• There is a consensus on all the actions related to Social Competencies, but only about 40% or fewer of Americans say most of the adults around them do these things.

- Passing down traditions, the one action related to Positive Identity, is considered highly important by a slight majority of adults, but less than 40% report the adults around them actually do this.

Overall, consistency between beliefs and actions by category of developmental assets is greatest for the actions that help young people feel support (mean gap 18 percentage points) and build their positive identity (one item with an 18-percentage-point gap). Next in order of consistency are the actions that could build commitment to learning (one item with a 21-point gap) and boundaries and expectations (mean gap of 24 points). The largest average gaps among the actions, when considered by category of developmental assets, occur among the actions that can help young people feel empowered (mean gap of 32 points), build their positive values (mean gap of 32 points), and strengthen their social competencies (mean gap of 38 points).

The actions examined in this study reflect a few of the many different ways adults can engage with kids and so help build assets in each of the developmental assets categories. The overall patterns offer some starting points for dialogue about areas where adults may be most ready to engage in relationships where they more intentionally focus on building such assets. The patterns may also help raise questions about how adults perceive young people and their role in communities and society.

Table 13 shows the relationship among beliefs, and among reports of adults around them doing the actions, for each of the seven developmental assets categories represented by an action. The correlation coefficients suggest a number of insights that may be useful for understanding these results and in considering how best to encourage more adult engagement with young people.

For example, Table 13 shows that the largest coefficients are typically found when considering the categories of Empowerment, Values, and Social Competencies. Those who believe these are important, and who say the adults around them do these things, also are more likely to say actions in other asset categories are important and that the adults around them do these as well. Not coincidentally, we reported above that these also are the asset categories in which the average gap is largest between adults' beliefs and the actions they report the adults around them take to engage with young people.

This suggests that adult beliefs about the importance of actions that build young people's sense of empowerment, values, and competencies are the best barometers for predicting how broad adults' senses of importance and social support for engaging with kids may be. In contrast, knowing how adults feel about the commitment to learning action (encouraging school success) tells us the least about how likely those adults are to believe other actions are important.

The same pattern holds when considering reports of being surrounded by adults who actually engage with kids in these ways. In fact, the coefficients are even stronger, across all asset categories, than they are for the ratings of importance. This suggests that there is more consistency in what adults are reported to do about engaging with kids, across the asset categories, than in what they believe it is important to do. Unfortunately, the consistency is in *lack of engagement* across the asset categories.

Table 13. *Correlation Coefficients Reflecting Relationship among Beliefs (B) and Actions (A) across Asset Categories (N = 1,425)*

	Support		Empowerment		Boundaries and Expectations		Commitment to Learning		Values		Social Competencies		Positive Identity	
	B	A	B	A	B	A	B	A	B	A	B	A	B	A
Support	—	—	.52	.58	.36	.43	.23	.38	.37	.47	.40	.49	.32	.33
Empowerment	.52	.58	—	—	.46	.54	.18	.32	.40	.53	.48	.52	.40	.36
Boundaries and Expectations	.36	.43	.46	.54	—	—	.24	.33	.44	.48	.46	.47	.33	.37
Commitment to Learning	.23	.38	.18	.32	.24	.33	—	—	.23	.42	.41	.48	.19	.27
Values	.37	.47	.40	.53	.44	.48	.23	.42	—	—	.40	.61	.35	.43
Social Competencies	.40	.49	.48	.52	.46	.47	.41	.48	.40	.61	—	—	.32	.41
Positive Identity	.32	.33	.40	.36	.33	.37	.19	.27	.35	.43	.32	.41	—	—

Note: The table should be read as follows: The correlation between belief in the Support actions and belief in the Empowerment actions is .52, but between belief in the Support actions and belief in the Empowerment actions, the correlation is smaller, .36.

The double-edged sword this represents, of course, is that if adults see others they know doing *some* of these actions, they are likely to see them doing *many* of the actions. That would produce not a special or isolated source of social support to engage with young people themselves in these ways but a broad source of support that is consistently experienced and therefore powerful in how it functions as a norm. On the other hand, perceiving a low level of other adults engaging with young people on a given action—which we actually found—is likely to mean adults are not seen as engaging with kids in other ways either. This broad absence of perceived adult engagement can be equally as reinforcing in keeping adults unengaged.

Adult Actions with Consensus on Importance: Norms and Values

To gain a deeper understanding of these actions and the related survey findings, we now highlight each action, starting with the nine about which there is the broadest consensus, the two genuine norms and seven social values.

Encourage Success in School

Because American adults consistently rate the quality of children's education as one of the nation's top priorities (*All for all,* 2000), it should be no surprise that the action that adults are most likely to strongly support is helping young people "take school seriously and do well at school." Across the spectrum, 9 out of 10 adults believe it is "most important" for adults to do this with both children and teenagers.

Even though 69% of Americans said most of the adults they know do encourage young people's school success, the highest proportion engaging in any of the 20 actions we studied, it is difficult to know how adults would act upon this general belief in specific situations. In our in-depth interviews with 100 of the survey respondents, we asked whether adults would feel any sense of responsibility if they saw "a group of middle school boys you know who should be in school, but are obviously just hanging out on the street corner." Many adults said that they would feel responsible. As one put it: "I don't think it's okay [to do nothing]. I think you have the responsibility to your neighbors and to your neighborhood." However, only 20% indicated that it was not their responsibility to do anything. One said, "It's none of my business."

Expect Parents to Set Boundaries

Eighty-four percent of U.S. adults believe it is important for parents to establish "clear and consistent rules and boundaries." We did not define what those "rules and boundaries" might be, so we must assume that a broad range of issues was represented in people's minds. Respondents might well have been thinking of such things as rules about watching television, doing chores, being home at certain times, getting homework done and done well, rules about friends, dating, drug use. Such a perspective reinforces the central role of family in young people's development, and it is consistent with the family boundaries asset. Among the important boundary-setting activities within a family are having clear rules and consequences, and keeping track of where young people are and who they are with. Supporting and reinforcing parents in these boundary-setting roles is one way a community strengthens families.

Setting boundaries is a complex task, as they must be appropriate to the young person's temperament and stage of development, consistent with cultural norms (with some cultures being more restrictive than others), and fitting within the context of community. Of course, the realm of behavior involved also adds to the complexity. Some boundary issues would doubtless be seen as solely the prerogative of parents, such as rules about TV watching or dating, whereas other boundary issues potentially or even necessarily involve support from other adults, such as those involving violence, drug use, or school attendance. In the framework of developmental assets, boundary setting in the family is reinforced by adults setting and enforcing boundaries in school and neighborhood. This consistency across different parts of the young person's life both reinforces the boundaries set by parents and increases the likelihood that he or she will live within those boundaries.

Unfortunately, we found that just 42% of Americans think the majority of parents around them actually set and enforce "clear and consistent" boundaries. This finding is similar to the Public Agenda finding that most adults think parents are not doing a good job teaching basic values to their children (Duffett et al., 1999). These are perceptions, of course, and may not gibe with what parents really are doing. It may be akin to the often-reported finding that people rate "America's" schools as doing a poor job but the schools in their own community as doing a very good job.

Our survey included another question related to boundary setting. It asked whether adults believe that parents should be able to discipline their children "without interference" from others. This is a difficult issue, as became apparent in our focus groups. It may tap into beliefs that parents are the most important people in kids' lives, that discipline is a preeminent issue, and that government and social welfare agencies dilute parents' authority by allowing young people to threaten parents and even accuse them of child abuse when no abuse has occurred. On the other side of this issue is the reality that substantiated child abuse and neglect do occur with numbing regularity in American families, and that modern society has determined that it has an interest in protecting children from harm. We chose to tilt to the protection side of this complex issue, and so reverse-scored this action. Unlike all the other items, study participants got lower scores if they said it was highly important for parents to have such an exclusive role over discipline, and if most of the adults they knew believed this.

But many adults (55%) believe that the exclusive discipline role for parents is very important. This support may reflect an ongoing cultural attitude that, when it comes to important things, parents have an exclusive role and responsibility in young people's lives. Such an attitude may be a significant barrier to other adults playing a role in guiding and setting boundaries for young people, and/or complicate what that role could or should be. It is important to note, however, that, while a slight majority of adults hold this position, it receives less support than 14 of the other 19 actions examined in this study. In addition, only 38% say the adults around them actually hold this belief.

Teach Shared Values

According to our survey, the vast majority of American adults (80%) believe it is important to teach young people a set of *shared,* core values, such as equality, honesty, and responsibility. While there is some variation across subgroups of adults, no group had less than 70 percent of the adults saying that teaching shared values is most important. Despite that broad agreement, however, just 45% say the majority of adults around them actually teach these shared values to young people.

There are inherent risks in seeking to identify and articulate shared values in a pluralistic, multicultural "nation of nations." The same certainly could be said, on a far different scale, of the geographic communities in which we live. In any given geographic community, on any given issue, there could be found a wide range of perspectives and values. However, true "community," in the sense of moral and ethical bonds uniting peoples, can occur at any level of geographic scale, but is possible only when people share a set of core commitments. As Gardner (1991, pp. 14–15) wrote: "To require a community to agree on everything would be unrealistic and would violate our concern for diversity. But it has to agree on something. There has to be a core of shared values. Of all the ingredients of community this is probably the most important."

Of course, a sense of "community," defined in part by shared values and norms, is not unchanging. Local, national, and global events affect our sense of connection to others. Involvement of Americans in war, especially wars that are perceived as just, particularly can unite us in defense of "our" way of life. At those historical moments, we put aside our differences, at least temporarily, in order to defeat a common enemy. Whether someone is a Republican or Democrat is irrelevant when we all are fighting for survival, as the widespread concerns over personal and national security have reminded us in the wake of the 2001 terrorist attacks on our nation. But in relatively more peaceful times, we examine more closely what "our" way of life really means, and the differences among us in the values we hold over a great range of issues can become quite important.

Despite the complexity of identifying, claiming, and passing on basic human values, this task is a critical part of contributing to young people's healthy development. Ianni's (1989) groundbreaking research underscores the importance of this consistency:

> Congeniality among their values and clarity and consistency in their guidance are essential to the adolescent, who is engaged in a *search for structure,* a set of believable

and attainable expectations and standards from the community to guide the movement from child to adult status. If the values expressed by different community sectors are at odds, if their directions are unclear or inconsistent, the teenager cannot be expected to accept their good will or trust their judgment. (p. 262; emphasis in the original)

Given the importance of this action as a reflection of the principles of democratic society, and its broad acceptance as highly important, it is distressing that less than half of Americans say the adults around them teach the shared values of equality, honesty, and responsibility to kids. This may be a particularly crucial action about which adults need to feel more support. On the other hand, this level of engagement in teaching shared values might be looked at as extraordinary in the context of the debates we have waged as a people over every one of those seemingly simple values of equality, honesty, and responsibility.

Values are explicitly mentioned in three of the top-rated nine actions: teaching children the core American values of equality, honesty, and responsibility; teaching them the value of respecting those from different cultural backgrounds; and openly discussing one's personal values with children and adolescents. The first two of those three actions have roots in broad democratic principles, but contain hints of significant cultural chasms that may not be tapped by the general wording of these questions.

The value of "equality" is a case in point. Of course, the Declaration of Independence notes only that "all men are created equal." But our history is filled with the struggles that have occurred to broaden the actual status of equality to include not only white men who were landowners, but women, people of all races and ethnicities, and those of all economic means. The meaning of "equality" even today is hotly debated in state and national legislatures and courts. Battles in recent years over the Equal Rights Amendment, the rights of gays and lesbians, affirmative action, the quality of education for children with special needs, equal employment access for those with disabilities, and countless other examples attest to our continuing struggle to address the meaning of "equality." Do all Americans, in their assent with the social value that says adults should teach the importance of equality, agree on all these meanings of the word, in theory and in practice? Of course not. And yet, our results suggest that adults seem ready to give each other more permission to talk about equality with children and adolescents outside their own families than may have been predicted.

Teach Respect for Cultural Differences

The importance of teaching shared values is appropriately balanced with the importance of teaching young people to respect the values and beliefs of different races and cultures—even when those values and beliefs conflict with their own. It ties to the developmental asset of cultural competence, which focuses on young people knowing and being comfortable with people of different cultural, racial, and ethnic backgrounds. Overall, 75% of adults surveyed across all cultural groups say that this kind of action is highly important. Little more than one-third, however (36%), say the adults around them actually do teach respect for cultural differences.

Given the overwhelming importance adults give to teaching young people about the shared values of equality, honesty, and responsibility, we must conjecture that teaching "respect for cultural differences" does not mean teaching respect for inequality, dishonesty, or irresponsibility. Perhaps our respondents meant "respect for cultural differences" as reflected in appearance, dress, or religious custom, but not really for great differences in how the values of equality, honesty, and responsibility are interpreted.

Almost certainly by ages six to eight (Leffert et al., 1997), and for some children as early as preschool (Hirschfield, 1995), children tend to develop an awareness of similarities and differences in people. As this awareness grows, it can lead either to an acceptance or tolerance, and even respect for others, or to the cultivation of prejudice. By modeling, talking about, and expecting respect for cultural differences, adults can contribute to that respect becoming part of a young person's values and identity. That barely more than one in three adults report the adults around them actually play this socialization role is an especially troublesome finding in a society that is rapidly becoming more culturally diverse. Perhaps the word "respect" contributed to some of these results. "Respect" certainly is not the same as acceptance or tolerance. The latter imply allowing, perhaps begrudgingly, the expression of a value or behavior, whereas respect implies that the value or behavior is due some honor, obedience, or even celebration. Respect is a more positive label to apply to a value or behavior than is the label of acceptance or toleration. We have no way of knowing if our respondents made such distinctions. We used the word "respect," and many respondents could have heard in that word "tolerate" or "accept."

Nevertheless, the level of agreement about the importance of this action is truly surprising, since our question explicitly asked adults how important it was to teach children and youth to respect differing races and cultures, *even when the values of the people in question differed from the adult's own values.* This result suggests that respect is due, not just to people who are unlike oneself in more obvious and perhaps also more superficial ways, such as skin color or place of birth, but to people whose *values* may be different (at least where they do not contradict the "shared" values of equality, honesty, and responsibility).

Is there a contradiction here? We have noted that there are clearly at least several specific values—we named equality, honesty, and responsibility in our question—that most Americans hold to be important enough that all adults should teach them to children and youth outside their own families. How does that square with respecting people whose values may be different? For example, although we did not specify which cultures' values ought to be respected, most adults' belief in teaching respect for "cultural" differences likely does not include "cultures" such as the Ku Klux Klan or neo-Nazis who preach hatred of others based on their race, religion, or other characteristics. The foundation of their philosophies contradicts the core, shared value of equality. Similarly, large numbers of American adults may want to teach young people not to blindly respect aspects of a corporate or consumer culture represented by tobacco companies, which in the pursuit of profits, also may be widely seen as having violated two of the three core values, honesty and responsibility.

One way of interpreting our results is that they may suggest most Americans recognize that honoring differences in values while preserving core values does not come without ongoing struggle, examination, and refining of personal and social attitudes and expectations. Reconciling those sometimes competing social values creates an ongoing social tension—it is a "messy" process inherent in democratic societies, and a responsibility of adults both to engage in themselves and also to teach the next generation that they too must take their place in that struggle.

Alternatively, of course, adults might not accept as necessary the idea they should be engaged in the task of *bargaining* about these social norms. Instead, we might also interpret these results as suggesting that adults merely accept the assumption that cultural differences should be respected, as long as core values are in place. As we have discussed earlier, thinking that both the teaching of shared values and the respecting of differences are important reflects the fundamental creative tensions of American life, namely, shared responsibility and upholding of the common good in balance with tolerance and the individual pursuit of life, liberty, and happiness. Other studies have shown that the public feels children and adolescents have been insufficiently exposed to basic values (Farkas & Johnson, 1997; Duffett et al., 1999). That public opinion perspective may partly explain the high level of support for those two actions that are values-oriented, and for the third more general one (discussed below) about adults "openly" discussing "their values" with children and youth.

Guidance on Decisions and Financial Matters

Adults may recognize that it is challenging for young people to define and live out values that are, at the same time, both personally meaningful and socially sanctioned and integrated. That recognition may also be partly why there is so much importance, surprisingly, given to two other actions: helping young people think through the consequences of possible decisions; and giving them guidance about sharing, spending, and saving money.

Adults can be important guides and resources in helping young people learn how to make responsible choices by, among other things, thinking through the possible consequences of their decisions. And, indeed, three-fourths (76%) of the adults surveyed believe that offering this kind of guidance is very important. Nevertheless, just 41% say most adults around them actually help young people with decision making.

The difference in the strong support for guiding decision making (considered most important by 76% of adults) and the low support for neighbors giving advice (considered most important by only 13% of adults) suggests meaningful nuances in adults' level of comfort with offering guidance. Adults appear to believe it is important to guide, share, help, and encourage young people in various ways, but they don't believe it's important to give them advice. What explains this difference? Here are some possibilities:

- Adults may believe that young people don't listen to adults' advice, so giving them advice is fruitless.
- Adults may be uncomfortable with neighbors giving advice because they don't really know their neighbors or what kind of advice they would give.
- Adults may worry that, if they do give advice, disapproval and negative consequences could follow.
- Adults may reason that, if they do give advice, they could themselves be held responsible or accountable for what the young person does.

As these possibilities suggest, there are some perceived risks involved in adults other than parents *promoting* rather than simply sharing a point of view that might affect young people's decision making. This may be one of the most important barriers to the deeper engagement of unrelated adults with other people's kids. These examples highlight some of the complex and problematic aspects of strengthening relationships between young people and unrelated adults in a society that, except in extreme cases, defers to parents' preferences and wishes. One interviewee put it this way when asked whether neighbors should give kids advice about using money: "It's up to the parent of the child because the parents, they might have set a goal for the child and [the neighbor's advice] might be different from what they wanted.... The parent might call or come and pay a visit and tell them to mind their own business."

Compounding the complexity, studies of adult–youth relationships show that, while young people generally prefer going to their parents for help, they often prefer to approach unrelated adults on some issues such as school concerns or sexual matters (reviewed in Scales & Leffert, 1999). These realities (coupled with the importance that adults place on offering guidance) present opportunities to initiate dialogue and reflection on how to address such questions so that more adults can play these roles. Such efforts to expand adult guidance around young people's decision making are particularly important given the large gap between the levels of belief that this role is important (76%) and how few adults report the adults around them actual play it (41%).

Similarly, perhaps more than any previous generation, today's young people face a dizzying array of financial choices and pressures. Possibly based on an understanding of that reality, three out of four adults we surveyed believe it is most important for adults to offer young people guidance on responsibly saving, sharing, and spending money. This consensus cuts across all economic levels among the adults surveyed.

Addressing saving, sharing, and spending money with young people clearly can help equip them to make responsible financial choices in a financially complex world. In addition, offering financial guidance can offer concrete issues around which to address several developmental assets, including those most clearly related to saving, spending, and sharing money, namely, the assets of caring, equality and social justice, responsibility, and planning and decision making. By helping young people examine their sense of financial responsibility, adults have the opportunity to strengthen all of these assets. But most adults apparently are missing that opportunity, since only half as many say the adults around them give this guidance—36%—as think it is important to do.

For years, one of the battlegrounds of the "culture wars" in America has been between two groups: those who have wanted to expand the ability young people have to make decisions, and those who want to preserve for adults the right and responsibility of making decisions for their own children, including the books they can read, the movies they can see, and the medical treatment they can obtain. One group of Americans has essentially argued, not for total autonomy for young people, but that young people increasingly must be given opportunities to make their own decisions as part of the process of preparing for adulthood. In contrast, the other group has essentially argued that until adolescents reach the legally defined age of adulthood, they are too immature to make many decisions for themselves, and that instead, primarily parents and society, through its laws regulating minors' behaviors, must make such decisions for young people.

The finding that a nationally representative sample of U.S. adults concurs that adults in general, not just parents, need to help young people do a better job in decision making was not necessarily predictable, given the history of those kinds of deep philosophical differences in our nation. Obviously, we would have observed greater disagreement had we asked about adult guidance on specific decisions such as those mentioned above (e.g., decisions about what books young people could read, movies they could see, or especially, medical treatment they could obtain). Our point is not that Americans think all adults should be helping young people on all sorts of controversial decisions. It is doubtful that is the case. Rather, this agreement on the importance of the general action—helping young people think through the good and bad consequences of decisions—suggests there may be more territory for adult engagement even in this complex area of decision making than many adults believe is socially safe or acceptable.

Of course, the consensus belief that it is important for adults to help young people in making decisions goes only so far. Guiding young people in decisions may be thought of as "objective" presence of adults and is supported, whereas giving advice to young people may be considered more of a "subjective" adult influence and is considered highly important only by a minority. In addition, as Figure 3 showed, we also asked Americans how important it was to ask for young people's *opinions* about decisions that would affect them, and only 48% thought that was highly important. The ambivalence between empowering and protecting the young, even while guiding them toward greater independence, is evident in the juxtaposition of these findings: Not surprisingly, adults would appear to be more comfortable guiding children and adolescents in thinking through decisions than actually asking young people to *contribute* to decisions.

It is significant that giving guidance about money matters was rated so important an adult action because it serves as a specific issue that unites the two more general actions concerning values and decision making. The values and decisions surrounding young people's financial choices are practically unlimited.

As we noted earlier, most young people say they do not get much financial guidance from parents or school on myriad financial questions. Such questions begging for adult guidance include: Whether one works for pay as a young person, or volunteers, or works and contributes part of one's pay to charity; how one deals with borrowing or lending money among friends; how one learns to be frugal without being thought cheap, generous without being gullible; whether one spends what one has or delays gratification to save for a highly desired purchase later on; what one spends money on; how important making money is in deciding how to spend one's time; how much money is enough to have; and so forth.

At the same time, the affirmation of the importance of talking about money is a surprise in a society in which money is typically viewed as private. Wuthnow (1994) reported on a nationally representative survey of more than 2,000 Americans in the workforce in which he found that 82% of adults had "never" or "hardly ever" discussed various aspects of personal finances with people outside their immediate family. Neither is communication within the family or in school common. Personal finance has been called the "last taboo topic for parents," and it has been estimated that only 10% of young people learn about personal finance in school (Bowman, 2000). Observers who have lived in other societies note that Americans are much more reluctant to talk about money than people elsewhere. It is considered impolite here to ask other people what their income is, for example. There are also cultural norms against revealing one's good or bad monetary fortunes. Many families feel it is important to shield their own children from knowing too much about the family budget— perhaps to keep them from worrying, but perhaps more often to keep them from asking for so much (Wuthnow, 1994).

That Americans of widely different economic means thought it highly important for adults to help children and adolescents deal with such issues is truly surprising. In many research studies, the question people most often refuse to answer is to identify their income level. In the current study too, it was the question people most often chose not to answer—6% refused, compared to no more than 1% for any other question. Yet people at all income levels agreed adults need to help young people better understand the personal and social implications of the decisions they make about money. This is rather remarkable consensus among Americans whose financial means force or permit them to live vastly different lives.

It is not surprising at all, of course, that most Americans of whatever economic standing think young people should be taught how to handle money "responsibly." At the very least, this is consistent with adults' support for teaching young people the core value of responsibility. And yet, there are two surprises in this finding. One is that values about "sharing, spending, and saving" money reflect possible deep differences among people based on family and cultural heritage, political leanings, and religious beliefs. Given the potential for serious differences of opinion over what young people should be taught about such sharing, spending, and saving, there is a second surprise, namely, *who* Americans think ought to be guiding young people: "all adults," not only parents.

Of course, as is the case with the consensus on values, the consensus on the importance of providing guidance about decisions and financial matters may break down when adults' frames of reference move from the abstract and theoretical to the concrete and specific. Our in-depth interviews based on hypothetical situations, for example, suggested that although most adults affirm the importance of generally offering financial guidance, they may be more hesitant in certain situations.

Specifically, only 23% of the 100 people who participated in the in-depth interviews said it would be "very common" for most adults to offer advice to dissuade a middle school boy from using for entertainment all the money he earned from raking leaves. In addition, only 20% of the adults who participated in the in-depth interviews for this study said it was a good thing for adults to give such advice or that all adults were responsible for providing such financial guidance. Most thought it was up to the boy and his parents to figure out what to do with the money, as suggested by one interviewee: "His parents should have told him what to do with the money. Not me—I'm just the employer."

Of course, it is possible that adults' reluctance to discuss financial matters, even though they rate it highly important, could also be due in part to their own limited knowledge of financial issues and vocabulary. Many adults do not themselves practice what they might preach when it comes to financial planning. After all, consumerism itself drives the average American to carry too much debt, wildly underestimate the resources it will take to retire comfortably, and not save enough for that eventuality (Conte, 1998).

These results suggest the complexity of the situational elements that affect whether adults do or don't do even an action they consider highly important. Perhaps Americans more strongly believe that all adults should have general conversations about financial values with young people, and teach them how to make various financial decisions, but not interfere when it comes to giving explicit advice about spending their own money. This is consistent with the notion that American adults seem more comfortable encouraging or guiding young people than specifically telling them what to do. It is no wonder that only a minority of adults do either of those things (guide decisions or give advice). After all, helping young people think through the possible good and bad consequences of various decisions requires considering what those decisions are about, that is, getting into specific situations. The more pointed the discussion gets, the more difficult it may be for many adults to refrain from saying what they would do, or what they believe the young person should do. The desire not to cross the line into advice giving may lead many adults to avoid providing even general guidance to young people.

Our results may also suggest that adults know that "teaching" young people about these things is not an easy process. Adults do not simply give young people our best lecture and then rest assured that the knowledge has been received and will be acted upon wisely. We support and guide young people, and those children and youth will watch and hear, or not, test or give our ideas a chance, or not, depending on whether they like and respect us more or less. Depending on our relationship with them, we may either come to learn that a child has taken our lesson and tried it out in real life, or not. At some point, it is simply up to the child or adolescent how much to reveal to an adult about the influence the adult has had on that child's life. These processes are repeated, endlessly, between the child and all the adults she or he knows.

Have Meaningful Conversations

Three-fourths of adults surveyed (75%) believe it is important for adults to have conversations with young people that help adults and young people "really get to know one another." In reality, though, such conversations occur infrequently. Search Institute surveys of 6th- to 12th-grade students find that only about half of young people (52%) have had a conversation with three or more adults they know well in the past month. And only about one-third of Americans in this current study (34%) say that most of the adults they know have meaningful conversations with young people.

Meaningful conversations are an essential part of a significant relationship. It is through such exchanges that adults not only share wisdom, traditions, skills, expectations, and priorities, but also allow young people to express themselves, their beliefs, realities, hopes, and dreams. Furthermore, meaningful conversations are an essential element of the other asset-building actions examined in this study. Only through meaningful conversations can adults teach shared values, discuss their own values, guide decision making, or give financial guidance—all actions that 70% or more of adults rate "most important."

The reality that adult influence in a child's life accumulates gradually as a relationship develops over time also may be partly why so much importance was given to adults having "meaningful conversations" with children and youth. For example, a study of volunteer mentoring reported by Rhodes and Roffman (2003) found that positive academic, behavioral, and psychological outcomes were more likely in mentor relationships that lasted more than one year, with decreasing likelihood of positive outcomes as the duration of mentoring relationships lessened. If the only interactions adults have with young people are brief, routine, and superficial, it is hardly possible to do some of the other actions Americans in large proportions think are highly important, such as teach core values, openly discuss one's own values, help young people think through decisions, and give them guidance on money matters. Thus, just any contact with adults probably is not by itself a salutary socialization influence. Sustained and meaningful interactions are more likely to have a positive impact on child and youth development.

Despite the support for the importance of having meaningful conversations, there is a caveat to note. Americans may want adults to talk more in-depth with children and youth, including young people outside their own families, but they don't think it's very important for adults to give advice to children and youth. Advice may be considered more directive, controlling, and intrusive. In contrast, what is important is for adults to guide, share, help, and encourage young people regarding the values and decision making discussed here. Those actions imply less imposition of the adult's point of view on the young person and, by extension, his or her family. As mentioned earlier, however, the line between helping young people think and suggesting to them what to think represents a thin boundary that probably is difficult for most adults to negotiate, leaving them less inclined to have meaningful conversations than they might be otherwise.

It could also be, as we have mentioned, that most adults are less comfortable with the idea of neighbors giving advice because they do not know all or even many of their neighbors that well and therefore do not really know what kind of advice they would give children or adolescents. Under those circumstances, one's trust in them to give what would be considered "acceptable" advice could be quite limited.

Discuss Personal Values

While it may not be surprising to learn that adults place priority on teaching shared values (see above), it may surprise some that 73% of adults believe it is also highly important for adults to "openly discuss their *own* values with children and youth" (emphasis added). Unlike shared values, personal values may not be shared by others; they may even be controversial. Or, more to the point, they may be values with which the child's or teenager's parent disagrees. As we have previously pointed out, however, perhaps support for this action was so high because adults assume others' personal values are the same conventional, uncontroversial ones that they themselves hold.

What is surprising about this high level of agreement for the third value-related action, discussing one's own values, is that there has been so much apparent conflict about values in social debates for decades. The conflicts have encompassed a large number of topics in education, health care, and other government policy. Examples include: What should be taught in sexuality education classes in schools; which books ought to be required reading in English; evolution versus creationism; which historical figures get how much space in social studies textbooks; issues such as abortion, euthanasia, and informed consent for health care; and policies on matters ranging from racial discrimination to welfare to immigration. Are Americans really giving permission to adults to talk with children and youth about their personal values on any subject? We doubt it.

Most likely, the values reflected in the other core actions are the ones Americans expect adults to do most of their sharing about: equality, honesty, responsibility, respect for cultural differences, respect for adults, abiding by rules, doing well in school. How all these get reflected in specific cases, not in their general importance, may be where differences emerge most. Perhaps too adults just don't imagine most other adults dealing with many other values in their relationships with kids. Perhaps the responding adults, in thinking about "personal" values, had their own values in mind, which they consider the "right" values, and so of course responded that it is important for adults to discuss those values with young people. They might also simply assume that other adults share the same "personal" values as do they, and so find it perfectly acceptable for "all" adults to share those values with young people.

But to an extent, the very importance adults gave to the action of all adults openly discussing their own unspecified values with children and adolescents may suggest that American adults expect young people to be exposed to a variety of values. Adults might recognize that kids also need guidance in coming to define for themselves a core set of values that is compatible with and supportive of the basic core of overarching democratic values. This requires exposing young people to differing values, even while assuming or hoping that they mainly will follow the values their parents have taught them. This creative tension about values socialization may be an implicit recognition that, even if adults would prefer to believe otherwise, young people can't simply be "taught" these things. Instead, life poses regular challenges to values and so young people need more help of a guiding, mentoring, facilitating nature from a wide spectrum of adults in securing a solid base of positive values for themselves, and in achieving the necessary balance between personal and shared values.

Whatever the reason for the high degree of support for discussing personal values, most adults miss the chance to have an impact on values development, since just 37% say the majority of adults they know actually discuss their personal values with other people's kids. A single conversation rarely affects a young person's deep-seated beliefs and values. Young people who learn from *many* adult perspectives, by talking with adults about their personal values and how they came to embrace those values, are able to catch glimpses into the process of values formation. This helps them learn how to shape their own values and beliefs in a complex world. But according to our results, only a minority of adults are contributing to the development of young people's values in this way.

Expect Respect for Adults

A great majority of adults believe that it is important to expect children and teenagers to respect adults and elders as authority figures. Sixty-eight percent of adults believe that this respect is highly important. The support for this expectation may speak to the widespread perception among adults that young people are disrespectful. One national poll reported that only 12% of adults think teenagers treat adults with respect (Farkas & Johnson, 1997). From a developmental perspective, it highlights that children ideally grow a sense of respect for others and an understanding of roles and authority that teaches them to accept reasonable boundaries and expectations. To the extent that they are seen not doing these things, they may be seen as disrespectful. This expectation also underscores the process of socialization in which the elders pass to the younger generations the wisdom and practices of the culture.

Expecting young people to respect adults also is one of only two actions that most adults (67%) think other adults actually do. And it is interesting that this is not even an adult action per se, but rather an *expectation* about how young people should act toward adults. "Expectation" in this sense means what adults want to happen, not what they predict will or does occur, since, as noted above, only a small minority of adults thinks adolescents actually do treat adults with respect.

Even at that relatively high level of "living" the action, however, about one-third of adults don't believe that the majority of adults around them hold even this most basic expectation for how young people should treat them. Had we asked how many adults actually do something when they witness disrespectful behavior, or are themselves the targets of it, it is reasonable to suspect far fewer than 67% would say most of the adults around them take such actions.

Why the Performance Gap between Beliefs and Actions?

Despite the core consensus that suggests a similarity of expectations across widely diverse Americans, there is an enormous gap between what Americans think is important for adults to do for and with kids, and what they report the majority of adults they know actually do. Despite the fact that 50% or more of Americans rated most of the actions—15 out of 20—highly important for "all adults, not just parents" to do, in practice their behavior belies this. This is hardly an unusual situation in contemporary culture. There are many things we think are important, but that sizable minorities or even majorities don't do at a correspondingly high level of consistency, such as eat right, exercise, plan for retirement, execute a will, vote, and be faithful in marriage.

But the size of the gap we report here between beliefs and actions is striking. For example, as Table 8 showed, for 13 of the 20 actions, there was a gap of at least 25 percentage points between how important it was rated and whether the majority of adults were thought to actually live the action. Disparities of this magnitude are found even among seven of the most important nine actions, and 11 of the most important 14.

These results make clear that adults attitudinally support engaging positively with children and youth at a far higher level than they engage with young people in real life. The consensus on abstract values obviously falls apart when people are faced with real-world, concrete situations in which they have to decide how to be engaged with young people, if at all. Of course, it is possible that the actions we inquired about may have artificially constrained the agreement between belief and action. Perhaps if we had asked more questions about adults' actions when they witness young people breaking laws, or acting in especially disruptive or especially heroic ways, we would have obtained more evidence of adult engagement and more consistency between beliefs and actions.

But that very possibility underscores the importance of our results: In the ordinary, unexceptional circumstances in which adults largely encounter young people, when young people are for the most part being neither especially disturbing nor unusually admirable, but just being normal, adults are not, as a rule, all that likely to be engaged in getting to know them, guiding them, or nurturing them.

It also is possible, of course, that the measure we used of "actions"—adults' estimate of the proportion of the adults they know that engage with young people in these ways—is simply something most adults cannot accurately judge. Had we asked what they themselves do, we arguably would have found a stronger alignment between personal beliefs and reported personal action (in future studies, we are asking about both their personal behavior and their perception of their social networks). But as we have also argued, that alternative measure could have suffered even more from social desirability bias to make the responding adult "look good." That risk of overestimation appeared more likely than the risk of bias in the other direction in the indirect measure we used, that is, understating how much adults really are engaged with young people.

Although we cannot definitively resolve the question of how biased—and in what direction—are our data on adults' reports of what the adults around them do, on balance the data seem reasonably accurate. There is no evidence of systematic bias in a positive direction of adults being made to look favorable in their engagement with kids, since for 18 of the 20 actions, no more than 30%–40% of adults at best report that most of the adults around them do the actions. On the other side of the coin, there is no evidence of a systematic bias in a negative direction of adults being made to look worse than they likely are in their engagement with young people. The low levels of reported engagement compare very well with the reports from the studies of young people we cited in Chapters 1 and 2, showing that only a minority of young people say they have a quantity and quality of relationship with adults conducive to building their developmental assets.

If the belief-action gap we report is a valid reflection of reality, then why might it be happening?

Lack of Perceived Permission

This large disparity between what adults think is important to do, and what they actually do, may well be due to a misperception of adults about how much permission they really have for engaging with other people's kids. Adults may have more social "permission" to get involved with the young in these ways than they think. Most people do believe it is important to become engaged with other people's kids in these ways. But if most adults don't realize that they share this belief, their misperception may lead to far fewer adults perceiving a social expectation or even permission to get involved with young people than may actually be the case.

Social psychologists have called this phenomenon "pluralistic ignorance," describing a situation in which most people privately reject a norm they subscribe to publicly. The explanation for this reasons that people act not simply on their own attitudes but on the attitudes they believe are held by everyone else (Miller, Monin, & Prentice, 2000). If most Americans believe that others think getting engaged with other people's kids is either not their responsibility or risky in terms of parents' or kids' reactions, then they won't get engaged. But our data show that the majority of Americans think 16 of the 20 actions are things "all adults, not just parents" should do, and an overwhelming 70% or more believe all adults should do nine of those actions. So the perceptions most Americans hold about how everyone else feels about engaging with kids may be false.

That is, most Americans may incorrectly believe everyone else thinks being unengaged with young people is the right way to behave. Our data show just the opposite: A considerable majority of Americans believe at least nine ways of adults engaging with kids are highly important to do. Therefore, a good deal of Americans' choices about engagement with kids is rooted in pluralistic ignorance. As long as most adults incorrectly perceive what most other adults really feel, and they shrink from deeper engagement with kids, everyone will continue to perceive that deep engagement is statistically unusual. That perception will confirm the original misimpression that unengagement is the "normal" expectation, and the circle of ignorance and unengagement will perpetuate itself.

The challenge is to break the cycle and motivate adults to act on these priorities. Absent perceived permission or expectation to get involved, the result may be a gap in adult interest and sense of responsibility for getting involved, which ultimately is reflected in the performance gap between beliefs and actions. Dispelling pluralistic ignorance about normative attitudes has been found to reduce college students' reports of heavy drinking (Miller et al., 2000). Thus, it could well be that making Americans aware that large majorities of them already strongly favor such engagement by all adults with young people could be one strategy that contributes to changes in more adults actually engaging more with kids.

Table 8 shows that, ironically, the largest gaps between adults' believing an action is important and reportedly taking the action can be found among the seven actions we categorize as social values. Indeed, the gap between stating that an action is important and actual involvement was at least 35 percentage points for all of those actions we describe as reflecting social values. Three other actions we conclude are effectively "personal preferences" had at least a 35-point gap as well: telling parents when their children do something right, providing young people opportunities for service, and volunteering or donating money monthly. Far more adults thought these actions were important than said they were surrounded by adults who do them.

If a lack of perceived permission to get involved with other people's kids is a big part of the belief-action gap, then parents may be able to play a particularly influential role in closing it. The results we discuss later in Chapter 8 show that parents are some of strongest supporters of a number of these adult actions. This result suggests that parents are basically giving permission for adults to do more than they are doing currently to help raise responsible and caring neighborhood children and youth. But most other adults are not receiving this message because it remains implicit in parents' attitudes, rather than explicit in their behavior.

As we mentioned earlier, how much more effective would this implicit permission be if it were made explicit in one-on-one conversations among adults and in community-wide discussions about an adult charter in which the expected involvement of most adults with kids was clearly defined? The potential would seem great for more adults to feel it acceptable to live these important actions if they knew more explicitly that they were what parents really wanted and/or expected of them. We will treat this issue more in depth in Chapter 9.

True Underlying Norms

In addition to the pluralistic ignorance dynamic, the large gap between the importance accorded many actions, and the proportion of adults who report that adults they know actually do them, also suggests that the power those favorable attitudes or beliefs have to promote adult engagement is perhaps undermined by two more powerful kinds of norms. One is the norm that "this is not my responsibility," as we have earlier discussed. A second norm may be related to that perception of little or absent responsibility. Even though someone considers these actions highly important to do, since it isn't really their responsibility, they shouldn't risk or sacrifice much to do them.

For example, the majority of Americans think teaching young people about core values such as equality, honesty, and responsibility is important, but the majority of us don't do this. Then the true norm governing our relationships with kids is, "Don't bother to teach them about values such as equality, honesty, and responsibility—leave that to the parents." Most adults say it is important to teach these values, but apparently, it is not important enough for adults actually to do it, not worth the likely trouble that may come from doing that action.

Each of the seven top actions that were considered important, but which most Americans don't do, can be read in its reverse as the true implicit norm that shapes how adults and kids relate: Don't bother to teach them about core values; don't bother to teach them about respect for cultural differences; don't bother to help them think through the consequences of decisions; don't bother to have more than casual conversations with them; don't bother to give them guidance on sharing, spending, and saving money; don't bother to openly discuss your values with them. Unless you're absolutely sure there is no risk involved, leave all these things to parents. And, if you're a parent, we understand if you don't bother to enforce clear rules and boundaries with your children.

This is not to say adults never do these things. Those who engage with kids in these ways are in the minority, but still a not insignificant minority—about one-third of Americans do many of the actions. So many of us engage with kids in these ways occasionally. But if these are indeed the true underlying norms guiding adults' behavior, then what we are suggesting is that for most adults, if they perceive that a situation with a young person involves any potential bother, discomfort, or uncertainty, the socially normal course is to then refrain from getting involved.

Perhaps there is shock value in reading the actions in the negative: Most people probably would think it irresponsible to intentionally choose *not* to do these things with children and adolescents. But the results of our nationwide study show that is exactly what we adults have done, in effect. These actions clearly are theoretically important to most Americans, and from that perspective they define elements of a reasonable responsibility all adults should have for engagement with young people. But in terms of being actual priorities that one does even if hassles and inconveniences come from doing them, these ways of engaging with young people fall far short of being genuine priorities for most Americans. In the next two chapters, we address further the gap between beliefs and actions. We also consider how differences among groups of Americans and across situational circumstances may affect how important adults think these actions are and how likely they are to be surrounded by adults who actually do engage with young people.

7 Normative Fragmentation: The Disappearance of Consensus

As we have seen, there is relative consensus on the importance of nine ways adults can engage with young people. Even within that consensus, however, there are divergent views about how important these "consensus" actions are. And once beyond that territory of relative consensus lies a more normatively fragmented American culture in which consensus on the importance of specific kinds of adult engagement fades and then disappears. In this chapter, we further discuss overall patterns of results for the actions that were not rated among the top nine in importance, and the gap between beliefs about those actions, and adults' actual behavior. In Chapter 8, we look more comprehensively at differences in beliefs and actions among different demographic groups of Americans.

Actions with Mixed Support: Social Values and Personal Preferences

The nine actions highlighted in Chapter 6 represent a solid core of ways that adults can engage in the lives of young people both in and outside their own families. They begin to help define the territory of reasonable responsibility that all adults might assume for child and youth well-being. Knowing that the vast majority of people (70% or more) believe these nine actions are highly important, many adults might get more engaged with young people in these ways. The fragility of this support, however, is suggested by the gap between belief and action, for seven of even these nine highly rated actions. One negative experience—a bad reaction from a parent or a child—may be enough to make even a motivated adult dealing with a highly important, agreed upon action wary of further or deeper engagement.

If that is the case for the most highly rated actions, how much more tenuous is the connection between belief and behavior for the actions beyond this core, some of which elicit considerable, but less, consensus among American adults?

Indeed, all but one of the 20 actions we studied was considered "most important" by nearly 50%–70% of adults, but even fewer adults were reported to do these actions than were reported to do the nine actions considered most important. These 11 actions with mixed support (with percentages of adults who believe they are "most important") are as follows:

- Tell parent(s) if they see a child or teenager doing something right (65%);
- Feel responsible to help ensure the well-being of the young people in their neighborhood (63%);
- Tell parent(s) if they see the child or youth doing something wrong (62%);
- Openly discuss their own religious or spiritual beliefs with children and youth (60%);
- Actively teach young people to preserve, protect, and pass down the traditions and values of their ethnic and/or religious culture (56%);
- Parents being the sole providers of discipline to their children (55%—as mentioned previously, this action was reverse-scored because it is not indicative of an "asset-building" approach to child and adolescent socialization);
- Know the names of many children and youth in the neighborhood (50%);
- Seek young people's opinions when making decisions that affect them (48%);
- Give young people lots of service opportunities to make their communities better places (48%);
- Volunteer time or donate money monthly to show young people the importance of helping others (47%); and
- Give advice to young people who are not members of the family (13%).

All of these interactions (except parents having the exclusive role over discipline, which we reverse-scored) can contribute to young people's well-being. And when we combine the responses of adults who say the action is "most important" and "very important," at least three-fourths of adults support all but one of these actions. The exception was neighbors giving advice to kids, which only 17% of adults say is most or very important, and which we discussed in the previous chapter.

Despite that solid level of support for most of the remaining actions, American adults clearly deem them less important than the top nine. As a result, it is likely that adults would generally be less likely to engage in these behaviors with young people. And as Table 8 indicated, just 13%–38% of adults say most of the adults they know actually do these other 11 actions. The difference in the perceived importance of and engagement in these actions, compared to the core nine, raises several questions about adults' priorities, roles, and capacity to make a difference:

- Are the overall lower ratings a result of significant disagreements in society about the importance of these actions? For example, people who are more religious are much more likely to affirm the importance of discussing religious values. Among those who attend services weekly or more, 75% say this action is very important, compared to 34% who rarely or never attend (see Chapter 8).

- Does the lower rating on these actions reflect adults' belief that they have less impact on young people's lives and thus are less important? For example, many adults may not recognize the impact of reporting positive behavior, knowing the names of young people in the neighborhood, and seeking their opinions as actions that help young people feel known, valued, connected, and empowered. Indeed, Public Agenda found that only 47% of adults believe that "neighbors spending more time with kids and watching out for them" is a very effective way to help young people (Farkas & Johnson, 1997).
- Do many adults see these actions as being even more than the nine top-rated actions the primary or sole responsibility of parents (and, perhaps, adults who work directly with children or teenagers)? Such an interpretation would be consistent with previous public opinion polls and focus group research (Duffett et al., 1999; Bales, 2001). As one interviewee put it, "Who are we to interfere and override what the parent thinks is best for their child in some circumstances?"
- Did some respondents feel that the action was too big for the average adult to have any impact? That may be the case, for example, with helping to ensure the well-being of neighborhood kids. Indeed, previous research has found that a significant barrier to people's involvement in the lives of children is their sense that the issues and challenges in young people's lives are too complex for them to be able to make a difference (Farkas & Johnson, 1997; Bostrom, 1999).

This study does not answer these questions directly; additional research could examine them in much greater depth. Yet perhaps it is more important to begin the dialogue within communities about these kinds of issues so that people can reflect upon their assumptions. Such reflection would help many adults arrive at an answer to the question, What do we agree upon and how can that consensus shape what adults expect of and support in each other when it comes to raising healthy children and youth?

This examination of individual and collective values and expectations takes on even greater importance when considering an additional message from our findings. Even though, as expected, the actions receiving lower ratings of importance generally are also done by fewer adults, the proportions engaging in most of even the agreed on important actions are not that different from the proportions engaging in many of the less-supported actions. For example, knowing the names of many neighborhood kids was considered highly important by just 50% of adults, and only 34% say most of the adults around them actually know many kids' names. Similarly, providing financial guidance was considered highly important by 75%, and yet just 36% said most adults they know actually provide that guidance to other people's kids. A very great challenge for building developmentally attentive communities, then, is that merely increasing the public's sense of how important an action is may have little practical effect on whether adults actually engage in that action. In Chapter 9, we deal in more detail with steps that might make more of a difference, not just in adults' beliefs, but also in their actions.

But first, in this and the next chapter, we deal with contextual and demographic differences in how important different adults think the actions are, and how many of the adults around them do those actions. In the current chapter, we examine in more detail the issue of the neighborhood as a locus of relationships among adults and young people, the influence of children's ages on adult actions, and other situational dimensions that affect how adults and kids relate.

Communities of Association versus Communities of Place

The relatively lower level of importance given to several actions may speak to the sense of responsibility for the common good being weaker than is otherwise suggested by the consensus on the core actions Americans considered most important. In theory, as expressed by their ratings of how important these actions are, most Americans seem to think they share responsibility for guiding the next generation. But in daily practice, as reflected in reports of the adults they know doing these actions, the nurturing of kids seems to be essentially left to their parents. In addition to the belief-action gap, this contradiction between seeming to acknowledge some responsibility, and acting on it in only a limited way, also is reflected in the lower levels of basic importance given to a number of actions. These include feeling responsibility to help ensure the well-being of all the children and youth in one's neighborhood, giving young people opportunities to make the community better, the acceptability of neighbors giving advice to children and adolescents, and volunteering or donating money monthly.

It is especially interesting to examine the results comparing actions that refer to the "neighborhood," or to "neighbors," with actions that made no such reference. Actions explicitly including a socialization role of adults for other people's kids generally received lower ratings of importance than actions where unrelated adults (e.g., "neighbors") were included in the general phrase "all adults," but not explicitly identified. This is an important distinction, and it reminds us again that the abstract belief among adults that engagement with young people is highly important often breaks down in real situations. The more specificity introduced to the hypothetical or abstract, the less the consensus on the importance of the action.

For example, we placed some emphasis in our questions on the importance of the "neighborhood," the geographical area nearest where adults live. We calculated the mean rating of importance and conformity on the five actions that explicitly referenced the "neighborhood," and compared those results to the mean ratings for the remaining 15 items that did not specify a location. Adults were not more likely to rate actions in one's neighborhood more important than those in other life settings. Nor did they report that adults around them did those "neighborhood" actions more than they reported adults did the other actions. In fact, the mean importance and conformity ratings were slightly higher for actions

Table 14. "Neighborhood" versus Other Actions: Means and Standard Deviations

	Importance		Conformity	
	Mean	SD	Mean	SD
Items Referencing Neighborhood				
Report positive behavior	4.42	1.61	2.41	2.33
Ensure well-being of neighborhood kids	4.46	1.44	2.96	2.32
Report misbehavior	4.40	1.60	2.87	2.40
Know names	4.23	1.65	2.90	2.40
Give advice	3.06	2.06	2.38	2.21
Neighborhood Items Mean	**4.10**		**2.70**	
(Without "Give advice")	**4.36**		**2.79**	
Items Not Referencing Neighborhood				
Encourage school success	4.87	0.82	3.95	1.88
Expect respect for adults	4.51	1.46	3.89	1.99
Expect parents to set boundaries	4.76	1.08	3.27	2.13
Teach shared values	4.69	1.27	3.32	2.17
Teach respect for cultural differences	4.65	1.33	3.04	2.18
Guide decision making	4.66	1.28	3.18	2.15
Have meaningful conversations	4.65	1.18	3.07	2.11
Give financial guidance	4.62	1.33	3.05	2.23
Discuss personal values	4.58	1.40	3.10	2.14
Discuss religious beliefs	4.30	1.81	2.99	2.32
Pass down traditions	4.34	1.59	3.12	2.17
Parents be sole discipliners	4.27	1.66	3.62	2.12
Provide service opportunities	4.18	1.71	2.16	2.09
Seek opinions	4.15	1.79	2.76	2.16
Model giving and serving	4.14	1.75	2.31	2.12
Nonneighborhood Items Mean	**4.49**		**3.12**	

that did *not* reference the neighborhood, both for importance and conformity. Table 14 shows those results.

Of course, each set of items (neighborhood and nonneighborhood) asked about different issues, and so we may not be tapping differences in perceptions about "neighborhood" here at all. For example, among the neighborhood group, there were four social values (tell parents when children do something right, or wrong; feel responsible to help ensure the well-being of all neighborhood kids; know the names of many neighborhood kids) and the lowest-rated item of all, a personal preference action (give advice to neighborhood kids). In contrast, the set of items without a location specified contained the remaining low-rated personal preferences, but also the higher-rated two genuine norms and 10 remaining actions we called social values. The result was that the average percentage rating the neighborhood items highly important was 51%, compared with the average importance of 64% for the items not specifying a location. Similarly, the average proportion who thought most of the adults they knew did these actions was 28% for the neighborhood items, compared with 36% for the set with an unspecified location.

Because the nature of the actions asked about was different in each set, the differences in means and average proportions could simply be a function of that different content, and have little or nothing to do with the neighborhood referent. We did remove the lowest-rated action, neighbors giving advice, and recalculated the neighborhood item importance and conformity means. Table 14 shows that although the difference became smaller, the nonneighborhood items were still rated higher both on importance and the degree to which adults were reported to do the actions.

Instead of being solely a function of variation in the content of the actions, there may be another partial explanation for these results. Our results may suggest that today, the geographical near neighborhood is no longer where many people live out their connections with kids. More importantly, that near neighborhood may not be where young people themselves feel the most connection. Adolescents especially will venture beyond the confines of their immediate neighborhood to encounter the social realities of other neighborhoods where their friends live, what have been called "neighborhoods of sociability" (Burton & Price-Spratlen, 1999, p. 82). Research also has shown that parents are not always privy to the neighborhoods that comprise their children's worlds (making them, and certainly unrelated adults, insufficient commentators on that issue). Moreover, children define neighborhood more by associational and relationship ties than by geography, the frame of reference parents use most (Burton & Price-Spratlen, 1999). Many adults may not know with great certainty which children and youth they see in their neighborhood are in fact from their neighborhood. These complexities may well have weakened the potential difference we could have found between "neighborhood" and "nonneighborhood" items.

In addition, the importance of neighborhood kinds of proximity in adult-child relationships may be lessened by other realities of the modern age. When most people travel to schools, workplaces, and consumer, civic, and leisure pursuits many miles from their home and neighborhood, when our extended families are more likely than ever to be spread across the country, and when millions establish virtual communities through the World Wide Web and Internet, geographical place of residence may simply mean less.

Communities of association may be more important than geographical community today. Perhaps if you care about kids, you mentor a lot, but not necessarily in your neighborhood. For example, a whopping 75% of Americans consider it highly important to have more than casual conversations with children and youth. But just 50% think it's highly important to know the names of many neighborhood kids, and only 34% say most of the adults they know do know many names of the young people in their neighborhoods. There is an obvious apparent contradiction here: How likely is it that an adult can have more than a casual conversation with a child or adolescent whose name he or she doesn't even know?

The only way we can make sense of this apparent contradiction is to note that in the question about adults having conversations with kids, we did not name neighborhood as the place where these conversations occur. In contrast, neighborhood was named in the question about the importance of knowing children's names. It is possible that many American adults think it's important to relate more than casually to children and youth whom they meet in various life circumstances, whether in their neighborhood or not, but make no special distinction about young people in their immediate neighborhood.

Perhaps the "sense of community" that is often referred to as having been lost in recent decades is not fully lost after all, but transferred to different domains, at least in part. Fukuyama (1999, p. 72) called the creation of individualized life spaces in technologically advanced societies the "miniaturization of community," as people join small, flexible interest groups they can get into and out of without much personal cost. Those adults may, instead of a neighborhood responsibility, feel more of a responsibility to help ensure the well-being of the young people they know from their broader community activities. These might include young people they know from their religious congregation, sports leagues, or volunteer work. The young people they know could largely be those who work at the places where adults shop, or be their own children's friends (many of whom, especially the friends of teenagers, may not live in the neighborhood or attend the school nearest their neighborhood).

In this sense, then, adults create their own communities of association, some face-to-face and even some "virtual villages." Whether in real space or cyberspace, they also may come into contact with other people's kids, but not necessarily kids from their own neighborhood. These interactions result from personal choices about time, place, and interests, as well as the impact of similar choices made by one's spouse and children. Indeed, only 63% of adults rated it highly important to feel personal responsibility for the well-being of neighborhood children and adolescents, and only about one-third (35%) said most of the adults they knew felt that responsibility for neighborhood kids.

The Importance of Children's Ages

Whether the children involved are younger children or adolescents, the kind of action involved, and adults' perceived intent in getting involved with kids, all affect levels of support for the importance of the actions and the extent to which the majority of adults are believed to relate to young people. For example, on the Importance scale, American adults felt these actions were more important for adults to do with children ages 5–10 than with young adolescents and older teenagers ages 11–18 ($F(1, 1356) = 14.16$, $p < .0002$). Adults also were slightly more likely to report being surrounded by other adults who live the actions (Conformity scale) when it comes to children than who do so in relationships with adolescents ($F(1, 1330) = 4.92$, $p < .02$).

Table 15 shows, however, that, overall, adults were no more unified in their views on how important the actions are for younger versus older children, nor were they any less variable in how they reported adults around them did or did not engage with kids based on their ages. Table 15 shows the means and standard deviations of the importance ratings and conformity ratings, a measure of dispersion around the mean, comparing adults who used children as a referent and adults who used adolescents as a referent. The results suggest that adults

Table 15. Children versus Adolescents: Comparative Consistency of Adult Beliefs and Actions (N = 1,425)

	Importance scale		Conformity scale	
	Mean	SD	Mean	SD
Engaging with children	4.31	0.68	2.93	1.13
Engaging with adolescents	4.22	0.73	2.85	1.10

were as varied in their responses when it comes to younger children as when it comes to adolescents. This similarity of standard deviations occurred even though adults thought it more important to relate to younger children in these ways, and even though they reported that the adults around them did so more than they did for adolescents.

In terms of specific actions, Table 16[5] shows that adults considered it more important to do the following with children than with youth:

- Teach children to respect people of different races and cultures;
- Help children see the consequences of their decisions;
- Feel responsible to help ensure the well-being of all neighborhood children; and
- Give children chances to improve their community.

These four adult actions included two that we labeled as social values (teaching respect for different races and cultures, and helping children with decision making). Recall that "social values" were considered important by 70% or more of Americans, but only a minority of adults said that they are surrounded by other adults who actually do these things. Of course, teaching respect for different races and cultures is a specific example of values in general. It appears that American adults feel they have more of a role in influencing the general value

[5] In order to be represented in a table or figure, comparisons among groups within the total sample (i.e., subsamples) had to satisfy two criteria. First, the difference between the *means* of the groups, analyzed by either t-tests or ANOVAs as appropriate, had to be significant at the .05 level. Additionally, because multiple t-tests were requested for two-group comparisons (e.g., children versus youth, men versus women), a Bonferroni correction (multiplying the observed *p* level by the number of t-tests requested in a single analysis) was applied to ensure against reporting as significant those findings that were significant by chance alone (*SPSS Base 8.0 Applications Guide,* 1998). A number of results were "significant" at the .05 level, but failed to reach that cutoff when the Bonferroni correction was applied. For example, a .005 level, multiplied by the number of t-tests in a typical analysis in this study, 20, yields a corrected value of .10, and is therefore no longer a significant finding. Only corrected figures are reported.

  Second, the difference between the percentage responses of the groups that are actually displayed in the figures had to be within the sampling tolerances for subsample comparisons. If a *mean* difference was statistically significant, but the *percentage* difference on norm importance or conformity was not within the sampling tolerance, we reported the statistically significant mean difference finding in the narrative, but did not display it in the figures. Appendix D provides tolerance tables that were used in assessing the meaningfulness of percentage differences between groups.

Table 16. *Children versus Adolescents: Proportions of Adults Rating Actions Important* (N = 1,424)

	Children	Adolescents	F
Teach respect for cultural differences	81%[a]	72%[b]	13.70**
Guide decision making	80%[a]	72%[b]	10.89*
Ensure well-being of neighborhood kids	68%[a]	58%[b]	14.94**
Provide service opportunities	55%[a]	40%[b]	32.89*

Note: Bonferonni correction applied to p values.
a, b = Percentages with different letters are significantly different from each other.
  * = Significant at $p \leq .02$.
 ** = Significant at $p \leq .004$.

orientation of younger children than adolescents, especially when it comes to views on race.

Although we can only speculate, perhaps when it comes to values adults imagine, correctly, that older youth will have more opinions of their own than younger children. Perhaps adults anticipate that it would be less enjoyable and more uncomfortable to enter into a conversation with middle school-and high school–age adolescents about matters regarding which there is the potential for views that conflict with those of adults. In addition, racial and ethnic identity begins to emerge at those older ages (Phinney, Cantu, & Kurtz, 1997). This developmental fact adds to the possibility that the young adolescent or older teenager might not simply accept adults' sharing of their values, but might debate or even react negatively to adults' opinions, neither of which outcome most adults apparently would find desirable. Even more sharply, as suggested by interviewee responses to several of our hypothetical situations, at least 20% of adults consider relating to older teens, compared to middle school–age youth or younger children, to be threatening or uncomfortable enough to be an immediate obstacle to adults' getting involved.

As fundamentally as concerns over discomfort with, or even fear of older youth, adults may feel that younger children's values are still being formed, and that they can play more of a role, whereas they may think that adolescents' values are already set. For example, from a series of focus groups conducted with adults, Bostrom (1999) concluded that the first words adults generate when they think of "children" and "teenagers" show that "children are full of potential and ready to be molded, while teens are already finished—for good or ill" (p. 31). Of course, adolescents' values, more so than younger children's, may be challenged by opportunity, circumstances, and experimentation. Ironically, those older children may have a greater developmental need for adults to openly discuss values with them than do the younger children who adults think may be more open to adult influence.

Finally, there is the matter of why adults thought it more important to give younger children chances to improve their communities than to do so for young adolescents and older teenagers. More than half of adults—56%—felt it was highly important to do so with children 5–10 years old, but less than half—only

40%—felt that way when it comes to children 11–18 years old. These responses were perplexing indeed. Since in many respects, those older children generally possess more awareness of the need to help others through community service, and more personal capacity to do so, why would adults think it even more important for younger children to be provided such opportunities? After all, Search Institute's studies show that only half of 6th–12th graders say they contribute service three hours a week or more, and only 20% feel they're given useful roles by their community. Furthermore, the younger middle school students are more likely to say they do community service and to report feeling useful than are the older high school youth (Benson et al., 1999). This is evidence that neither the interest nor the capacity of older youth to contribute is close to being fully tapped in most American communities, and we discuss some possible reasons for these results below.

Of course, as we have already described, there is a gap between what is considered important and what adults actually do. Adults report that the adults around them do just two of the actions more for children than for youth: ensure the well-being of all kids in the neighborhood ($F(1, 1424) = 12.08$, Bonferonni corrected $p < .01$), and give advice to kids ($F(1, 1424) = 14.83$, corrected $p < .002$). Thus, even though younger children may be more likely to experience positive relationships with unrelated adults, those relationships still are not common. Interestingly, although parents are no more likely to be involved with younger children outside their families than are nonparents, parents are more likely than nonparents to be involved with *adolescents* outside their families, as we discuss in more detail in the next chapter.

Variation by Content, Situation, and Adults' Perceived Intent

In addition to children's ages affecting how important adults feel it is to do various asset-building actions, support for the importance of different actions seems to decline as a function of two other dimensions. First is the *kind of action* involved.

The continuum of adult comfort in ascribing importance to these individual actions may be at its highest point concerning school issues, followed by teaching shared values, discussing money, talking about values in general, and talking about religious/spiritual beliefs. Some actions involve issues that may seem more acceptable than others for adults to discuss, teach, encourage, or model. Encouraging commitment to school, parents enforcing boundaries, teaching core values and cultural respect, helping young people with decision making, and giving guidance on money matters all were rated highly important by more than 70% of American adults. Receiving considerable but less strong support (between 60% and 70%) were questions about other adults enforcing boundaries (telling parents when children are doing either wrong or right things) and discussing religious or spiritual beliefs with kids. Teaching kids to preserve their own culture was considered highly important by somewhat fewer (56%), and seeking kids' opinions about decisions that would affect them was considered by fewer than 50% to be highly important. But these ratings of importance are just one way to look at the results. The pattern of the gaps between those beliefs and reported actions of American adults is perhaps more telling. Regardless of their levels of rated importance, the actions related to some categories of developmental assets seem more difficult to do than actions in other categories.

As we discussed earlier, in decreasing order of gap size, the average belief-action gap is largest for actions related to the asset categories of Social Competencies, Empowerment, and Positive Values, and least for Boundaries and Expectations, Commitment to Learning, Support, and Positive Identity. Apart from their level of rated importance, perhaps it is those categories of Social Competencies, Positive Values, and Empowerment where the favorable abstract idea of getting engaged collides most with the specifics of the circumstances adults and young people are in at the moment when adults could choose to act. If those categories do reflect more gray areas where specifics may not align well with abstractions, then they may well be among the areas about which adults must most explicitly discuss their expectations of each other.

The Lesser Importance Given to Empowerment of the Young

Two of the lowest-rated actions deserve further mention. As Table 8 showed, less than half of adults thought it highly important to give children and youth opportunities to make the community a better place. Only 13% said they're surrounded by adults who give kids such opportunities, despite all the federal and local policies providing such service opportunities, and mounting evidence of the positive effects of service and service-learning (e.g., Kielsmeier, 2000; Billig, 2000; Scales, Blyth, Berkas, & Kielsmeier, 2000; Melchior, 1997). Adults thought it was more important for children ages 5–10 to have service opportunities (but even so, fewer than 60% gave it that high a rating of importance for younger children). And as we shall discuss in Chapter 8, women, African Americans, and Hispanics thought it more important than men or non-Hispanic white Americans.

In addition, less than half of adults thought it highly important to seek children and youths' opinions about decisions that will affect them, with no difference when considering relationships with adolescents or with younger children. Only among women did a majority think it highly important to ask young people their opinions about decisions that will affect them. And just one-fourth of adults said most of the adults they knew did seek out young people's opinions.

Providing service opportunities and soliciting young people's opinions are behaviors related to Search Institute's conceptualization of the developmental assets that reflect "empowerment" among young people. Empowerment is the sense young people have that they are valued, that they have important roles to play, and that they can contribute to the broader community. These are among the assets young people are least likely to report experiencing, with just 20%–25% of

6th–12th graders feeling that they are treated as resources or that the community values them (Benson et al., 1999). Given these data, it is telling but not surprising that a Gallup poll in 2000 found that, among the five "promises" put forward by America's Promise as a framework for raising healthy and productive young people, having opportunities to give back to their community was rated the least important by national samples of both adults and adolescents ages 12–17: Only 48% of adults and 40% of youth thought contributing to the community was extremely important (comparable to our results), versus 87% and 84%, respectively, who thought it extremely important for young people to have caring adults in their lives (America's Promise, 2001). That contributing to the community may be a means of increasing the number of interactions young people have with adults, and even of increasing the number of caring adults in their lives, seems to be a missing connection for the majority of Americans, young people and adults alike.

An especially provocative illustration of youth empowerment is provided by an initiative in Alaska. Thanks to a lobbying effort by youth themselves as part of an effort of the Alaska Association of School Boards, youth representatives will for the first time be included on five committees that establish the "cut scores" for the Alaska High School Qualifying Exam (e-mail from Derek Peterson to HC · HY listserv, February 27, 2001). Graduating seniors must pass that test in order to receive a high school diploma. Given the high stakes involved in the decision about where to set the pass and fail points, this is an example of youth empowerment that is noteworthy as much for its authenticity (they are making a real impact on society) as for its rarity.

Why would most adults not think it important to help young people feel more useful and valued in such ways? Perhaps there is a clue in the comments we have made about the distinction between adults encouraging young people, and adults giving advice. Encouragement of young people by adults is rated more important than giving them advice. Giving encouragement is perhaps a less direct, assertive, and forceful action than giving advice.

In the same way, most adults may be more comfortable with the idea of young people gaining their sense of being valued and useful by being responsible, working hard at school, managing money well, and treating people from different races with respect. These actions suggest accommodation, acceptance, tolerance, and respectfulness. They all may tap into adults' sense of maintaining community and societal values, perhaps more so than providing young people opportunities to help make things "better" in the community. Making things "better" implies that things are perhaps not so good right now. It also suggests directiveness, assertiveness, and forcefulness in working for community change. Many adults may be unconvinced that such activism for social change is desirable.

If this reasoning has some foundation, it may partly explain why adults thought it more important for younger children to have service opportunities, even though older youth are cognitively and socially more able and ready to make such contributions. For younger children, we asked whether it was important for them to be able to do things such as feed the homeless or clean up a park, activities developmentally appropriate to their ages. In contrast, in the questions referring to adolescents, we asked about the importance of young people working on political or civic campaigns to change laws or policies, activities that would not be unusual for adolescents but generally would be for younger children. In each case, the examples were preceded by the phrase "to make their communities better places."

It could be, however, that adults responding to the question on youth rated working on campaigns to change laws less important than they would have rated the question about younger children (feeding the homeless or cleaning up a park). So, in some respects, the overall rating would perhaps have been higher if our wording had been identical for youth and for younger children. Nevertheless, even if adults had rated the adolescent item equally as important as the child item, only slightly more than half would have rated it highly important. We still must conclude that, in general, adults are split on the question of how important it is for children and adolescents to have explicit opportunities to intentionally try to make their communities better places. Yet the fact that about half of adults consider those service opportunities highly important, and the importance of such experiences to young people's development, suggests that there is a large foundation of public support and rationale that could be tapped to connect those favorable adults and young people. In so doing, as a Portland parent put it, "a whole generation might grow up seeing adults and youth working together in the community as 'just what normal people do' " (Sullivan, 2001).

Situational Elements Affecting Adult Beliefs and Actions

There also are clear differences in how adults relate to young people depending on the situation they are in together. Recall that we inquired about four hypothetical situations (being asked by youth to volunteer for a flood cleanup, doing something about boys skipping school, advising a young person about spending earned money, and dealing with skateboarders outside a local business). In all but the situation about a youth's spending money, the great majority of the 100 interviewees said most adults would feel a responsibility to do something. However, the great majority (86%) also said it was okay to not get involved at all in the flood relief scenario. Of course, these data were collected in spring 2000. One wonders whether most adults would respond the same way in the wake of the September 11, 2001 terrorist attacks on the United States. It is possible that, at least for a time, appeals for all sorts of relief situations may be met with more generous response than before the national tragedy.

An additional contextual variation was revealed in asking about the flood situation: Although most said it was acceptable to say no to volunteering or donating money, 29% said adults would indeed be more likely to volunteer or donate *if someone else were watching* when the girls approached the adult with the request to help. Another adult's presence might apply implicit social pressure to help out, especially since 25% of the respondents said adults would feel guilty about not helping or that others would criticize them for their lack of involvement.

Another source of variation in rated importance seems to stem from perceptions or assumptions about how directive the adult behavior might be. Actions about "encouraging" or about "sharing values" got more support than those mentioning "guiding," and the least support was for adults explicitly "giving advice." For example, about 75% or more of adults thought it was highly important for adults to discuss values in general with children and youth, especially equality, honesty, and responsibility. The same proportion thought it highly important to give kids guidance on how to share, save, and spend money, and to help them think through the consequences of decisions. Nevertheless, only 13% thought it very important for neighbors to give advice to children and youth. To the extent adults can share, encourage, model, and guide, there is widespread support for their positive engagement with young people. But "giving advice" appeared to be considered too directive an action for most adults to take.

Despite the overwhelming support for the theoretical importance of getting involved with young people in these ways, it seems apparent that, for most of the actions, that support is a mile wide and an inch deep. The imaginary line separating "sharing, encouraging, modeling, and guiding" from "giving advice" would seem, in many instances, to be quite subtle. It might be difficult for most adults to feel confident knowing where to draw that line. Rather than risk crossing it, they stay far away from it.

Much of the difference between guiding and advising is also a matter of perception and definition: What one adult might consider guiding, another might call advice giving. Perhaps given that most Americans don't think giving advice to other people's children and youth is very important, they also imagine that, if they do give advice, this would be disapproved and negative consequences would follow. Following that sequence of cause and effect, it is then hardly surprising that, despite the overwhelming importance given at least nine of these actions, the majority of Americans still don't act to engage with kids even in those most supported ways.

In the next chapter, we expand on the discussion of how Americans' beliefs and actions may vary, not so much by situation as across differing groups in society. Together, Chapters 7 and 8 set the stage for our discussion in the final chapter of how the results of this study can be used to build on areas of consensus, create bridges across differences, and more sharply define the territory of reasonable responsibility that most adults could share for the well-being of all kids.

8 Multiple Normative Americas: The Differences among Us

The most important message of this study is that across the great diversity of American society there is a broad consensus on a number of specific ways in which adults should be engaged with other people's children to raise a next generation that is healthy, responsible, involved, and productive. The results of our study confirm that these expectations are not the province of any one group or type of community in America, but are widely supported by a diverse spectrum of Americans.

This finding reflects the stereotypical "melting pot" image of America—that despite our differences, there are some values about nurturing children and youth around which we congregate as one people. That message should not be lost in this chapter as we examine some of the different threads that make up the fabric of American culture.

But our results also reflect divisions, which sometimes are deep, in how American adults think they ought to know and help nurture the children and adolescents of their neighborhoods and communities. There are significant differences among groups of Americans in the extent of support even for the core social norms and social values. Thus, while support for the nine core actions is high across all subgroups, some groups of Americans accord them significantly greater importance than do others. These differences suggest that the consensus should not be taken for granted (i.e., we found significant differences even regarding "consensus" actions among different groups of Americans, all of whom agree that those actions are "highly important"). Consensus should not be mistaken for unanimity.

Some groups of American adults are more likely to consider most of these actions important, and to report being surrounded by other adults who actually relate to kids in these ways. The shorthand we use to describe these adults is that they are personally and socially "motivated" to engage with young people. In a sense, they are "kid-oriented," prompted by personal attitudes and social reinforcement (perhaps even pressure) toward engagement with young people. We recognize that calling these adults "motivated" may be too extreme and may disregard too much the degree of care and involvement that other adults have for and with kids. Calling "less motivated" or even "uninvolved" those who express limited support for these actions, or who are not surrounded by adults who are involved with young people, or both, may be an inelegant oversimplification.

But, in a gross sense, such interpretive distinctions may accurately capture an orientation, a weltanshauung or worldview, if not necessarily a lifestyle. For some identifiable groups of Americans, it seems it is just more normal to place a higher priority on positively relating to other people's children and to perceive that other adults also do so. It might not be fair to make these judgments, but it is clear from our results that meaningful differences do exist in how important various groups of Americans think it is for all adults to be engaged with young people. And although they are fewer, there also are some clear differences in the extent to which different groups of adults report that the adults around them actually are engaged with kids.

Psychological and sociological research over the past 150 years has repeated countless variations on a single theme: For optimal development, human beings need both comfort and challenge, security and growth, connection and autonomy (National Research Council and Institute of Medicine, 2000). As much as the consensus among Americans is comforting, the differences among us also are challenging.

In the following pages, we discuss some of those differences. These differences do not suggest divisiveness, but they do suggest that we as a people clearly are not of one mind when it comes to how we ought to each share in the collective nurturing of young people. Our data and other studies cited in this book show that Americans clearly believe parents are primarily responsible for their own children, but also that parents are not solely responsible.

Yet we seem unsure how to clearly define even a parent's role in terms of daily social activities, much less the responsibilities the rest of us have and under what circumstances we have them. Whether we are parents ourselves or not, there is precious little guidance about what we are supposed to do to help guide and nurture *other people's children*.

Adults agree on the importance of the core nine actions we've discussed, but even among those actions, some groups of Americans, as we discuss in this chapter, think they're even more important than do others. On the rest of the actions, even where the majority rate the action highly important, there are sometimes great disparities in how differing groups of American adults think and report the adults around them act.

What Proportion of Adults Are Motivated to Be Engaged with Young People?

Within every community are people of all ages and from all walks of life who are actively involved in the lives of children and youth both in and outside their own families. While some adults from all demographic categories are engaged with other people's kids, doubtless some are more deeply engaged. We wondered who those more engaged adults are, and how many of them there are. Most of this chapter is spent answering the former question. To answer the latter, we created a "consistency of motivation" score for each survey participant.

Based on the theory of planned behavior (Azjen, 1988), discussed in Chapter 3, we would predict people to be more likely to do a certain behavior if they have favorable attitudes toward it, and if they feel they people around them support their doing that behavior, that is, that the behavior is the norm. Thus, adults would be more motivated to actually engage with young people if they thought doing so was important, and if their social networks supported that engagement. We considered adults' ratings of importance for the actions to reflect favorable or unfavorable attitudes that could serve as a measure of "personal motivation" to be engaged with kids. Similarly, we considered their reports of the engagement of the adults they knew with young people to reflect normative support for their own engagement that could serve as a measure of "social motivation" to be engaged with young people. Together, the personal and social motivation measures could be said to reflect relative consistency (personal and social motivation to engage both high or both low) or inconsistency (one higher and one lower). In this sense, adults with high levels of personal and social motivation for engagement would be the most likely actually to be engaged with young people.

To derive the consistency of motivation score, adults received two points if they said an action was both "most" important and that almost all or a great majority of the adults in their lives lived this action. On the question of parents as sole providers of discipline, the scoring was reversed. Those who said it was "least" important and that most of the adults around them did *not* believe in parents having the sole right to discipline their children were the ones who received two points. Study participants received one point if they said either that an action was highly important or that most of the adults in their lives did the action. If they neither said an action was highly important, nor said most of the adults in their lives did the action, they received a zero for that action (see Table 17).

Thus, across 20 asset-building actions, scores could range from zero to 40. A score of 20, for example, might suggest that the adult considered *all* the actions highly important, but the adults around them did not live *any* of the norms. More likely, that score also could signify that they considered some of the actions highly important and that some, but not many, of the actions were actually lived by most of the adults around them. Based on this reasoning, as Table 17 indicates, we call people with scores of 0–10 "uninvolved," as their scores were evidence of consistently low personal and social motivation to be involved with young people. Adults with scores of 11–20 are called "receptive," because their scores suggested mild and inconsistent motivation. We use the label "inclined" to describe adults with scores of 21–30. Those scores suggested moderate but still somewhat inconsistent motivation. Scores of 31–40 reflected high and consistent personal and social motivation; we call adults with those scores "engaged."

Table 17. Identifying Levels of Adult Engagement

To identify the people in our survey who have the greatest motivation to be involved with children and teenagers, each adult's responses were analyzed to determine her or his beliefs about the various ways of engaging with young people, and how much they said the adults they knew were engaged in those ways. For each of 20 statements,* survey respondents were scored as follows:

- If they said the action was most important *and* that most adults around them were involved in that action: 2 points
- If they said the action was most important *or* that most adults around them were involved in that action: 1 point
- If they said *neither* that the action was important *nor* that most adults around them were involved in that action: 0 points

Thus, an individual's score could range from zero to 40 points. Then we divided the sample into four categories (quartiles) as follows:

Label	Score (out of 40)	Description
Engaged adults	31–40 points	Adults who consistently see most of the asset-building actions as important *and* say most adults around them are actively involved with young people, suggesting a high level of engagement with young people in the community.
Inclined adults	21–30 points	Adults who are inconsistent in their commitment to or sense of involvement with young people by adults they know, suggesting a moderate level of connections to young people, but not a deep consciousness and engagement.
Receptive adults	11–20 points	Adults who are mildly committed to or surrounded by adults involved with young people, suggesting a basic level of awareness, but not a strong commitment.
Uninvolved adults	0–10 points	Adults who do not see most of the actions as important and are not involved in asset-building actions.

*This scale included the 19 asset-building actions plus a question on parents as sole discipliners. On this additional question, the scoring was reversed, so that those who said it was "least" important *and* that most of the adults around them did *not* believe in parents having the sole right to discipline their children received two points.

Based on these categories, the results suggested that very few American adults can be called *engaged*—those who experience strong and consistent personal and social motivation for getting involved with young people. Figure 5 shows that only 5% of American adults both considered these actions, overall, to be highly important and reported that, overall, the great majority or almost all of the adults around them actually did these actions. Thirty-four percent of our national sample were *inclined* adults who experienced moderate but still inconsistent personal or environmental motivation for these intergenerational relationships. Half of American adults (51%) were just *receptive*: They experience mild but inconsistent motivation for being engaged with young people. The

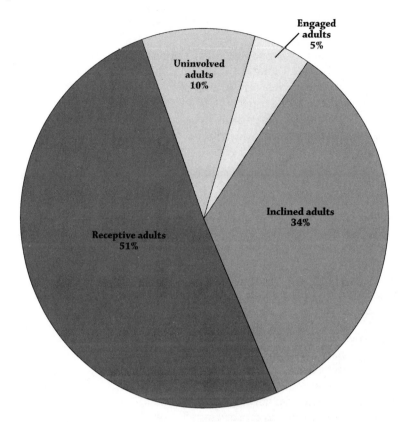

Figure 5. Levels of Engagement with Children and Teenagers

remaining 10% of adults were *uninvolved*, experiencing consistently low motivation to be engaged with kids.

These results are both heartening and distressing. On the one hand, nearly 4 in 10 American adults (39%) show at least moderate or even high levels of personal and environmental motivation for getting engaged with kids. They already consider it highly important to relate to young people in these specific ways, and carry on their lives in social networks of adults who, more often than other adults report, seem to live up to many of these expectations. Such a combination of favorable personal attitudes and strong social models and support for acting in these ways should together provide a considerable proportion of American adults the motivation to engage positively with young people in ways that will promote young people's healthy development. Even though only a small percentage of Americans already can be called engaged, a sizable minority seems potentially movable from an inclination to be engaged to actual engagement.

Of course, the flip side of this hopeful result is that 61% of American adults experience, at best, inconsistent and, at worst, quite limited personal and social motivation for engaging positively with young people. Some adults among the "receptive" group, the largest group of Americans, likely find strong motivation in their lives for doing some of the actions that can promote healthy development in young people, but do not experience strong motivation for doing many other actions.

But, overall, we must conclude that for most Americans, relating to young people is probably best thought of as not routinized and generalized across young people and situations, but instead highly dependent on specific circumstances and situations being especially favorable to getting involved. The result, as our data illustrate, is the pervasive inconsistency between beliefs and reported adult actions that best describes how most American adults relate to kids.

In a sense, through either their highly favorable attitudes or highly supportive social networks, or both, engaged people may be able to give themselves permission to be more deeply involved with young people. Perhaps engaging with young people is either so important in their own minds, or they already see so many adults they know engaging in these ways, that they feel relatively safer and more risk-free with the possibility of connecting more deeply with young people than do those who are only receptive or inclined. These engaged adults may perceive both fewer risks and greater rewards for their engagement. By engaging with young people, which they consider highly important, they achieve a more integrated self-image in which their beliefs and actions are in harmony. In addition, by engaging with young people in the same ways as the adults they know do, they are doing something valued by the groups they belong to. Thus, they are able to strengthen their identification and relationships with those adults, and affirm their connectedness and identity within important reference groups.

Overview of Differences among Groups: Statistical and Substantive Significance

A gap between beliefs and actions may be the most usual state of affairs for adult relationships with young people, but some adults, of course, do think that engagement is more important than other adults do, and some adults live those beliefs to a greater degree. We used a variety of analysis strategies (see Appendix A) to identify demographic groups that were more likely to be engaged or concerned than merely aware or even uninvolved with young people, and we discuss these results in the remainder of this chapter.

In general, the results of these analyses are consistent with Search Institute's previous research with a statewide sample of adults in Colorado (Scales et al., 1998). For example, in that study we found that women, parents, people of color, the less educated and affluent, and longer-time community residents all reported more engagement with young people. We found all those statistically significant results in the current study, and more. In a comprehensive analysis of the social currents transforming American communities, Putnam (2000) offered support for some but not all of these same trends. He reported that informal social connections were much more common among women than men, and among older adults more than middle-aged Americans. He did not report on racial/ethnic differences in informal social connections, but he did note that the findings were mixed regarding education and income differences and length of residency.

To better understand which demographic groups of adults might be more likely to experience consistent personal and environmental motivation to engage with young people outside their families, we conducted canonical discriminant analysis of the consistency of motivation scores described above across the various demographic variables. Based on these discriminant analysis results, as well as the other data analyses, the following groups are the most likely to be both personally favorable to engagement with young people and report living in a social network where engagement with kids is more the norm:

- Women;
- Those who interact with children ages 5–10 more so than with adolescents ages 11–18;
- Those with a high school education or less;
- Those who attend religious services weekly;
- Adults over age 35;
- Those who have lived in their community for at least 10 years;
- Those who have regular contact with at least one to two children or youth;
- Married adults;
- Those who volunteer at least monthly;
- Those who attend community or neighborhood meetings often;
- African Americans and Hispanics;
- Those who make less than $60,000 per year; and
- Parents.

It should be noted that some of these variables had a relatively greater or lesser contribution to the discrimination among groups than would have been suggested when looking at the influence of that demographic category alone, as we do in the following pages. For example, income, examined by itself, appeared to have a greater impact on engagement with young people than did marital status. However, the discriminant analysis is a multivariate procedure that takes into account all the variables and their interactions *simultaneously*. Therefore, marital status (which is associated with several key variables, including income, education, parental status, attendance at religious services, and contact with kids among them), yielded a larger standardized canonical coefficient than did income (see the following section and Table 18).

Discriminant Analysis Details

Discriminant analysis defines the linear combination of variables that best explains differences among groups (i.e., the combination that has the highest possible multiple correlation with the groups). The procedure then defines a second linear combination that provides the next best explanation for differences and is uncorrelated with the first set of variables, and so on. Although not fully comparable, the various canonical functions may be viewed as analogous to

Table 18. Canonical Discriminant Analysis: Groups Most Consistently Motivated to Be Involved with Young People

Variable	Canonical function 1	Canonical function 2
Gender	.56	−.16
Children vs. adolescents	−.40	−.33
Education	−.27	.05
Frequency attend religious services	−.26	−.68
Age	.39	.08
Length of neighborhood residency	.25	.18
Number of kids interact with	.20	.17
Marital status	−.18	.16
Frequency volunteer	.18	−.15
Frequency attend neighborhood meetings	.17	.52
Race/ethnicity	−.12	−.32
Annual household income	−.12	.16
Parental status	−.002	−.18
Canonical correlation	.33	.17
Approx. standard error	.03	.03
Likelihood ratio	.87	.97
Approx. F	6.74	2.83
DF	26	12
p	.0001	.0008

factors extracted in a principal components analysis (*SAS/STAT User's Guide,* 1990; *SPSS Base 8.0 Applications Guide,* 1998).

Dividing the consistency of motivation scores into four groups as we had done to separate adults into engaged, inclined, receptive, and uninvolved groups produced relatively small subsamples (about 100 each) in either the high- or low-motivation group. Because using extreme scores could make it relatively easier for the analysis to produce discrimination results, and we wanted to avoid falsely characterizing some adults as more motivated toward engagement with young people than others, we instead adopted a more conservative approach by dividing the sample arbitrarily into thirds. Because not all possible scores were actually received, the cutoff scores used meant that the "thirds" varied somewhat from 33% each. The top third (actually 38% of the scores) were considered to have relatively more consistent personal and environmental motivation for doing these actions; the middle third (actually 30%) were considered to have mild and inconsistent motivation; and the bottom third (actually 32%) were considered to have low and inconsistent motivation.

Table 18 shows the standardized canonical coefficients for the entire sample on the two canonical functions. The standardized coefficients (with means standardized to zero and variance to 1) reflect the relative importance of each demographic variable in discriminating among those Americans who said (1) that they experienced consistent personal and environmental motivation for relating to children and youth, (2) that they experienced some personal or environmental motivation, but inconsistently, or (3) that they experienced little personal or environmental motivation for relating to young people in these ways.

Table 19. Class Means on Canonical Variables: Consistency of Personal and Environmental Motivation for Engagement with Young People

Group	Canonical function 1	Canonical function 2
High, consistent motivation	.27	.05
Mild, inconsistent motivation	−.06	−.12
Low, inconsistent motivation	−.23	.10

Table 18 shows that the first canonical function had a moderate and significant (at $p < .0001$) canonical correlation of .33 with the consistency of motivation scores, and the second function had a weaker but still significant (at $p < .0008$) correlation of .17. This suggests that, as required by discriminant analysis, the first canonical function and the arithmetic combination of the variables in it had a stronger linear relationship with consistency of motivation for engagement than did the second function, using the same variables but with different arithmetic weights attributed to each. The table also presents the standardized canonical coefficients. The standardized coefficients (ignoring the signs) represent the relative importance of each variable in distinguishing among those with higher and lower levels of motivation for normative involvement with young people.

Finally, Table 19 displays the class means on canonical variables, showing that the first function clearly discriminated in a linear fashion the different levels of motivation for involvement that adults reported experiencing, whereas the second function offered a smaller and less easily interpreted discrimination. The mean on the first canonical function for the consistent motivation group was far higher than the mean for the inconsistent motivation group (.27 versus −.06), whose mean was far higher still than the mean for the low motivation group (−.06 versus −.23). The second canonical function did not distinguish groups well on the basis of how it combined the variables, with the low motivation group having a higher class mean than either the inconsistent or consistent motivation groups (.10 versus −.12 and .05, respectively).

Thus, if we wanted to predict how much an adult might be motivated to engage with young people, applying the first canonical function would provide a more accurate prediction than would the second function alone. The second function, however, which places more emphasis on variables such as parental status, frequency of volunteering, and frequency of participation in neighborhood meetings than did the first, would improve the initial prediction by a small but significant amount. Obviously, some of these variables cannot be changed, or at least not changed easily (gender, race/ethnicity). But people can choose to readily change some of the variables that predict motivation to engage. Religious involvement, volunteering, and participating in community meetings, for example, all are activities that add to the likelihood of adults being motivated to engage with young people (see also Scales, Benson, Roehlkepartain, Hintz, Sullivan, & Mannes, 2001). Efforts to increase adults' levels of involvement in those activities could contribute to higher levels of adult engagement with kids, through two paths. They could heighten the importance those adults give to engaging with young people (positively affecting their attitudes or personal

motivation). Perhaps even more powerfully, increased participation in those activities could strengthen the normative support adults feel for engagement by
deepening their involvement in reference groups of adults for whom connection with kids is more the norm (positively affecting their social motivation for
engagement).

In addition, some differences among groups were more substantively meaningful than were other differences. We present a considerable amount of detail
in the following pages in order to paint the fullest picture possible of these variations in engagement, but the broader outlines should not be lost. There were
three broad classes of statistically significant differences:

1. Those that were quite substantively strong and consistent across large
   numbers of the 20 engagement actions, and therefore meaningful;
2. Those that were moderately strong but less consistent, and so less meaningful, although still notable; and
3. Those that were statistically but weakly significant, or difficult to interpret because of their inconsistency across the actions, and therefore of
   marginal or unclear meaningfulness.

One additional summary note is in order as an introduction to this detailed
discussion. As we reported in Chapter 6, the connection between adults' beliefs
and the reported actions of the adults around them, is not always strong or
predictable.

For example, women, African Americans and Hispanics, and parents were
among the four groups (the other being frequent attendees of religious services)
who were most substantively differentiated from their counterparts (i.e., men,
non-Hispanic whites, and nonparents) on the importance they assigned these actions. But in only limited circumstances did those differences in beliefs translate
into differences in how the adults around them were reported to act.

On the other hand, frequent volunteers, those who participate often in
community or neighborhood meetings, longtime neighborhood residents, and
Americans over age 55 showed less pervasive belief differences with their counterparts than women, African Americans and Hispanics, and parents did with
their counterparts. But those frequent volunteers, meeting participants, longtime
residents, and older adults (along with frequent attendees at religious services)
did say they were surrounded more by adults who actually did these actions.
Those people may not have been more likely to believe these actions are important, but they were more likely to be in social networks where engaging with
kids in these ways was the norm.

How Meaningful Are the Differences across Groups?

Most Substantively Meaningful Differences on Beliefs and Actions

The strongest and most consistent differences in how important groups considered the various actions to be occurred on the basis of gender, race/ethnicity,
parental status, and frequency of attendance at religious services. Women were

much more likely than men, both African Americans and Hispanics were more likely than non-Hispanic white Americans, parents were more likely than non-parents, and those attending religious services weekly were more likely than those who sometimes or rarely/never attended to consider it important for all adults to engage with young people. There were, however, minimal differences in how much women and men, whites, African Americans and Hispanics, and parents and nonparents reported being surrounded by people who actually engaged with kids. Religious involvement was the only one of these four variables that made a substantive difference on both the rated importance of the actions and the degree to which people reported that the adults around them actually lived these actions.

Notable but Less Meaningful Differences on Beliefs and Actions

We also found statistically significant, but somewhat less consistent and meaningful, differences in beliefs about the importance of the actions based on involvement in volunteering and participation in neighborhood or community meetings, as well as on age of adult and how long adults had lived in their current neighborhood. Monthly volunteers, frequent participants in neighborhood meetings, adults over age 35, and neighborhood residents of 10 or more years tended to rate it more important for all adults to engage with young people.

Most of the groups that showed the most pervasive differences (the "most substantively meaningful" group described above) on the importance of the actions, did not show comparable differences in how much they said the adults around them did the actions. However, several groups in the category of notable but less meaningful differences in importance beliefs showed meaningful differences in adults saying they were surrounded by others who lived the actions.

For example, like weekly religious service attendees, those who participated often in community or neighborhood meetings were especially likely to report being surrounded by adults who actually were engaged with young people. Adults who had resided in their neighborhood for 10 or more years, and those age 55 or over also were substantively more likely to report the adults around them were engaged with kids.

Least Meaningful Differences

Finally, we also found statistically significant, but not nearly as clearly consistent and meaningful differences across the various actions on the basis of education and income, marital status, and level of contact with young people. Adults with less than a college education, those making less than $60,000 per year, married and widowed adults, and those who had regular contact with at least one to two young people all rated it somewhat more important than other adults to engage with kids in the ways we studied. As we have seen, however, beliefs and actions were even less in sync across these groups than in the groups in the notable and meaningful difference categories described above. Married and widowed Americans were somewhat more likely to report that the adults around them were engaged with young people, but none of the other variables in this category was associated clearly with differences in how much the adults around respondents were reported to be engaged with young people.

Detailed Results on Differences: Most Substantively Meaningful

Gender

Given traditional gender-linked roles regarding nurturing children, we expected that women would both rate these actions more important than men would and report that the adults around them were more likely to live the actions than men would report that to be the case. Women did score higher than men on the Importance scale ($F(1, 1356) = 74.23$, $p < .0001$) and rated 15 of the 20 asset-building actions more highly important than did men, though not always by large proportions. The only actions women did not consider more important than men were encouraging success in school, discussing personal values, feeling responsible to help ensure the well-being of neighborhood kids, parents being the sole discipliners of their children, and giving advice.

Table 20 shows that of the 15 actions women rated more important than men did, they rated 10 of them more highly important by 10 or more percentage

Table 20. Proportion of Men and Women Designating Action as "Most Important" (N = 1,424)

	Men	Women	F
Top-Rated Actions			
Expect respect for adults	60%[b]	74%[a]	34.59***
Expect parents to set boundaries	81%[b]	87%[a]	12.21**
Teach shared values	77%[b]	83%[a]	9.14***
Teach respect for cultural difference	72%[b]	81%[a]	17.47***
Guide decision making	70%[b]	82%[a]	29.21***
Have meaningful conversations	69%[b]	79%[a]	18.02***
Give financial guidance	67%[b]	81%[a]	38.73***
Actions with Majority Support			
Report positive behavior	54%[b]	74%[a]	67.68***
Report misbehavior	54%[b]	68%[a]	30.23***
Discuss religious beliefs	53%[b]	65%[a]	22.63***
Pass down traditions	47%[b]	64%[a]	46.37***
Know names	45%[b]	55%[a]	13.35***
Actions with Less than Majority Support			
Provide service opportunities	40%[b]	55%[a]	35.01***
Seek opinions	43%[b]	52%[a]	9.46*
Model giving and serving	39%[b]	54%[a]	36.40***

a, b = Percentages with different letters are significantly different from each other.
   * = Significant at $p \leq .05$.
  ** = Significant at $p \leq .01$.
 *** = Significant at $p \leq .006$.

points, including four of the top-rated nine actions. Women also rated several other actions significantly more important than did men, but with less than a 10 percentage point difference between them, including three of the top-rated nine actions.

Women scored slightly higher as well on the general Conformity scale measuring how much the adults around them were reported to do these actions $(F(1, 1330) = 8.44, p < .003)$. But, in looking at the individual actions, on only one of those actions were women more likely than men to be surrounded by adults who actually lived the action. Women were somewhat more likely than men (38% to 31%) to report being surrounded by adults who discussed their religious or spiritual beliefs with children $(F(1, 1330) = 9.13$, Bonferroni corrected $p < .04)$.

Men are not missing in these results: The majority of men, like women, also considered most of the asset-building behaviors to be highly important. But consistently, regardless of the content of the action, they expressed that sense of importance in significantly lower proportions; on none of the 20 actions did more men than women say they were highly important. For example, 68% of men thought it highly important for adults to give children and adolescents guidance on sharing, spending, and saving money, but 79% of women accorded financial guidance that much importance. On the average, American men seem to regard these expectations about relationships with young people as reasonably important, but not as vitally important as do women. Not surprisingly then, although the differences are smaller than on ratings of importance, men were also less likely than women to report on the overall Conformity scale that they were surrounded by adults who actually lived these actions with young people.

Similar gender differences show up in young children and persist into middle school and high school (reviewed in Scales & Leffert, 1999). For example, a study of more than 1,000 6th–8th graders found that girls more significantly than boys felt it was their duty to help others, and were also more concerned with others' social welfare (Scales, Blyth, et al., 2000). Data from a statewide survey of Colorado adults (Scales et al., 1998) found that women were significantly more likely than men to say that they knew the names of many youth, that the media depicted youth in an overly negative way, and that they would likely do something if they saw youth hanging out and skipping school.

A review of animal and human research studies also concluded that females across species may even react to stress, not only by fleeing or fighting, as the traditional paradigm has described the options, but also by seeking personal support from and giving support to others. The behaviors of seeking and offering support obviously are more consistent with building children's healthy development than either aggression or withdrawal (Taylor et al., 2000).

Then too, there are similar well-documented differences between men and women on various values and on the importance of domestic policy issues relating to caring for others. For example, the *New York Times* 2000 poll of adults found that women were more likely than men to think that it was a moral problem for there to be income inequality and to say that people should take care of their aging parents (Wolfe, 2000). A survey of U.S. women found that these personal concerns and tendencies extend even to American women's views on global policy issues: More significantly than men, women think it is an extreme or high priority to give girls an education equal to that boys receive, to promote fair labor practices, to make birth control available, and to work to prevent childhood diseases (Crossette, 2000).

Are these traditional attitudinal differences by gender likely to continue? Although it is speculation, we suspect there may be some changes in the disparity of female-male views among young adults. A recent national survey of 1,000 21- to 65-year-old adults by the Radcliffe Public Policy Center reported that nearly equal proportions of men (82%) and women (85%) 21 to 39 years old put family ahead of power, money, or prestige in importance. Given that the sample included both parents (who presumably would be more likely to agree) and nonparents, those figures are quite high, suggesting that these sentiments cut across differences in parental status. A similarly surprising 71% of men in that 21- to 39-year-old age group said they would give up some pay in order to spend more time with their families. In fact, men in their 20s were even more likely than women to say they would forgo pay in order to get more family time (Radcliffe Public Policy Center study . . . , 2000). It remains to be seen, of course, whether such views will be acted upon by these younger adults, and whether the cultivation of such family-first attitudes might increase the level of men's attentiveness to their own children, and, ultimately, to the children of others. Since these attitudes seem to be in flux among today's young men, one might expect eventually to find greater numbers of men becoming more actively engaged in th1e lives of children and youth.

Race/Ethnicity

Based on our earlier study of Colorado adults, we did expect that non-Hispanic white adults would rate the actions less highly important, and would be less likely to say the adults around them lived the actions, than would African American or Hispanic respondents. We found that African American adults, more than both Hispanic or non-Hispanic white adults, rated the actions more highly important on the Importance scale ($F(2, 1356) = 9.72$, $p < .0001$). African Americans and, to a lesser extent, Hispanic adults seemed to place a greater value on everyone having a role in contributing to child development. For example, both African Americans and Hispanics rated the following actions as being more highly important than did non-Hispanic white adults: discussing religious beliefs, teaching kids to preserve and pass down their ethnic and religious culture, giving children and adolescents opportunities to improve their communities, and neighbors giving advice to young people (see Table 21).

Blacks also were more likely than both Hispanic adults and non-Hispanic whites to consider the following actions highly important: encouraging young people to take school seriously and do well, expecting young people to respect adults as authority figures, telling parents if children or adolescents do something right, feeling responsible for the well-being of all the neighborhood's kids, telling parents if children or adolescents do something wrong, knowing the

Table 21. Proportion of Adults Designating Action as "Most Important," by Race/Ethnicity
(N = 1,424)

	Black	Hispanic	White	F
Top-Rated Actions				
Encourage school success	98%[a]	82%[b]	90%[b]	10.59**
Expect respect for adults	80%[a]	71%[b]	66%[b]	6.72*
Actions with Majority Support				
Report positive behavior	76%[a]	68%[b]	63%[b]	4.91*
Ensure well-being of neighborhood kids	80%[a]	70%[b]	60%c	14.05**
Report misbehavior	74%	60%	60%	5.45*
Discuss religious beliefs	69%[a]	69%[a]	57%[b]	6.35*
Pass down traditions	71%[a]	65%[a]	53%[b]	11.81**
Know names	72%[a]	50%[b]	47%[b]	16.87**
Actions with Less than Majority Support				
Provide service opportunities	57%[a]	58%[a]	46%[b]	6.81**
Model giving and serving	62%[a]	44%[b]	45%[b]	7.66*
Give advice	35%[a]	18%[b]	10%c	39.45**

a, b = Percentages with different letters are significantly different from each other.
* = Significant at $p \leq .007$.
** = Significant at $p \leq .0001$.

names of many kids in their neighborhoods, and volunteering and donating money monthly.

These findings from our nationally representative sample generally echo those from our earlier survey of Colorado adults. In that survey, people of color were more likely than non-Hispanic white respondents to say they would intervene if they saw youth skipping school, and had a greater interest in receiving information about getting more involved with youth (Scales et al., 1998).

However, on the Conformity scale, despite a borderline significant F value, there were no significant differences overall across racial/ethnic groups in the degree to which adults said they were surrounded by adults who relate to kids in these ways ($F(2, 1330) = 2.91$, $p < .05$).

Only a few individual actions showed a racial/ethnic difference in whether the adults around respondents were reported to be actually engaged with young people. African Americans and non-Hispanic white adults were more likely than Hispanics to be surrounded by adults who expected young people to respect adults (70% Blacks, 68% Whites, 56% Hispanics, with $F(2, 1424) = 3.89$, $p < .02$). Blacks and non-Hispanic whites were more likely than Hispanic adults to report that adults around them knew the names of many neighborhood kids (36% Blacks, 34% whites, 23% Hispanics, with $F(2, 1424) = 4.02$, $p < .01$). Finally, both African American and Hispanic respondents were more likely to live in networks where adults felt parents should discipline their kids without interference from others (27% African Americans, 26% Hispanics, 14% whites, with $F(2, 1424) = 13.46$, $p < .0001$).

It may be that race/ethnicity interacts with religious involvement and gender (African Americans and Hispanics are more likely to be religiously active, and those who are religiously active, as well as women, also tend to give many of the same responses). Thus, we conducted multiple analyses of variance and concluded that these racial/ethnic differences were largely independent and not accounted for by interactions with those other variables (see sidebar titled Interactions among Race/Ethnicity, Gender, and Involvement in Religion).

Those differences between African Americans (especially) and Hispanics, as compared with non-Hispanic white adults, may reflect what anthropologists have described as a difference between the value of "collectivism" predominant in most nonindustrialized cultures (and culturally inherited by many African American and Hispanic peoples) and the value of "individualism" that is common in European American culture (culturally inherited by many non-Hispanic white peoples) (Phinney, Ong, & Madden, 2000). We hasten to add that the unfortunate term "collectivism," as anthropologists use it, does not imply and should not be confused with political socialism. Collectivism is defined in part by the importance of interdependent relationships among community members and by "conformity to group norms" (p. 529). It does not require the formal, state-sponsored suppression of individual initiative and achievement that characterizes socialist governments. Rather, the term describes an informal but powerful social balance between satisfying individual and group needs that tilts more to the group than to the individual. Behaviors such as "helping," for example, may be important within both value systems, but within an individualistic tradition helping others is a personal choice predicated on the assumption that members of a society are free to mutually negotiate best solutions to situations. In contrast, in a more collectivist or community-oriented tradition, expectations for behavior are "mutually understood" as a part of a primary goal of forming relationships with other group members. Within such a value system, helping others is considered to be not a choice but a reciprocal obligation (Raeff, Greenfield, & Quiroz, 1998).

Among Hispanic and especially African American adults, our results suggest that there are more clearly defined roles for everyone in the socialization of the next generation. Children are expected to respect all adults as authority figures. All adults are expected to teach the young to preserve, protect, and pass down their ethnic and religious traditions, feel a responsibility for ensuring the well-being of the kids in their neighborhood, and give advice to young people as needed. African American adults especially expect their neighbors to keep them informed about their children and adolescents, both when their children do something right as well as when they do something wrong.

These expectations among African Americans and Hispanics combine to define cultural (although not necessarily neighborhood) communities in which the mutual and interdependent reinforcement brought to bear by family, school, neighborhood, and community might give rise to a collective strength that is less common among non-Hispanic white Americans. Among the people of color we surveyed, the connection between community and child development seems a more important ideal or value than appears to be the case among white Americans.

The study by Raeff et al. (1998) suggests, however, that for immigrant Hispanics, there may be various dimensions of cultural conflict that both undermine the redundancy of these socialization efforts in Hispanic/Latino communities and make more difficult the passing down of such understandings to the next generation. For example, they studied Los Angeles elementary schoolchildren, half from a predominantly Anglo school, and half from a predominantly Latino school in which most of the students were from immigrant families (largely from Mexico). The researchers found different systemic dynamics reflected in how parents, children, and teachers described what the right thing to do would be in several hypothetical situations designed to tap either individualistic or collectivist values. In the mostly Anglo school, children, parents, and teachers all gave mostly individualistic responses, with no significant differences among them. In the Latino school, however, parents and children were more collectivist than teachers, and parents were more collectivist than their children were. The education system might be seen by these parents as undermining their goals for the social development of their children, and teachers, on the other hand, might see these parents as undermining their goals for their students' social development.

Certainly, the explanation we offer here of the influence of cultural heritage on such attitudes is only one possibility. Another factor could be that residents of communities that are in greater distress are more likely to band together and help each other out; African American and Hispanic adults have a higher probability of living in such poverty. For example, the white, non-Hispanic poverty rate in 1999 was 7.7%, versus 23.6% for African Americans and 22.8 % for Hispanics (Dalaker & Proctor, 2000). Perhaps communities whose residents are wealthier are less likely to experience crime and other social problems, have more access to resources, and are less driven to seek out and rely on each other. For example, wealthier residents may purchase the child care they need, whereas less-well-off residents rely on extended family and neighbors.

Again, however, African American and Hispanic respondents were no more likely than non-Hispanic white respondents to report being surrounded by people who actually engage with young people in most of these ways. Thus, although both the "distressed community" explanation and the inherited culture explanation may have some application in specific circumstances, it appears that race and ethnicity are related more to beliefs about engagement with young people than to actions. These results seem to support an explanation for these differences in beliefs that is rooted more in cultural norms transmitted across generations and geographies than in adaptive reactions to current economic circumstances.

In fact, when it comes to the disjunction between how favorably African Americans and Hispanics seem to be to all adults being engaged with kids, and how much they report that the adults they know do these actions, one might argue just the opposite. That is, instead of distressed circumstances making it more likely for people to help each other out, living in neighborhoods with high levels of poverty and/or crime may make parents *more reluctant* to allow children access to adults seen as dangerous influences, or at best, poor role models. Thus, the adults those respondents are reporting on, if in similar circumstances, may be acting to protect their children more than maximize children's relationship "opportunities" with other adults that they don't define as positive opportunities at all. This reasoning is consistent with previous studies on parents' adapting their child-rearing practices to such circumstances (e.g., Furstenberg, 1993; Cochran et al., 1990).

A final qualification also is necessary. Obviously, there is no "people of color" culture. Nor can various African American cultures be lumped together with the many Hispanic cultures we did not further identify among our study participants (e.g., Mexican American, Puerto Rican, Cuban, Central American, etc.), each of which has its own cultural values and norms regarding adults' relationships with young people. And since people of Hispanic origin can consider themselves to be either white or black, "Hispanics" as a group cannot accurately be included in a racial umbrella term such as "people of color" (Patterson, 2001). Yet we are led to posit that there are indeed some cross-cultural similarities among many African American and Hispanic adults that distinguish them on these child and youth engagement issues from their non-Hispanic white peers.

The differences on how important it is for adults to engage with young people strongly and consistently show that African American and Hispanic adults find them more important than do non-Hispanic whites. This is a pervasive pattern, not something observed on one, two, or three actions. Although we did not observe differences across racial/ethnic groups in actually relating to kids in these ways, that finding partly may also be an artifact of question wording.

In an earlier study of a statewide sample of Colorado adults (Scales et al., 1998), we found that Latino and African American adults were more likely than white adults to report being engaged with young people. But that study was limited to relationships with adolescents (not younger children), and the measure of involvement included volunteering in formal programs for youth, as well as somewhat different measures of informal relationship than the actions we studied in the current research. In the current study, we considered a broader age range of young people, and there may well be fewer differences in how adults relate to younger children, with whom adults seem to find it easier to relate. In this national study, we also did not include formal volunteering as part of our assessment of adult involvement with young people. Nevertheless, this national study's findings and those of the earlier Colorado study are consistent in suggesting that African American and Hispanic/Latino adults at the very least may hold it more important than do non-Hispanic whites for all adults to share in nurturing and guiding young people.

Parental Status

We would expect parents, more so than nonparents, to say they are surrounded by adults who engage with other people's kids, if only because, through their own children's activities, they likely encounter more young people outside their families than do most nonparents. It does not necessarily follow, however, that parents would be more likely to *believe* that all adults engaging with young people is highly important. Perhaps parents concur with what we have described as the overarching norm about adult-child relationships today, namely, that it is overwhelmingly their responsibility to nurture and guide young people, not the role of other adults, especially those outside the family.

Although these seem to be reasonable hypotheses, we were somewhat surprised to find the opposite results. In general, parents supported the involvement of all adults with kids more than nonparents did. Parents were more likely than non-parents on the Importance scale to rate the actions highly important overall ($F(1, 1354) = 18.13$, $p < .0001$), and to rate 11 of the individual actions more important, six of them by 10 or more percentage points (see Table 22). Perhaps parents particularly value this kind of engagement because they know it will be helpful to their children and to them, but don't see enough adults engaged positively in their children's lives.

Parents were *not* more likely, however, to report being surrounded by adults who lived the actions (Conformity scale: $F(1, 1329) = 0.83$, $p < .3610$). After applying Bonferroni corrections to the multiple F tests, on only two actions were parents more likely than nonparents to be surrounded by adults who did the action: (1) give advice to neighborhood kids (20% parents, 11% nonparents, with $F(1, 1413) = 14.85$, corrected $p < .002$), and (2) tell parents if their children do something right (24% parents, 13% nonparents, with $F(1, 1413) = 19.48$, corrected $p < .002$).

Interestingly, although parents rated it somewhat more important than nonparents for adults to expect parents to set and enforce clear boundaries for their children (by 86% to 79%), it was *nonparents* who reported somewhat more that they were surrounded by adults who believed parents should set clear boundaries (49% nonparents, 40% parents, with $F(1, 1413) = 8.97$, corrected $p < .04$).

Table 22. *Proportion of Parents versus Nonparents Designating Action as "Most Important"*
(N = 1,413)

	Nonparents	Parents	F
Top-Rated Actions			
Encourage school success	84%[b]	92%[a]	17.89**
Expect respect for adults	60%[b]	71%[a]	15.62**
Expect parents to set boundaries	79%[b]	86%[a]	10.01*
Teach shared values	71%[b]	83%[a]	26.70**
Guide decision making	70%[b]	79%[a]	11.26*
Have meaningful conversations	68%[b]	77%[a]	10.03*
Actions with Majority Support			
Report misbehavior	55%[b]	64%[a]	9.90*
Discuss religious beliefs	50%[b]	63%[a]	18.99**
Pass down traditions	46%[b]	60%[a]	20.27**
Parents be sole discipliners	44%[b]	58%[a]	19.11**
Actions with Less than Majority Support			
Model giving and serving	38%[b]	51%[a]	16.88**

a, b = Percentages with different letters are significantly different from each other.
  * = Significant at $p \leq .02$.
 ** = Significant at $p \leq .002$.

Perhaps parents, being faced daily with bargaining, negotiating, and the recon-
sideration of their rules, define the setting of clear boundaries somewhat more
flexibly than do nonparents, whose ideas about setting and especially enforcing
clear boundaries are not tested every day through interactions with children.

Differences by Age of Parents' Children

Do parents respond differently depending on whether they have older
or younger children? The brief answer is some, but not much. Parents whose
youngest child was 19 or older were more likely than nonparents, but not more
than parents of children 18 or younger, to rate the actions highly important overall (Importance scale: $F(2, 1354) = 3.56$, $p < .02$). However, as was the case for
the parent versus nonparent comparison, there were no significant differences
among adults by parental status on whether they reported being surrounded by
adults who actually lived the actions (see Table 23).

Beliefs

Results Favoring Parents in General. When comparing those three groups of
adults on the individual actions, all parents were more likely than nonparents
to rate it highly important for adults to expect young people to respect them as

Table 23. *Proportion of Adults Designating Action "Most Important," by Parental Status and Age of Youngest Child (N = 1,413)*

	Nonparents	Parents youngest child 18 or under	Parents youngest child 19 or over	F
Top-Rated Actions				
Encourage school success	85%[b]	91%	94%[a]	4.64**
Expect respect for adults	60%[b]	70%[a]	72%[a]	7.80***
Teach shared values	71%[b]	80%[a]	87%[a]	8.44***
Discuss personal values	67%[b]	74%	75%[a]	3.04*
Actions with Majority Support				
Report positive behavior	59%[b]	62%	73%[a]	4.88**
Ensure well-being of neighborhood kids	57%[b]	67%[a]	64%	3.42*
Report misbehavior	55%[b]	62%[a]	67%[a]	6.55**
Discuss religious beliefs	50%[b]	55%[b]	72%[a]	13.13***
Pass down traditions	46%[b]	58%[a]	61%[a]	8.37***
Know names	46%[b]	52%[a]	52%[a]	4.74**
Actions with Less than Majority Support				
Model giving and serving	38%[b]	51%[a]	51%[a]	5.33**

a, b = Percentages with different letters are significantly different from each other
 * = Significant at $p \le .05$.
 ** = Significant at $p \le .008$.
 *** = Significant at $p \le .0004$.

authority figures; teach young people the same shared values, such as equality, honesty, and responsibility; tell them if their children do something wrong; teach young people to preserve their cultural traditions; know the names of many neighborhood kids; and volunteer or donate money monthly.

Results Favoring Parents of Grown Children. Parents whose youngest child was 19 or older were also more likely than nonparents, but not parents whose youngest child was 18 or younger, to say it was highly important for adults to encourage young people to do well in school, (marginally) discuss their own values with young people, and tell parents if their children do something right. Those parents of grown children also were more likely than all adults to say adults should discuss their religious or spiritual values with young people.

Results Favoring Parents of Children 18 or Younger. Parents whose youngest child was 18 or younger were more likely than nonparents, but not parents of older children, to say it was highly important for adults to feel responsible for the well-being of all the neighborhood's kids.

Actions

In terms of differences in adults reportedly living the actions, the only significant findings favored parents whose youngest child was 19 or older. Those parents were more likely than all other adults to say they were surrounded by adults who told parents when their children did something right (30% older, 19% younger, 13% nonparents, with $F(2, 1413) = 10.07$, $p < .0001$), and who volunteered or donated money monthly (21% older, 14% younger, 14% nonparents, with $F(2, 1413) = 6.80$, $p < .001$). They were also more likely than nonparents, but not parents whose youngest child was 18 or younger, to be surrounded by adults who provided kids opportunities to improve the community (19% older, 10% younger, 9% nonparents, with $F(2, 1413) = 5.23$, $p < .005$), and who gave advice to neighborhood kids (23% older, 17% younger, 11% nonparents, with $F(2, 1413) = 4.22$, $p < .01$).

Parental Status Relations with Beliefs and Actions: Children versus Adolescents

As reported above, on the Importance scale, parents were more likely than nonparents to think that engaging in these actions generally was important. That difference held true both when the child was an adolescent or grade school aged. On the Conformity scale as well, parents were no more likely than nonparents to be surrounded by adults who lived the actions when it came to younger children.

However, parents were more likely than nonparents to say that, overall, the adults around them lived the actions when it came to *adolescents* (Conformity scale: $F(1, 639) = 5.86$, $p < .01$). Among the separate relationship actions, parents were more likely than nonparents to say the adults around them:

1. Had meaningful conversations with adolescents (35% parents, 22% nonparents, with $F(1, 683) = 9.87$, Bonferroni corrected $p < .02$);

2. Told other parents when their adolescent children did something good (26% parents, 6% nonparents, with $F(1, 683) = 31.41$, corrected $p < .002$); and

3. Gave advice to neighborhood adolescents (16% parents, 7% nonparents, with $F(1, 683) = 9.36$, corrected $p < .04$).

Further research needs to more deeply explore the possible reasons for these results, especially since the clear negative image most adults hold of adolescents is one not much more positive among parents (Farkas & Johnson, 1997). We can speculate, however, that parents may in their daily lives recognize better than nonparent adults the need these older children continue to have, and may increasingly need (Scales & Gibbons, 1996) for positive connections with adults outside the family.

It is intriguing that parents were no more likely than nonparents to think it important for adults to tell them when young people did something right, but that parents were more likely to say the adults around them actually told parents about positive behavior when it concerned adolescents. It may be that parents understand that, given the poor image most adults, including parents, may have of teenagers, it is even more critical for parents to have counter-vailing information for those older children when it is available. Parents may know more deeply from their own experience as parents how important it is to be told when their adolescent children are observed behaving in admirable and responsible ways that encourage others, including parents, to view them with pride and respect, as well as a not insignificant measure of relief. Perhaps, holding such insights, parents send signals, explicit or implicit, of the type we have alluded to, that let other adults know parents would welcome hearing such things about their adolescent children. In other words, parents may be both more in need of and more willing to accept help from others in nurturing and guiding their older children than they are when it comes to their younger children.

In sum, these results suggest that parents overall are more supportive than nonparents of all adults being engaged with young people. However, only in specific circumstances (e.g., when it involves adolescents, or when they are parents of grown children) are they any more likely than nonparents to report being surrounded by adults who actually do these actions.

Frequency of Attendance at Religious Services

Religious congregations are one of the few places where many adults can interact in a safe and organized setting with young people who are not in their families. Thus, it is reasonable to suspect that those who are more involved with religious congregations also will find such adult engagement with young people to be more important, and to report being surrounded by other adults who engage with young people in these ways. We looked at differences among three categories: those who attended religious services weekly or more, compared to

Table 24. Proportion of Adults Designating Action as "Most Important," by Religious Involvement (N = 1,411)

	Weekly or more	Sometimes	Rarely or never	F
Top-Rated Actions				
Expect respect for adults	71%[a]	62%[b]	66%	4.45**
Expect parents to set boundaries	87%[a]	80%[b]	83%	4.95***
Teach shared values	83%[a]	76%[b]	77%[b]	5.00***
Respect cultural differences	80%[a]	73%[b]	74%[b]	4.96***
Guide decision making	79%[a]	72%[b]	76%	3.31*
Have meaningful conversations	77%	72%	71%	2.88*
Give financial guidance	79%[a]	68%[b]	72%	7.29****
Discuss personal values	79%[a]	68%[b]	64%[b]	15.91****
Actions with Majority Support				
Report positive behavior	71%[a]	58%[b]	59%[b]	12.78****
Ensure well-being of neighborhood kids	68%[a]	62%	56%[b]	7.56****
Report misbehavior	67%[a]	54%[b]	59%[b]	9.62****
Discuss religious beliefs	75%[a]	54%[b]	34%[c]	98.34****
Pass down traditions	62%[a]	54%[a]	46%[b]	13.36****
Know names	55%[a]	51%[a]	41%[b]	9.31****
Actions with Less than Majority Support				
Provide service opportunities	55%[a]	45%[b]	38%[b]	14.82****
Model giving and serving	55%[a]	41%[b]	37%[b]	19.17****
Give advice	17%[a]	11%[b]	8%[b]	8.45****

a, b = Percentages with different letters are significantly different from each other.
* = Significant at $p \leq .05$.
** = Significant at $p \leq .01$.
*** = Significant at $p \leq .007$.
**** = Significant at $p \leq .0007$.

those who attended sometimes (monthly, or a few times every few months), or rarely or never (a few times a year or less).

As expected, we found that frequency of attendance at religious services made a substantial difference in how important adults rated the various actions they could take in relating to young people, and in how much the adults around them were reported to engage with young people (see Tables 24 and 25). On the Importance scale, frequent attendees rated the actions more important overall than did all other adults ($F(2, 1352) = 30.56$, $p < .0001$). On the Conformity scale, both frequent and merely occasional attendees were more likely than those who attended rarely or never to report the adults around them actually did these actions, but weekly attendees were no more likely than occasional attendees to say so ($F(2, 1326) = 10.41$, $p < .0001$).

On the individual actions, those who attended services weekly or more rated all of the top nine actions except encouraging school success more important than did adults who attended services only sometimes, although they rated only two (providing financial guidance and discussing personal values) more important by a margin of 10 or more percentage points. On those top-rated actions with substantial consensus across all Americans, however, weekly attendees' importance

Table 25. Proportion of Adults Saying Most Adults around Them Do Action, by Religious Involvement (N = 1,411)

	Weekly or more	Sometimes	Rarely or never	F
Top-Rated Actions				
Encourage school success	65%[b]	74%[a]	72%[a]	5.61***
Respect cultural differences	39%[a]	31%[b]	34%	3.26*
Guide decisions	41%	47%[a]	38%[b]	2.96*
Have meaningful conversations	35%	39%[a]	29%[b]	4.12**
Actions with Majority Support				
Report positive behavior	26%[a]	20%	14%[b]	10.71****
Ensure well-being of neighborhood kids	39%[a]	41%[a]	24%[b]	15.32****
Discuss religious beliefs	41%[a]	32%[b]	26%[b]	13.68****
Actions with Less than Majority Support				
Provide service opportunities	16%[a]	11%[b]	9%[b]	6.71***

a, b = Percentages with different letters are significantly different from each other.
* = significant at $p \leq .05$.
** = Significant at $p \leq .01$.
*** = Significant at $p \leq .003$.
**** = Significant at $p \leq .0001$.

ratings were generally not higher than the ratings of those who rarely or never attended.

It is on the remaining actions, those with less clear consensus across all Americans (i.e., less than 70% and even less than 50% thinking they were highly important), that weekly attendees generally rate the action more important than both those who attend sometimes and those who rarely or never attend. Five of these nine remaining actions on which there are significant differences show differences of 10 percentage points or more between frequent attendees and all other adults.

The picture is a little less clear when considering differences in reports that adults around them actually did these actions. It appears that attending services just monthly, or even a few times every few months, seems more conducive to engaging with kids than rarely or never attending.

Weekly attendees were more likely than those who rarely or never attended to report being surrounded by adults who did several of the actions, including telling parents when children did something good, feeling responsible for ensuring the well-being of the neighborhood's kids, discussing religious beliefs, and providing service opportunities for young people. On the latter two actions, as well as on teaching kids to respect cultural differences, frequent attendees also were surrounded more than those who attended sometimes by adults who did these things. But those who attended services just sometimes were more likely than those who attended rarely or never to be surrounded by adults who guided young people's decision making and who had meaningful conversations with them. They were also as likely as frequent attendees to feel responsible for ensuring the well-being of the neighborhood's kids.

An unexpected finding was that frequent attendees were less likely than all adults who attended services less often to say the adults around them encouraged young people to do well in school. Perhaps the latter result occurs because the young people frequent attendees most often encounter also are regular participants in the activities of religious congregations, and such participation is associated with better school performance (reviewed in Scales & Leffert, 1999). Thus, those adults may not feel as pressing a need to emphasize that commitment on the part of young people.

Our results showing the generally positive relationship between religious participation and engagement with young people are consistent with previous research that has reported attendance at religious services to be associated with prosocial attitudes and behaviors such as caring and generosity (Mattis et al., 2000). These results are hardly unexpected, since all major religious traditions—including Judaism, Christianity, Islam, Mormonism, Buddhism, and Native spirituality—"emphasize compassion, generosity, service, and justice as priorities—even obligations—for people of faith" (Roehlkepartain, 2002). Religiously active people vote more, give blood more, trust others more, and socialize more with neighbors (Saguaro Seminar, 2001). In our study, frequent participation in religious services—at least weekly attendance—apparently has an association with both favorable attitudes toward adults engaging with kids and the reported behavior of the adults around them. However, a lower level of participation—monthly—also is related to being in networks of adults who live these actions. Why would a less frequent level of participation among adults be associated with perceived differences in the engagement behavior of other adults around them, when it was insufficient to be related to differences in personal beliefs or attitudes?

We can speculate, but not confirm, that monthly participation affords increased opportunities for interaction with young people and with other adults who are so engaged with kids, but perhaps does not stimulate as much reflection about the meaning of those opportunities as weekly participation does. More frequent participation in religious community may be required for adults to think more deeply about the critical role of these adult behaviors in young people's lives. Perhaps additional examination of oneself in relation to one's religion and society is afforded by more frequent participation in religious community. Through that added reflection, adults may have a greater chance of incorporating these principles for nurturing the young into their philosophical understanding of what their religious tradition asks them to believe as well as do.

This reasoning takes on additional salience if we consider that the very tenets of a faith community can play a formative role in shaping adults' sense of responsibility for young people. The context for developing a social expectation for involvement with the young may reflect an even broader ethic of caring for others as well as the expectation that believers have a responsibility to imbue the young in their fold with the principles of their faith. The shared vision of priorities and values, emphasis on social interaction, and high degree of social trust that exist in a faith community make it a "rich moral milieu that can contribute to the development of character," in adults as well as young people (King, 2000, p. 7). Regular attendance at religious services may reflect both a deeper social connection with others and a deeper religious commitment, both of which could motivate individuals to be connected to kids. Because we did not have a measure of the importance of religion in adults' lives, we cannot tease out the relative contributions each may have made to connection with young people, but it is likely both greater social connection and greater religious commitment play roles in that greater engagement.

Because religious involvement clearly is associated with a variety of prosocial attitudes and behaviors, including the engagement with young people investigated in our study, it might be tempting for intentional efforts to mobilize adults around engaging with young people especially to target the religiously active as a core group. Although these results suggest there is much that recommends such a strategy, the Social Capital Community Benchmark Survey (Saguaro Seminar, 2001) also sounded a note of caution. Religiously involved Americans in that national study were reported to be more socially and politically conservative and intolerant of those who are different. The researchers concluded that their outreach tended to be more to build bridges to people who were like them than people who were unlike them. These findings led the researchers to observe, even while noting that faith-based communities have "some matchless strengths" for civic engagement, that the "special challenge" of faith-based civic engagement is to "encourage greater tolerance for minority viewpoints and greater sensitivity to imperatives of social reform" (p. 2). That caution is appropriate to note, of course, but history also demonstrates that religious commitment has motivated countless individuals to action on behalf of social justice and civil rights. The religiously involved, in short, are not a homogeneous group in terms of their social or political convictions. We did not study the effect on engagement of holding particular religious beliefs. But our data clearly suggest that religiously involved people in general are more likely than the less involved to think it important to be engaged with young people, and to say they are surrounded by adults who actually are engaged with young people in their daily lives.

Interactions among Race/Ethnicity, Gender, and Involvement in Religion

Because women, African Americans, and Hispanics tend to be more involved with religious activities, we also conducted multiple analyses of variance on the Importance and Conformity scales to test whether there were any significant interactions among gender, race/ethnicity, and religious service attendance. (Later in this chapter we present a more detailed treatment of the effects of attendance at religious services on engagement with young people.) Both MANOVAs produced significant overall results (Importance: $F(35, 1352) = 5.37$, $p < .0001$; Conformity: $F(35, 1326) = 3.10$, $p < .0001$).

For Importance, gender, race, and attendance at religious services all were significant, with women ($F(1, 1326) = 78.64$, $p < .0001$), African Americans ($F(2, 1326) = 11.99$, $p < .0001$), and weekly attendees at religious services ($F(5, 1322) = 9.53$, $p < .0001$) all rating the actions more important for all adults to do. The only significant interaction was a relatively weak interaction of gender by race: African American women were somewhat more likely than other groups to rate the actions highly important ($F(2, 1352) = 1.93$, $p < .03$). Thus, race, gender, and attendance at religious services, taken individually as well as together, all have separate effects on how important these actions are rated, and race has an additional interaction effect with gender.

For Conformity, each variable also produced a significant main effect, with women ($F(1, 1326) = 9.57$, $p < .002$), weekly attendees at religious services ($F(5, 1322) = 5.33$,

$p < .0001$), and, more weakly, African Americans ($F(2, 1326) = 3.31$, $p < .03$) being more likely than others actually to report that adults around them lived the actions. The only significant interaction effect for norm conformity also was gender by race, but it was *white* women who were more likely than other groups to say that adults they know actually lived the actions ($F(2, 1326) = 3.10$, $p < .0001$). This result is consistent with the findings from a study of Boston families (mothers) with children in grades 1–4 (Marshall et al., 2001). Although social class was confounded with ethnicity in that sample, and so it was not clear which was the primary contributor to the results, the researchers reported that the European American mothers were more likely than Hispanic or African American mothers to involve nonrelatives in activities with their children.

Detailed Results on Differences: Notable but Less Substantively Meaningful

Frequency of Volunteering and Charitable Giving

Those who volunteer in their communities might be expected to be generally more involved with others and committed to acts of caring, of which being engaged with young people is an example. Although less than half the sample thought it highly important to volunteer or donate money monthly to show young people the importance of giving, this proportion could have been limited due to question wording. We asked about "monthly" volunteering or donating, which may be an unrealistic level to expect more than a minority of Americans to agree is vital. That level of frequency may be considered less important than *periodically* volunteering or donating *occasionally* to charity as a model for kids.

But that monthly level of volunteerism did seem related to how important adults considered the actions to be, and how much they reported the adults around them did those actions. We divided the sample into those who said they were "regular" volunteers (at least a few hours a month), those who were "occasional" volunteers (a few hours every few months, or a few hours a year), and those who said they "never" volunteered. Overall, the results suggest that monthly volunteering has a moderate impact on the importance adults attach to these actions, and on the likelihood of their reporting that the adults around them do engage with kids in these ways (Tables 26 and 27).

Those "regular" volunteers (i.e., volunteering at least a few hours per month) were more likely than all other adults to rate the actions highly important on the Importance scale ($F(2, 1350) = 15.25$, $p < .0001$). On the Conformity scale, both the regular and merely occasional volunteers also were more likely than those who never volunteered to be surrounded by adults who engaged with children and adolescents in these various ways ($F(2, 1323) = 13.73$, $p < .0001$). Regular volunteers were not more likely to say this than occasional volunteers, however.

Looking at the actions separately, regular volunteers rated several actions more important than did all other adults: discussing personal values with young people, discussing religious beliefs, and, not surprisingly, showing young people

Table 26. Proportion of Adults Designating Action as "Most Important," by Frequency of Volunteering (N = 1,409)

	Never	Occasional	Regular	F
Top-Rated Actions				
Discuss personal values	66%[b]	70%[b]	77%[a]	7.51**
Actions with Majority Support				
Report positive behavior	63%	58%[b]	70%[a]	9.10**
Ensure well-being of neighborhood kids	61%	60%[b]	67%[a]	3.36*
Discuss religious beliefs	52%[b]	51%[b]	68%[a]	20.40**
Pass down traditions	56%	49%[b]	61%[a]	7.10**
Actions with Less than Majority Support				
Provide service opportunities	48%[a]	39%[b]	54%[a]	13.21**
Seek opinions	59%[a]	39%[c]	47%[b]	13.86**
Model giving and serving	40%[b]	36%[b]	58%[a]	28.76**

a, b = Percentages with different letters are significantly different from each other.
  * = Significant at $p \leq .03$.
  ** = Significant at $p \leq .0009$.

the importance of charitable giving and volunteering. The importance attached to discussing religious beliefs also was not surprising because frequent volunteers may be more likely to contribute that significant time helping others through their religious congregation. But these differences were relatively modest: Regular volunteers rated only two actions higher in importance than all other adults by 10 or more percentage points—discussing religious beliefs and modeling giving and serving.

Those regular volunteers also were more likely than occasional volunteers to rate it important to tell parents when children do something good, to feel

Table 27. Proportion of Adults Saying Adults around Them Do Action, by Frequency of Volunteering (N = 1,409)

	Never	Occasional	Regular	F
Top-Rated Actions				
Encourage school success	63%[b]	73%[a]	69%	3.85*
Discuss shared values	37%[b]	43%	49%[a]	6.28**
Discuss personal values	28%[b]	39%[a]	40%[a]	5.93**
Actions with Majority Support				
Ensure well-being of neighborhood kids	29%[b]	36%	38%[a]	3.29*
Parents be sole discipliners	22%[a]	15%[b]	16%	3.33*
Know names	24%[b]	39%[a]	35%[a]	8.70***
Actions with Less than Majority Support				
Provide service opportunities	9%[b]	10%[b]	16%[a]	6.18**
Model giving and serving	10%[b]	12%[b]	22%[a]	13.99***

a, b = Percentages with different letters are significantly different from each other.
  * = Significant at $p \leq .03$.
  ** = Significant at $p \leq .002$.
  *** = Significant at $p \leq .0002$.

responsible for ensuring the well-being of all neighborhood kids, and to pass down cultural traditions. However, people who said they never volunteered were no less likely than the regular volunteers to rate those three actions highly important. In addition, those who never volunteered were more likely than occasional volunteers (but not regulars) to rate it important to give young people chances to serve their communities, and more likely than *all* adults to say it was important to seek young people's opinions.

If our speculation is correct that frequent volunteers may be contributing that time predominantly through their religious congregations, then it is not so surprising that regular volunteers considered it less important to seek young people's opinions than did those who never volunteered. Those belief differences would align well with the greater importance regular volunteers attach to discussing religious and spiritual beliefs and passing down traditions. These actions all help maintain the solidity of a belief system, and seeking young people's opinions may be seen as inviting questioning and skepticism that could be considered threatening to the integrity of those belief systems. We have no such plausible explanation for why occasional volunteers would be less likely than those who never volunteer to say it is important to give young people opportunities to serve their communities. Perhaps those occasional volunteers (who volunteer only a few hours a year) feel guilty because they believe they ought to be volunteering more than they are (they are volunteering a little, after all, so it seems to be an important action in their value system). Did they then attempt to assuage that guilt by rating it not that important to give young people similar opportunities, in effect saying contributing service is not all that important? This is high speculation indeed. We simply have no satisfying explanation for this finding.

The differences in importance ratings generally do favor regular volunteers. Nevertheless, when we examine how much adults say they are surrounded by others who do these actions, the regular volunteers are no more likely to say the adults they know actually discuss religious beliefs or pass down traditions than do other adults. The regular volunteers are significantly more likely, however, than *all* adults to report that the adults around them provide service opportunities to young people, and model the importance of giving and volunteering.

Along with occasional volunteers, regular volunteers also are more likely than those who never volunteer to report they are surrounded by adults who discuss their personal values with young people, and who know the names of many kids in their neighborhoods. Regular volunteers also are more likely than those who never volunteer to discuss shared values with young people, and feel responsible for ensuring the well-being of all neighborhood kids. As was the case for the Importance ratings, however, most of these differences are relatively modest. For example, on only one action, modeling giving and serving, are regular volunteers more likely by 10 or more percentage points to say the adults around them do the action.

Occasional volunteers, but not regular ones, are more likely than those who never volunteer to say that the adults around them encourage school success. But it is those who never volunteer who are most likely to say the adults around them believe parents should be the sole discipliners of their children.

Regular volunteers may reflect more relative conservatism of values through the higher importance they attach to discussing religious beliefs and passing down traditions. But perhaps those who never volunteer also do not feel quite the same embeddedness as those who volunteer do within an embracing social support system of like-minded others. Even if parents are effectively making the same discipline decisions across levels of volunteering, those who at least occasionally volunteer may feel supported in their discipline decisions by the values of the social systems within which their volunteer activities place them, and so feel "helped" by others in that regard. The relative absence of those experiences and perceptions may lead those who never volunteer to perceive that more of the adults around them are "going it alone" on matters of discipline.

Frequency of Participation in Neighborhood or Community Meetings

As we discussed in regard to attendance at religious services and participation in volunteering, participation in community or neighborhood meetings may reflect a more general orientation adults have to civic engagement and connection with others. Concomitantly, those active, more generally "connected" adults may attach greater importance to engaging with young people and report a greater likelihood of being in social networks of adults who do engage with kids (Tables 28 and 29).

Table 28. Proportion of Adults Designating Action as "Most Important," by Community Involvement (N = 1,409)

	Often attend community meetings	Sometimes attend community meetings	Never attend community meetings	F
Top-Rated Actions				
Respect cultural differences	73%^{b}	75%	81%^{a}	3.80*
Give financial guidance	72%^{b}	71%^{b}	80%^{a}	7.16****
Actions with Majority Support				
Report positive behavior	72%^{a}	64%	62%^{b}	3.63*
Ensure well-being of neighborhood kids	71%^{a}	61%^{b}	62%	3.68*
Report misbehavior	68%^{a}	59%^{b}	62%	3.18*
Know names	63%^{a}	49%^{b}	46%^{b}	10.34****
Actions with Less than Majority Support				
Provide service opportunities	54%^{a}	45%^{b}	49%	3.16*
Model giving and serving	55%^{a}	46%^{b}	45%^{b}	4.00**

a, b = Percentages with different letters are significantly different from each other.
  * = Significant at $p \leq .04$.
 ** = Significant at $p \leq .01$.
 *** = Significant at $p \leq .002$.
**** = Significant at $p \leq .0008$.

Table 29. Proportion of Adults Saying Most Adults around Them Do Action, by Community Involvement (N = 1,409)

	Often attend community meetings	Sometimes attend community meetings	Never attend community meetings	F
Top-Rated Actions				
Teach shared values	50%^{a}	47%^{a}	39%^{b}	5.57***
Guide decision making	44%	45%^{a}	36%^{b}	4.51**
Have meaningful conversations	49%^{a}	34%^{b}	27%^{b}	18.68****
Discuss personal values	42%^{a}	39%^{a}	32%^{b}	5.09***
Actions with Majority Support				
Report positive behavior	26%^{a}	21%	18%^{b}	2.98*
Ensure well-being of neighborhood kids	49%^{a}	31%^{b}	34%^{b}	13.39***
Pass down traditions	44%^{a}	40%^{a}	33%^{b}	5.85***
Know names	47%^{a}	31%^{b}	30%^{b}	13.76****
Actions with Less than Majority Support				
Provide service opportunities	23%^{a}	10%^{b}	10%^{b}	17.72****
Seek opinions	30%^{a}	28%^{a}	20%^{b}	6.19***
Model giving and serving	26%^{a}	17%^{b}	11%^{c}	14.31****
Give advice	21%^{a}	14%^{b}	19%^{a}	4.93***

a, b = Percentages with different letters are significantly different from each other.
* = Significant at $p \leq .05$.
** = Significant at $p \leq .01$.
*** = Significant at $p \leq .007$.
**** = Significant at $p \leq .0001$.

As expected, we found that meeting attendance does matter. Those who attended meetings often or even just sometimes rated these actions, overall, as more important for all adults to do than did those who attended neighborhood meetings rarely or never, but frequent attendees did not rate them significantly more important than merely occasional participants did ($F(2, 1351) = 4.05$, $p < .01$).

On the Conformity scale, however, those who participated often in community meetings were more likely than *all* others to say they were surrounded by adults who live the actions. In addition, those who attended neighborhood meetings just sometimes were more likely to report being surrounded by adults who engaged with kids than those who never attended ($F(2, 1325 = 20.86$, $p < .0001$). Thus, unlike the ratings of importance, where greater participation beyond the occasional level does not seem associated with higher ratings of importance, more frequent participation in community or neighborhood meetings does seem related to adults reporting that they are embedded in a network of adults who engage with young people.

On individual actions, ratings of importance did not always vary as expected with frequency of meeting participation. For example, those who participated often in neighborhood or community meetings were more likely than all other adults to say it is highly important to know the names of many neighborhood young people. They also rated it more important than did those who attended rarely or never for adults to tell parents when children do something good.

However, frequent participants were more likely than occasional participants, but not more than those who participated rarely or never, to believe it important for adults to feel responsible for helping ensure the well-being of neighborhood young people, tell parents when children do something wrong, and provide service opportunities for kids. In addition, it was rare participants who thought teaching respect for cultural differences was more highly important than frequent participants thought, and that giving financial guidance to kids was more important than all other adults did.

It is with regard to how much the adults around them are reported to be engaged with young people that differences more consistently appear in the expected direction. On 10 of the 12 actions on which there are any significant differences, adults who often attend community or neighborhood meetings report being in such engaged social networks more than those who rarely or never attend. On the majority of these, the differences are at least 10 percentage points. And on six of those 12 actions, frequent meeting participants also exceed those who participate just sometimes in their reports of adult engagement around them.

For example, those frequent participants are much more likely than other adults to report that the adults around them have meaningful conversations with young people, feel responsible for helping ensure the well-being of all the neighborhood's kids, know the names of many neighborhood young people, provide service opportunities, and model giving and serving. These actions would seem to distinctly emphasize the building of support and empowerment assets in young people.

It appears that the effect of community meeting participation may be even greater on behavior—on being in a network where the norm is engagement with kids—than it is on attitude. Even just *occasional* attendance is related to being in a network of adults who live some of these actions. For example, those who attended community meetings just sometimes were, along with those who attended often, more likely than those who never attended community meetings, to say the adults around them discussed both shared and personal values with young people, sought out young people's opinions, taught young people to pass down their traditions, and modeled giving and serving. In addition, those occasional participants were more likely than those who rarely or never participated in meetings to say the adults around them guided young people's decision making.

Participating at least occasionally in community meetings is an indication that one is more inclined to engage positively with young people than if one never attends. And yet, participating quite often in community meetings, though clearly related to reported behavior of adults, seems to add little to an overall sense of the importance of these adult behaviors beyond what occasional participation already contributes. Frequent attendance may not have much additional impact beyond occasional attendance on favorable attitudes toward adult engagement with kids. Frequent attendance does seem related, however, to experiencing greater social support and motivation overall for actually being involved with young people.

But why would there not be stronger overall effects of frequent participation in neighborhood or community meetings on favorable beliefs or attitudes about engaging with kids? Why would just occasional attendance be associated with as much support for these actions as frequent attendance was? After all, organizational involvement has been found to predict a positive psychological sense of community membership, which affects a person's feeling of influence at the neighborhood level (Caughy, O'Campo, & Brodsky, 1999). Greater participation in community meetings, therefore, should promote feelings of responsibility for the welfare of those in the community, and a sense that one can effectively do something about those needs.

Although the reasoning is speculative on our part, it may be that the high degree of social fragmentation in contemporary society allows a relatively low level of community meeting involvement—"sometimes"—to do two things: satisfy many individuals' needs for or reinforce their sense of belonging to the "community" or "neighborhood" group, and draw their attention to key issues of common concern.

As the 1999 Knight Foundation community indicators survey found, adults generally do not know even the names of many of their neighbors. Under those circumstances, a relatively small improvement in getting to know them, especially in considering, in a public meeting, issues of shared importance, may begin to raise not only senses of belonging and influence but also senses of trust in each other, as people who share similar values. Even occasional participation may well also bring more sharply to their attention issues that affect many or all residents, and so raise the perceived importance of those issues.

It may take frequent participation, however, for these dynamics of increased trust and issue awareness to contribute to an interpersonal climate more conducive to neighbors actually playing a deeper and more active role in relating to children and youth outside their own families. But even occasional exposure to one's neighbors in dealing with issues of common interest may heighten the attitudinal salience of matters that affect families and children as being among the top priorities for collective action. Our results are consistent with previous research. For example, studies have reported that participation in neighborhood meetings, volunteerism, and attendance at religious services is associated with both prosocial attitudes and behaviors (Mattis et al., 2000). The absence of those community involvement activities also is associated with such undesirable health outcomes as low birth weight among neighborhood infants (Caughy et al., 1999).

In summary, participation in religious services, attendance at community meetings, and volunteering all have separate effects on how important adults consider the actions to be and how likely it is they are surrounded by others who live the actions. When considered together (see sidebar below), these activities also reinforce each other on the importance attributed to adult engagement, such that those who participate most frequently in both religious services and volunteering or community meetings consider it more important for all adults to be engaged with young people. Different analysis techniques suggested that either religious service attendance or volunteering was the most important contributing variable, but frequency of meeting attendance was significant in each of the different analyses.

Interactions among Involvement in Religion, Volunteering, and Neighborhood Meetings

Because it may be that the adults who often attend community meetings are the same adults who frequently volunteer and frequently attend religious services, we also conducted multiple analyses of variance on the Importance and Conformity scales to examine the possible interaction among those variables. Each MANOVA was significant (Importance: $F(131, 1342) = 2.04$, $p < .0001$); Conformity: $F(131, 1315) = 2.22$, $p < .0001$). For Importance, all three main effects were significant: attendance at religious services ($F(5, 1342) = 121.93$, $p < .0001$), participation in community meetings ($F(3, 1342) = 3.41$, $p < .01$), and frequency of volunteering ($F(5, 1342) = 2.56$, $p < .02$).

There was a strong interaction between attendance at religious services and volunteering ($F(24, 1342) = 2.24$, $p < .0005$), with those who attended services daily and who volunteered a few hours a week considering the actions more important. A weaker interaction was observed between religious services and community meeting participation ($F(16, 1342) = 1.69$, $p < .04$), with those who attended services at least weekly and community meetings at least sometimes more likely to rate the actions important.

Looking at the MANOVAs on conformity to the actions, there were significant main effects for religious service attendance ($F(5, 1315) = 6.17$, $p < .0001$) and community meeting attendance ($F(3, 1315) = 11.58$, $p < .0001$), but not for volunteering. There was a spurious three-way interaction effect caused by two-thirds of the 64 combinations having Ns of less than 10.

Because of the small cell sizes in these MANOVAs, we also conducted a regression analysis with the Importance and Conformity scales as dependent variables, entering attendance at religious services, volunteering, and meeting participation as independent variables, as well as the products of each with the others as interaction terms. Volunteering was a more meaningful predictor of Importance in this analysis than in the MANOVA, and meeting attendance also was significant, with the interaction among three also significant. All three variables significantly contributed to Conformity, and, as with the MANOVA results, there were no significant interaction effects.

Years Living in the Neighborhood and Age of Adult

Neighborhood Stability

For purposes of analysis, adults were arbitrarily divided into those who had lived in their neighborhoods for 10 or more years, five to nine years, and less than five years. On the Importance scale, longer-term residents of 10 or more years were more likely than relative newcomers of less than five years' residency to rate the actions overall as highly important ($F(2, 1356) = 11.20$, $p < .0001$).

On individual actions, the longtime residents were more likely than all adults to rate it highly important to teach children and youth to discuss religious and spiritual beliefs with young people, and to teach them to pass down their cultural traditions (Table 30). They also were more likely than newcomers (but not residents of five to nine years) to think it highly important for adults to

Table 30. Proportion of Adults Designating Action as "Most Important," by Years in Neighborhood (N = 1,419)

	5 or Fewer years	5–9 Years	10 or More years	F
Top-Rated Actions				
Expect respect for adults	63%[b]	68%	71%[a]	4.58*
Actions with Majority Support				
Report positive behavior	59%[b]	65%	70%[a]	6.68**
Report misbehavior	56%[b]	60%	67%[a]	8.16***
Discuss religious beliefs	56%[b]	51%[b]	66%[a]	10.79***
Pass down traditions	49%[b]	52%[b]	64%[a]	16.18***
Know names	44%[b]	48%	56%[a]	9.18****

a, b = Percentages with different letters are significantly different from each other.
* = Significant at $p \leq .01$.
** = Significant at $p \leq .001$.
*** = Significant at $p \leq .0003$.

expect kids to respect adults, tell parents if their children do something right or wrong, and know the names of many neighborhood children. On two of those six actions—discussing religious beliefs and passing down traditions—longtime residents exceeded all other adults by 10 or more percentage points in ratings of importance.

A slightly different pattern emerged in looking at how length of community residency affects being in a network of adults who are engaged with young people (Table 31). On the Conformity scale, long-term residents were more likely than residents of five to nine years, but *not* more likely than newcomers, to be surrounded by adults who did these actions ($F(2, 1330) = 4.64, p < .009$).

In terms of conformity to the individual actions, there were significant differences on only five actions. Longer-term residents were more likely than *all* other adults to say adults around them gave young people chances to improve their communities and modeled the importance of volunteering or donating

Table 31. Proportion of Adults Saying Most Adults around Them Do Action, by Years in Neighborhood (N = 1,419)

	5 or Fewer years	5–9 Years	10 or More years	F
Top-Rated Actions				
Have meaningful conversations	31%[b]	32%	38%[a]	4.13*
Actions with Majority Support				
Report positive behavior	19%[b]	19%	25%[a]	3.96*
Ensure well-being of neighborhood kids	30%[b]	36%	39%[a]	5.33**
Provide service opportunities	10%[b]	9%[b]	16%[a]	7.16**
Model giving and serving	13%[b]	12%[b]	21%[a]	9.76***

a, b = Percentages with different letters are significantly different from each other.
* = Significant at $p \leq .01$.
** = Significant at $p \leq .008$.
*** = Significant at $p \leq .0001$.

money to charity each month. They were also more likely than newcomers, but not residents of five to nine years, to say the adults around them had more than casual conversations with young people, told parents when their children did something right, and felt responsible for helping ensure the well-being of all neighborhood kids. These differences are relatively modest, however, as on none of these actions did the differences across years of residency reach 10 or more percentage points.

It is possible that longer-term residents are more likely to be parents, and so it is really the parental status variable affecting these differences more than residence length per se. The two are positively related, but the correlation co-efficient between residence length and parental status was only .18, suggesting at best a mild relationship. As we shall see (see sidebar on page 184), much of the differences around length of residency may be due instead to the fact that longer-term residents also are likely to be older residents. That is, length of resi-dency may be important in its own right, but an adult's age may be even more of a contributor to differences in how important adults rate these actions and how much they are embedded in social networks of other adults who are engaged with young people. (We also tested whether age effects were explained by the fact that older adults also are more likely to be married and parents, and found age continued to have independent effects—see sidebar on page 186.)

Length of neighborhood residence seems therefore to have a modest impact on the likelihood that adults both rate these actions highly important and are surrounded by other adults who live the actions. In general, residents of 10 or more years seem to experience more personal and environmental support for engaging in these actions. Even though length of residency does interact with age, as we shall describe below, how long adults have lived in their neighborhood appears to have some positive relationship to their engagement with young people.

These results are consistent with other research. Studies have found greater residential stability to be associated with outcomes such as lower adolescent risk taking and violent, aggressive behavior, regardless of the level of neigh-borhood disadvantage (Kowaleski-Jones, 2000), as well as lower neighborhood rates of child abuse (Garbarino & Sherman, 1980). Neighborhood stability also is related to higher levels of collective efficacy, which in turn is related to lower rates of perceived and actual neighborhood violence (Sampson et al., 1997). These results, along with the similar patterns of results found for religious ser-vice participation, volunteering, and participation in community/neighborhood meetings, lend support to the conclusion that "the more stable an adult's stake in the neighborhood . . . the more they are engaged with young people as well" (Scales, Benson, Roehlkepartain, Hintz, et al., 2001, p. 724).

Age of Adult

In examining the individual actions by adults' ages, the most predominant trend was for adults age 35 and over to rate them more highly important. Specifi-cally, on the Importance scale, adults age 35 and older were more likely than 18- to

Table 32. Proportion of Adults Designating Action as "Most Important," by Age of Adult
(N = 1,405)

	Age 18–34	Age 35–54	Age 55+	F
Top-Rated Actions				
Expect respect for adults	61%[b]	69%[a]	74%[a]	8.35***
Teach shared values	72%[b]	82%[a]	87%[a]	16.26**
Guide decision making	72%[b]	80%[a]	77%	4.98**
Give financial guidance	71%[b]	77%[a]	76%	3.19*
Discuss personal values	69%[b]	72%	76%[a]	3.29*
Actions with Majority Support				
Report positive behavior	60%[b]	64%[b]	72%[a]	7.44**
Report misbehavior	56%[b]	64%[a]	66%[a]	4.97**
Discuss religious beliefs	47%[b]	61%[a]	71%[a]	28.12***
Pass down traditions	46%[b]	59%[a]	64%[a]	14.86***

a, b = Percentages with different letters are significantly different from each other.
 * = Significant at $p \leq .04$.
 ** = Significant at $p \leq .007$.
 *** = Significant at $p \leq .0002$.

34-year-olds to rate the actions highly important ($F(2, 1346) = 9.28, p < .0001$). Although we found a number of differences on individual actions (see Table 32), the magnitude of the differences is not large. For only one action—the importance of discussing religious beliefs—did older adults exceed all others by 10 or more percentage points.

Adults 35 and older were more likely than 18- to 34-year-olds to rate as highly important these ways of getting involved with young people: expecting adults to respect adults, teaching the same shared values to young people, volunteering once per month, discussing religious and spiritual beliefs with kids (especially among those 55 and older), telling parents when their children did something wrong, and passing down religious and ethnic cultural traditions.

Adults 55 and older were more likely than 18- to 34-year-olds, but not more likely than 34- to 54-year-olds, to rate it highly important to discuss their personal values with young people. Older adults were more likely than all other adults, however, to say it was important to tell parents when children did something good. Adults 35–54 were more likely than 18- to 34-year-olds, but not adults 55 and older, to rate it important to help young people with decision making and to give them guidance about money matters.

These patterns of importance attributed to various ways of engaging with young people may suggest one of two things, or perhaps both. First, the higher importance adults over age 35 give to numerous engagement actions may signify that there has been a cultural shift over the past few decades in the norms that frame what adults think it is right to do in their relationships with other people's kids. Younger Americans seem less certain about their roles and responsibilities in the nurture and guidance of all children and youth. Of course, the current study was a cross-sectional one in which the data were collected at one point in time. The possibility that these results reflect cultural shifts must remain speculative until subsequent national surveys can illuminate trends over time that can either support or raise questions about that speculation.

But another possibility suggested by our findings is not as readily dismissed. That is a developmental explanation. For example, with the average age at first marriage and parenthood in the United States advancing over the past few decades (for example, from 21 and 23 years of age for women and men in 1970 to 25 and 27 today; see Fields, 2001), younger adults ages 18–34 are increasingly less likely than adults of similar ages in previous generations to be parents themselves.

Indeed, in our data, the correlation of age and parental status is .31, suggesting that young adults ages 18–34 are somewhat less likely to be parents than adults age 35 and older. The differences in importance that adults at different ages ascribe to these actions may then also be due in part to these developmentally differing experiences adults of differing ages have with children, including their own children, children in their extended families, and other people's kids. We have already mentioned that in one of Search Institute's previous studies (Scales et al., 1998), the more adults were involved with young people, the more positive their image of young people, and the less they accepted as accurate the common negative media portrayals of young people. In the current study, we also found (see sections titled Parental Status, above, and Exposure to/Contact with Kids, below) that being a parent and having greater regular contact with young people outside the family were both associated with attributing greater importance to these adult engagement actions.

A second developmental possibility is that with increasing age adults are more likely to be concerned with influencing the quality of the next generation. Indeed, a small study of adults found support for the hypothesis that older adults are more likely to be motivated by "healthy" or "intrinsic" values "consistent with assumed innate needs to grow, connect with others, and expand into the community" (Sheldon & Kasser, 2001, p. 492). The pursuit of such goals also was associated with greater psychological well-being than the pursuit of approval, status, or material wealth. Thus, organismically, adults meet an important psychological need by being more connected to young people as they get older.

In terms of conformity to the actions, adults ages 55 and older also were more likely overall than 35- to 54-year-olds, but not 18- to 34-year-olds, actually to be surrounded by adults who live the actions (Conformity scale: $F(2, 1322) = 6.90, p < .0001$). Contrasting patterns emerge, however, when we look at the individual actions.

For example, those older adults age 55 and over were more likely than all other ages to be surrounded by adults who taught young people to respect people from different cultures, told parents when their children did something good, gave young people chances to improve the community, volunteered or donated money monthly, and gave neighborhood young people advice. They were also somewhat more likely than 18- to 34-year-olds, but not 35- to 54-year-olds, to report that adults around them had meaningful conversations with young people and felt responsible for the well-being of neighborhood kids (Table 33).

Table 33. Proportion of Adults Saying Adults around Them Do Action, by Age of Adult (N = 1,405)

	Age 18–34	Age 35–54	Age 55+	F
Top-Rated Actions				
Encourage school success	78%^{a}	66%^{b}	63%^{b}	13.41****
Expect respect for adults	73%^{a}	66%	63%^{b}	5.11**
Expect parents to set boundaries	46%^{a}	42%	38%^{b}	3.14*
Respect cultural differences	34%^{b}	33%^{b}	41%^{a}	3.61*
Have meaningful conversations	31%^{b}	34%	39%^{a}	3.42*
Give financial guidance	41%^{a}	31%^{b}	36%	5.34***
Actions with Majority Support				
Report positive behavior	18%^{b}	18%^{b}	30%^{a}	12.34****
Ensure well-being of neighborhood kids	31%^{b}	36%	41%^{a}	4.52**
Report misbehavior	37%^{a}	30%^{b}	32%^{b}	3.19*
Actions with Less than Majority Support				
Provide service opportunities	9%^{b}	8%^{b}	24%^{a}	30.95****
Model giving and serving	12%^{b}	16%^{b}	23%^{a}	9.20****

a, b = Percentages with different letters are significantly different from each other.
  * = Significant at $p \leq .04$.
 ** = Significant at $p \leq .01$.
 *** = Significant at $p \leq .004$.
**** = Significant at $p \leq .0001$.

However, younger adults ages 18–34 were somewhat more likely than all other ages to say the adults around them told parents if children or adolescents did something wrong, and encouraged young people to do well in school. They also were somewhat more likely than older adults, but not 35- to 54-year-olds, to be surrounded by adults who expected parents to enforce clear rules and boundaries, and by adults who expected young people to respect adult authority. Finally, they were more likely than 35- to 54-year-olds, but not older adults, to be surrounded by adults who gave financial guidance to the young.

As for the pattern with ratings of importance, the differences in reports that the adults around them did these actions were not consistently large, despite being statistically significant. For example, older adults exceeded all other adults by 10 or more percentage points on only two actions: saying the adults around them told parents if children did something good, and providing service opportunities to young people. Likewise, younger adults exceeded all others by 10 or more percentage points on only two actions: saying the adults around them encouraged school success and expected young people to respect adults.

These mixed results suggest that the impact of an adult's age on whether she or he is surrounded by others who live these actions varies considerably with the action in question, and does not vary consistently by age across all actions. Where there are differences in adults living the actions, younger adults under age 35 seem more likely to be surrounded by adults who reinforce boundaries and expectations for young people. In contrast, older adults age 55 or over seem more likely to be in networks where adults provide more support and empowerment to young people.

Our data also suggest that life stage may be relevant in another respect. Adults 35 to 54 years old were (like adults 55 and older) more likely than younger adults to rate the actions as important, but they were less likely than either younger or older adults to be surrounded by people who are so engaged with young people.

Perhaps this disparity between belief and action among 35- to 54-year-olds is due to two factors. People in this age group are influenced by the same normative and cultural dynamics as everyone else, which we have discussed throughout this book (e.g., belief that nurturing the young is the parents' responsibility, negative images of kids inhibiting interaction, etc.). In addition, however, those adults typically are in the busiest stage of their lives. The majority of adults between age 35 and 54 are married, raising their own families, working their longest hours at what for most will include their jobs of greatest responsibility and financial compensation, saving for retirement, dealing with the health and emotional needs of their own aging parents, and so on. In that developmental context, it is not surprising that their beliefs and the reported actions of the adults around them may not be as consistent as they are among older adults. Older adults may be less busy (or simply feel more in control of their schedules), and may be able to pick and choose better than those 35–54 years old the adults in their social networks. That may make it easier for them to associate with people like themselves, and so increase the alignment between their personal beliefs about engaging with kids and what the adults around them do.

Interactions between Age and Years in Neighborhood

As we have mentioned previously, it is likely that age and length of residency are connected. To test for an interaction effect between age and years residing in the community, we conducted multiple analyses of variance on the Importance and Conformity scales. Each yielded a significant overall F (Importance: $F(14, 1346) = 3.90$, $p < .0001$; Conformity: $F(14, 1322) = 2.45$, $p < .002$), but only the main effects for age were significant (Importance: $F(2, 1346) = 9.44$, $p < .0001$; Conformity: $F(2, 1322) = 6.96$, $p < .001$).

The interaction of age and residence produced a significant result on both Importance ($F[8, 1346] = 2.93$, $p < .003$) and Conformity ($F[8, 1322] = 2.40$, $p < .01$). In each case, adults age 35 or older *and* who were residents of their current neighborhood for 10 years or more tended to have the highest ratings of importance and greater proportions of adults in their social networks who reportedly lived these actions. Together, the main effects and interaction results suggest that age is the more meaningful contributor to differences in Importance and Conformity ratings, but that length of residency also is related to those differences.

Detailed Results on Differences: Least Substantively Meaningful

Marital Status

On marital status, we compared three groups of adults: married, single, and divorced/separated/widowed. Overall, on the Importance scale, divorced/separated/widowed adults rated the actions somewhat more important than did single adults ($F(2, 1351) = 3.86$, $p < .02$). But despite a marginally significant F value overall on the Conformity scale ($F(2, 1325) = 2.90$, $p < .05$), Tukey multiple comparisons yielded no significant differences among adults by marital status on reports of the adults they knew actually living these actions overall.

There were significant differences by marital status on the importance given nine actions. The results tended to suggest that divorced/separated/widowed people placed a greater emphasis on neighbors letting parents know when kids were transgressing, on inculcating in children a sense of their traditions, and on all adults giving advice to kids. On all but one of the actions on which there were any significant differences, divorced/separated/widowed adults either rated them more important than did all other adults, or along with married people, rated them more important than did single adults. For example, married and divorced/separated/widowed adults were more likely than single adults to say it was important to expect young people to respect adults, expect parents to set boundaries, teach young people shared values, guide their decision making, and discuss religious beliefs with the young. All but the last of those were among the actions rated most important overall by the entire sample. Married people also were more likely than single people to say it was important to tell parents if children did something good (Table 34).

On two actions with majority support among the total sample, divorced/separated/widowed adults rated them more important than did married or single adults: telling parents if children did something wrong, and passing down traditions. Single people considered passing down traditions less

Table 34. *Proportion of Adults Designating Action as "Most Important," by Marital Status* ($N = 1,411$)

	Married	Single	Divorced/Separated/Widowed	F
Top-Rated Actions				
Expect respect for adults	70%[a]	60%[b]	71%[a]	7.39****
Expect parents to set boundaries	86%[a]	77%[b]	87%[a]	9.06****
Teach shared values	83%[a]	71%[b]	83%[a]	13.11****
Guide decision making	78%[a]	71%[b]	79%[a]	4.34**
Actions with Majority Support				
Report positive behavior	67%[a]	60%[b]	66%	2.90*
Report misbehavior	61%[b]	57%[b]	69%[a]	5.45***
Discuss religious beliefs	61%[a]	51%[b]	65%[a]	8.08****
Pass down traditions	56%[b]	48%c	65%[a]	9.06****
Actions with Less than Majority Support				
Give advice	15%	11%[b]	17%[a]	4.45**

a, b = Percentages with different letters are significantly different from each other.
  * = Significant at $p \leq .05$.
 ** = Significant at $p \leq .01$.
 *** = Significant at $p \leq .004$.
**** = Significant at $p \leq .0006$.

Table 35. Proportion of Adults Saying Most Adults around Them Do Action, by Marital Status
(N = 1,411)

	Married	Single	Divorced/Separated/ Widowed	F
Top-Rated Actions				
Encourage school success	71%[a]	72%[a]	61%[b]	6.80**
Expect respect for adults	68%[a]	72%[a]	60%[b]	5.93**
Expect parents to set boundaries	41%	48%[a]	39%[b]	3.20*
Actions with Majority Support				
Know names	36%[a]	34%	28%[b]	3.35*
Actions with Less than Majority Support				
Provide service opportunities	14%[a]	8%[b]	17%[a]	6.22**

a, b = Percentages with different letters are significantly different from each other.
  * = Significant at $p \leq .04$.
 ** = Significant at $p \leq .002$.

important than all adults, but even married people considered it less important than did divorced/separated/widowed adults. Those adults who were divorced/separated/widowed also considered it more important than did single people to give advice to neighborhood kids.

In contrast to those results on Importance ratings, married people seemed somewhat more likely than divorced/separated/widowed adults to report actually being surrounded by adults who did some of these actions, specifically, knowing the names of many neighborhood kids, and, with single adults, encouraging school success, expecting young people to respect adults, and expecting parents to set boundaries. Single people were less likely than all other adults to say the adults around them gave young people chances to serve their communities (Table 35).

Overall, on both importance, and the degree to which adults around them are seen as conforming to these actions, the data suggest that people who are currently married or have ever been married have greater degrees of personal and social support for engaging with kids in these ways. However, nearly all the significant differences are relatively modest, less than 10 percentage points. Thus, although there seems to be some relationship between marital status and adult engagement with kids, it is likely not as pervasive or strong as some of the other relationships discussed earlier (e.g., gender, race/ethnicity, parental status).

Interactions among Age, Marital Status, and Parental Status

Given that parental status is positively and moderately related to both age and marital status (correlation coefficients of .31 and .40, respectively, with older and married people more likely to be parents), we also conducted a MANOVA to test for the interaction among age, marital status, and parental status. On the Importance scale, the overall F was significant ($F(25, 1343) = 3.61$, $p < .0001$), and there were significant main effects for age ($F(2, 1343) = 9.50$, $p < .0001$), with adults over age 35 rating the actions more highly important than did 18- to 34-year-olds. Parental status also was significant ($F(1, 1343) = 7.64$, $p < .005$), with parents rating the norms more important. Marital status produced a borderline significant F, with widowed adults rating the actions more important than did single adults ($F(4, 1343) = 2.33$, $p < .05$). There was only one significant, non-spurious interaction effect (small cell sizes caused two other spurious interaction effects): The interaction of age and parental status was significant, with 35- to 54-year-olds who were not parents having the lowest Importance ratings of any age x parental status group ($F(2, 1343) = 4.89$, $p < .007$).

On the Conformity scale, the overall F also was significant ($F(25, 1318) = 3.03$, $p < .0001$), and there were significant main effects for age ($F(2, 1318) = 7.05$, $p < .0009$), with adults age 35 and older more likely to live the actions than 18- to 34-year-olds, and for marital status ($F(4, 1318) = 5.22$, $p < .0004$), with married and widowed adults more likely to live the actions than divorced adults. For both Importance and Conformity, there also was a spurious interaction effect among age, marital status, and parental status, caused by 13 of the 23 cells containing fewer than 20 respondents.

Because the small subsample cell sizes precluded us from definitively exploring interaction effects with the MANOVAs, we also conducted a regression analysis with the Importance and Conformity scales as dependent variables, entering age, marital status, and parental status as independent variables, as well as the products of each with the others as interaction terms. Age and parental status again were significant predictors for the Importance scale, but marital status, which had a marginal significance in the MANOVA, was not significant in the regression. Several interaction terms were significant, however, including the age x parental status relationship already discussed (35- to 54-year-olds who were not parents had the lowest Importance scale scores). Additionally, married people who were also parents rated the actions more important, as did older respondents who were both married and parents. The regression results more fully confirmed the MANOVA results for Conformity, with age and marital status significant, and no interactions significant.

Thus, when it comes to reports of being surrounded by adults who do these actions, the effects of age, marital status, and parental status generally seem to occur separately and do not seem to be confounded with each other. Regarding the importance attributed to these actions, each of the different analysis procedures showed age and parental status as significant, with marital status borderline in one procedure and not significant in the other. Therefore, the main effect results obtained by the different procedures seem essentially the same. The MANOVA showed one of the interactions was significant, and the regressions confirmed that result as well as suggested that two other interactions also were significant, with married parents, and older, married parents rating the actions more important than did other adults.

Exposure to/Contact with Kids

We can imagine that adults who already have regular contact with young people outside their families would rate it highly important to do so. Perhaps they would be motivated by nothing nobler than decreasing the dissonance between how they act and how they say all adults should act; that is, their favorable responses on importance would be the result at least in part of an identity-protection dynamic. Perhaps also, more hopefully, their greater contact with young people, compared to that of other adults, would leave them with a better impression of children and youth, and a genuine belief that other adults could contribute value to young people's lives through more deeply connecting with them. We asked adults whether they saw young people at all on a regular basis, if they saw them but had little personal contact, or if they talked, played,

Table 36. Proportion of Adults Designating Action as "Most Important," by Level of Regular
Contact with Kids (N = 1,399)

	3+ Kids	1–2	See, but no contact	Don't see	F
Top-Rated Actions					
Expect respect for adults	71%	65%	65%	67%	4.09**
Teach respect for cultural differences	78%	80%^{a}	69%^{b}	75%	3.39*
Have meaningful conversations	78%	73%	67%	73%	3.77*
Actions with Majority Support					
Pass down traditions	63%^{a}	53%^{b}	49%^{b}	51%^{b}	6.08**
Know names	59%^{a}	45%^{b}	45%^{b}	43%^{b}	10.49***
Actions with Less than Majority Support					
Provide service opportunities	51%^{a}	50%	36%^{b}	48%	4.52**

a, b = Percentages with different letters are significantly different from each other.
  * = Significant at $p \leq .01$.
 ** = Significant at $p \leq .006$.
*** = Significant at $p \leq .0001$.

or worked with one or two, or three or more young people outside their families on a regular basis.

The level of contact adults have with young people has some impact on how important the actions are considered to be. Adults who talk, play, or work with three or more children or adolescents on a regular basis are more likely than adults with either no exposure to kids, or those who see children and youth around but don't interact with them, to consider the norms overall to be highly important (Importance scale: $F(3, 1343) = 7.09$, $p < .0001$). Adults with regular contact with one or two young people also rate the actions more important than do adults who are exposed to kids but don't interact with them (Table 36). More regular contact with even a small number of young people may promote greater importance being accorded these actions because those adults have come to care about the well-being and success of at least some particular children. Adults who do not have regular interaction with even one or two kids may view these actions more in the abstract, and so rate them less important.

Despite a significant F value, however, high-contact adults were not more likely to report being surrounded by a majority of adults who engaged with young people in these ways (Conformity scale: $F(3, 1318) = 2.95$, $p < .03$).

On the individual actions, adults with the highest level of regular contact with young people (i.e., with three or more young people regularly) thought it more important than *all* other adults did to know the names of many neighborhood kids. In addition, those with high levels of regular contact were more likely than those with limited contact to say it was important to help young people preserve and pass down their religious and ethnic traditions. Those high-contact adults also were more likely than adults with no regular contact with kids to say it was important to help kids improve their communities and have meaningful conversations with young people. Adults who had the highest level of contact with young people also attributed greater importance to young people respecting adults than did those with limited contact or regular contact with only one or two young people. But regular contact with just one or two young people was associated with adults giving greater importance to teaching respect for cultural differences than if they had no regular contact with kids.

In terms of environmental motivation or social pressure for engaging with kids, there were few differences. Adults having regular contact with three or more young people were more likely (40%) than those with either no exposure to kids (28%) or no regular contact with them (26%) to be surrounded by adults who had more than casual conversations with kids ($F(3, 1399) = 6.06$, $p < .0004$). Those high-contact adults also were more likely (38%) than adults having no contact with young people (31%) or whose contact was limited to one or two young people (26%) to tell parents if children did something wrong ($F(3, 1399) = 4.95$, $p < .002$).

Considering all the actions together, regular contact with even one young person is related to rating the actions more important. Those who had regular contact with three young people were barely distinguishable in their Importance ratings from those who had regular contact with just one or two children or youth. High contact does make some difference on whether adults are embedded in a network in which most adults live a couple of the individual actions, but it does not make a pervasive difference in actual engagement.

On the average then, even minimal contact elevates the importance of these actions. Greater contact may add some personal and social motivation to engage with kids, but perhaps not as much as might have been expected. This may suggest that adults who engage with young people in these ways are making highly individualistic choices and not conforming to a strong perceived social norm calling for such engagement. In addition, it may be that they are not sharing significantly with other adults about how much they are engaged with young people, why they do so, the positive feelings they experience from that engagement, and so forth. Those all are communications that might help their personal engagement contribute more considerably to establishing a more widespread expectation or social norm for engagement (we consider these issues more in Chapter 9).

It may appear tautological to say that adults with more contact with young people are more "engaged" with them. Isn't "engaged" just another way of saying they have contact?

Not necessarily. Recall that earlier in this chapter we used two components to define whether Americans were "engaged," "inclined," "receptive," or "uninvolved": how important adults said it was for all adults to act in these ways, and how much they reported they were surrounded by other adults who related to young people in those ways. It is not at all certain that increased contact with young people would necessarily cause adults to think these actions were important. Perhaps the more contact they had with young people, the more some adults would conclude that what young people needed was more *family* contact and influence, not more contact with unrelated adults who cannot substitute for loving family.

It is also not unimaginable that one could have a high degree of contact with young people, as we measured it, and not be surrounded by other adults who also did. For example, what if one's contact was informal and part of one's daily life, and not primarily through volunteering in a program or attending a group meeting? Could one then experience a lot of contact with young people, but not be part of an adult network for whom such levels of contact were the norm? For engagement with young people to be a norm—that is, something one does intentionally and on most of the opportunities that present themselves—both components were necessary. In these senses then, it is predictable but not inevitable that greater self-reported "contact" with kids would be associated with ascribing greater importance to these actions, as well as having more adults around oneself who do those actions. Finally, of course, we did not corroborate adults' self-reports of their own level of regular contact with young people (such as by asking them to name young people, and then asking those young people to name the adults). Therefore, the weaker than expected relations we saw among levels of regular contact and reported engagement of other adults with young people may be partly a function of adults estimating poorly (i.e., underestimating) the levels of "regular" contact adults in their social networks have with young people.

Similarly, perhaps we would have observed greater effects from the "contact with kids" variable had we defined it more precisely. Instead of lumping together the examples of "contact" that we gave ("talk, play, or work with"), we could have separated out those different kinds of contact. We also did not define the time frame, "on a regular basis." For example, it is likely that working with three or more young people on a "regular" basis, for example, encompasses quite different activities than playing with them, or simply talking with them outside the shared frame of reference of a work setting. Combining those very different kinds of relationships may have blurred the importance of the contact variable, as could have the absence of a concrete, shared time frame for defining "on a regular basis." Monthly contact is certainly regular, but arguably not as impactful in a young person's life as weekly contact. These possibilities underscore that connection or engagement with young people is only a first step in building a developmentally attentive relationship. Simply having even regular "contact" with one or two young people makes some difference. But what adults do with and for the young people with whom they have such regular contact, how they actually use the time, as reflected in the specific actions we studied, surely is more important than mere contact.

Nevertheless, although it awaits more precise empirical inquiry than we conducted here, having three children or youth in one's life with whom one has "regular contact" still may be theoretically important. It may represent the difference between adults whose engagement with kids has become part of their routine, versus those whose involvement is idiosyncratic or mostly due to special circumstances. Those circumstances might include the child being the son or daughter of a close friend, or the child living right next door, or happening to share an adult's hobby interest. Instead, adults relating regularly with three or more kids may be applying a broader sense of responsibility for all young people, and feeling more capacity to act on that sense, as reflected by the other adults around them also being involved with young people in the ways we studied.

Education and Income

It is not clear what the possible relation of education and income might be to beliefs and actions regarding engagement with the young. On the one hand, those with higher levels of formal education likely have been more exposed to formal courses, such as psychology and sociology, that help them better understand the science of human development and the role that many adults outside the family can play in positive child and youth development. Thus, they should consider the actions all adults can take to be more important than those actions are rated by adults with less education. On the other hand, those with more years of formal education likely delayed marriage and parenthood longer than those with fewer years of schooling, and being a parent is associated with attributing greater importance to these adult actions. Thus, those with fewer years of education could well consider them more important.

Looking at all the actions together, education made a small difference on ratings for the Importance scale ($F(1, 1352) = 5.12$, $p < .02$) and no difference on the Conformity scale ($F(1, 1326) = 0.22$, $p < .6383$).

On the Importance scale, those with incomes between \$20,000 and \$59,999 per year were more likely than all other adults (i.e., those making less than \$20,000 or \$60,000 or more) to rate the actions overall as highly important ($F(2, 1244) = 7.03$, $p < .0009$). On the Conformity scale, however, income overall made no difference ($F(2, 1221) = 0.39$, $p < .6754$).

Where education and income differences did occur, on both the overall scales and individual actions, they tended toward the *less* educated (no college) and less affluent (under \$60,000 and in some cases under \$20,000 annual income) rating the actions more highly important. For example, this pattern was the case on the Importance ratings for 12 of the actions when comparing those with and without a college education. Some of these differences were not marginally significant either: On six of the 12 actions with significant differences, differences favoring less-educated adults rating the actions more important were at least 10 percentage points (having meaningful conversations, ensuring the well-being of all neighborhood kids, passing down traditions, knowing many neighborhood kids' names, providing them service opportunities, and seeking their opinions). (See Table 37.)

However, the more highly educated adults were more likely actually to be surrounded by adults who expected young people to respect adult authority ($t = 3.26$, $1409df$, Bonferroni corrected $p < .02$). This was the only significant difference between education groups in conformity to individual actions.

Individual differences on the importance of the asset-building actions based on *income* levels also tended to suggest those making less than \$60,000, especially those making less than \$20,000 per year, considered six actions more

Table 37. Proportion of Adults Designating Action as "Most Important," by Level of Education (N = 1,410)

	Noncollege	College	F
Top-Rated Actions			
Expect respect for adults	74%[a]	62%[b]	21.05**
Teach shared values	84%[a]	77%[b]	9.76*
Have meaningful conversations	80%[a]	69%[b]	22.06**
Give financial guidance	78%[a]	71%[b]	10.70**
Actions with Majority Support			
Report positive behavior	70%[a]	61%[b]	12.20*
Ensure well-being of neighborhood kids	69%[a]	58%[b]	20.97**
Report misbehavior	66%[a]	58%[b]	10.95*
Pass down traditions	63%[a]	50%[b]	23.98**
Know names	57%[a]	44%[b]	25.79**
Actions with Less than Majority Support			
Provide service opportunities	54%[a]	42%[b]	20.43**
Seek opinions	58%[a]	38%[b]	55.65**
Give advice	18%[a]	9%[b]	22.51**

a, b = Percentages with different letters are significantly different from each other.
∗ = Significant at $p \leq .02$.
∗∗ = Significant at $p \leq .002$.

important than did more affluent adults. The lowest-income adults, for example, considered it much more important than *all* others for adults to give advice to neighborhood kids and to feel responsible for the well-being of all young people in the neighborhood (Table 38).

On *conformity* to the individual actions, adults making less than $20,000 per year were more likely than all others (and those making $20,000–$59,999 more likely than those making $60,000 or more) to be surrounded by adults who provided opportunities for young people to improve their community (55% lowest

Table 38. Proportion of Adults Designating Action as "Most Important," by Income (N = 1,291)

	More than $60,000/Year	$20,000–$59,999/Year	Less than $20,000/Year	F
Actions with Majority Support				
Ensure well-being of neighborhood kids	57%[b]	63%[b]	70%[a]	6.51*
Report misbehavior	54%[b]	62%[a]	67%[a]	6.03*
Pass down traditions	43%[b]	60%[a]	57%[a]	13.71**
Know names	40%[b]	53%[a]	54%[a]	9.53**
Actions with Less than Majority Support				
Provide service opportunities	40%[b]	49%[a]	55%[a]	6.92*
Give advice	6%[b]	12%[b]	23%[a]	21.82**

a, b = Percentages with different letters are significantly different from each other.
∗ = Significant at $p \leq .002$.
∗∗ = Significant at $p \leq .0001$.

income, 48% middle, 40% upper income, with $F(2, 1291) = 11.57, p < .0001$. The lowest-income adults also were somewhat more likely than all adults to feel responsible for the well-being of all neighborhood kids (70% lowest income, 63% middle, 57% upper income, with $F(2, 1291) = 3.14, p < .04$), and to be surrounded by adults who felt parental discipline without interference was important (22% lowest income, 15% middle, 17% upper, with $F(2, 1291) = 3.28, p < .03$).

The primary differences that occurred on both the overall scale and the individual actions consistently showed Americans with less education and less annual income to be more engaged with young people than were more highly educated and affluent Americans. Why would this be so? It would seem more logical that high levels of education would be associated with greater awareness of the developmental needs of children and adolescents, and greater affluence would be associated with greater ability to provide for those needs, both directly and indirectly.

One reason may be the relationship of education and income to each other, and to other variables. The accompanying sidebar shows that both education and income, examined separately, have independent effects on how important adults feel these actions are. The interactions between education and income appear insignificant. But when education, income, and race are considered together, it appears to be race that has the most significant impact on whether adults consider the actions highly important. None of these variables has a significant impact on whether adults actually are engaged with young people.

Interactions among Education, Income, and Race/Ethnicity

Because education and income are highly correlated with each other, and also with race, we conducted a multiple analysis of variance to examine the interactions among those variables to determine if factors other than education and income operating alone were responsible for these results. For the Importance scale, the MANOVA was only marginally significant ($F(105, 1243) = 1.26, p < .04$), and the only significant effect was a main effect of race ($F(2, 1243) = 9.61, p < .0001$), with African Americans, as we have already discussed, more likely to rate the actions overall as highly important. No other main or interaction effects were observed.

The MANOVA for the Conformity scale, however, was insignificant overall ($F(104, 1320) = 0.94, p < .6466$), just as the separate ANOVAs had been for race, education, and income. Race, education, and income each have a separate impact on whether adults consider the actions important, but none has an impact on the degree to which adults report that the adults around them actually are engaged with young people.

It is worth repeating that some of these results are counterintuitive. After all, national opinion polls have reported that poor people and people with less formal education, along with African Americans and immigrants, are significantly more distrustful of social institutions and other people than are whites, the affluent, and the college-educated (National Opinion Research Center data, cited in Fukuyama, 1999, p. 70). If that is the case, why were African Americans, Hispanics, less affluent, and undereducated adults in this study among the Americans who considered engagement with kids to be most important?

Even though those groups were no more likely actually to conform to those norms in their behavior, they were more likely to give high importance to various ways of relating to children and youth. They agree not only with the high importance of the core nine actions but also that it is highly important for all adults to do such things as pass on cultural traditions to young

people, tell parents what their children are up to, give advice to kids, and feel responsible for
the well-being of the neighborhood's young.

All those qualities reflect the difference in collectivist and individualist societies discussed
earlier. Among people who do not hold a cultural majority status, there may be a greater sense
of interdependence and shared norms with their culturally close nonkin than is characteristic
of other Americans. This may lead many people in nonmajority status to trust those within
their cultural group (although not necessarily in their neighborhood, which could explain why
there were so few differences on conformity to these actions) more than outsiders. This may be
less true of our $20,000–$59,999 income category, which clearly includes some Americans with
above-average incomes. But that income category also includes many lower-income adults, so
for a sizable proportion of that category, these speculations may well be reasonable.

In any case, however, we must repeat that all this speculation concerns beliefs or attitudes.
There are scant differences across these education and income groups in whether they report
being surrounded by adults who relate to kids in these ways.

How Much of Engagement with Young People Could This Study Explain?

There is much we cannot explain about why some adults seem to experience
a stronger personal and social motivation to be involved with young people than
do other groups. We conducted stepwise multiple regression analysis, with the
consistency of motivation score as the dependent variable, and the demographic
subgroups as independent variables, in order to determine the amount of variance in the consistency of motivation for engagement that could be explained
by these variables.

Together, those demographic variables could explain just 12% of the consistency of motivation score. And if we use a 1% contribution as a cutoff level
signifying a potentially *meaningful* contribution to variance, then we can explain
only 11%. Two questions arise: Is this an unusually low proportion of variance
explained, and why couldn't we explain more?

First, this is not an unusual result when using demographic variables alone
as predictors. Eleven percent is about the level of contribution we have found
demographic variables contribute to explaining 6th–12th graders' levels of risk
behavior patterns and thriving indicators (Leffert et al., 1998; Scales, Benson et al.,
2000). Similarly, Blum et al. (2000) reported on the relationship of risk behaviors
and demographics in the National Longitudinal study of Adolescent Health, a
nationally representative survey of 7th–12th graders. They found, controlling
for the well-established relation of gender to adolescent risk behaviors, that
race/ethnicity, income, and family structure explained no more than 10% of the
variance for any of the five risk behaviors studied for middle school students,
and no more than 7% for high school students.

A second explanation is that the consistency of motivation score we calculated was only partly based on adults' reports of their own attitudes or behavior
(the Importance ratings that served as a measure of favorable or unfavorable
attitudes). The score was partly based on adults' reports of *other* people's behaviors (what they perceived the adults they knew doing). As explained earlier, we

adopted this measurement strategy to get a sense of the norms they perceived in their social networks. We did so also in order to lessen the likelihood that adults would respond in socially desirable ways, by saying that of course they personally related to kids in all these positive ways. Our concern with the possibility of biased, socially desirable responses was prompted in part by a finding in our previous study of Colorado adults. Although 75% of those adults thought other adults didn't spend enough time with kids, 75% of adults thought they personally did spent sufficient time (Scales et al., 1998), a kind of "I'm OK, you're not" alignment of self-other perceptions.

Thus, we wanted to use a more indirect measure. We reasoned that because the members of one's everyday social network are most often quite like oneself in important values and aspects of lifestyle (e.g., Berscheid & Walster, 1969; Newcomb, Bukowski, & Bagwell, 1999), an indirect measure would give us a less distorted lens through which to view adults' behavior. We believe we did get responses that were not unduly biased in a positive direction. It also could be, however, that the demographic variables would have had more power to explain adults' *own* reported involvement with young people than they did in explaining our indirect measure (i.e., adults' assessment of the proportion of *other* adults in their lives who are engaged with kids). In our 2002 replication of this national study, we asked about the behavior of the social network, as we did in the current study, but we also will ask about adults' own engagement with young people. That additional data will both clarify the relationship among perceived normative pressures and personal behavior and, we predict, enable us to explain a greater proportion of engagement.

Of course, other variables we did not measure at all also are likely to be sources of a considerable amount of the variance in people's experiencing personal and especially social or environmental motivation for relating to young people in these ways. Other demographic variables might have added some explanatory power, such as adults' general political leanings, or the kind of community where they live (not just the years they've lived there). Another factor could be the pressure people feel to work so many hours that they feel they have little time for relationships outside work and family. Although we noted early in this book that time availability is likely not a reasonable explanation for why most adults seem so unengaged with young people, it is probably a valid explanation for at least some adults' lack of engagement.

But even adding other demographic variables such as those probably would not have contributed too much more explanation, since demographics considered alone, as we noted above, just don't seem to contribute that much in other studies. Other nondemographic variables we did not measure probably contribute even more explanation. These could include adults' consumer patterns and lifestyles, their personal sense of efficacy in engaging "successfully" with young people, the developmental assets they experience in their own lives, or other dimensions of their overall attitude framework about engaging with young people. For example, adults might imagine favorable or unfavorable outcomes if they engaged more with young people. If unfavorable outcomes are imagined, their rating of importance for that action might decline commensurately, much in the same way a person might rationalize that a promotion that was desired but not received really wasn't that important anyway.

Attitude, values, and lifestyle clusters that affect engagement with young people also may exist that we did not measure. For example, market researchers have found that buyers of minivans and sport utility vehicles present different psychological profiles. Minivan buyers seem more likely to be involved in their communities and families, doing more volunteer work, attending religious services more often, and having fewer reservations about being parents, often thinking of their parenting role as extending to "all the kids in the neighborhood" (Bradsher, 2000). The relationship of such lifestyle niches to traditional demographics is often tenuous, and so such data could have added explanatory power.

The Role of Adult's Own Experience of Developmental Assets

Another contributor to whether adults are more or less engaged with young people may be adults' own history and current experience of developmental assets appropriate to various stages of development. For example, adults who experienced plentiful caring connections with adults in their own childhood and adolescence might consider that engagement more important, and be more likely to live in social networks in which it is the norm, than adults who had less of that adult connection when they were young.

That question remains for future research to answer, as well as the question of how adults' current experience of assets affects connection with kids. But it is likely to be an important "missing ingredient" in explaining adult engagement with the young. For example, among young people, our studies have shown that their level of reported experience of developmental assets adds much more than demographics—up to another 33% of the variance—in explaining different risk behavior patterns and thriving outcomes (see Leffert et al., 1998; Scales, Benson, et al., 2000). Adults may also analogously experience developmental assets appropriate to their stage of development that, if we had measured them, also would have added considerably more explanation.

For example, adults experience a variety of relationships, opportunities, values, skills, and self-perceptions that influence their avoidance of risky behavior and their ability to thrive, just as children and adolescents do. Instead of engagement with and bonding to schools, adults need to feel engaged in the work they do and connected to their coworkers and colleagues. They need to feel caring and support, not so much from their own parents anymore, but from their spouse, partner, and children. They need not so much to develop their value system but to be able to make life choices that for the most part are consistent with those values. They need not only to feel a sense of purpose in their lives but to come to terms with their own mortality, and what that eventuality means for how they live today.

Developmentally healthy adults also must be concerned with what Erik Erikson called "generativity," the "concern for establishing and guiding the next generation" (1968, p. 138). There is no comparable database on adults to compare with the database Search Institute has built for adolescents, and is now planning to build for younger children. Thus, much of the discussion we offer here is speculative. And yet it is hardly wild speculation to suggest that adults who possess high levels of developmental strengths or assets appropriate to their stage of life might be more likely also to be more engaged with young people.

Adults whose lives are as developmentally rich and nurturing as the developmental ecologies we hope young people experience may in turn be more likely to be active builders of young people's assets, engaging with them in many of the specific ways we have studied. For example, a study done for the National Commission on Children found that parents who were more nurturing and supportive of their children were happier in their marriages, and were more likely to consider their child's school to be safe, caring, and involving of parents (Voydanoff & Donnelly, 1998). Those findings were correlational, and certainly, happier marriages may also lead to parents' being more nurturing and supportive of their children. But the research we have cited on altruism and on the effect of religious involvement, for example, suggests that nurturing others, giving to others, and serving others, whether children or adults, may also help contribute to greater ego integrity, personal happiness, and overall well-being. A recent small study of 108 mostly white, middle-class adults lends further support to our reasoning. In that study, older adults were indeed found to try to construct their lives, more so than younger adults, to meet needs for generativity, emotional intimacy, and community contribution (Sheldon & Kasser, 2001).

Perceived Self-Efficacy as a Barrier

Another variable that may be at work in distinguishing adults who engage deeply with other people's kids and those who have less engagement is perceived self-efficacy. According to the theory of planned behavior (Azjen, 1988), it should take a certain amount of felt self-efficacy for adults to take relatively complex actions such as teaching young people about respect for cultural differences, guiding them about money management, or discussing values openly with them. We have made much of one potentially important barrier to doing these things: That many adults may feel limited permission, social expectation, approval, or pressure to be so involved with other people's kids.

But a related barrier may be that, regardless of the strength of the norm calling for engagement, many adults do not feel they would be effective in that involvement with young people. In terms of Azjen's theory of planned behavior (1988), which we discussed briefly in Chapter 3, they might not perceive that they have sufficient behavioral control to undertake these actions. They might feel it is acceptable or even expected to get involved with kids in these ways, but lack confidence that they actually can teach kids effectively about respect for cultural differences, or managing money wisely. Perhaps they think they could tell a parent if a child does something wrong, but worry that they don't know how to do so in a way that would keep the parent from feeling angry, hurt, or otherwise upset with them as neighbors. Similarly, they might feel efficacious in the sense that they could do these actions, but not very effective in the sense that, as one person, they might not be able to make much of a difference.

We can only speculate about such possibilities, because we did not measure such aspects of adults' sense of self-efficacy as builders of young people's developmental assets. Nevertheless, the theory of planned behavior reasons that such feelings of efficacy, or lack thereof, do play a role in the degree to which someone is motivated to perform a behavior or take an action. Therefore, there is no reason to think that a measure of self-efficacy regarding engaging with young people would not have meaningfully contributed to the explanation of variance in the variable we call consistency of motivation to be engaged.

In a small, unpublished study we conducted of asset-building initiative leaders in several Colorado communities, for example, we found some potential support for this reasoning about efficacy. Initiative leaders' ratings of how efficacious they thought their community's adults believed themselves to be as asset builders were strongly related to the leaders' assessment of how much asset-building action was going on in their communities (Scales, Shavender, & Halvorson, 1999). It is somewhat of a leap to go from that finding to suggesting that a measure of adults' own perceived self-efficacy as asset builders would be related to their actually taking those actions. Nevertheless, the theoretical research on the relationship between self-efficacy and motivation for behavior (e.g., Azjen, 1988; Bandura, 1997), as well as the data from that small Colorado study, are certainly consistent with such a speculation. Had we measured adults' perceived self-efficacy about positively engaging with young people, it is possible that a not insignificant increase in explaining motivation for engagement could have been achieved.

The foregoing also suggests that, for many adults, the desire and even a sense that it is socially acceptable to get more positively involved with children and adolescents may be there, but their perception may be that their skills for doing so are lacking. For example, many adults may be unsure of how to initiate a conversation about values, when to provide guidance about financial matters, under what circumstances to linger for a deeper conversation with young people and when to just say a brief hello. For those adults, increasing the sense that the environment supports their getting more involved may not be enough to move them to higher levels of behavioral motivation. They also may need a chance to increase their repertoire of *skills* for building relationships with young people, and thereby feel more confident about how they would handle such situations and opportunities. We will consider these issues more in-depth in the final chapter.

Reprise: The Gap between Beliefs and Actions

It is important to reiterate that even among the groups that more significantly thought these ways of engaging with kids were highly important for all adults to do, it was extremely rare for majorities of American adults to say they were surrounded by adults who actually did them. That is, it was not a social norm to be so involved with young people.

For example, women were the most consistently likely to rate it highly important for adults to relate to young people in these ways. Yet in only the two genuine social norms—encouraging young people to take school seriously and expecting young people to respect adults—did a majority of women say that most of the adults around them actually lived the actions. And although parents gave higher ratings of importance to these actions, they were not, in general, more likely than nonparents actually to be surrounded by adults who were engaged with young people (parents *were* more likely specifically to relate to *adolescents* outside their own families than were nonparents). Thus, the actions we studied may represent potential asset-building norms, but that potential has yet to be realized for the great majority of Americans.

The clear conclusion we must draw is that the gap between what most adults think is important when it comes to engaging with kids, and what most adults are reported to do, is both broad and deep. The gap cuts across numerous ways of getting involved with young people, and it runs through all the demographic groups we studied.

Yes, there are some groups who are relatively more likely than others to be surrounded by adults who are engaged with young people. But even those who more often experience what we called "consistent motivation" for engagement with young people don't usually see the great majority of adults around them being involved with kids in the ways most Americans say are highly important for all adults to be involved. Simply put, our *real* relationships with children and adolescents are much more limited and superficial than we adults think they ought to be. If we really want to create a new superordinate norm such as developmental attentiveness to young people, then our data suggest several strands of effort are necessary that together are likely to build the motivational likelihood of most adults relating to young people in more positive, sustained, and meaningful ways.

First, adults must perceive there to be greater permission than they currently do, from parents especially but from others as well, for them to be engaged positively and meaningfully with young people outside their own families. They must feel it is a social expectation that is welcomed and rewarded, not an unusual and risky action that will be greeted with suspicion, disapproval, or anger.

Second, the sense most adults have of their personal capacity to assume a reasonable responsibility for the well-being of young people needs to be strengthened. A key strategy for facilitating that heightened sense of self-efficacy is for adults in a community to more explicitly define what is a reasonable responsibility to expect most adults to assume, as we have begun to do in reporting these findings. If adults knew there were some specific actions most other adults expected them to take in nurturing and guiding children and adolescents in their community, the prospect of relating in deeper and more sustained ways with kids might not seem as daunting as it could without such specificity. Providing adults with simple ideas for connecting with young people that they can use in their everyday lives likely helps increase that sense of efficacy as well.

Most adults already consider many positive ways of engaging with young people to be highly important things to do. There is a place for efforts that communicate how important such relationships are to young people's development. But those campaigns probably will not provide the principal stimuli for moving inclined and receptive adults to becoming engaged, or the uninvolved to becoming more receptive to engagement. Probably more important are adults feeling they have explicit permission from fellow residents to engage with kids, and that they personally are capable of doing so, in part because what "reasonable responsibility" is expected of them has been clearly specified through community-wide dialogue. In the final chapter, we consider strategies for increasing personal and social motivation to engage with young people, and for promoting a better fit between the positive beliefs adults hold about engaging with kids and the actions most adults take every day.

9 Strategies for Increasing Adult Engagement with Other People's Kids

Our study suggests that there is indeed a core group of at least two social norms (encouraging kids to take school seriously and expecting them to respect adults as authority figures) and seven social values that represent a beginning basis for clarifying adults' reasonable responsibility to nurture and guide young people. Doubtless there are other values we did not measure (such as the value of hard work) to which the majority of Americans also would ascribe high importance. But these nine actions represent the beginnings of a definitional foundation for how we would like all adults, not just parents, to relate to children and adolescents.

The caveat, of course, is that our data also show that fewer than 10% of American adults can be said consistently to experience both strongly favorable attitudes (a component of personal motivation to engage) and a perception of collective permission (social motivation) for engaging with young people in these ways. We also have argued that self-efficacy, in the sense of feeling confident in one's ability to engage with young people in socially acceptable ways, may also be a component of personal motivation, so that limited self-efficacy further helps to lessen adult engagement. Even among the actions large majorities of adults think are highly important for them to take in helping guide children and youth, only two are statistically normal, reportedly done by a majority of adults.

As we have discussed, genuine norms aren't just things we think are important. Norms imply social expectations. They also are backed up with social rewards if supported and consequences of some kind if violated. It is only in encouraging kids to take school seriously and do well, and expecting them to respect adults as authority figures, that the majority of adults believe the people around them "walk their talk." Adults who don't encourage young people to take school seriously or who don't expect them to respect adults are in a distinct minority.

But even considering those two actions, adults probably enjoy or incur few social consequences, positive or negative, regarding whether they encourage young people to do well at school or whether they expect respect. There may be too little reward or positive consequence in American communities for adults who do get more deeply engaged with young people in the ways we have studied and, although it is a less desirable motivating factor, too little punishment or negative consequence for their indifference.

In Chapters 1 and 2 especially, we have discussed the research showing that young people derive considerable benefits from relationships with other adults in addition to parents, including extended family as well as adults outside their families. Those relationships seem to contribute toward young people being more emotionally healthy, socially competent, and academically successful, as well as less likely to engage in a variety of risk behavior patterns. Thus, ideally, more Americans can be encouraged to act on the positive beliefs we found they have about engagement with young people in everyday life. To reach that goal, new norms need to be forged and nurtured in most communities so that it becomes socially expected for adults to be involved with other people's kids in positive ways. Thus, a dual challenge confronts us. It is important not only to change what we have called the underlying "true implicit norms" that are antithetical to positive child and adolescent development (e.g., it's the parents' responsibility, not mine; someone else should take care of it). It also is important to promote the transformation of what we have called "social values"— expectations that are widely supported but acted on only by a minority—into genuine normative expectations that are broadly shared and carry meaningful rewards if lived (and, to a lesser extent, meaningful negative consequences if violated). In the rest of this chapter, we discuss some strategies suggested by this study and others' research that might help develop new personal and social motivations for most adults to be engaged with young people.

The Practical Context for Defining Reasonable Responsibility and Changing Expectations

Before discussing strategies, we should consider in greater detail some of the points we have made so far, in order to delineate the practical boundaries within which the strategies we discuss need to operate. To begin with, as we noted in Chapter 1, we are trying to define what the reasonable responsibility might be for most, but not necessarily all, adults to nurture and guide young people. But even within that less universal population of interest, it is not likely that most adults will in fact ever be deeply engaged with numerous young people outside their own families. In practical terms, it is probably not possible to achieve a goal of most adults deeply connecting with kids. But it may be possible to move the engagement needle from its current position, in which only a small minority of adults positively engage with young people outside their families in meaningful and sustained ways. Where would the needle be if all the strategies we discuss here were successfully implemented throughout the nation over a period of several years? Instead of 5% being "engaged," 34% "inclined," and 51% "receptive," as we found adults to be in this 2000 survey, perhaps 20% might be engaged and 50% inclined. That would be a significant increase in caring adult connections with the young, and thus would represent a meaningful improvement in the positive developmental possibilities of children and youth.

But even after such notable improvement, only a minority of adults still would be highly motivated, personally and socially, to consistently be deeply engaged with young people outside their families. The point of drawing out these hypotheticals is not to sound a discouraging note but rather to lay the groundwork for understanding how this situation might change. Connecting with kids—except for parents and those who have a legal caregiving role to play, however temporary (such as teachers and child-care workers)—is a voluntary endeavor. No matter how valuable relationships with unrelated adults might be to young people, adults should not (indeed, cannot) be forced to have such relationships if they don't want them.

Thus, as we discussed earlier, when we speak of "consequences" being necessary for true norms to exist, especially negative ones for "violation" of norms, we refer neither to legal consequences nor to highly public manifestations of disapproval and rejection. Instead, we mean the more subtle forms of social expectations and feedback that help shape most of our relationships, in the family, at work, at play, in the community. In our daily lives, we learn, through uncountable facial expressions and body movements, as well as offhand remarks and secondhand accounts of others' nonverbal and verbal expressions, how people feel about us, the values we stand for, and the actions we take.

Because connecting with other people's kids is a voluntary action, the balance of the consequences available to encourage people to engage with the young should be positive, and the negative consequences should consist of those subtle forms of social disapproval and feedback just described. It is highly unlikely that a diet of sanctions would prompt many adults to engage positively with kids. Even if those negative consequences did "work," what would the developmental influence be like when offered under duress from an adult who felt so socially pressured to do so?

So the predominant "consequences" adults should experience regarding relating to young people are social rewards for doing so, not punishments for failing to do so. Experiencing some subtle negative feedback for not connecting, as described above, undoubtedly will help facilitate positive engagement, because that feedback will activate feelings of guilt that can be motivating. But recall our discussion of guilt and shame in Chapter 3: Too much emphasis on negative consequences for not engaging with kids is likely to produce emotions such as shame or anger, which are not conducive to promoting desired behavior.

There is a final practical point to underscore here before we discuss strategies more specifically. Throughout this book, we have stressed the limited informal, everyday relationships both young people and adults report they have with each other. It is those informal actions adults could take in daily life on which our study focused, and that the strategies we discuss below are meant to increase, through changing the social norms that support engagement with young people.

But the social norms that help shape informal relationships do not exist in a vacuum. They are affected by formal entities such as policies, resources, programs, organizations, advocacy efforts, and community initiatives. Moreover, a developmentally attentive community needs to express its attentiveness through both its formal policies and programmatic structure, and the more informal structure of the relationships its residents have with each other and with young people. Thus, although we do not emphasize them, we discuss some implications that formal entities and efforts have for affecting the normative climate in which adults and young people relate.

What Can Be Done?

In Chapter 8, we discussed two components of adults' consistency of motivation to engage with young people: their personal motivation to do so, and the social motivation that they experience from the adults around them. The remainder of this chapter addresses strategies that might increase adults' personal and social motivation to engage with young people. It should also be reiterated that, although we present those discussions separately, personal and social motivations to connect with young people are intertwined. For example, as more and more neighborhood or community opinion leaders discuss and model such engagement, the chance increases for social expectations or norms that favor engagement to be promoted, thereby theoretically strengthening adults' social motivation to engage more deeply with young people. At the same time, seeing how other adults are engaging with young people, and noting the benefits they derive in terms of pleasure and respect from others, may also influence how favorable adults' attitudes are toward engagement, as well as their assessment of their own capability to be engaged (self-efficacy). Both of those outcomes are theorized to be components of personal motivation. In similar ways, a number of the strategies we discuss here, although mentioned in either the personal or the social motivation discussion, could in effect have a positive impact on both kinds of motivation to engage.

Strategies That May Increase Adults' Personal Motivation to Engage

In Chapter 8, we noted that personal motivation to engage with young people was measured in this study by how favorable adults' attitudes were toward the various engagement actions—that is, how important they rated it for all adults to do those things. The discussion in Chapter 3 also suggests that there are other elements that comprise personal motivation. These might include the balance of costs and benefits adults perceive for getting engaged with kids versus keeping more distant; the extent to which getting engaged reinforces their sense of personal identity; the degree to which they have internalized expectations to get involved, such that being too little involved with young people contributes to feelings of guilt, thereby motivating them to become more involved; and adults' sense of how capable or effective they would be to get involved in the acceptable ways with other people's kids. In the following pages, we address how advocates of greater engagement might contribute to increasing some of these dimensions of personal motivation.

- **In both personal conversations and public communications, challenge assumptions that interfere with adult engagement, especially concerning the actions receiving majority, although not consensus, support in this study.**

Several assumptions adults may hold can represent formidable obstacles to their engagement with young people outside their own families. We have speculated at length on these earlier, including (also see a detailed treatment in Benson, 1997, and Bales, 2001):

- Parents have primary responsibility for how their children are raised. Other adults may be involved because they choose to be (as volunteers) or it's their job (such as teachers). But they are not accountable for young people's well-being.
- People in general have a "live and let live" approach to others, and so in a conflict between the values of tolerance and shared responsibility, the balance usually tilts toward live and let live.
- Young people, particularly teenagers, are viewed as "aliens" from a different generation who can't relate to adults. They don't want to connect with adults, and adults don't want to connect with them.
- Adolescence is, by definition, a turbulent, conflict-ridden time, and engaging in negative, even dangerous behavior is inevitable; it is not something adults, for the most part, can prevent.
- It takes lots of time as well as professional expertise to make a difference for young people. This is partly because the primary way adults currently know how to help young people is to reduce risks or intervene when problems emerge.

Challenging assumptions such as these could begin to reduce some attitudinal barriers to adults getting involved. For example, a community initiative might focus on increasing adult connection with young people by countering the widespread negative images of teenagers. The underlying belief of those community change agents in this case might be as follows. Once adults understood that most teenagers hold the positive values adults wish they did, and that most want to contribute positively to their families, schools, and communities, then more adults would become open to building relationships with young people. (Ironically, asking young people to join in contributing to the community good, such as through service or leadership projects, is so uncommon that young people themselves might not take an adult's first invitations seriously. As one of the respondents to our 2000 survey of Healthy Communities · Healthy Youth initiatives observed, "Even some of our most confident, capable young people seem surprised when we ask them to be involved in community projects. They say things like 'you mean you want me?' ")

Similarly, personal motivation in the sense of favorable attitudes toward engagement might be increased by public communications that addressed the importance of several actions we studied that received majority, but not consensus, support. There are six such positive actions that have less support than the consensus top nine, but that still are considered highly important by majorities of Americans. Communications regarding these could focus on expanding and intensifying the degree to which American adults think these actions are highly important for all adults to do.

Those six actions—telling parents when children do something right, telling them when their kids do something wrong, feeling responsible for the well-being of all neighborhood kids, discussing religious and spiritual beliefs with young people, teaching young people to preserve their cultural and religious traditions, and knowing the names of many neighborhood kids—were considered highly important by 50%–65% of Americans. Although below our arbitrary cutoff point of 70% (+/− 4 percentage points) for defining beliefs that can be considered representative of a consensus, those six actions clearly have widespread support. A communications strategy of noting those study results, reinforcing how important most Americans feel these actions to be, and providing information about why they are important, could over time expand the proportion of adults in a given community whose attitudes toward doing these actions are favorable.

- **Provide convincing information about the benefits—to both individuals and to the community—of adopting this new norm of engagement (and to a lesser extent, subtly note the social consequences of *not* relating to other people's kids in these ways).**

As we have repeatedly observed in this book, a significant barrier to adults' engagement with young people may be the perceived consequences of getting— or not getting—involved. Without clear benefits, too many adults simply conclude, albeit unconsciously, that involvement simply isn't worth the trouble. Many adults likely believe that the negative consequences of getting engaged with other people's kids are greater than the benefits of involvement. Those anticipated consequences might range from discomfort and embarrassment to suffering physical harm or lawsuits. Adults also could simply feel that connecting more with kids would be a waste of time because it wouldn't be effective or even appreciated. In the focus groups we conducted early in this study with adults in Minneapolis, we found that a major barrier to involvement was fear of rejection by young people themselves—a fear that grows out of the assumption that young people don't want to connect with adults.

The negative perceptions adults have of young people also influence adults' perceptions about the consequences of getting involved. Some of the 100 national survey participants who also reacted to the hypothetical situations we developed took it further. When asked about the possible consequences of getting involved in setting boundaries, one adult said adults would hold back out of "fear that those children or those young teens would come and try to wreck their home or something—take the air out of their tires. I know that kids have done things like that."

One way of countering such perceptions, for example, is for change agents to focus more in both their personal and public communications on the kinds of positive consequences that could very well occur if adults did get involved with kids. Public communications could be shaped that remind adults not just that their engagement with young people is good for kids but also of other personal, short-term, and tangible benefits (such as having a new, interesting, caring friend with shared interests, or feeling younger by associating with younger people) that can accrue *to them* from getting involved. Too often, getting involved with young people is "marketed" as something that people should do only because it's a responsibility of adults. Although we believe most adults can define a "reasonable" responsibility for that involvement, it is also the case that most people, adults and the young alike, already have enough things they "have" to do. Some of those positive consequences, generated by our interviewees, included:

- General feelings of goodness and happiness;
- Feelings of self-satisfaction and accomplishment;
- Intrinsic reward of helping those in need;
- Improved relationships among adults and young people through teaching kids responsibility;
- Giving young people ideas to think about;
- Helping young people make the right choices or do the right things; and
- Showing young people that others care about them.

The underlying message of such communications to adults might be summed up as "get involved with kids because you'll feel good." It is not an appeal to self-interest in the sense that adults are told that helping kids can help themselves, such as in pointing out that healthy and productive young people are increasingly needed to support our aging population. Research shows that such "naked" self-interest appeals, no less than appeals to pure altruism, or the use of "shocking" statistics, rarely are effective (Bales, 2001; Ad Council, 2001). But it does suggest that there are positive personal outcomes from getting involved with kids, not only positive benefits to the young people. For example, it was reported in a qualitative study of informal mentoring relationships in Scotland that part of the positive feelings adults get from being a mentor is that the experience helps them make better sense of the issues they face as adults, providing a form of social capital for those adult mentors (Philip & Hendry, 2000). In so describing adult engagement, it may help modify the frame of reference for adult engagement from a more purely altruistic one that is easier to ignore, to one that has more personal salience.

So adult engagement with kids might be stimulated in part by casting it as something one chooses to do, not only because it's good for kids or the community, but because of the "selfish" benefits to oneself. For example, being friends with a young person can afford adults the opportunities to play games that are fun and that many adults no longer get the chance to play. Being friends with a young person gives adults additional chances to give and receive affection and caring, qualities that enhance the joy of living and that few would argue most people have enough of. Friendships with young people also can keep adults in touch with trends in music, language, and fashion, and expose them to fresh ways of seeing the world. Not all of this is always comfortable, of course, but it provides a source of renewal and vitality to adults. It is doubtful that most adults think about those positive benefits of engaging with young people, but perhaps public communications that prompted these thoughts would be effective.

Of course, adult worries of their tires being slashed if they get too involved with young people represent a concrete and threatening perception that will be difficult to counter with messages about how good one can feel from relationships with young people. That is why the ways in which such messages about positive benefits are communicated may be at least as important as the messages themselves.

For example, Elster (1989) argued that the emotional aspects of norms (the feelings of guilt over possible violation of a norm) are even more important than their rational aspects (e.g., obeying is in one's self-interest). If emotions are so important, then a clue is offered for changing true underlying norms that limit positive engagement with kids, and for turning the social values that support getting engaged with young people into genuine social expectations.

Getting people to *feel* differently about their capacity and responsibility for nurturing children and youth may be even more important than getting them to *think* differently. Therefore, rational appeals or arguments may be relatively less successful than indirect approaches that elicit more emotional responses. Such communications might make better use of visual and auditory images, which, because they are processed by more primitive areas of the brain, more fully capture the essence of such messages. For example, a technique market researchers often use to get beneath the cognitive surface to deeper emotions is to have research participants gather pictures they associate with a product, and then discuss what the pictures mean to them. In one application of this technique, marketers discovered that Nestlé Crunch lovers brought in pictures evoking *time*, everything from pictures of clocks to photos from long-ago eras in their own lives. The researchers concluded that the candy bar was "less a workday pick-me-up than a time machine back to childhood" (Pink, 1998, p. 224). The company was then able to use simple cues about time to get readers/viewers more instantly and viscerally engaged in the message about their product.

- **Around the core or "consensus" nine actions, reinforce adults' sense of themselves as already being people who care for and support children and adolescents in these ways.**

Around the nine core actions, the problem is not caring, in the abstract, but acting. Shorr (1999) argued, for example, that it is "futile" for campaigns promoting child well-being simply to exhort Americans that "they should care more about children" (p. 1). Rather, she recommended that messages for action be built around issues already prominent on the radar screens of voters and taxpayers. In terms of encouraging adult engagement with young people, the nine actions receiving 70% or greater support as being highly important for all adults to do would seem to qualify as issues already high on priority, if not exactly prominent. Communications that focus on those nine consensus actions might best concentrate on helping people move from supportive beliefs to action. Public information campaigns to promote adult engagement with young people might be more effective with a focus on using these data to reinforce the positive images people have of themselves, the "kind of person we think you already are" phenomenon we discussed in Chapter 3. Rather than criticizing adults, explicitly or implicitly, for how little they appear to be engaged with children and youth, it might be more effective to communicate, both directly and more nonverbally and imagistically that:

1. (You) (adults) already are caring and supportive (as reflected in the overwhelming importance they give to the nine consensus ways of all adults engaging with kids);
2. (You) (they) *want* to do more for kids;
3. Most (of your friends) (other adults) feel the same way (i.e., there is considerable social support for adults to act on their sense that getting involved with kids is highly important);
4. (You) (others) have the time and know-how to get involved—little things can make a big difference (see more detailed discussion later);
5. Good things will happen if (you) (adults) get engaged with other people's kids; and
6. Bad things will happen if (you) (adults) don't.

As referenced earlier, research has shown that both children and adults are more likely to take actions to protect the environment if they are told they already care about the environment and do those things. This approach is more effective than scolding, ridiculing, or being made to feel guilty about not being sufficiently environment-centered (Allen, 1982; Miller et al., 1975). If that is the way to increase people's involvement in environmental protection, why should it not also be an effective public communication strategy for increasing adults' positive involvement with children and adolescents? Indeed, the Ad Council (2001) concluded that messages meant to shock or "humiliate" adults into acting on behalf of children were notably *ineffective*.

At least for the core nine actions, the great majority of American adults do think it is highly important for all adults to play a role in helping socialize, nurture, and guide children and youth other than their own. For the most part, they do not positively act on those beliefs, but the belief that all adults should nurture and guide young people—the favorable attitude toward engagement— is present to a high degree. Communications that reinforced this positive sense adults have of themselves as caring and responsible might be highly effective in encouraging greater action by reinforcing positive personal identity through messages to get involved with kids because that is the kind of person they already are.

- **Segment messages to different groups of people based on their existing "attitude context" and the self-identity or lifestyle functions those attitudes serve, especially when communicating about actions beyond the core nine.**

DeBono (1987) shed light on the complexity of attitude change in his report of two studies involving a total of 160 university students enrolled in introductory psychology courses. Although such a sample is not representative of the adult population, there is no reason to suspect the students' educational or cognitive status contributed to highly unique findings. Students for whom attitudes served mainly as vehicles for social acceptance changed their attitudes most when messages referred to the social appropriateness or inappropriateness of their attitudes. In contrast, students whose attitudes served more to express their own values changed those attitudes most when confronted with messages that said a different attitude would better communicate and be in better alignment with the underlying values the individual held. If the messages didn't explicitly address the functional role of the attitude the researchers were trying to change—whether social acceptance or personal integrity—then the messages were relatively less successful as persuasive communication. The focus of the messages had to be correctly varied to match students' differing attitude orientations. No single message worked for all students.

In the 1990s and beyond, marketers began to adopt a strategy that moved away from "mass market" advertising. In the 21st century so far, truly "mass" marketing is increasingly rare. Instead, appeals now are customized to increasingly narrow consumer niches; one executive, commenting more than a decade ago at the cusp of this sea change in public communications strategies, called the emerging trend "pleasing one person at a time" (Eder, 1990).

The principles of social marketing found to be effective in promoting behavior change around a variety of consumer health habits go beyond efforts to change social norms. That broader social marketing approach includes messages about (1) the desired behavior (the product, e.g., in our case, specific ways of adults getting positively engaged with children and adolescents), (2) changing perceptions about the price (costs and benefits of getting more involved with kids), (3) reframing the place (creating or pointing out settings or situations where the desired actions can most easily be lived, i.e., with more benefits and less cost), and (4) broad promotion (not just advertising, but intentionally sparked word-of-mouth campaigns, contests, etc.). All these are carefully tailored to specific groups of people who share similar beliefs, values, or lifestyles (Andreasen, 1995).

For example, as we discussed in the preceding chapters, some Americans report more positive attitudes toward and/or more social network support for being engaged with young people than do other adults. Women, African Americans and Hispanics, parents, older adults, and those making annual incomes of less than $60,000 were some of those who considered engagement with kids more important, and adults age 55 and older were more likely to be in social networks where actual engagement was the norm. Might it make sense for public communications around engagement with young people to be somewhat different when targeted at those adults than for men, whites, younger adults, nonparents, and wealthier Americans? The former certainly do not need to be convinced of the importance of such engagement, but perhaps helped to act on those positive beliefs more consistently.

Once beyond the core nine actions that 70% or more of adults thought were highly important (what we have defined as a consensus), different groups of Americans are likely to hold differing values, and experience differing expectations, about relating with children and adolescents. To the extent communities are interested in encouraging more adults to take those actions with less consensus, differing appeals to differing groups of people, or "segmenting the market" may be called for, based on coherence among various norms and attitudes and the functions they play in reinforcing people's self-conceptions. It is unlikely that most communities will have the resources to undertake massive communications campaigns tailored to numerous target group segments. But a community's particular makeup and culture may point to some segmentation along the lines we suggest here as one of the more essential strategies for promoting changes in norms about adult engagement with young people in that community.

Segmenting Messages by the Contribution of Behavior to Regulatory Fit

Higgins (2000) described how, when we evaluate the success of our decisions, the process is not simply a function of the costs and benefits accrued in reaching ends or outcomes. The "value" we accord our decisions, in retrospect, is a function also of how well the means we use to pursue our goals "fits" our overall style of approaching the world.

Fundamentally, some people have a regulatory focus that emphasizes their security and safety; others, a style that emphasizes growth and nurturance. According to regulatory focus theory, people with a nurturant focus are concerned more with gaining or losing positive outcomes. Put another way, they don't want to lose opportunities for growth or for the fulfillment of aspirations. On the other hand, those with a regulatory focus on security tend to be more concerned with avoiding negative outcomes than with gaining positive ones. They are concerned more with protection and prevention.

Our data do not shed light on such clear distinctions in regulatory focus among different demographic groups of Americans. Nor can we say with confidence that a nurturant-focused person is more likely than a security-focused person to be engaged with kids. Both could be involved, but for different reasons.

Further, one can imagine that most people could employ different regulatory foci as needed, much as research has shown that people do not use a single moral reasoning framework (e.g., caring versus justice), but rather are generally capable of employing either. The fact that women, for example, are significantly more involved with young people than men may be a function both of deeply held senses of responsibility in a society that socializes females to assume such roles, as well as a greater orientation among many women to personal growth. Similarly, those who attend religious services more often are relatively more involved with young people than less frequent attendees. But this could be a function of opportunity (congregations are one of the few places where intergenerational activities regularly occur) and sense of duty (helping to nurture and teach the young being one's responsibility according to one's faith), as much as being due to their being more focused on nurturance.

But the issue of decisions fitting with one's regulatory style is an important one, and our recommendation is that communications need to focus on *both* classes of reasons for being engaged with young people. The more data are available about the balance among the residents of a community or other "targets" of communication in how they prioritize growth versus security, the more judgment can be made about the possible relative strength of one kind of appeal over another. But it is likely that most communities need both kinds. The concepts of regulatory fit theory are simply another way of looking at how norm change might be facilitated, depending on what knowledge is available about the predominant regulatory style people in a target neighborhood or community may use in different situations.

> The implication for promoting deeper relationships among adults and the young is similar to the earlier implications around message segmentation based on "lifestyles." Messages about doing particular actions will appeal more to people when those messages "fit" better with their regulatory style. Consequently, people will give a higher value to those actions and be more motivated to do more of those actions.
>
> People who are security focused, for example, may not be much affected by public communications that stress all the wonderful, positive feelings that can be experienced when adults were more deeply engaged with other people's kids. They might, however, engage in exactly the same relationship actions if the appeal were to their sense of duty and responsibility, with the implication that others would think badly of them if they failed to meet that responsibility. Similarly, messages about how building assets in young people today can help reduce violent behavior, or help provide for their own future in their old age, might be more effective for security-focused individuals.
>
> Likewise, people with a growth or nurturant focus might be less concerned with the potential reaction of parents or with other fears, since they inherently are people more inclined to take reasonable risks. They might, in contrast, be most responsive to communications that focused on how becoming more involved with young people can bring them both a personal satisfaction they cannot get in other ways and experiences that are unique to those who have such intergenerational relationships.

- **Show adults how even little ways of engaging with kids can make a big difference.**

As we have noted before, reminding people of the positive feelings or other benefits of getting involved with young people is only part of the change equation; the other is helping them overcome barriers to action. It may be even more effective to focus on removing barriers to action, since a majority of Americans thought most of the actions we studied were highly important for all adults to do. For example, focus groups we conducted in Minneapolis found that the message that "little things can make a big difference" was the most effective in getting people to act on their values. Focus groups in Kansas found that the best way to communicate the benefits of engagement was to ask adults to think about someone who had been there for them when they were children. Based on the concreteness and personal meaningfulness of that recollection, subsequent media communications encouraged adults to play that same role for a young person today.

A key strategy may be to identify those actions for which there is broad support (and thus, less risk, such as doing the nine actions rated most highly important in this study), and then encourage people to do something small that connects to a particular priority action or actions. A study of young adults' civic involvement by the Ad Council and MTV: Music Television reinforces the wisdom of encouraging small steps. The study tested a variety of messages designed to encourage young adults to get involved in their community. The message that resonated most strongly with the focus group participants was: "By getting involved in a social cause, I know that I can't change the world, but I might be able to make a small difference in someone else's life" (Ad Council and MTV: Music Television, 2000). Similarly, Search Institute focus groups with parents in low-income communities found that the most effective message was that "some small things can make a big difference in the lives of kids" (Saito, Sullivan, & Hintz, 2000). Focus group participants in Kansas did not want to feel like they were making an enormous commitment, and once they grasped that a public communications campaign was asking adults to do small and simple things with kids, most people understood and liked the concept (*Children's Health Campaign research summary report*, 2000).

People also need reminders to do and/or keep on doing the simple things they already are doing or disposed to doing. "Foot in the door" techniques (encouraging people to take a small action that makes their taking a bigger action more likely) and the use of prompts to remind people to do things they already are motivated and attitudinally receptive to doing are examples. These have been shown to be two effective tools for social marketing campaigns aimed at fostering sustainable behavior (McKenzie-Mohr, 2000).

Hundreds of examples of people finding solutions and ways of putting these recommendations into practice, in both formal and informal ways, have emerged from Search Institute's Healthy Communities Healthy Youth initiative. As thousands of students returned to school in the fall of 2000 in St. Louis Park, Minnesota, for example, hundreds of residents chose to greet students as they entered their schools. The goal of the effort was simply to have each student addressed by name by at least one community adult.

Such stories remind people that change is possible and that they can make a difference, even if only for one person. And when such gestures—though small—become a way of life and a social expectation, these molecules of "developmental attentiveness" begin to reshape norms and expectations and create a web of connection that is crucial for the healthy development of young people, of adults, and of the community.

Why does reminding adults that even a little action can make a big difference seem to be an effective approach both for mobilizing people and for helping to change broader norms about involvement? Perhaps such a strategy strengthens personal motivation for engagement in two ways. First, taking even a small action to connect with kids may reinforce an adult's sense of positive identity, as being a caring, giving, responsible person who does morally good things.

Second, it may bolster one's sense of self-efficacy. One reason we have mentioned that adults do not get involved with children and teenagers is that they have become overwhelmed by the headlines about the problems and challenges young people face. A Coalition for America's Children focus group report concluded: "Currently the public views only negative and sensational stories about children. This causes them to feel overwhelmed by the problems and apathetic about the issues that seem too difficult to solve. They need to see some success stories so that they understand that there are solutions for problems that appear to be overwhelming" (Bostrom, 1999, p. 27). In the face of that reality, the Ad Council's focus groups and public opinion research concluded that two of the most effective approaches for motivating Americans to act on behalf of children were (1) reminding them how much their help could make a difference, and

(2) highlighting success stories that contribute some hope to what otherwise is a sense that children's problems seem so overwhelming (Ad Council, 2001). By showing how getting engaged with kids in small ways can help, adults may be encouraged to feel effective as nurturers and guiders of young people, and that enhanced self-efficacy should further increase their personal motivation to engage.

Moreover, reminding people that small actions can make a big difference helps to address what has been called the "bystander problem" (Darley & Latane, 1968). Theories of collective action suggest that when individual involvement is seen as contributing a great deal to the collective good, then optimism about others' potential involvement motivates one's own involvement (Oliver, 1984). In contrast, as more people get involved in solving a problem, then individual involvement is perceived to make little difference to the collective good ("diminishing marginal returns"). As groups expand, optimism that others will take care of things then can lead to increasing numbers of individuals taking a "free ride" on those other persons' labors.

For example, Darley and Latane (1968) put volunteers into staged situations and recorded their reactions. One situation was coming to the aid of someone who was experiencing a (staged) epileptic seizure, and another staged event was whether one would report smoke coming from underneath a door. The researchers found that the great majority of people would do the right thing (i.e., help, report the fire) if they were alone. However, if they thought even four other people heard or observed what they did, that is, optimistically thought others would take care of it, only a minority would help. Reminding people how much their individual effort matters, however small that effort might be, could help counter this social phenomenon.

In addition to those possible impacts on personal motivation, each seemingly small engagement of an adult with young people also can contribute to changing people's perceptions of the overall normative climate, and thus affect social motivation to engage. For example, Gladwell (2000) argued that the best way to understand the "emergence of fashion trends, the ebb and flow of crime waves . . . the transformation of unknown books into bestsellers . . . is to think of them as epidemics" (p. 7). An idea becomes contagious, such that small changes can contribute to large effects, and sudden transformations can occur when a critical mass is reached that Gladwell called the "tipping point."

Picker's (1997) model society simulation (discussed in more detail below) neatly illustrates what Gladwell (2000) meant about tipping points and sudden transformations. Changes occurring at the margins, incremental changes, can have sudden, dramatic effects when they occur at about the same time. As an example, Gladwell pointed to New York City's above-average reduction in crime in the 1990s being related to several smaller but not insignificant contextual changes (e.g., the crack trade declining, the police getting better at enforcement, the drug-using population aging). In fund-raising, Cialdini and Schroeder (1976) also showed that a campaign adding a single phrase, "Even a penny will help," to standard donation requests resulted in significantly more donations to the American Cancer Society.

Strategies That May Increase Adults' Social Motivation to Engage

We have seen that a variety of strategies may help to increase personal motivation to engage with young people. But what can neighborhoods and communities do to strengthen adults' social motivation, their sense that there is an expectation among friends, neighbors, and fellow residents, a collective permission, for adults being engaged with young people outside their own families?

- **Define a shared vision of reasonable responsibility—a social contract—for most adults to participate in the nurture and guidance of young people.**

The foundation for overcoming the gap between belief and action reported in this study is for community members to unite behind a shared vision for adult engagement with young people. One of the most important findings of our study is that even though group differences can be cited, there is profound national consensus across differences of race, religion, education, and income, among other variables, on how adults ought to engage in the lives of children and youth.

This finding suggests the clear possibility in many if not most communities of making explicit a *shared vision* that appears already to be implicit for the reasonable responsibility most adults could assume for engagement in the lives of children and adolescents. Perhaps the top nine actions that 70% or more of Americans thought were highly important in our study might serve as a beginning framework for shaping that vision. By defining what neighborhood and/or community residents consider adults' reasonable responsibilities for helping nurture and guide young people, this shared vision can promote social trust and collective efficacy (see Figure 6).

In essence, developing this shared vision of reasonable responsibility might take the form of a social contract, an "adult charter" that would articulate for all residents the behavior toward children and adolescents that adults expect of most adults. This charter would be analogous to the call others have issued for communities to develop "youth charters" that describe for youth the behavior adults expect of youth (Damon & Gregory, 1997; Damon, 1995; Ianni, 1989). In this case, however, an adult charter would describe for adults the behavior toward children and youth that other adults expect of them. The community dialogue might begin around defining shared values and a common vision of the community's aspirations for young people. But an essential part of this vision building would be to make explicit the expected roles of adults in the positive development of young people. Such a shared vision, operationalized through an adult charter, could serve as a representation of collective permission, formally encouraging positive engagement among adults and young people at a neighborhood level or within a school, congregation, or other organizations. It could be a step in building a social contract for engagement across a whole town or city, a state, or, eventually, the nation.

This study focuses on creating a culture and communities in which young people are surrounded by a sustained network of caring adults who are committed to asset building. These adults choose to know, name, support, affirm, acknowledge, guide, teach, and include children and adolescents as part of their daily lives. Over time, hundreds or thousands of small gestures of support and care are woven into a pattern, a way of life, in a community. They create a web of connection crucial for healthy development.

This process is complex. At the core, however, we suggest that the mobilization of these webs of connection can be understood as follows:

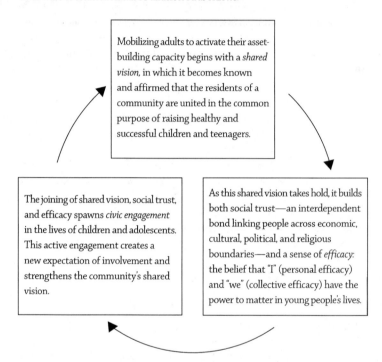

Mobilizing adults to activate their asset-building capacity begins with a *shared vision,* in which it becomes known and affirmed that the residents of a community are united in the common purpose of raising healthy and successful children and teenagers.

The joining of shared vision, social trust, and efficacy spawns *civic engagement* in the lives of children and adolescents. This active engagement creates a new expectation of involvement and strengthens the community's shared vision.

As this shared vision takes hold, it builds both social trust—an interdependent bond linking people across economic, cultural, political, and religious boundaries—and a sense of *efficacy:* the belief that "I" (personal efficacy) and "we" (collective efficacy) have the power to matter in young people's lives.

Figure 6. Mobilizing a Web of Connections

- **Encourage parents explicitly to give other adults permission to get involved in the lives of their children and youth.**

We have argued in this book that positive child and adolescent development might be advanced if most adults, not only parents and those with legally defined, temporary caregiving roles such as teachers and child-care workers, perceived a reasonable responsibility for themselves in helping to nurture and guide young people. But it is not only those "other" adults who can be the focus of intentional norm-changing efforts. Parents may be the primary audience for efforts to change the normative climate in which adults and young people relate. For example, one commentator (Cizek, 2000) argued that, in issues such as education, the persistent use of phrases such as "for the children" to motivate adult action obscures the possibility that education reform might not be "about" the children at all, but rather about their parents as the primary consumers.

Similarly, "norm reform" regarding adults engaging more with other people's kids may be about parents as much as it is about those other adults.

Parents are a critical part of developing in a neighborhood or community a widespread sense of collective permission for adults to get involved with young people. We have already alluded to this recommendation a number of times. We found that parents are more likely than other adults to believe it is highly important for all adults, not just parents, to be engaged with kids. Therefore, there is an important role parents could play in changing the context in which adults decide whether to get involved with other people's children and adolescents: Actually make explicit their permission, which is implicit in their high levels of support reported in our study, for neighbors or other adults to do so. Parents might name the kinds of issues or circumstances concerning which they not only would not mind but also would actually welcome neighborly support and involvement with their children. Among adults who already have a favorable attitude toward getting involved with children and youth (personal motivation), such parental permission might well increase a sense of greater social expectation and motivation for getting involved.

A neighborhood undertaking both individual efforts, such as parents giving more permission and neighbors asking for it, and collective efforts, such as development of an adult charter, would have a comprehensive set of forces working to create a new norm of expected engagement with young people. Many if not most communities could benefit from such adult sharing among themselves of their expectations for engaging with young people, in order to build trust among parents and other adults. Increased trust should in turn facilitate parent and other adult comfort in adults having deeper relationships with children and adolescents outside their own families.

Parents can be encouraged to make it clearer to the adults around them how they expect those adults to be involved with their children. If they particularly value the way a neighbor volunteers or supports charities financially, for example, they might tell that neighbor they would like it if the neighbor would occasionally talk with their son or daughter about volunteering and donating to help others. They might let an even larger group of neighbors know that they as parents would appreciate it if they were told when the neighbors see their child doing not just wrong things, but also when neighbors "catch" their child doing something good.

Parents can take other steps that could increase the collective permission adults feel to engage with kids, and so strengthen their social motivation for doing so:

- Reflect on how they interact with their children's friends as well as other kids in the neighborhood. Are parents themselves engaging with other people's kids in all the positive ways they can?
- Tell the parents of their children's friends about the positive things *their* children do, as well as report misbehavior.
- Encourage their children to seek other adults' guidance on important decisions such as jobs and careers, education, faith, and financial choices.

- Ask their children about their adult friends to make sure they are comfortable with how they treat the children, the values of those adults, and how they spend time together with the children.
- Take advantage of or create opportunities to get to know neighbors, such as block parties. Plan events in ways that include and connect all generations.
- Mentor and encourage younger parents to do the same kinds of things.

The effect of parents giving permission, in effect "asking" neighbors to be more involved with their children, could be profound, because our data and that of other studies show that most Americans already want to be involved with young people and know it is important. The effect could be akin to that reported in studies of volunteerism, in which by far the strongest predictor of volunteering was whether someone was simply asked to volunteer (America's Promise—The Alliance for Youth, 2001; Ad Council and MTV: Music Television, 2000). For example, a Gallup poll for America's Promise found that, of the adults who were asked in the preceding year to volunteer to help young people, 72% currently reported volunteering, compared to only 26% who volunteered without being asked (America's Promise, 2001). Unfortunately, just one in four American adults reported being asked, reflecting a tremendous number of missed opportunities for stimulating more adult engagement with young people in formal programs. If parents more explicitly asked their neighbors to get involved with their kids, it is not unreasonable to imagine a comparable *informal, everyday engagement effect* being stimulated.

This is more explicit parental permission giving than is customary in contemporary American society. Our data suggest that many of the concerns adults have about getting negative reactions to their involvement with young people may prove unfounded. On the contrary, such involvement may well generate support and encouragement from other adults, especially from parents. Publicizing this fact could lead to greater adult engagement. But parents' proactively and explicitly giving permission for that involvement will go even further to stimulate adults' relationships with kids outside their own families.

As we have discussed, Bostrom (1999) and others have concluded that a key reason for adult inaction on behalf of young people is the belief that it is parents' responsibility to nurture and guide their children. If so, then what more powerful counterpoint to that existing norm can be made than for parents themselves to communicate what their responses showed in our study, namely, that they themselves don't believe it is only parents who have a responsibility to nurture the young?

In our study, parents gave significantly greater importance to nearly a dozen ways in which all adults should be involved with young people. More so than other adults, parents thought all adults should be having meaningful conversations in which adults and young people really get to know each other, interactions through which adults can discuss both religious and secular shared values, pass on cultural traditions, and help young people with their decisions.

Parents believe more than do nonparents that all adults should know the names of many young people in the neighborhood, show young people the importance of volunteering and donating money to help others, and tell parents when their children do something wrong. And parents with children 18 or younger also felt it more important for all adults to feel responsible to help ensure the well-being of all neighborhood kids.

These are not superficial actions for adults to take, and significantly greater proportions of adults are unlikely to take them than do so today unless there is a sweeping change in the normative context. That sweeping change could result in part from parents assuming a more intentional responsibility to be explicit about their desire for other adults to more get engaged with their kids. Parents with older, perhaps grown children, are not left out of these suggestions either. Our data suggest they can offer unique contributions as leaders, mentors, and guides for other parents in their neighborhoods and the organizations to which they belong in order to encourage both informal and formal adult roles in nurturing the next generation.

Neighborhood adults also can *ask* parents for permission in ways that are not artificial and "out of the blue" but similarly opportunistic. A neighbor who has essentially a "wave and say hi" relationship with a nine-year-old girl might one day ask the pro forma "how are you doing?" and experience the girl responding honestly, seeming upset. The adult may then be uncomfortable pursuing the reasons why the girl is upset.

Could that neighbor not tell the girl's parents, say he or she wanted to help more but was concerned with whether the parents would approve of her or his getting involved, and ask how the parents would want the neighbor to respond, if at all? That kind of communication from unrelated adults also acknowledges appropriate boundaries in their involvement with young people outside their families. Parents may need to invite other adults more explicitly to be part of their children's lives, but those adults also must show that they understand their supplemental role. In the time they spend with young people, the activities they do together, the conversations they enjoy, there is ample room for unrelated adults to help young people develop positively without having the relationship become worrisome for parents. Parents may be uneasy, not because they fear an adult's improper behavior, but because an unrelated adult may, ironically, so succeed in connecting with their child that he or she may seem to be almost playing a pseudoparental role instead of an adult friend role. In terms of perceptions, that relationship may then be seen as too much of a good thing. Unrelated adults need to demonstrate to parents in a variety of ways that they appreciate and respect these more subtle forms of parents' primary responsibility for their children.

One adult-adult interaction at a time, one adult-child or adult-youth relationship at a time, such communications among parents and other adults in the neighborhood could informally help define reasonable responsibilities for most adults to assume. The ultimate result would be to create a new norm of expected involvement with children and adolescents outside of one's own family. That new social expectation would strengthen adults' social motivation to

get involved with other people's kids, and thereby expand the intentional positive socialization role played by multiple adults in different domains of young
people's lives.

- **Rebuild neighborhood trust and civic engagement.**

Putnam (2000) concluded that neighborhood ties at the beginning of the
21st century were probably only half as strong as they had been 50 years earlier,
especially in the arena of the informal social connections that are at the heart
of the study we report in this book. He wrote that "although neighborhoods at
the end of the twentieth century were occasionally mobilized for political purposes, organized social life at the neighborhood level—street carnivals, amateur
theatricals, picnics, potlucks, dances, and the like—was much more vibrant in
the first half of the twentieth century than in its waning years" (p. 107). There
probably is no more clichéd recommendation one can make than to suggest that
we need more trust in our neighborhoods and engagement in our communities.
And probably nothing that requires more of what Lisbeth Schorr (1997) called
a "new synthesis" in which social and community problems are addressed by
"combining physical and economic development with service and education
reform, and all of these with a commitment to building community institutions
and social networks" (p. 319).

Increasing neighborhood trust will not alone solve deep-rooted problems
of poverty, discrimination, and resource depletion in many American communities, nor is it likely that increasing neighborhood trust by itself will dramatically
increase adults' engagement with kids outside their own families. But even the
simpler among our recommendations, such as parents making more explicit
to neighbors their permission for other adults to get involved with their kids,
requires that parents *know* their neighbors at some threshold level.

People will not be comfortable connecting with neighborhood kids—or letting neighbors connect with *their* kids—unless there is a basic level of trust and
relationship among neighbors. The McKnight Foundation survey showing that
most Americans don't even know the names of most of their nearest neighbors is
a stark reminder that adults have considerable work to do to build greater community among themselves, much less among themselves and all the children and
adolescents in their neighborhoods. The Social Capital Community Benchmark
Survey (Saguaro Seminar, 2001) showing that half of Americans don't trust their
neighbors also lends credibility to this reasoning. Many parents do not know or
trust their neighbors enough to want them to report their children's behavior, or
give them decision-making guidance. Similarly, many adults may not know the
children and adolescents in their neighborhoods, or their parents, well enough
to take a chance on getting involved.

Likewise, our research suggests the same conclusion, that is at once both
banal and telling: Americans need to get to know their neighbors more. All these
studies suggest that both a broader, more public community dialogue about
adults' reasonable responsibility for kids would be useful (a social contract)
and that increased informal conversation and relationship among neighbors
(a neighborhood compact) would have value. Both the broader and the more

informal neighborly dialogue would involve adults explicitly naming the ways they want each other to engage positively with all children and youth in the neighborhood and/or community.

Many communities obviously need a long-term, widespread, "new synthesis" of large-scale physical, financial, and human capital. But seemingly small actions can, over time, in virtually any community or neighborhood, contribute to large differences in the social trust and collective efficacy people experience. One could simply make a point of knocking on all neighbors' doors and introducing oneself. Or one could choose to wave hello more, take walks around the neighborhood, and say hello and talk with fellow residents. Even in economically distressed communities, in many of which residents' senses of safety and trust are so badly compromised it is difficult to imagine anyone randomly knocking on doors and saying hello, there are strengths on which to build formal and informal actions that can increase connectedness and trust.

For example, a Search Institute study of two economically distressed neighborhoods suggested, as a foundation, "finding and supporting neighborhood leaders who are willing and able to be catalysts for neighborhood-based activities—whether focused on recreation, seasonal or holiday celebration, neighborhood improvement efforts, or parent-to-parent support. These events can serve as the sparks that, given enough time and fuel, may well become the warming fire that re-creates community and turns neighbors from strangers to supporters" (Saito et al., 2000).

For a smaller group of people, another naturally occurring event may be quite important as well. In Chapter 8, we reported that a moderately strong discriminator between people who are relatively more and less engaged with kids is how frequently they participate in neighborhood or community meetings. The power of such political participation should not be underestimated. For example, in a study of Baltimore neighborhoods, it was reported that poor pregnancy outcomes were *twice as likely* in neighborhoods with limited political organization as they were even in neighborhoods with high crime rates (Caughy et al., 1999).

Neighborhood and community meetings are by definition about common concerns. Those concerns might start as apparent special interests that most then realize could affect them too (e.g., soil erosion from too many homes built on too steep a hill, or too many liquor stores opening up in the immediate area). They also can start out as immediately obvious shared issues, such as a recent increase in the neighborhood crime rate or the need for a stop sign to keep cars from speeding through a neighborhood.

Our study showed that people who often or even just sometimes participated in neighborhood or community meetings were more likely than those who didn't to say getting involved with kids was highly important. They also were more likely actually to be engaged with kids than people who never participated in such meetings.

People who participate in neighborhood or community meetings are, of course, more socially or politically active than those who do not attend. Because they tend to attract and be gathering places for people who are already engaged in strengthening community, these meetings also provide a powerful forum for addressing common interests in taking steps to enhance the healthy development of young people.

It is likely, however, that this accounts for only part of the association between meeting participation and being engaged with children and youth. As we discussed in Chapter 8, attending these kinds of meetings also increases the chances of getting to know one's neighbors and fellow residents, and of thereby promoting greater social trust among residents. With greater trust and knowledge of how one's neighbors think and what their values are in general, may come a greater willingness to engage with *their* kids and a greater belief in one's ability to do so. Thus, these potential outcomes can boost individual and collective efficacy, as well as social motivation for engagement. There may also be an accompanying greater willingness to have neighbors engage with one's own children, even without having a specific conversation about any of the actions we studied. Association with neighbors in these ways also may create a support network that helps provide adults with the emotional and social resources they need to be engaged with young people.

Of course, only about 20% of a neighborhood's residents are likely to be involved in neighborhood meetings in the course of a year (Saguaro Seminar, 2001). So those positive dynamics that build trust apply most directly among that group of residents. But those active in neighborhood meetings also set examples for other residents and carry the messages and benefits of meeting participation into their other informal relationships with neighbors. That is, their impact is multiplied well beyond their fellow residents who also attend meetings. Thus, even a small increase in the degree to which residents participate in neighborhood meetings may yield a significant improvement in perceived neighborhood trust.

In their work on strengthening neighborhoods, Kretzmann and McKnight (1993) also noted that there are many formal and informal associations at the neighborhood level that are overlooked in community organizing efforts. These groups are the "vehicles through which citizens in the U.S. assemble to solve problems or to share common interests and activities" (p. 6). While these groups may have a specific focus such as cultural heritage, religious activity, recreation, or other purposes, they also can be tapped to play a vital role in connecting individuals to each other and uniting neighbors around a common vision and strategy. For example, change agents could work within these existing groups to spread the message about the value of getting involved with young people. In that way, they could "seed" clusters of adults who already are connected to each other by virtue of the association's specific interests. Those already-connected adults might not yet have considered action to increase adults' engagement with young people to be a high priority of their group.

The caveat to this line of reasoning, however, is that not all associations have the same impact on community engagement. For example, Marcello and Perrucci (2000) conducted a secondary analysis of more than 1,000 adults who participated in three kinds of small groups: secular (e.g., Parents Without Partners), religious (e.g., Bible study groups), or mixed secular and religious (e.g., Alcoholics Anonymous). Although higher education did have an association with greater civic engagement, other individual demographic characteristics were less important than the type of group and what went on in the group.

Members of mixed groups (i.e., that had both secular and religious purposes) were more likely to be involved in civic affairs, and members of religious groups least so. The researchers speculated that most of the religious group members' volunteer energies were devoted to activities connected to their own congregations, not with the broader community. In addition, the more formal the structure a group had, the more members were involved in the community. The explanation the researchers offered was that the more formal structure allows for greater opportunities for modeling and learning group-process skills that are then transferred to settings outside the small group. Overall, the study's findings caused the researchers to issue a "general warning against assuming that all civic engagement has the same social impact" (p. 73).

Nevertheless, both increased informal connection among neighbors, and greater resident participation in formal public dialogues seem necessary to heighten the degree of trust Americans experiences in their neighborhoods and communities. Based on the work of Sampson et al. (1997) on collective efficacy, that increased trust should also be related to subsequently improved collective efficacy in actually making the neighborhood the kind of place residents wish it to be. In other words, improved articulation of an agenda for, and action geared toward, building a healthy community for young people could well lead to improved collective action on other community issues as well, from environmental conditions to racial reconciliation. In fact, it was reported in the Social Capital Community Benchmark Survey (Saguaro Seminar, 2001), which included both a national sample and surveys in three dozen communities, that such social connectedness was a much stronger predictor of perceived quality of community life and of personal happiness than were the community's educational and income levels.

- Leaders of efforts such as Healthy Communities · Healthy Youth initiatives could add a neighborhood mobilization strategy in addition to community-wide efforts, in which the goal would be to nurture the development of small numbers of engaged adults who know and coordinate intensively—cluster—with each other in local neighborhoods. This could produce areas where there are relatively higher concentrations of adults engaging with young people, that is, where such engagement actually becomes more the norm.

Florini (1996) wrote that norms operate in a noisy, competitive cultural environment. Those that become most successfully entrenched (Gladwell [2000] referred to the "stickiness" of an idea) are those that can achieve sufficient public attention, are coherent with enough existing norms, and are supported by fortunate environmental circumstances and contingencies. Prominence is most often achieved through the efforts of "norm entrepreneurs," individuals and organizations who are role models. Sometimes, but not always, they may be people with high levels of prestige, who set out to change behaviors, and whose prestige and/or persuasiveness encourage others to emulate them.

In the language of the developmental assets framework, such people have been called "asset champions" (Benson, 1997). Among the messages those change agents might champion is the desirability of adults' defining a reasonable responsibility for most adults in nurturing and guiding young people, perhaps beginning with the nine actions our study showed had consensus support. In his journalistic treatment, Gladwell (2000) took it further and divided norm entrepreneurs or asset champions into three kinds of people, all of whom he considered necessary for an idea to break through the social "tipping point" and suddenly spread as in a viral epidemic. "Connectors" are those whose acquaintances or weak ties occur in countless social worlds, who seem literally to be connected with everyone. "Mavens" are the data banks of an idea, fad, or trend, those who have both the knowledge and the innate need to spread it. "Salespeople" are just that—people who quickly can gain the trust of others, overcome objections to commitment, and infuse others with their energy for the idea. The presence of all three types of people can contribute to the rapid diffusion and acceptance of new ideas. People are needed who bring each kind of orientation to the goal of reaching a working consensus on values and establishing norms to increase positive engagement among adults and young people.

Effective social marketing efforts that seek to change people's behavior often have a two-step strategy. Those campaigns "first communicate their messages to key individuals in communities called opinion leaders, and these individuals then pass on this information to target customers through word of mouth" (Andreasen, 1995, p. 158). In some cases, these individuals serve as silent sources of information by simply being role models of the desired behavior. Once opinion leaders have been inspired to action, they often spread the key messages (e.g., "it's reasonable to expect most adults to get more connected with young people") by word of mouth through their relationships and networks. The interpersonal network of an opinion leader enables him or her "to serve as a social model whose innovative behavior is imitated by many other members of the system" (Rogers, 1995, p. 27). Thus, opinion leaders' buy-in, advocacy, and modeling can play a powerful role in convincing other community members to engage with young people. Also playing a role in the "convincing" of others to engage with the young is the social learning that can occur as adults see those asset champions or opinion leaders being rewarded for their efforts. In the current normative climate, where engagement is not highly rewarded, those "rewards" may be quite modest, such as the perception that engaged adults seem highly respected by other adults or seem to be having a lot of fun when engaging with young people. But some adults are likely to emulate those actions, even in a low-reward environment, if for no other reason than to experience similar rewards. As more and more positive benefits of engaging with young people become visible, the likelihood should increase of adults engaging with young people so that they too can experience those rewards.

Examples of Intentional Norm-Changing Campaigns in U.S. Communities

In Portland, Oregon, the asset-building initiative, spearheaded by the Multnomah County Commission on Children, Families, and Community, is called "Take the Time." It features a media campaign based on the approach we discussed earlier in this chapter, of telling people they already are the kinds of people who engage with kids and already are the "experts" they often erroneously assume are the only adults who can be positive nonfamily influences in the lives of young people. The spots feature messages such as "You ARE a teacher" and "You ARE a philosopher," with images of adults and young people doing everyday activities together such as flying a kite, taking a walk, or playing soccer. The initiative offers minigrants and "coaches" to numerous groups to help them build the promotion of developmental assets and deeper relationships among adults and kids into their systems and informal networks.

Similarly, the Kansas Health Foundation launched a statewide initiative under the theme Community Development for Healthy Kids. The core goal is increasing positive connections among adults and young people, through spreading the recognition that even small actions adults take can make big differences in the lives of the young. A basic communications strategy is their "Take a second. Make a difference" campaign. Spots feature people telling stories about adults who were there for them when they were growing up, and in a personal way making the connection between those relationships, the simple things those adults did, and positive child and adolescent development. The stories connect listeners, viewers, and readers with their own pasts by reminding them of the adults who were there for them, and then the spots ask, "Whose story are *you* in?" The media campaign is buttressed by community organizing and technical assistance work being done with leaders in 17 Kansas communities to expand community-wide efforts to get adults more engaged with young people.

Another outgrowth of our national study is that the Kansas Health Foundation enabled Search Institute to begin in 2001 a deeper study of how normative change may occur. In a statewide telephone poll, Kansas adults who already are leaders of asset-building initiatives in their communities—asset champions—are being presented with an "action vignette" similar to the hypothetical situations we explored in this study. Their reactions to the vignette are helping researchers learn how adults identify and respond to realistic situations in which decisions have to be made about getting involved with young people. Those asset champions also respond to a forced-choice survey of the kind we used in the national study, and have a chance to describe in a more open-ended manner their vision of how their community can become a healthier place for child and adolescent development. In addition, researchers are studying several Kansas communities more in depth, with surveys of "typical" residents, interviews, focus groups, and analysis of critical events occurring in those communities. Interviews with asset champions explore the many pathways different people have taken as they came to be so highly engaged. The interviews also are used to investigate how people have moved from believing in the importance of engaging with young people, to materially changing the intentionality of how they relate with young people in their personal lives. The goal of that case study research is to understand how the social norms adults hold regarding caring for and nurturing young people may shift over time as communities launch initiatives to build their formal and informal developmental attentiveness to kids.

Together, the results of the Kansas statewide and case study research on normative change, and what is learned from the campaigns in Portland and elsewhere that focus on getting adults more involved with young people will extend the lessons already gleaned from this study. The national study was repeated in 2002 and we hope to do the same in subsequent years between 2004 and 2010, so that a nationally representative perspective may be gained on how American adults' relationships with kids, and the social expectations for that engagement, may change over the first decade of the 21st century.

In essence, this strategy might involve focusing first on engaging a small core of individuals in a given neighborhood in shaping a shared vision of reasonable responsibility for kids, building trust, and making a positive difference.

Over time, cluster by cluster, neighborhood by neighborhood, this circle of influence and shared vision can expand throughout the community. Of course, this strategy alone, like all the others we discuss, is not likely to bring about significant social change. But as part of an intentional effort in which multiple strategies like those discussed in this book are implemented, considerable movement in personal and social motivation to engage with young people might be achieved.

Finally, in the process of identifying and cultivating champions and opinion leaders for changing how adults engage with young people, it is important to consider young people themselves as prime candidates to play significant roles. Young people have been instrumental in numerous social movements, from environmentalism to antismoking campaigns and the promotion of civil rights. The possibility of adults being led by young people into more active involvement is heightened by findings from another national survey of 1,000 adults. Twice as many adults (63%) said they would agree to being a volunteer in a youth program if a youth or friend asked them to volunteer as said they would volunteer if recruited through a TV program or advertisement (Youth involvement, 1998).

- **Provide more widespread information about how "more and more adults" are getting involved with children and youth.**

Picker (1997) used computer simulation techniques to create "model" societies and study social change. From those experiments, he derived a triumvirate of conditions that social movements ultimately may affect and that seem to favor norms becoming "robust," in Legro's (1997) sense of the word (i.e., specific, enduring, and broadly accepted). Picker called this set of conditions the norm's "basin of attraction" (p. 1227). Those conditions include (1) how much neighbors are connected, (2) the amount of information neighbors have when making decisions, and (3) the rules neighbors use to assess and evaluate that information.

"Norm cascades" or the rapid transition from old to new norms, can occur when norm entrepreneurs undertake the "seeding of norm clusters" under the favorable conditions Picker described (p. 1228). In simpler terms, things can change dramatically and suddenly under these conditions: A concentrated group of people doing and saying the same things (e.g., the importance of getting engaged with kids) can offer to others around them a lot of information about what they're doing and help or support for those other adults to make the same commitment. In Picker's simulations, choices had to be made as to which "move" to make in a model society "game" (i.e., which "norm" to adopt), to show how rapidly new "norms" can take hold when those conditions are satisfied (see the accompanying sidebar for more details).

Picker's game theory exercise was artificial and laden with assumptions. Nevertheless, the results yielded clear implications for changing norms affecting adults' engagement with other people's kids. Picker recommended a strategy of small-scale interventions for "seeding norm clusters so as to perturb an existing equilibrium" (p. 1286). In this way, clusters of asset champions in close proximity to each other in neighborhood and community could establish the conditions suitable for the existing norm of relative uninvolvement of adults to change. But in addition, Picker's research suggested the importance of getting larger and larger numbers of people to perceive the benefits of living the new norm (getting engaged with kids), as well as the consequences of failing to adopt the new norms (which we have argued is a far less preferable strategy).

Computer Simulations of Norm Change

Several concepts are integral to understanding Picker's model society simulations. First, each individual is surrounded by what Picker called a "payoff neighborhood," the immediately local area (perhaps the immediate blocks of a neighborhood) that determines what benefits or consequences are gained from choosing what to do in given situations. The payoff neighborhood basically is a measure of "how linked we are with our neighbors" (p. 1239). Schweigert (1999) described an interpersonal unit analogous to a payoff neighborhood as a "moralnet," a band of up to several dozen people who serve as an individual's primary normative reference group because of their personal knowledge of each other and their patterns of cooperation. This might be, for example, a geographic block in a neighborhood, a religious congregation, or a military unit.

Second, each payoff neighborhood is surrounded by a larger "information neighborhood," which is the arena in which people can observe the results of their own and others' decisions. We use that information to maintain or modify how we act in subsequent similar situations. If we see neighbors deriving benefits from doing something we have not yet done, we are more likely to emulate them the next time we get a chance. For example, even people who don't buy lottery tickets are more likely to do so if the family three houses down the block just won big. This information neighborhood might be only slightly larger than the payoff neighborhood. But it could be as big as a school district, a television viewing area, or the Internet. Any communications entity through which adults can see the impact on others of engaging with kids can constitute an information neighborhood for those adults. In certain special circumstances, the payoff and information neighborhoods may be identical. Consider the casts of the TV "reality" show *Survivor*. The benefits and consequences of their decisions, and their ability to get information about the results of their own and others' decisions, *all* occur within their own "tribes," or within the single tribe left when enough people have been voted out of the game.

By running numerous simulations using different assumptions, Picker demonstrated that a bigger payoff neighborhood increases the odds of the rest of the "society" adopting the desirable norm. But even a small cluster of people doing the "target" behavior or living by the new norm can be quite influential, depending on how much the benefits of the new norm improve over the benefits of the existing norm. For example, if acting in accordance with the new norm is assumed to have a 65% higher benefit than the old norm (or if violating the new norm now has a 65% greater chance of being punished), only *six individuals* holding that new norm and *clustered together*, eventually will result in 100% of the remaining 10,195 "players" making the choice of acting in accordance with the new norm.

So the Picker models are not directly translatable into neat equations that help identify which actions reflecting adults' reasonable responsibility for kids might have the greatest chance of being rapidly emulated. But those models do show that larger payoff neighborhoods—larger clusters of individuals near each other who do engage with young people—might stimulate social change if people imagined even a modest increase in benefits (15%–33%) from engaging with kids. In addition, as social learning theory would predict, the bigger the information neighborhood (the more individuals a person can observe reaping the results—positive or negative—of their choices), the more likely the new norm—engaging with young people—is to be widely adopted. So, the more people there are who sense rewards for getting engaged with young people, the more likely they too will expand their engagement.

Finally, if people emulate the norm choice that gives the "highest average" payoff rather than the single highest payoff, even relatively modest benefit improvements of the new norm over the old will eventually lead to wide adoption of the new norm. For example, getting an award for longtime volunteer work for kids might be the highest, most visible and tangible single payoff for engagement. But fewer people are likely to be successfully encouraged to volunteer for years than are likely to be successfully encouraged to smile at young people every day. In the end, that easier action, repeated frequently, may even have a higher average payoff, since everyone can feel good about smiling at young people or accrue respect from others for their relationships with kids, and only a handful can get awards for formal volunteer service.

- **Include in public communications messages the rewards of engaging with young people in order to socially "fit in."**

Picker's "model society" simulations suggest another important implication: The more adults become aware that the great majority of other adults think it is highly important to get engaged with kids, and the more they perceive that other adults are in fact getting engaged with young people (through the cluster seeding approach described above, for example), the more additional adults are likely to begin changing their behavior too, and increase their involvement with the young. The underlying message of communicating this fact might be phrased as "get involved with kids so that you'll fit in."

It may seem that this recommendation conflicts with our earlier discussion of some theories of collective action. That research has found that the more people perceive others are taking responsibility for action, the less likely they are to take that responsibility themselves, when it comes to assuming leadership in organizations. But the difference lies in the nature of the two examples (organizational leadership versus informal engagement with young people). If only a relatively small number of leaders are needed (such as committee members or officers for an organization), and the costs of involvement are seen as far greater than the rewards, most individuals are likely to think that others will "take care of it." But what if getting engaged with kids informally, in one's daily life, is increasingly seen as what "everybody" is doing, not just a relatively small number of leaders? In that case, the risks of getting involved obviously must not be great (or else the majority of people would not be involved). Under those conditions, perceptions about the relative reward of fitting in socially could be an important element in heightening social motivation to engage with kids.

The motivation to change behavior that is stimulated by concern about *negative* consequences for being indifferent to children and youth, or appearing to be so by lack of positive engagement with them, is not as effective as messages about positive benefits or about how to overcome barriers to action. But messages about negative consequences might operate most strongly among the people with whom an adult has his or her closest relationships (in other words, Picker's payoff neighborhood). Messages about the *positive* benefits that can accrue to adults who do engage with young people can also work at this level, but are probably the *only* effective message at a mass communication (i.e., information neighborhood) level.

The dynamics may work as follows. People's concern about others' approval of them matters only as a function of their networks of relationships. In this sense, a stranger may have little or no power or influence over what happens to a person. In that case, that stranger's negative evaluation will typically have little motivational value in getting the other adult to change his or her behavior. On the contrary, the stranger's disapproval is likely to stimulate a defensive or dismissive reaction. However, negative evaluations from people whom we care about and interact with often can be quite motivating. On the other hand, *positive* reasons for doing something, even if offered by strangers to us, may encourage us to listen with little defensiveness and greater openness to their message.

Thus, *personal* communications about getting more engaged with kids can effectively address either the positive consequences of involvement or, occasionally, even the negative consequences of indifference. *Public* communications, such as print or electronic media campaigns, seem most likely to move people toward greater engagement with young people if they focus on positive messages about the targeted adults, and about the benefit—to adults and to young people—of that greater engagement with other people's kids.

Further Ideas for Making It Normal for Most Adults to Be Engaged with Kids

- To ensure sustainability, weave ideas for adults getting more engaged with kids into policies, practices, programs, and ongoing communications of organizations and systems. Use these to model, remind, inform, encourage, support, and reward adult engagement.
- Help already-engaged adults become more intentional about their involvement. Help them inspire, support, and reward engagement among people who are already "concerned" or "aware" of how important such connections are, but who are not consistently engaged with kids.
- Encourage local schools and religious congregations to offer and publicize more opportunities for adults and kids to get connected. Schools and congregations are generally safe places where it may be easier for many adults to get more engaged with kids outside their own families, and easier for parents to encourage such engagement.
- Tell positive stories about young people to the media and to each other so that attitudes about young people become more positive.
- Share the results of this study with other adults to demonstrate that Americans already have a shared set of values and expectations around how adults should connect with young people. Use the study to start discussions about the realities of the local community, and how adults can make it an even better place for kids.
- Better still, conduct the study in your community—people who may dismiss the results of a "national" study as not relevant in their community are hard-pressed to disregard the voices of the adults in their own area.
- Ask young people in the community what they think of these results, or the results of doing this study locally: Do the findings ring true in their experience? Ask them how they would like most adults to relate to them.
- Find ways to make positive consequences of interacting with young people more visible and tangible through public recognition of those who are engaged. For example, a statewide initiative to build child and youth assets in Indiana is planning to encourage young people to "catch" caring adults "in the act" of being involved with kids, and present them with a special pin that recognizes them as an adult who really cares about young people.
- Encourage people from all cultures to think about their own communities when they were growing up—who was there for them, what was good and what was bad about how they interacted with adults. Help them think about what's the same and different for kids today, and about the kinds of adult connections they want kids today to have.

Collective Actions to Change Norms Regarding Engagement

The challenge for boosting the developmental attentiveness of a community is twofold. One is to increase the individual, informal, everyday actions most adults can take in relationship with young people. That has been the focus of this book. Another step is to expand the proportion of adults contributing energy to formal efforts that help create a community climate more conducive to adult engagement with the young. The influence of each level should not be confused with the numbers of adults involved in each, however. It is possible that, one day, the majority of adults in a community might engage more deeply with kids on an everyday level, whereas it is highly unlikely that a majority of adults would be involved in formal collective actions. But each level of action may be needed for truly systemic change to occur. For example, small numbers of influential policy makers can stimulate broad change through laws, regulations, and policies that formally alter how adults relate with the young (e.g., funding of widespread after-school opportunities and instituting leave policies allowing employees to volunteer for kids during work hours). They also can use their access to the "bully pulpit" to be voices of advocacy for greater adult engagement with young people.

But those policy makers also are influenced by broader social norms and by their sense of the pulse of the people who elect and appoint them. Moreover, laws and policies that allow, encourage, and facilitate adult connections with the young only contribute to creating a favorable environment for positive personal action. They do not make personal action happen. Thus, the more long-term foundation for *sustained* change in social norms may occur at the grassroots level, in individual residents and in neighborhoods, as people change how they relate with the young in their everyday lives. In the long run, "mobilizing" communities to do more with and for kids might be most effective when it entails at least as much emphasis on people making changes in their personal, daily behavior as on getting people to commit time in formal volunteering, helping leaders advocate for kids, or trying to change public policies. In that way, both the formal and informal infrastructures of a community are energized, activating more sources of personal and social motivation for adult engagement with the young than either infrastructure by itself could achieve.

Conclusion: Developing New Personal and Social Motivations to Engage with Kids

Together, the approaches we have described in this chapter may encourage new personal and social motivations for engagement with young people to be created throughout American culture. In that new climate, both the social expectations and the rewards of engaging positively with children and youth, as well as the personal and collective benefits of doing so (and to a lesser extent, the costs of being uninvolved), would have three key features: They would be clearly apparent, consistently experienced, and substantively meaningful. As we have discussed throughout this book, developing social expectations that are clearly apparent starts with communities defining their vision for their young people and the reasonable responsibility of most adults, not only parents, in helping that vision become a reality. For many communities, the nine actions we found 70% or more of American adults think are highly important can serve as the beginning of that definition of reasonable responsibility. In some communities, other actions that received majority, but not consensus, support in our national sample perhaps also might reflect local consensus.

Once communities have clearly defined their vision, adults need to create an environment in which they experience consistency of expectations and rewards around engaging with kids. Such consistency helps young people experience healthy development, and there is no reason to think such environmental redundancy is not also important for adults. When all the social systems of which an adult is a member reinforce the same expectations and provide similar rewards for engaging with young people (and more subtle negative consequences for uninvolvement), then engagement with young people may become the norm across all the pieces of an adult's life, not just with one group of friends, neighbors, or coworkers.

Increasing the rewards and supports adults receive for getting more positively involved with children and adolescents is important and is a strategy that is certainly more conceptually and philosophically in keeping with the developmental assets approach of focusing on strengths and positives. To the extent that the great majority of Americans believe in the importance of the nine core ways to engage with the young, adults who live up to and reinforce the norms for involvement implied by those actions might reasonably expect other adults to approve of their engagement.

Ideally, engaging with young people is something most adults would do because they perceive it to be a positive, personally rewarding thing to do, and not simply an obligation. Selznick (2000) puts it this way: "An ethic of responsibility calls for understanding as well as conformity; it looks to ideals as well as obligations . . . we expect [responsibility] to be based on an inner sense of rightness" (p. 57). A person who is responsible in this sense feels a "unity of self and other," a morality in which "the well-being of another becomes a condition of one's own satisfaction and self-esteem" (p. 60).

And yet, the reality of the social order is that doing what one is expected to do rarely brings special recognition, whereas failing to do the right thing often does bring special, usually undesired, recognition and attention (Elster, 1989). Therefore, those who would increase adults' engagement with young people might place a greater emphasis on making clear to adults what the rewards and benefits are of their connecting more deeply with young people. Some adults will undoubtedly be moved to engagement more by the presence of social costs of not getting positively involved with other people's kids (e.g., social disapproval, embarrassment, rejection by others, isolation). But direct appeals to people to behave so as to avoid the negative are not likely to be effective for the majority of adults.

In contrast it is likely that efforts to inform, encourage, and reward residents for positive engagement, rather than punish them for its absence, will more subtly help create a new norm of engagement. If a new norm of engagement with young people becomes strong and evident, then a natural pressure to conform to the norm will also develop. Concomitantly, people will be more likely to experience a natural discomfort if they do not live up to the social expectation that so many other adults seem to be living up to.

In our study, we found and have discussed some of the differences among groups of Americans in how normatively important adults think it is to engage positively with other people's children, and how much they say they are surrounded by other adults who act that way. But the differences, although real, tend to be less compelling than the similarity in views and behaviors across a broad spectrum of Americans. It is this consensus that provides the basis for our conclusion that it may be possible to effect a change in the prevailing norms governing how adults relate to and with other people's kids.

In commenting on the landmark breaking of the human genetic code in 2000, President Bill Clinton noted that "all human beings, regardless of race, are 99.9 percent the same . . . The most important fact of life on this earth is our common humanity" (Wade, 2000, p. D1). Our genetic heritage reveals that we human beings, despite the surface differences among us, are more alike than different. So too have we found that Americans are more alike than different in how important we consider various ways of nurturing young people to be, and how likely it is that we are surrounded by adults who actually are engaged with young people in these ways.

We seem more united than has been realized around our collective sense that it is important to play a more active and involved role in helping socialize, nurture, and guide children and adolescents outside our own families. For all the cliché status that "it takes a village" has assumed, and despite all the criticism leveled against this overused phrase, Americans do believe that it takes more than parents to nurture the next generation. They believe it takes a community of shared values, social trust and cohesion, meaningful communication, and involvement of most adults around the socialization of the young about values, decisions, and cultural diversity.

In these findings, we reflect a great American tradition. Alexis de Tocqueville visited the United States nearly 175 years ago and observed that Americans had a unique quality of needing simultaneously to be independent and self-reliant, as well as to be connected with others and helpful to those in need. Even while honoring our tradition of privacy and independence in the form of acknowledging primary parental responsibility for nurturing and guiding their children, our results show that Americans recognize a reasonable responsibility for most adults also to play roles in the positive development of the next generations.

Our study has provided the most comprehensive, nationally representative look yet at adults' beliefs and experiences that define the social expectations shaping their relationships with young people. It has helped illuminate how the continuing American ambivalence between the individual and the group, between private benefit and common good, between independence and interdependence, between tolerance and responsibility, is played out in how most adults contribute to the socialization of children and youth. What has been learned in this study might eventually contribute to new social expectations about connecting deeply with young people. On that new day, there would be more explicit rewards for adults getting more deeply engaged, and adults who are uninvolved would feel more sharply what they are missing. It might then become normal for most adults to experience personal motivation and widespread collective permission, social expectation, and approval for nurturing not only their own children and youth, but also other people's kids, for the betterment of us all.

Appendix A: Study Methodology

Telephone polling was chosen as the most feasible way of obtaining a high response rate from a nationally representative sample of U.S. adults. In designing the telephone survey instruments (both a forced-choice poll and a more in-depth interview based on responses to hypothetical scenarios or situations), we used a multipath approach in which we identified norms discussed in peer-reviewed journal articles, books, and reports; created original forced-choice survey questions and open-ended, hypothetical scenarios/situations in which key norms might operate; consulted with experts in child and adolescent development, and in positive youth development programming; pretested individual questions and drafts of the survey instruments with staff; and solicited feedback from positive youth development practitioners.

Literature Review

We generated a list of potential social norms regarding adult relationships with young people by conducting an extensive literature search. The key terms used to define the preliminary search were based on the definitions of the word "norm" and "value" that were obtained from social science dictionaries. Key words used in this search included standards, expectations, rules, boundaries, shared beliefs, shared values, social influence, customs, and habits. The initial definitions of "norm" we used from the disciplines of social science, sociology, and anthropology are presented at the end of this appendix.

Few explicit statements of norms concerning relating to children and youth were yielded from an extensive literature search. There were very few scientific studies about norms relating to children and youth from which to collect possible questions or statements describing specific norms adults may hold. Observations about adult behavior toward children and adolescents certainly are present in the literature, but most of this content is advocacy-oriented or rhetorical, not empirical studies.

Staff Rating of Initial Items

"Norm statements" were essentially actions that adults might take to relate to the young that might or might not be found to be social expectations with consequences. These statements or actions gathered from the literature search were compiled into a draft forced-choice survey instrument. Staff members were asked to rate 131 items on their clarity and priority for use in the study. Responses were used to eliminate many items and revise others.

Focus Groups

On many occasions, the Research Subcommittee discussed the need to more deeply integrate knowledge and perspectives from individuals in communities of color to help inform the rating instrument. The great majority of those who had reacted to draft items were non-Hispanic whites. Thus, to create a comprehensive list of adult engagement actions that reflected issues of relevance to adults from a variety of cultural and ethnic backgrounds, the subcommittee conducted five focus groups in three cities (Minneapolis, Minnesota, Bridgeport, Connecticut, and Denver, Colorado) to identify norm, value, and belief statements. The goals of the focus groups were to:

1. Learn about the values, beliefs, and norms held by African American, Latino (largely Mexican American), Asian (Cambodian), and Native American (nations/tribes represented included Red Lake, White Earth, Sistan Wahpeton, and La Cordelous in Minnesota, and San Idelfonsa, Pueblo, Mescarlero Apache, Pawnee, and Turtle Mountain Chippewa in Denver) adults about their relationships with children and adolescents;
2. Be respectful of cultural diversity; and
3. Truly integrate this input into the shaping of the research, and not use it merely as an add-on.

Indigenous cultural partners were identified in each site and contracted to form and help run the focus groups. The partners were responsible for recruiting individuals for the focus groups, identifying a location for the focus group, helping to facilitate the focus groups (together with a Search Institute staff person), and supplying refreshments at the focus groups. After the first focus groups were held with individuals from each of the four communities of color, audiotapes of the focus group discussions were translated and transcribed. Findings from the focus groups were analyzed, and participants from each focus group were invited to review and verify their accuracy. This second focus group was led by the partner facilitator in each site. A stipend of $30 was given to each participant who attended the series of two focus groups.

A total of 56 participants took part in the focus groups. Like all focus groups, these were not representative of all our targeted audiences' opinions. This was due not only to self-selection of the focus group sample but also to the difficulty in translation, cultural diversity in comfort expressing such opinions in group settings with strangers present, and variance in facilitators' styles, among other issues. Nevertheless, the focus groups with Native American, African American, Latino, and Asian adults were invaluable and resulted in the integration of a half-dozen key adult actions or norm statements to the draft instrument.

Several interesting findings informed and advised our understanding of norms about other people's kids in these communities of color. For example, Native American adults focused on issues of respecting, understanding, and participating in cultural activities with young people. They placed high value on the extended family and having respect for elders. They talked at length about how values of respect, culture, education, honest communication, and family are foundational to Native cultures. Similarly, Latino families placed a high value on their extended families, the importance of the young respecting their elders, and their participating in cultural and religious ceremonies. Most Latino parents wanted to recapture strong cultural values such as a sense of family (often including extended family under one roof), respect for brothers and sisters, trust, communication, and caring neighbors. Expanded support networks that reinforce the same values also were very important in African American cultures. Black focus group participants spoke of appreciating it when other adults in the family and neighborhood kept an eye on kids, correcting young people if they were out of line, and telling parents if kids were getting into trouble. Both Latino and African American adults said that ultimately, it's the parents' business, and certainly not the government's, how they raise their kids. The patterns of their comments suggested the coexistence among those participants of a primary socialization role for parents and extended family, but also a definite supportive socialization role for unrelated adults.

In general, throughout these focus groups there was considerable discussion about such topics as the desirability of young people being seen and not heard; their culture's views of appropriate discipline being perceived by focus group participants as different from the norms of the majority culture; and the challenge of passing on their culture's norms when the norms of the broader culture are seen as at odds with many culturally specific norms. Several of the items in our study specifically were suggested in the focus groups held with African American, Cambodian, Native American, and Latino adults. These included protecting, preserving, and passing down ethnic/religious culture; expecting children and youth to respect adults as authority figures; and parents being able to discipline their children without interference from others.

Healthy Communities · Healthy Youth Initiative Practitioners

In August 1999, 38 leaders in HC · HY community initiatives—nominated by Search Institute and Lutheran Brotherhood staff as potentially knowledgeable for the task—were identified to review the list of 47 adult actions or norm statements that resulted as a result of the staff ratings and focus group discussions. The purpose of asking the practitioners about the list was to establish face validity of the items among a group of individuals highly active at the grassroots level in mobilizing their communities to become more asset-building places for children and adolescents. After follow-up, a total of 13 people (34%) responded to the request with suggestions and guidance.

Expert Advice

We also sought the counsel of two recognized experts on the social worlds of children and adolescents, Francis Ianni, Ph.D. (Professor Emeritus at Columbia University), and William Damon, Ph.D. (Stanford University), on conceptual and substantive issues regarding the study. They provided substantial feedback that further affected the evolving research strategy and items.

The responses from each expert both verified and validated our general thinking and also posed challenges. In particular, Ianni and Damon questioned whether the items as then worded on the forced-choice survey draft would elicit responses that went beyond superficial public opinion polling and would instead provide deeper data on how and why particular norms might operate. Those reflections led to further revision of wording for the forced-choice survey items. We also added a follow-up interview, to be conducted with a randomly selected 100 of the respondents to the national forced-choice poll. The follow-up interview focused on respondents' open-ended reactions to hypothetical situations in which norms about relating to other people's kids might operate.

Healthy Communities · Healthy Youth Listserv Question Posting

Finally, a question asking which broad categories of adult engagement actions should be the focus was posed to the HC · HY listserv maintained by Search Institute. A summary of the study and nine categories in which adult action items had then been developed were posted to the listserv, and subscribers were invited to offer their views on which norm categories should be emphasized in the final protocol. Listserv subscribers could be anyone from youth to adults, those deeply trained in the issues of interest and those simply with opinions to share. The 25 responses suggested further refinements of the survey.

Sample

A national cross section of households was systematically selected from all telephone-owning households in the continental United States. A random digit dialing technique was used to ensure the inclusion of households with both listed and unlisted telephone numbers. Within each household one person 18 years of age or older was interviewed. A total of 1,425 interviews were completed from March 7 through April 26, 2000, representing a 60% participation rate from the population of those eligible. (Approximately 65% of all phone numbers called three times resulted in contact with an eligible adult. Of the adults actually reached, the participation rate was approximately 92%. According to Gallup researchers, those figures are quite typical for Gallup polls [e-mails from Harry Cotugno, Gallup Organization, to Peter C. Scales, Search Institute, July 27–28, 2000].)

Within the total sample, Hispanic and African American households were oversampled to obtain a minimum of 300 respondents within each group. The sampling frames for those groups were created by assigning all U.S. telephone numbers in area codes and exchanges that have 50% or more African American or Hispanic population to a "high density" group, from which a higher proportion of numbers was called. In addition, a split sample format was used: half the respondents were asked about children ages 5 to 10 and the other half about youth ages 11 to 18.

Intentional oversampling and differential contact and refusal rates produced a sample that in some respects differed from a representative sample of all adults 18 and over in telephone households. Gallup then applied weighting procedures to correct results for distributional differences. Demographic adjustments were made to align the sample with the demographic proportions reported in the March 1999 Current Population Survey released by the U.S. Census Bureau. The QUANTUM computer package was used to apply weights.

All results reported here are weighted and are not distorted by a group's representation in the sample that is different from that group's distribution in the U.S. population of telephone-owning households. The characteristics of the national sample are presented in Table 39.

Percentages reported for the total sample have a +/−margin of error of 2–4 percentage points at the 95% confidence interval; i.e., in 95 out of 100 similar samples, the true result would lie within +/−2 to 4 percentage points of the results

Table 39. Overview of National Sample

		Actual respondents		Weighted correction* (in %)
		Number of respondents	Percent of total sample	
Total Sample		1,425	100	
Gender	Female	894	63	54
	Male	531	37	46
Race/ethnicity	Hispanic/Latino	310	22	10
	African American	307	22	11
	All other**	808	57	80
Age	Ages 18 to 34	471	33	31
	Ages 35 to 54	585	41	40
	Ages 55+	350	25	27
Marital status	Single, never married	430	30	25
	Married	691	49	53
	Separated, divorced, or widowed	291	21	22
Parental status	Parent***	1,060	74	73
	Nonparent	354	25	26
Education	No college	573	40	48
	Some college****	838	59	51
Annual household income	Less than $20,000	329	23	21
	$20,000–$59,999	649	46	46
	$60,000 or more	314	22	23

*All results reported are weighted, and are not distorted by a group representation in the sample. Percentages may not sum to 100 due to missing data and rounding.
**Overwhelmingly non-Hispanic whites.
***Includes parents whose youngest child is age 19 or older.
****Includes any post–high school education.

[""]

reported here. The range of 2 to 4 percentage points is dependent on the percentage response reported; for example, a sample response of 33% would have a margin of error or sampling tolerance of $+/-3$ points, whereas a percentage of 60% would have a margin or error of $+/-4$ points. Margins of error for subgroups (e.g., comparing males to females, making comparisons across different racial/ethnic groups) vary from $+/-4$ percentage points to $+/-11$ percentage points, with the range dependent on the size of the subgroup samples involved as well as the size of the percentage responses reported.

Procedure

Polling was conducted by the Gallup Organization over a several-week period from late March to mid-April 2000.

Search Institute's studies (e.g., Benson et al., 1999; Scales et al., 1998) as well as research done by others (see review in Scales & Leffert, 1999) strongly suggest that the age of young people makes a difference in the developmental assets they are likely to experience. Younger children consistently report closer, more frequent, and more satisfactory connections with parents and other adults. Therefore, half the sample, randomly selected by computer, used "children" (defined as ages 5–10 or kindergarten–5th grade) as the referent, while the remainder of the sample used "youth" (defined as those ages 11–18, or 6th–12th grades).

Instruments

Two instruments were created for this study: a forced-choice telephone poll averaging 16 minutes in duration, for use with the nationally representative sample of U.S. adults. In addition, a second, 25-minute interview based on hypothetical situations was developed for use with 100 respondents who had participated in the national forced-choice poll.

The Forced-Choice National Poll

The final forced-choice poll contained 20 substantive statements about adult actions (e.g., "some adults know the names of many youth in their neighborhood"), as well as 12 background or demographic items (e.g., level of weekly contact with children and youth, involvement in volunteering, race/ethnicity, gender). The forced-choice poll protocol is found in Appendix B. Respondents were asked two questions about each of the 20 actions: (1) How important is this for adults to do or believe (5 = most important, 1 = least important); and (2) how many of the adults you know actually do or believe this (5 = almost all, 4 = a large majority, 3 = about half, 2 = some, 1 = very few)?

Adults "you know" was defined as "adults you know from your family, neighborhood, workplace, community activities you might be involved with, and so forth." Thus, two different dimensions of these adult actions were tapped:

the *importance or worthiness* of the action as a normative expectation (personal motivation to do the action), and the *degree of conformity* to the normative expectation that adults in the respondent's world of regular contacts are believed to exercise. The latter dimension may be considered a measure of environmental motivation or implied social pressure for the respondent also to engage in the action and so abide by the norm the action implies.

It has been observed for decades that people have a tendency to respond in socially desirable ways when they feel that, in today's term, there is a "politically correct" way to respond (Webb, Campbell, Schwartz, & Sechrest, 1972). We were concerned that asking directly whether adults personally were engaged with young people in these ways might elicit socially desirable responses. An extensive research tradition has described the role that similarity of background, interests, and values plays in both adult and adolescent friendships (Bersheid & Walster, 1969; Newcomb et al., 1999). Given that they probably are similar in many important attitudinal and value respects to other adults they "know from your family, neighborhood, workplace, community activities, and so forth," asking adults how many of those adults they "know" did these actions, seemed a reasonable and less biased proxy for reporting on their own behavior.

Moreover, since the central interest of this study was in the very social pressure that the idea of norms reflects, asking about the degree to which adults feel surrounded by others doing these actions is a more appropriate measure of normative expectation than even asking about their own behavior. The fact that so few adults said the majority of the adults they knew engaged with young people in these ways (see Chapter 6) clearly suggests we were successful in obtaining responses that were not exaggerated in a positive direction. Of course, it is possible that, if norms for engaging with young people are perceived to be weak, the results may have been exaggerated in a negative direction, that is, to increase the proportion of adults who said the adults they knew did not engage with kids. What if our respondents were themselves not very engaged with kids (which we did not ask because of social desirability concerns)? Then, by lessening the dissonance between their own actions and those of valued others, it might have served the function of maintaining acceptable personal identity if those respondents underestimated how much the adults around them were engaged. We have no way of determining whether this occurred, but we can say with a reasonable degree of confidence that adults at least did not portray the adults they knew as highly engaged with kids.

Thus, several combinations of responses were possible, each combination shedding light on the degree to which an adult action functioned as an implied social norm:

- Social Norms: Actions were considered both important and conformed to by most adults the respondent knew
- Social Values: Actions were considered important by a majority but not conformed to by most adults
- Personal Preferences: Statements were not considered important by a majority and not conformed to by most adults.

A fourth combination was theoretically possible: Actions were considered unimportant but conformed to by most adults anyway. This was not observed in our study.

Scales on Importance of Relationship Actions and Conformity to Relationship Actions

Each of the 20 actions had two parts, a question about the importance of the action, and one about the proportion of adults in the respondent's life who actually lived the action, a measure of whether the adult was surrounded by environmental motivation to also live the action. The 20 importance questions and the 20 conformity questions were combined into an Importance of Relationship Actions scale and a Conformity to Relationship Actions scale. Scale scores were created by summing the individual item scores. The scores for parents disciplining their children without interference were reversed, as it was considered more desirable for adults *not* to believe this was highly important and *not* to be surrounded by adults who believed in parental exclusivity over discipline. Alpha reliabilities were computed, showing very good internal consistency reliability for both scales (Importance scale = .82, Conformity scale = .85).

The Situation-Based Interview

The time limitations imposed on the forced-choice survey prevented asking respondents the reasons for their thoughts about the various norm statements. To gain a deeper understanding of the influences on adult decision making about whether or not to get more involved with children and youth, a second poll was conducted.

A pool of hypothetical situations was created and a subsample of 100 adults who had participated as part of the nationally representative sample in the forced-choice poll, and who indicated their willingness to be called back for a subsequent interview, was asked to react to those situations. As part of the national quantitative survey, all respondents were asked to give their consent for a second in-depth interview. Of those originally interviewed, 990 (69%), gave consent for a reinterview. The 100 in-depth interviews were completed between May 15 and June 5, 2000. Interviews were tape-recorded, transcribed, and content analyzed by the Gallup Organization. Interviewers instructed the respondent that "some of these things may have happened to you, and some may not have happened," but that the respondent should "just imagine yourself in each of the situations" and "tell me what you imagine you would most likely do." The four situations and follow-up questions posed to interviewees are found in Appendix C.

Analysis Procedures

The forced-choice poll yielded the primary data for this study. We analyzed these data in several ways. First, we examined percentage responses to each item, for the whole sample and across demographic subgroups (i.e., by gender, parental status, etc.). To better understand the degree of personal and environmental support for these actions among American adults, we were especially interested in the proportion that rated each norm a "5," or most important. Similarly, we were most interested in the proportion that said either *almost all* adults they knew (a response of "5") or a *great majority* of them ("4") actually lived the norm in question. We also examined differences in means, on both individual actions, and the action Importance and Conformity scales.

Where two groups were compared, we computed two-group analyses of variance (ANOVAs, with a p level of .05). As is the case in conducting multiple t-tests, we included a Bonferroni correction applied when multiple two-group ANOVAs were conducted in the same analysis; where more than two groups were compared, we conducted analyses of variance (ANOVAs) with Tukey multiple comparisons on all ANOVAs with significant overall F values. As explained in Chapter 6, we were most interested in the intensity of respondents' importance ratings, and whether they perceived normative support in their environment for doing these actions. Thus, even though it decreased the possible variability of responses, we recoded individual item responses so that there were only two responses for these analyses: Either respondents rated a norm "most important" or they did not, and either they said the majority of adults around them lived the norm or they did not. Those rating an action at the highest level, and those surrounded by a majority of adults doing the action, would themselves be considered most likely to experience personal and environmental motivation to get engaged with kids. The recoding thus allowed us to examine in a more focused way the differences between groups in their likely motivation to get engaged with young people. The means created by that binary recoding were used in the t-tests and analyses of variance.

In cases in which variables were likely to be moderately or strongly correlated, we conducted multiple analyses of variance (MANOVAs) to assess simultaneous main and interaction effects on norm importance and conformity. Finally, in order to get an overall picture of which adults were most likely to rate the actions important *and* be surrounded by adults who lived the actions, we combined the importance and conformity ratings to yield a "consistency of motivation score" (we detail how this score was derived in Chapter 6). We then conducted canonical discriminant analysis to determine which variables discriminated among adults experiencing high, medium, and low degrees of consistency in their personal and environmental motivation to get engaged with other people's kids.

Initial Definitions of "Norms" Used to Guide Literature Search

Social Science

"A norm is a rule, standard, or pattern for action. Social norms are rules for conduct. Norms are the standards by reference to which behavior is judged and approved or disapproved. A norm in this sense is not a statistical average of actual behavior but rather a cultural definition of desirable behavior. To the extent that a particular social norm actually is effective, one will be able, of course, to observe a marked actual regularity of social acts in recurrent situations of a particular kind. Thus there will be more or less standardized ways in which people are seen to behave when conducting trade, engaging in religious worship, or playing games. Social pressures arising from group acceptance of norms have definite consequences for behavior. Norms are learned by individuals in social intercourse with others—that is, in the process of socialization. The answer seems to be that norms arise to meet recurrent problems. They tend to be initiated or proposed-by someone who finds an immediate agreement to be in some way advantageous" (Sills, 1968, pp. 204–205).

Sociology

"In *everyday* usage, a norm is a standard that is considered by most people to be usual practice in a statistical sense. For example, eating three meals a day is considered the norm in most Western societies. In *sociology,* however, a norm is a cultural rule that associates people's behavior or appearance with rewards or punishments. Norms create social consequences that have the effect of regulating appearance and behavior. Norms make a connection between an act on one hand and social sanctions on the other. Neither the behavior nor the sanction is the norm; rather the norm is the entire rule that connects the two" (Johnson, 1995, pp. 190–191).

Anthropology

"A norm is simply a shared standard of a social group to which members are expected to conform. Homans (1950) defines norm as "an idea in the minds of members of a group, an idea that can be put in the form of a statement specifying what the members or other men should do, ought to do, are expected to do under given circumstances." They are standards to which people are expected to conform, probably because they are believed beneficial for the group. Faced with an ambiguous situation, a group of individuals initially will have widely divergent opinions, but then the opinions gradually converge, thus giving rise to normative behavior" (Hunter & Whitten, 1976, p. 288).

"[A norm is] usually in any given culture the established mode of behavior to which conformity is expected. Sometimes the term [norm] refers to the average or typical behavior referred to as the statistical norm, rather than the expected behavior, or ideal norm" (Barnard & Spencer, 1996).

Appendix B: Forced-Choice National Survey Questions

This appendix lists a summary of the actual questions asked in the survey. For space reasons, the actual survey protocol is not reproduced here but can be obtained from the author. The national research study of American adults interviewed 1,425 men and women to learn about the values and norms that have the strongest influences on how adults relate with children and youth. The telephone interview took approximately fifteen minutes. A series of screening questions (e.g., age and ethnicity) were asked of the participants before the interview. Following the interview participants were asked some final questions about themselves as well as some demographic questions.

The body of the interview consisted of 20 questions. Interviewers from the Gallup Organization read statements to the participants that described things American adults might do with or believe about young people. Two interview protocols were used: one about children and the other about youth. We defined "children" as young people in grades kindergarten through 5, or ages 5 to 10. We defined "youth" as young people in grades 6 through 12, or ages 11 to 18. By "parents," we meant the main adults who are raising children or youth, including biological parents, adoptive or stepparents, grandparents, or unrelated guardians. We explained that we were interested in learning how they thought the statements might be rules about the behavior that is expected of all adults, not just parents. For each of the statements, the interviewers asked two things—first, how important it is for adults to do this; and second, how many of the adults you know actually do this.

The Likert Scale used for the "importance" questions was:

With "5" being the most important, and "1" being the least important, how important is this for adults to do?

5   Most important
4
3
2
1   Least important

The scale used for the "adults you know" questions was:

5   Almost all
4   A large majority
3   About half
2   Some
1   Very few

The Interview Questions:

1. Some adults volunteer some time each month or donate money to show children/youth the importance of helping others. With "5" being the most important, and "1" being the least important, how important is this for adults to do?

   1a. How many of the adults you know actually do this? Would you say almost all, a large majority, about half, some, or very few?

2. Some adults stress to children/youth the importance of respecting people of different races or cultures, even when the values and beliefs of those people conflict with adults' own values and beliefs. With "5" being the most important, and "1" being the least important, how important is this for adults to do?

   2a. How many of the adults you know actually do this? Would you say almost all, a large majority, about half, some, or very few?

3. When some neighbors see children/youth doing something right, they tell the parents of those children/youth. With "5" being the most important, and "1" being the least important, how important is this for neighbors to do?

   3a. How many of the adults you know actually do this? Would you say almost all, a large majority, about half, some, or very few?

4. When some neighbors see children/youth doing something wrong, they tell the parents of those children/youth. With "5" being the most important, and "1" being the least important, how important is this for neighbors to do?

   4a. How many of the adults you know actually do this? Would you say almost all, a large majority, about half, some, or very few?

5. Some adults know the names of many of the children/youth in their neighborhood. With "5" being the most important, and "1" being the least important, how important is this for adults to know?

   5a. How many of the adults you know actually know this? Would you say almost all, a large majority, about half, some, or very few?

6. Some adults think it is okay for neighbors to give advice to children/youth who are not members of their family. With "5" being the most important, and "1" being the least important, how important is it for adults to think this?

   6a. How many of the adults you know actually think this? Would you say almost all, a large majority, about half, some, or very few?

7. Some adults encourage children/youth to take school seriously and do well at school. With "5" being the most important, and "1" being the least important, how important is this for adults to do?

   7a. How many of the adults you know actually do this? Would you say almost all, a large majority, about half, some, or very few?

8. Some adults often have conversations with children/youth that allow the adult and child/youth to really get to know one another. With "5" being the most important, and "1" being the least important, how important is this for adults to do?

8a. How many of the adults you know actually do this? Would you say almost all, a large majority, about half, some, or very few?

9. Some adults seek children's/youth's opinions when making decisions that affect children/youth. With "5" being the most important, and "1" being the least important, how important is this for adults to do?

9a. How many of the adults you know actually do this? Would you say almost all, a large majority, about half, some, or very few?

10. Some adults give children/youth guidance on what it means to save, share, and spend money in responsible ways. With "5" being the most important, and "1" being the least important, how important is this for adults to do?

10a. How many of the adults you know actually do this? Would you say almost all, a large majority, about half, some, or very few?

11. Some adults openly discuss their values with children/youth. With "5" being the most important, and "1" being the least important, how important is this for adults to do?

11a. How many of the adults you know actually do this? Would you say almost all, a large majority, about half, some, or very few?

12. Some adults openly discuss their religious and spiritual beliefs with children/youth. With "5" being the most important, and "1" being the least important, how important is this for adults to do?

12a. How many of the adults you know actually do this? Would you say almost all, a large majority, about half, some, or very few?

13. Some adults give children lots of opportunities to make their communities better places, such as by feeding the homeless or cleaning up a park. (Children) Some adults give youth lots of opportunities to make their communities better places, such as working on political or civic campaigns to change laws or policies. (Youth) With "5" being the most important, and "1" being the least important, how important is this for adults to do?

13a. How many of the adults you know actually do this? Would you say almost all, a large majority, about half, some, or very few?

14. Some adults help children/youth think through possible good and bad consequences of their decisions. With "5" being the most important, and "1" being the least important, how important is this for adults to do?

14a. How many of the adults you know actually do this? Would you say almost all, a large majority, about half, some, or very few?

15. Some adults actively teach children/youth to preserve, protect, and pass down the traditions and values of their ethnic and/or religious culture. With "5" being the most important, and "1" being the least important, how important is this for adults to do?

15a. How many of the adults you know actually do this? Would you say almost all, a large majority, about half, some, or very few?

16. Some adults believe that parents should decide how to discipline their children/youth, without interference from others. With "5" being the most important, and "1" being the least important, how important is this for adults to believe?

16a. How many of the adults you know actually believe this? Would you say almost all, a large majority, about half, some, or very few?

17. Some adults feel a responsibility to help ensure the health and well-being of children/youth in their neighborhood. With "5" being the most important, and "1" being the least important, how important is it for adults to feel this responsibility?

17a. How many of the adults you know actually feel this responsibility? Would you say almost all, a large majority, about half, some, or very few?

18. Some adults in the places children/youth live, play, and work teach children/youth the same core values as other adults do, such as equality, honesty, and responsibility. With "5" being the most important, and "1" being the least important, how important is it for adults to teach children/youth the same core values as other adults do?

18a. How many of the adults you know teach children/youth the same core values? Would you say almost all, a large majority, about half, some, or very few?

19. Some adults and elders expect children/youth to respect them as authority figures. With "5" being the most important, and "1" being the least important, how important is it for adults to expect children/youth to respect them?

19a. How many of the adults you know have this expectation? Would you say almost all, a large majority, about half, some, or very few?

20. Some parents enforce clear and consistent rules and boundaries for their children/youth. With "5" being the most important, and "1" being the least important, how important is this for parents to do?

20a. How many of the parents you know actually do this? Would you say almost all, a large majority, about half, some, or very few?

Appendix C: Hypothetical Situations Posed for In-Depth Interviews

Introduction:
Hello, this is _____ from _____. As you remember, we talked with you recently for our research study on the values and norms that influence how children and youth grow up. We're calling now for our second conversation.

In this part of the study, I'm going to read you a few hypothetical situations in which people sometimes find themselves. Some of these things may have happened to you, and some may not have happened. Just imagine yourself in each of the situations described, and then I'll ask you a few questions about your reaction to each situation. There are no right or wrong answers—we'd just like you to have a conversation with us about these hypothetical situations.

If you've been in a similar situation, I'd like you to tell me how you handled it. If you've never been in a situation like the ones I'll read, just tell me what you imagine you would most likely do and what you think other adults would do. Just as in our other interview, your answers are totally anonymous and confidential—no one but the researchers will know how you responded. Okay?

Imagine skateboarders hang out around a local business (restaurant, grocery store, or doctor's office) on a regular basis because of the ramps and inclines available in the parking lot. The business owner gets complaints from customers about the disruption and inconvenience. If you were the owner of the store, how would you react to the skateboarders? What would you tell the customers? Why?

- Do adults, whether the business owner or the customers, feel any responsibility to do something in this situation? Why or why not?
- Would most adults try to accommodate the skateboarders or instead try to get rid of them? Why?
- Is it OK for adults to do nothing in this situation? Why or why not?
- What kinds of consequences, good or bad, do adults think will happen if they do nothing? What about if they decide to get to know these young people more and see if they can work this situation out—what consequences, good or bad, do they imagine would happen?
- Has this ever happened to you? If so, what did you do? Why?
- What difference would it make in this situation if the youth were of a different race or ethnicity than the adult? How about if the adult and youth were of a different sex or gender? How about if the children involved were younger, say ages 5 through 10 or grades K through 5 instead of being young adolescents? What if the children were older teens in high school? Why would it make a difference?

- What would make it more likely for an adult to get to know the youth in this situation and try to work out a compromise?

Imagine there has been a devastating flood in a neighboring county, which has been well documented for several days. Two neighborhood middle school girls appear at your door, representing a local congregation that is not your own. They ask if you would participate with youth in a cleanup day they are sponsoring and if you can donate cleaning supplies and drinking water. What would you do? Why?

- Is it unusual for an adult in those situations to take part in those activities?
- Do adults feel any responsibility to do something in these situations? Why or why not?
- Is it OK for adults to say no to these invitations? Why or why not?
- What kinds of consequences, good or bad, do adults think will happen if they say no? What about if they say yes and actually participate in these events—what good or bad consequences do they imagine happening?
- Has this ever happened to you? If so, what did you do? Why did you react that way?
- What difference would it make in this situation if someone else were watching, versus if no one else is watching? How would that affect what the adult did?
- What difference would it make if the youth were boys instead of girls? Why?
- What difference would it make in this situation if the youth were of a different race or ethnicity than the adult? How about if the adult and youth were of different sexes or genders? How about if the children involved were younger, say ages 5 through 10 or grades K through 5 instead of teenagers? What if they were older teens in high school? Why would it make a difference?
- What would make it more likely for an adult to participate in these activities than to say no to the invitation?

Imagine you see a group of middle school boys you know who should be in school, but are obviously just hanging out on the street corner. What would you do? Why?

- How common would it be for adults to do something in this situation?
- What would hold them back?
- If they decided to do something, what would they do?
- Do adults feel any responsibility to do something in this situation? Why or why not?
- Is it OK for adults to do nothing in this situation? Why or why not?
- What kinds of consequences, good or bad, do adults think will happen if they do nothing? What about if they decide to do something—what consequences, good or bad, do they imagine would happen?
- Has this ever happened to you? If so, what did you do? Why did you react that way?

- What difference would it make if the youth were girls instead of boys? Why?
- What difference would it make in this situation if the youth were of a different race or ethnicity than the adult? How about if the adult and youth were of different sexes or genders? How about if the children involved were younger, say ages 5 through 10 or grades K through 5 instead of young adolescents? What if the children were older teens in high school? Why would it make a difference?
- What would make it more likely for an adult to do something in this situation?

Imagine a 12-year-old boy from your neighborhood has agreed to rake your yard on a regular basis. The youth intends to spend all the money earned on some CDs. Should you counsel the boy to consider other uses for the money, such as saving it, or donating part or all of it to charity? Why?

- How common would it be for adults in this situation to give advice to the youth on other ways of using the money?
- What would hold them back?
- If they decided to give such advice, what would they do?
- Do adults feel any responsibility to give advice in this situation? Why or why not?
- Is it OK for adults to do nothing in this situation? Why or why not?
- What kinds of consequences, good or bad, do adults think will happen if they do nothing? What about if they decide to give advice—what consequences, good or bad, do they imagine would happen?
- Has this ever happened to you? If so, what did you do? Why did you react that way?
- What difference would it make if the youth were a girl instead of a boy? Why?
- What difference would it make in this situation if the youth was of a different race or ethnicity than the adult? How about if the adult and youth were of different sexes or genders? What if the child involved was younger, say 5 through 10 or grades K through 5 instead of a young adolescent? What if the child was an older teen in high school? Why would it make a difference?
- What would make it more likely for an adult to give advice on alternative ways of using the money in this situation?

Appendix D: Sampling Tolerance

In interpreting survey results, it should be borne in mind that all sample surveys are subject to sampling error, that is, the extent to which the results may differ from what would be obtained if the whole population had been interviewed. The size of such sampling errors depends largely on the number of interviews.

The following tables may be used in estimating the sampling error of any percentage in this report. The computed allowances have taken into account the effect of the sample design upon sampling error. They may be interpreted as indicating the range (plus or minus the figure shown) within which the results of repeated samplings in the same time period could be expected to vary, 95 percent of the time, assuming the same sampling procedures, the same interviewers, and the same questionnaire.

Table 40 shows how much allowance should be made for the sampling error of a percentage: Let us say a reported percentage is 33 for a group which includes 1000 respondents. Then we go to row "percentage near 30" in the table and go across to the column headed "1000." The number at this point is 3, which means that the 33 percent obtained in the sample is subject to a sampling error of plus or minus 3 points. Another way of saying it is that very probably (95 chances out of 100) the true figure would be somewhere between 30 and 36, with the most likely figure the 33 obtained.

In comparing survey results in two samples, such as, for example, men and women, the question arises as to how large a difference between them must be before one can be reasonably sure that it reflects a real difference.

Table 40. Recommended Allowance for Sampling Error of a Percentage (in Percentage Points—at 95 in 100 Confidence Level)*

	Sample size									
	1425	1000	800	700	600	500	400	300	200	100
Percentages near 10	2	3	3	3	3	4	4	5	6	8
Percentages near 20	3	3	4	4	5	5	6	6	8	11
Percentages near 30	3	4	4	5	5	6	6	7	9	13
Percentages near 40	4	4	5	5	6	6	7	8	10	14
Percentages near 50	4	4	5	5	6	6	7	8	10	14
Percentages near 60	4	4	5	5	6	6	7	8	10	14
Percentages near 70	3	4	4	5	5	6	6	7	9	13
Percentages near 80	3	3	4	4	5	5	6	6	8	11
Percentages near 90	2	3	3	3	3	4	4	5	6	8

*The chances are 95 in 100 that the sampling error is not larger than the figure shown.

Table 41. *Recommended Allowance for Sampling Error of the Difference between 20% and 80% (in Percentage Points—at 95 in 100 Confidence Level)**

	Sample size									
	1425	1000	800	700	600	500	400	300	200	100
1425	4									
1000	5	5								
800	5	5	6							
700	5	5	6	6						
600	5	6	6	6	6					
500	6	6	6	6	7	7				
400	6	7	7	7	7	7	8			
300	7	7	7	8	8	8	8	9		
200	8	9	9	9	9	9	10	10	11	
100	11	12	12	12	12	12	12	13	14	16

*The chances are 95 in 100 that the sampling error is not larger than the figure shown.

Table 42. *Recommended Allowance for Sampling Error of the Difference between 50% and 50% (at 95 Percentage in 100 Confidence Level)**

	Sample size									
	1425	1000	800	700	600	500	400	300	200	100
1425	5									
1000	6	6								
800	6	7	7							
700	6	7	7	7						
600	7	7	7	8	8					
500	7	8	8	8	8	9				
400	8	8	8	9	9	9	10			
300	9	9	9	10	10	10	11	11		
200	10	11	11	11	11	12	12	13	14	
100	14	14	15	15	15	15	15	16	17	20

*The chances are 95 in 100 that the sampling error is not larger than the figure shown.

In Tables 41 and 42, the number of points that must be allowed for in such comparisons is indicated.

Table 41 is for percentages near 20 or 80; Table 42 is for percentages near 50. For percentages in between, the error to be allowed for is between those shown in the two tables.

References

Abell, Ellen, & Gecas, Victor. (1997). Guilt, shame, and family socialization. *Journal of Family Issues,* *18*, 99–123.

Ad Council. (2001). *Summary of the Advertising Council's Strategic Task Force research* (downloaded March 15, 2001, from www.adcouncil.org).

Ad Council and MTV: Music Television. (2000). *Engaging the next generation: How nonprofits can reach young adults.* New York: Authors (www.adcouncil.org).

Alaska Governor's Interim Commission on Children and Youth. (1988). *Our greatest natural resource: Investing in the future of Alaska's children.* Juneau: Office of the Governor.

All for all: Strengthening community involvement for all students. (2000). Washington, DC: Public Education Network.

Allen, Chris T. (1982). Self-perception based strategies for stimulating energy conservation. *Journal of Consumer Research, 8,* 381–390.

Allison, Paul D. (1992). The cultural evolution of beneficent norms. *Social Forces, 71,* 279–301.

America's Promise—The Alliance for Youth. (2001). *A Gallup poll social audit.* Washington, DC: Author.

America's Promise. (2000). *Who is responsible for helping America's youth?* (www.americaspromise.org/Files/misc/wirthlinFacts.pdf, accessed Nov. 21, 2000).

Andreasen, Alan B. (1995). *Marketing social change: Changing behaviors to promote health, social development, and the environment.* San Francisco: Jossey-Bass.

Anna Quindlen says . . . (2000). *Child Care ActioNews, 17* (3), 6.

Archer, Jeff. (2000, April 26). Volunteer push leaves its mark, but extent of impact still unclear. *Education Week, 19* (33), 1, 22–23.

Azjen, Icek. (1988). *Attitudes, personality, and behavior.* Chicago: Dorsey Press.

Azjen, Icek. (2001). Nature and operation of attitudes. *Annual Review of Psychology, 52,* 27–58.

Bales, Susan Nall. (2001). Perceptual barriers to valuing and supporting youth. In Peter L. Benson and Karen Johnson Pittman (Eds.), *Trends in youth development: Visions, realities and challenges* (pp. 55–75). Norwell, MA: Kluwer Academic Publishers.

Bandura, Albert. (1989). Human agency in social cognitive theory. *American Psychologist, 44,* 1175–1184.

Bandura, Albert. (1997). *Self-efficacy: The exercise of control.* New York: W.H. Freeman.

Barber, Brian K., & Olsen, Joseph A. (1997). Socialization in context: Connection, regulation, and autonomy in the family, school, neighborhood, and with peers. *Journal of Adolescent Research, 12,* 287–315.

Barnard, Alan, & Spencer, Jonathan. (Eds.). (1996). *Encyclopedia of social and cultural anthropology.* New York: Routledge.

Batson, C. Daniel. (1994). Why act for the public good? Four answers. *Personality and Social Psychology Bulletin, 20,* 603–610.

Belkin, Lisa. (2000, July 23). Your kids are their problem. *New York Times Magazine,* 30–35, 42, 56, 60–63.

Bem, Daryl J. (1967). Self-perception: An alternative interpretation of cognitive dissonance phenomena. *Psychological Review, 74,* 183–200.

Bengston, Vern L. (2001). Beyond the nuclear family: The increasing importance of multigenerational bonds. *Journal of Marriage and the Family, 63,* 1–16.

Benson, Peter L. (1997). *All kids are our kids: What communities must do to raise caring and responsible children and adolescents.* San Francisco: Jossey-Bass.

Benson, Peter L., Leffert, Nancy, Scales, Peter C., & Blyth, Dale A. (1998). Beyond the "village" rhetoric: Creating healthy communities for children and adolescents. *Applied Developmental Science, 2,* 138–159.

Benson, Peter L., & Saito, Rebecca N. (2001). The scientific foundations of youth development. In Peter L. Benson & Karen Johnson Pittman (eds.), *Trends in youth development: Visions, realities and challenges* (pp. 135–154). Boston: Kluwer Academic Publishers.

Benson, Peter L., Scales, Peter C., Leffert, Nancy, & Roehlkepartain, Eugene C. (1999). *A fragile foundation: The state of developmental assets among American youth.* Minneapolis: Search Institute.

Benson, Peter L., Scales, Peter C., & Mannes, Marc. (2003). Developmental strengths and their sources: Implications for the study and practice of community-building. In Richard M. Lerner, Francine Jacobs, & Donald Wertieb (Eds.), *Promoting positive child, adolescent, and family development: A handbook of program and policy innovations:* Vol. 1, *Promoting developmental assets: Community-based approaches.* Thousand Oaks, CA: Sage.

Berkowitz, Marvin W., & Grych, John H. (1998). Fostering goodness: Teaching parents to facilitate children's moral development. *Journal of Moral Education, 27,* 371–391 (www.uic.edu/~Inucci/MoralEd/aotm/fosterin.htm).

Berscheid, Ellen, & Walster, Elaine H. (1969). *Interpersonal attraction.* Reading, MA: Addison-Wesley.

Billig, Shelley H. (2000). Research on K–12 school-based service-learning: The evidence builds. *Phi Delta Kappan, 81,* 658–664.

Blum, Robert W., Beuhring, Trisha, Shew, Marcia L., Bearinger, Linda H., Sieving, Renee E., & Resnick, Michael D. (2000). The effects of race/ethnicity, income, and family structure on adolescent risk behaviors. *American Journal of Public Health, 90,* 1879–1884.

Blyth, Dale A., Hill, John P., & Thiel, Karen. (1982). Early adolescent significant others: Grade and gender differences in perceived relationships with familial and nonfamilial adults and young people. *Journal of Youth and Adolescence, 11,* 425–450.

Bostrom, Margaret. (1999). How people talk about children's issues: A focus group report. In Coalition for America's Children, *Effective language for communicating children's issues* (pp. 27–60). Washington, DC: Benton Foundation.

Bowen, Gary, & Richman, Jack. (1997). *Contextual risks, social capital, and internal assets among Communities in Schools participants: Comparisons to the national School Success Profile.* Chapel Hill: Jordan Institute for Families, School of Social Work, University of North Carolina.

Bowman, Darcia Harris. (2000, Oct. 4). Schools urged to teach value of money. *Education Week, 20* (4), 8.

Bradsher, Keith. (2000, July 17). Was Freud a minivan or S.U.V. kind of guy? *New York Times,* A1, 16.

Bridges, F. Stephen, & Coady, Neil P. (1996). Urban size differences in incidence of altruistic behavior. *Psychological Reports, 78,* 307–312.

Britt, Thomas W. (1999). Engaging the self in the field: Testing the triangle model of responsibility. *Personality and Social Psychology Bulletin, 25,* 696–706.

Brody, Gene H., Ge, Xiajia Ge, Katz, Jennifer, & Arias, Ileana. (2000). A longitudinal analysis of internalization of parental alcohol-use norms and adolescent alcohol use. *Applied Developmental Science, 4,* 71–79.

Bronfenbrenner, Urie. (1979). *The ecology of human development: Experiments by nature and design.* Cambridge, MA: Harvard University Press.

Broyde, Michael J. (2000). The power and purpose of Jewish law. *Responsive Community, 10* (2), 45–50.

Bruce, Neil, & Waldman, Michael. (1990). The rotten-kid theorem meets the Samaritan's dilemma. *Quarterly Journal of Economics, 105,* 155–165.

Buckingham, Marcus. (2001). Focus on your strengths or fix your weaknesses? *Gallup Poll Releases* (downloaded May 9, 2001, from www.gallup.com/poll/releases/pr010316b.asp).

Bugental, Daphne Blunt, Lyon, Judith E., Lin, Eta K., McGrath, Emily P., & Bimbela, Alfred. (1999). Children "tune out" in response to the ambiguous communication style of powerless adults. *Child Development, 70,* 214–230.

Burton, Linda W., Price-Spratlen, Townsend. (1999). Through the eyes of children: An ethnographic perspective on neighborhoods and child development. In Ann S. Masten (Ed.), *Cultural processes in child development: The Minnesota Symposia on Child Psychology* (Vol. 29, pp. 77–96). Mahwah, NJ: Lawrence Erlbaum.

Carlson, Darren K. (2000, Nov. 10). *Americans today more skeptical of young people than they were 50 years ago.* Princeton, NJ: Gallup Organization, Poll Releases (www.gallup.com/poll/releases/pr001110b.asp, accessed Nov. 14, 2000).

Casper, Lynne M., & Bryson, Kenneth R. (1998). *Coresident grandparents and their grandchildren: Grandparent-maintained families.* Population Division, Working Paper Series No. 26. Washington, DC: U.S. Bureau of the Census.

Caughy, Margaret O'Brien, O'Campo, Patricia, & Brodsky, Anne E. (1999). Neighborhoods, families, and children: Implications for policy and practice. *Journal of Community Psychology, 27,* 615–633.

Chaskin, Robert J., & Hawley, Theresa. (1994). *Youth and caring: Developing a field of inquiry and practice.* Chicago: Chapin Hall Center for Children, University of Chicago.

Cherlin, Andrew J. (1999, Oct. 17). I'm OK, you're selfish. *New York Times Magazine* (www.nytimes.com/library/magazine/millennium/m5/poll-cherlin-html).

Child Welfare League of America. (1999). *Assessing public opinion and perceptions regarding child abuse in America.* Washington, DC: Author (final report from Liberman Research Worldwide).

Children's Health Campaign research summary report. (2000). Wichita, KS: Sullivan Higdon & Sink.

Cialdini, Robert B., & Schroeder, David A. (1976). Increasing compliance by legitimizing paltry contributions: When even a penny helps. *Journal of Personality and Social Psychology, 34,* 599–604.

Cizek, Gregory A. (2000, Dec. 6). School politics 101: It's not really about the children. *Education Week, 20* (14), 35–36.

Clary, E. Gil, & Snyder, Mark. (1993). *Transmitting the values of a caring society: What, when, and how.* Paper delivered at Independent Sector Research Forum, San Antonio, March 18–19, 1993.

Cochran, Moncrieff, Larner, Mary, Riley, David, Gunnarsson, Lars, & Henderson, Charles H., Jr. (1990). *Extending families: The social networks of parents and their children.* Cambridge: Cambridge University Press.

Cohen, Dov, Vandello, Joseph, Puente, Sylvia, & Rantilla, Adrian. (1999). "When you call me that, smile!" How norms for politeness, interaction styles, and aggression work together in southern culture. *Social Psychology Quarterly, 62,* 257–275.

Collins, W. Andrew, Maccoby, Eleanor E., Steinberg, Laurence, Heatherington, E. Mavis, & Bornstein, Marc H. (2000). Contemporary research on parenting: The case for nature and nurture. *American Psychologist, 55,* 218–232.

Community Indicators Survey—National. (1999, Nov. 30). Princeton, NJ: Princeton Survey Research Associates, for the John S. and James L. Knight Foundation (www.knightfdn.org/indicators).

Connell, James P., & Kubisch, Anne C. (2001). Community approaches to improving outcomes for urban children, youth, and families: Current trends and future directions. In Alan Booth & Ann C. Crouter (Eds.), *Does it take a village? Community effects on children, adolescents, and families* (pp. 177–201). Mahwah, NJ: Lawrence Erlbaum.

Conte, Christopher. (1998). *The National Summit on Retirement Savings: Agenda and background materials* (June 4–5, 1998, in Washington, DC). Washington, DC: American Savings Education Council (downloaded August 12, 2001, from www.asec.org/saversummit/1998summit/).

Cooter, Robert D. (1997). Punitive damages, social norms, and economic analysis. *Law and Contemporary Problems, 60,* 73–91.

Crossette, Barbara. (2000, June 7). Women's global views examined by survey. *New York Times,* A12.

Csikszentmihalyi, Mihaly. (2000, April 19). Education for the 21st century—Mapping the field of forces that shape children's lives. *Education Week, 19* (32), 64, 46–47.

Dalaker, Joseph, & Proctor, Bernadette D. (2000). *Poverty in the United States: 1999.* Washington, DC: U.S. Department of Commerce, Bureau of the Census.

Damon, William. (1995). *Greater expectations: Overcoming the culture of indulgence in our homes and schools.* New York: Free Press.

Damon, William. (2001, April 27–29). The gap generation. *USA Weekend,* 6–9.

Damon, William, & Gregory, Anne. (1997). The youth charter: Towards the formation of adolescent moral identity. *Journal of Moral Education, 26,* 117–130.

DARE to revamp its anti-drug strategy. (2001, Feb. 15). *Public Agenda Alert* (downloaded July 9, 2001, from www.publicagenda.org).

Darley, John, & Latane, Bibb. (1968). Bystander intervention in emergencies: Diffusion of responsibility. *Journal of Personality and Social Psychology, 8,* 377–383.

DeBono, Kenneth G. (1987). Investigating the social-adjustive and value-expressive functions of attitudes: Implications for persuasion processes. *Journal of Personality and Social Psychology, 52,* 279–287.

Dryfoos, Joy G. (1990). *Adolescents at risk: Prevalence and prevention.* New York: Oxford University Press.

Duffett, Ann, Johnson, Jean, & Farkas, Steve. (1999). *Kids these days 1999: What Americans really think of the next generation.* New York: Public Agenda.

Duncan, Greg J., & Raudenbush, Stephen W. (1999). Assessing the effects of context in studies of child and youth development. *Educational Psychologist, 34,* 29–41.

Eagly, Alice H., & Chaiken, Shelly. (1993). *The psychology of attitudes.* Orlando, FL: Harcourt Brace.

Eccles, Jacquelynne S., Roeser, Robert, Wigfield, Allan, & Freedman-Doan, Carol. (1999). Academic and motivational pathways through middle childhood. In Lawrence Balter & Catherine S. Tamis-LeMonda (Eds.), *Child psychology: A handbook of contemporary issues* (pp. 287–317). Brighton and New York: Psychology Press.

Eder, Peter F. (1990). Advertising and mass marketing: The threat and the promise. *Futurist, 24,* 38–40.

Elster, Jon. (1989). *The cement of society: A study of social order.* Cambridge: Cambridge University Press.

Ensminger, Jean, & Knight, Jack. (1997). Changing social norms: Common property, bridewealth, and clan exogamy. *Current Anthropology, 38,* 1–14.

Erikson, Erik H. (1968). *Identity: Youth and crisis.* New York: W.W. Norton.

Falomir, Juan Manuel, Mugny, Gabriel, & Perez, Juan Antonio. (2000). Social influence and identity conflict. In Michael A. Hogg & Deborah J. Terry (Eds.), *Attitudes, behavior, and social context: The role of norms and group membership* (pp. 245–264). Mahwah, NJ: Lawrence Erlbaum.

Farkas, Steve, Duffett, Ann, Johnson, Jean, Foleno, Tony, & Foley, Patrick. (2000). *Necessary compromises: How parents, employers, and children's advocates view child care today.* New York: Public Agenda.

Farkas, Steve, Foley, Patrick, Duffett, Ann, Foleno, Tony, & Johnson, Jean. (2001). *Just waiting to be asked? A fresh look at attitudes on public engagement.* New York: Public Agenda.

Farkas, Steve, & Johnson, Jean. (1997). *Kids these days: What Americans really think of the next generation.* New York: Public Agenda.

Farver, JoAnn M., Ghosh, Chandra, & Garcia, Christine. (2000). Children's perceptions of their neighborhoods. *Journal of Applied Developmental Psychology, 21,* 139–163.

Feiring, Candice, & Lewis, Michael. (1991). The transition from middle childhood to early adolescence: Sex differences in the social network and perceived self-competence. *Sex Roles, 24,* 489–509.

Felmlee, Diane H. (1999). Social norms in same- and cross-gender friendships. *Social Psychology Quarterly, 62,* 53–67.

Few "good Samaritan" laws in America. (1997, Sept. 5). *Salt Lake Tribune* (www.sltrib.com/97/sep090597/nation_w/2594.htm).

Fields, Jason. (2001). *America's families and living arrangements, 2000: Population characteristics.* Washington, DC: U.S. Department of Commerce, Bureau of the Census.

Fishbein, Martin. (1966). The relationship between beliefs, attitudes, and behavior. In Shel Feldman (Ed.), *Cognitive consistency: Motivational antecedents and behavioral consequents* (pp. 199–223). New York: Academic Press.

Florida court frees retirement community from school levy. (2000, May 20). *New York Times,* A10.

Florini, Ann. (1996). The evolution of international norms. *International Studies Quarterly, 40,* 363–389.

Folbre, Nancy. (1998). The neglect of care-giving: Interview with Nancy Folbre. *Challenge: The Magazine of Economic Affairs, 41,* 45–58.

Forsyth, Donelson R. (1999). Norms: Coercive sources of influence? Course materials, Virginia Commonwealth University (www.vcu.edu/hasweb/psy/psy341/norms.html).

Freedman, Jonathon L., & Fraser, Scott C. (1966). Compliance without pressure: The foot-in-the-door technique. *Journal of Personality and Social Psychology, 4,* 195–202.

Fukuyama, Francis. (1999). The great disruption: Human nature and the reconstitution of social order. *Atlantic Monthly, 283,* 55–80.

Furstenberg, Frank F. (2000). The sociology of adolescence and youth in the 1990s: A critical commentary. *Journal of Marriage and the Family, 62,* 896–910.

Furstenberg, Frank F. (1993). How families manage risk and opportunity in dangerous neighborhoods. In William Julius Wilson (Ed.), *Sociology and the public agenda* (pp. 231–258). Newbury Park, CA: Sage.

Galley, Michelle. (2000, May 31). Chicago to size up parents with "checklists." *Education Week, 19* (38), 3.

Gallup Organization. (2000). *National study of American social norms around children and youth conducted for Search Institute/Lutheran Brotherhood.* Princeton, NJ: Author (narrative report).

Garbarino, James, & Sherman, Deborah. (1980). High-risk neighborhoods and high-risk families: The human ecology of child maltreatment. *Child Development, 51,* 188–198.

Gardner, John W. (1991). *Building community.* Washington, DC: Independent Sector.

Gibbons, Keith, & Walker, Iain. (1996). Social roles, social norms, and self-presentation in the quiz effect of Ross, Amabile, and Steinmetz. *Journal of Social Psychology, 136,* 625–634.

Gladwell, Malcolm. (2000). *The tipping point: How little things can make a big difference.* Boston: Little, Brown.

Goldberg, Carey, & Connelly, Marjorie. (1999, Oct. 20). Fear and violence have declined among teen-agers, poll shows. *New York Times,* A1, A20.

Gordon, Sol. (2001). *How can you tell if you're really in love.* Holbrook, MA: Adams Media.

Haines, Michael, & Spear, Sherilynn F. (1996). Changing the perception of the norm: A strategy to decrease binge drinking among college students. *Journal of American College Health, 45,* 134–140.

Harris, J.R. (1995). Where is the child's environment? A group socialization theory of development. *Psychological Review, 102,* 458–489.

Hersch, Patricia. (1998). *A tribe apart: A journey into the heart of American adolescence.* New York: Ballantine.

Higgins, E. Tory. (2000). Making a good decision: Value from fit. *American Psychologist, 55,* 1217–1230.

Hirschfield, Lawrence A. (1995). Do children have a theory of race? *Cognition, 54,* 209–252.

Hofferth, Sandra L., & Sandberg, John F. (2001). How American children spend their time. *Journal of Marriage and the Family, 63,* 295–308.

Horatio Alger Association. (1998). *The state of our nation's youth 1998–1999.* Alexandria, VA: Author.

How do adults view sex ed? (1999). *Family Planning Perspectives, 31,* 210.

Hunter, David E., & Whitten, Phillip (Eds.). (1976). *Encyclopedia of anthropology.* New York: Harper & Row.

Ianni, Francis A.J. (1989). *The search for structure: A report on American youth today.* New York: Free Press.

It's About Time for Kids. (2001). *Other caring adults = kids with fewer problems, greater success: A social marketing campaign to influence action.* Seattle: Author (www.timeforkids.org).

Jaccard, James, Dittus, Patricia J., & Gordon, Vivian V. (2000). Parent-teen communication about premarital sex: Factors associated with the extent of communication. *Journal of Adolescent Research, 15,* 187–208.

Jackson, Kristina M., & Aiken, Leona S. (2000). A psychosocial model of sun protection and sunbathing in young women: The impact of health beliefs, attitudes, norms, and self-efficacy for sun protection. *Health Psychology, 19,* 469–478.

Jacobson, Linda. (2000, Oct. 11). Poll finds gap in child-rearing know-how. *Education Week, 20* (6), 3.

Jessor, Richard. (1993). Successful adolescent development among youth in high-risk settings. *American Psychologist, 48,* 117–126.

Jetten, Jolanda, Spears, Russell, & Manstead, Antony S.R. (1996). Intergroup norms and intergroup discrimination: Distinctive self-categorization and social identity effects. *Journal of Personality and Social Psychology, 71,* 1222–1233.

Jimerson, Jason B. (1999). "Who has next?" The symbolic, rational, and methodical use of norms in pickup basketball. *Social Psychology Quarterly, 62,* 136–156.

Johnson, Allan G. (1995). *The Blackwell dictionary of sociology: A user's guide to sociological language.* Cambridge: Blackwell.

Kasser, Tim, Ryan, Richard M., Zax, Melvin, & Sameroff, Arnold J. (1995). The relations of maternal and social environments to late adolescents' materialistic and prosocial values. *Developmental Psychology, 31,* 907–914.

Kett, Joseph F. (1993). Discovery and invention in the history of adolescence. *Journal of Adolescent Health, 14,* 605–612.

Kielsmeier, James C. (2000). A time to serve, a time to learn: Service-learning and the promise of democracy. *Phi Delta Kappan, 81,* 652–657.

King, Pamela. (2000). *Adolescent religiousness and moral outcomes: A proposed model of social capital resources and moral behavior.* Doctoral dissertation, Graduate School of Psychology, Fuller Theological Seminary, Pasadena, CA.

Kominski, Robert, Jamieson, Amie, & Martinez, Gladys. (2001). *At-risk conditions of U.S. school-age children.* Population Division, Working Paper Series No. 52. Washington, DC: U.S. Bureau of the Census.

Kowaleski-Jones, Lori. (2000). Staying out of trouble: Community resources and problem behavior among high-risk adolescents. *Journal of Marriage and the Family, 62,* 449–464.

Kretzmann, John P., & McKnight, John L. (1993). *Building communities from the inside out: A path toward finding and mobilizing a community's assets.* Evanston, IL: Center for Urban Affairs and Policy Research, Northwestern University.

Krueger, Curtis. (2001, July 16). State cuts parents' bill for youths in detention. *St. Petersburg (FL) Times* (downloaded July 17, 2001, from www.sptimes.com:80/News/07601/news_pf/State/State_cuts_parents_b.shtml).

Kuhn, Thomas S. (1962). *The structure of scientific revolutions.* Chicago: University of Chicago Press.

Larson, Reed W., & Richards, Maryse H. (1989). Introduction: The changing life space of early adolescents. *Journal of Youth and Adolescence, 18,* 501–509.

Lee, Nancy. (2001). *It's About Time for Kids: Caring adult relationships focus groups.* Seattle, WA: Social Marketing Services, Inc.

Leffert, Nancy, Benson, Peter L., & Roehlkepartain, Jolene L. (1997). *Starting out right: Developmental assets for children.* Minneapolis: Search Institute.

Leffert, Nancy, Benson, Peter L., Scales, Peter C., Sharma, Anu, Drake, Dyanne, & Blyth, Dale A. (1998). Developmental assets: Measurement and prediction of risk behaviors among adolescents. *Applied Developmental Science, 2,* 209–230.

Legro, Jeffrey W. (1997). Which norms matter? Revisiting the "failure" of internationalism. *International Organization, 51,* 31–63.

Lerner, Richard M. (1992). Dialectics, developmental contextualism, and the further enhancement of theory about puberty and psychosocial development. *Journal of Early Adolescence, 12,* 366–388.

Lerner, Richard M., Lerner, Jacqueline V., De Stefanis, Imma, & Apfel, Alison. (2001). Understanding developmental systems in adolescence: Implications for methodological strategies, data analytic approaches, and training. *Journal of Adolescent Research, 16,* 9–27.

Leventhal, Tama, & Brooks-Gunn, Jeanne. (2000). The neighborhoods they live in: The effects of neighborhood residence on child and adolescent outcomes. *Psychological Bulletin, 126,* 309–377.

Lewin, Tamar. (2001, March 7). Legal action after killings at schools often fails. *New York Times,* A14.

Luthar, Suniya S., Cicchetti, Dante, & Becker, Bronwyn. (2000). The construct of resilience: A critical evaluation and guidelines for future work. *Child Development, 71,* 543–562.

Mandell, Lewis. (1998). *Our vulnerable youth: The financial literacy of American 12th graders.* Washington, DC: Jump$tart Coalition for Personal Financial Literacy.

Manstead, Antony R.S. (2000). The role of moral norm in the attitude-behavior relation. In Michael A. Hogg & Deborah J. Terry (Eds.), *Attitudes, behavior, and social context: The role of norms and group membership* (pp. 11–30). Mahwah, NJ: Lawrence Erlbaum.

Marcello, Melissa K., & Perrucci, Robert. (2000). Small groups and civic engagement: All about me? *Responsive Community, 10,* 67–73.

Marshall, Nancy L., Noonan, Anne E., McCartney, Kathleen, Marx, Fern, & Keefe, Nancy. (2001). It takes an urban village: Parenting networks of urban families. *Journal of Family Issues, 22,* 163–182.

Masten, Ann S. (2001). Ordinary magic: Resilience processes in development. *American Psychologist, 56,* 227–238.

Mattis, Jacqueline S., Jagers, Robert J., Hatcher, Carrie A., Lawhon, G. Dawn, Murphy, Eleanor J., & Murray, Yohance F. (2000). Religiosity, volunteerism, and community involvement among African American men: An exploratory analysis. *Journal of Community Psychology, 28,* 391–406.

McKenzie-Mohr, Doug. (2000). Fostering sustainable behavior through community-based social marketing. *American Psychologist, 55*, 531–537.

McKnight, John. (1995). *The careless society: Community and its counterfeits.* New York: Basic Books.

Melchior, Alan. (1997). *Interim report: National evaluation of Learn and Serve America school and community-based programs.* Washington, DC: Corporation for National Service.

Miller, Dale T., Monin, Benoit, & Prentice, Deborah A. (2000). Pluralistic ignorance and inconsistency between private attitudes and public behaviors. In Michael A. Hogg & Deborah J. Terry (Eds.), *Attitudes, behavior, and social context: The role of norms and group membership* (pp. 95–113). Mahwah, NJ: Lawrence Erlbaum.

Miller, Kim S., Kotchick, Beth A., Dorsey, Shannon, Forehand, Rex, & Ham, Anissa Y. (1998). Family communication about sex: What are parents saying and are their adolescents listening? *Family Planning Perspectives, 30*, 218–222, 235.

Miller, Richard L., Brickman, Philip, & Bolen, Diana. (1975). Attribution versus persuasion as a means for modifying behavior. *Journal of Personality and Social Psychology, 31*, 430–441.

Missing the basics. (2000, April 16). *New York Times*, BU14.

Moore, Kristin A. (1992). *National Commission on Children: 1990 survey of parents and children.* Washington, DC: Child Trends.

National Commission on Children. (1991). Beyond rhetoric: A new American agenda for children and families. Washington, DC: Author.

National Research Council and Institute of Medicine. (2000). *From neurons to neighborhoods: The science of early child development.* Jack P. Shonkoff and Deborah Phillips, eds. Board on Children, Youth, and Families, Commission on Behavioral and Social Sciences and Education. Washington, DC: National Academy Press.

New York Times/CBS News. (1999, Oct. 17). What's the word on health? Complete magazine poll results. *New York Times* (www.nytimes.com/library/national/101799mag-poll-results.html).

Newcomb, Andrew F., Bukowski, William M., & Bagwell, Catherine L. (1999). Knowing the sounds: Friendships as developmental contexts. In W. Andrew Collins & Brett Laursen (Eds.), *Relationships as developmental contexts* (pp. 64–84). Mahwah, NJ: Lawrence Erlbaum.

Oliver, Pamela E. (1984/1997). "If you don't do it, nobody else will": Active and token contributors to local collective action. *American Sociological Review* (1984), 49, 601–610. Reprinted in Doug McAdam & David A. Snow (Eds.). (1997). *Social movements: Readings on their emergence, mobilization, and dynamics* (pp. 207–215). Los Angeles: Roxbury.

Parcel, Toby L., & Dufur, Mikaela J. (2001). Capital at home and school: Effects on child social adjustment. *Journal of Marriage and the Family, 63*, 32–47.

Patterson, Orlando. (2001, May 8). Race by the numbers. *New York Times*, A31.

Philip, Kate, & Hendry, Leo B. (2000). Making sense of mentoring or mentoring making sense? Reflections on the mentoring process by adult mentors with young people. *Journal of Community and Applied Social Psychology, 10*, 211–223.

Phinney, Jean S. (1996). When we talk about American ethnic groups, what do we mean? *American Psychologist, 51*, 918–927.

Phinney, Jean S., Cantu, Cindy Lau, & Kurtz, Dawn A. (1997). Ethnic and American identity as predictors of self-esteem among African American, Latino, and White adolescents. *Journal of Youth and Adolescence, 26*, 165–185.

Phinney, Jean S., Ong, Anthony, & Madden, Tanya. (2000). Cultural values and intergenerational value discrepancies in immigrant and non-immigrant families. *Child Development, 71*, 528–539.

Picker, Randall C. (1997). Simple games in a complex world: A generative approach to the adoption of norms. *University of Chicago Law Review, 64*, 1225–1287.

Pink, Daniel H. (1998). Metaphor marketing. *Fast Company, 14*, 214–229.

Powers, Richard. (2000, May 7). American dreaming. *New York Times Magazine*, 66–67.

President's Council of Economic Advisors. (2000). *Teens and their parents in the 21st century: An examination of trends in teen behavior and the role of parental involvement.* Washington, DC: The White House.

Price, Richard H., Ciocci, Madalyn, Penner, Wendy, & Trautlein, Barbara. (1993). Webs of influence: School and community programs that enhance adolescent health and education. In Ruby

Takanishi (Ed.), *Adolescence in the 1990s: Risk and opportunity* (pp. 29–63). New York: Teachers College Press.

Prilleltensky, Isaac. (1999). *Columns on children, psychology, and values.* (www.radpsynet.org/docs/pril-children.html).

Profiles of general demographic characteristics, 2000: 2000 census of population and housing. (2001). Washington, DC: U.S. Department of Commerce, Bureau of the Census.

Putnam, Robert D. (1996). The strange disappearance of civic America. *American Prospect, 24,* 34–50.

Putnam, Robert D. (2000). *Bowling alone: The collapse and revival of American community.* New York: Touchstone/Simon & Schuster.

Radcliffe Public Policy Center study finds new generation of young men focusing on family first. (2000, May 3). Press Release. Cambridge, MA: Radcliffe Public Policy Center (www.radcliffe.edu/news/pr/ooo503ppc_harris.html).

Raeff, Catherine, Greenfield, Patricia Marks, & Quiroz, Blanca. (1998). Conceptualizing interpersonal relationships in the cultural contexts of individualism and collectivism. *New Directions for Child and Adolescent Development,* no. 87, 59–74.

Rhodes, Jean E., & Roffman, Jennifer G. (2003). Nonparental adults as asset builders in the lives of youth. In Richard M. Lerner & Peter L. Benson (Eds.), *Developmental assets and asset-building communities: Implications for research, policy, and programs.* New York: Kluwer Academic/Plenum.

Roehlkepartain, Eugene C. (2002). Is there room at the table for everyone? Interfaith engagement in positive child and adolescent development. In Richard M. Lerner, Francine Jacobs, & Donald Wertlieb (Eds.), *Promoting positive child, adolescent, and family development: A handbook of program and policy innovations,* Vol. 3. Thousand Oaks, CA: Sage Publications.

Rogers, Everett M. (1995). *Diffusion of innovations* (4th ed.). New York: Free Press.

Romer, Daniel, Black, Maureen, Ricardo, I., Feigelman, Susan, Kaljee, L., Galbraith, Jennifer, Nesbit, R., Hornik, Robert C., & Stanton, Bonita. (1994). Social influences on the sexual behavior of youth at risk for HIV exposure. *American Journal of Public Health, 84,* 977–985.

Rosen, Craig. (2000). Is the sequencing of change processes by stage consistent across health problems: A Meta-Analysis. *Health Psychology, 19,* 593–604.

Rosen, Jeffrey. (1997, Oct. 20). The social police: Following the law, because you'd be too embarrassed not to. *New Yorker,* pp. 170–181 (www.stuaff.niu.edu/uhs/scPolice.htm, pp. 1–10; Web page 2).

Rosen, Jeffrey. (2001, Feb. 4). In lieu of manners. *New York Times Magazine,* 46–51.

Saam, Nicole J., & Harrer, Andreas. (1999). Simulating norms, social inequality, and functional change in artificial societies. *Journal of Artificial Societies and Social Simulation, 2,* 1–21 (www.soc.surrey.ac.uk/JASSS/2/1/2.html).

Saguaro Seminar. (2001). Social Capital Community Benchmark Survey. Cambridge, MA: Harvard University, John F. Kennedy School of Government (downloaded April 4, 2001, from www.cfsv.org/communitysurvey/results/html).

Saito, Rebecca, Sullivan, Theresa K., & Hintz, Nicole. (2000). *The possible dream: What families in distressed communities need to help youth thrive.* Minneapolis: Search Institute.

Sampson, Ralph J. (1997). Collective regulation of adolescent misbehavior: Validation results from eighty Chicago neighborhoods. *Journal of Adolescent Research, 12,* 227–244.

Sampson, Ralph J., Raudenbusch, Stephen W., & Earls, Felton. (1997). Neighborhoods and violent crime: A multilevel study of collective efficacy. *Science, 277,* 918–924.

Sanders, Mavis G. (1998). The effects of school, family, and community support on the academic achievement of African American adolescents. *Urban Education, 33,* 385–409.

SAS/STAT User's Guide, Volume 1, Version 6, 4th Ed. (1990). Cary, NC: SAS Institute, Inc.

Scales, Peter C. (1997). The role of family support programs in building developmental assets among young adolescents: A national study of services and staff training needs. *Child Welfare, 76,* 611–635.

Scales, Peter C. (2001). The public image of adolescents. *Society, 38,* 64–70.

Scales, Peter C., Benson, Peter L., Leffert, Nancy, & Blyth, Dale A. (2000). Contribution of developmental assets to the prediction of thriving among adolescents. *Applied Developmental Science, 4,* 27–46.

Scales, Peter C., Benson, Peter L., & Roehlkepartain, Eugene C. (2001). *Grading grown-ups: American adults report on their real relationships with kids.* Minneapolis: Lutheran Brotherhood and Search Institute.

Scales, Peter C., Benson, Peter L., Roehlkepartain, Eugene C., Hintz, Nicole R., Sullivan, Theresa K., & Mannes, Marc. (2001). The role of neighborhood and community in building developmental assets for children and youth: A national study of social norms among American adults. *Journal of Community Psychology, 29*, 703–728.

Scales, Peter C., Blyth, Dale A., Berkas, Thomas H., & Kielsmeier, James C. (2000). The effects of service-learning on middle school students' social responsibility and academic success. *Journal of Early Adolescence, 20*, 332–359.

Scales, Peter C., & Gibbons, Judith L. (1996). Extended family members and unrelated adults in the lives of young adolescents: A research agenda. *Journal of Early Adolescence, 16*, 365–389.

Scales, Peter C., & Leffert, Nancy. (1999). *Developmental assets: A synthesis of the scientific research on adolescent development.* Minneapolis: Search Institute.

Scales, Peter C., Leffert, Nancy, & Vraa, Renee. (2003). Community developmental attentiveness and adolescent health. *American Journal of Health Behavior* (in press).

Scales, Peter C., Lucero, María Guajardo, & Halvorson, Holly. (1998). *Voices of hope: Building developmental assets for Colorado youth: Results of the Colorado adult and youth polls.* Minneapolis: Search Institute.

Scales, Peter C., Shavender, Kimberly, & Halvorson, Holly. (1999). *The role of perceived efficacy in mobilizing communities to build developmental assets among children and youth: The experience of communities in Colorado.* Minneapolis: Search Institute, unpublished paper.

Schine, Joan (Ed.). (1997). *Service learning: Ninety-sixth yearbook of the National Society for the Study of Education.* Chicago: University of Chicago Press.

Schorr, Lisbeth B. (1997). *Common purpose: Strengthening families and neighborhoods to rebuild America.* New York: Anchor.

Schorr, Lisbeth Bamberger. (1999, March). Turning voter will into successes for kids. *Next Generation Reports* (2–page insert). Santa Monica, CA: Children's Partnership.

Schwartz, Shalom H. (1970). Elicitation of moral obligation and self-sacrificing behavior: An experimental study of volunteering to be a bone marrow donor. *Journal of Personality and Social Psychology, 15*, 283–293.

Schweigert, Francis J. (1999, Feb. 2). *Mending the moral net: Moral education on strengthening personal and family networks.* St. Paul: University of St. Thomas, Dept. of Philosophy (unpublished paper).

Seligman, Martin E.P., & Csikszentmihalyi, Mihaly. (2000). Positive psychology: An introduction. *American Psychologist, 55*, 5–14.

Selznick, Phillip. (2000). Reflections on responsibility: More than just following rules. *Responsive Community, 10*, 57–61.

Sheeran, Paschal, Conner, Mark, & Norman, Paul. (2001). Can the theory of planned behavior explain patterns of health behavior change? *Health Psychology, 20*, 12–19.

Sheldon, Kennon M., & Kasser, Tim. (2001). Getting older, getting better? Personal strivings and psychological maturity across the life span. *Developmental Psychology, 37*, 491–501.

Shurnow, Lee, Vandell, Deborah L., & Posner, Jill. (1999). Risk and resilience in the urban neighborhood: Predictors of academic performance among low-income elementary school children. *Merrill-Palmer Quarterly, 45*, 309–331.

Sills, David L. (Ed.). (1968). *International encyclopedia of the social sciences.* New York: MacMillan & Free Press.

Simmons, Roberta G. (1991). Presidential address on altruism and sociology. *Sociological Quarterly, 32*, 1–22.

Small, Stephen, & Supple, Andrew. (2001). Communities as systems: Is a community more than the sum of its parts? In Alan Booth & Ann C. Crouter (Eds.), *Does it take a village? Community effects on children, adolescents, and families* (pp. 161–174). Mahwah, NJ: Lawrence Erlbaum.

Smiley, Jane. (2000, May 7). The good lie. *New York Times Magazine*, 58–59.

Software industry unites for kids. (2000). *Children's Voice* (Child Welfare League of America), *9*, 15.

SPSS Base 8.0 Applications Guide. (1998). Chicago: SPSS, Inc.

Stattin, Hakin, & Kerr, Margaret. (2000). Parental monitoring: A reinterpretation. *Child Development, 71*, 1072–1085.

Steinberg, Laurence. (2001). We know some things: Parent-adolescent relationships in retrospect and prospect. *Journal of Research on Adolescence, 11*, 1–19.

Stevenson, Howard C. (1998). Raising safe villages: Cultural-ecological factors that influence the emotional adjustment of adolescents. *Journal of Black Psychology, 24*, 44–59.

Stille, Alexander. (2000, May 20). A happiness index with a long reach. *New York Times*, A17, 19.

Sullivan, Terri. (2001). A new breed of youth volunteers. *Pregnancy Prevention for Youth: An Interdisciplinary Newsletter, 4* (2), 3–4.

Sylvester, Kathleen. (2000). *Listening to families: The role of values in shaping effective social policy.* Washington, DC: Social Policy Action Network.

Takanishi, Ruby, Mortimer, Allyn M., & McGourthy, Timothy J. (1997). Positive indicators of adolescent development: Redressing the negative image of American adolescents. In Robert M. Hauser, Brett V. Brown, & William R. Prosser (Eds.), *Indicators of children's well-being* (pp. 428–441). New York: Russell Sage Foundation.

Taylor, Shelley E., Klein, Laura Cousino, Lewis, Brian P., Greenwald, Tara L., Gurung, Regan A.R., & Updegraff, John A. (2000). Biobehavioral responses to stress in females: Tend-and-befriend, not fight-or-flight. *Psychological Review, 107*, 411–429.

Teaching financial values that last a lifetime. (1999, Sept. 30). *Northern Funds Quarterly Portfolio Update*, 4–5.

Teachman, Jay D., Tedrow, Lucky M., & Crowder, Kyle D. (2000). The changing demography of America's families. *Journal of Marriage and the Family, 62*, 1234–1246.

Time with mothers and fathers. (2001, May 23). *Education Week, 20* (37), 4.

Tocqueville, Alexis de. (1835/2000). *Democracy in America.* New York: Bantam.

Trends in the well-being of America's children and youth, 1998. (1998). Washington, DC: U.S. Department of Health and Human Services, Office of the Assistant Secretary for Planning and Evaluation.

Turow, Joseph. (1997). Breaking up America: The dark side of target marketing. *American Demographics, 19*, 51–54.

Tyson, Ben, & Coulter, Robin. (1999). Marketing enlightened self-interest: A model of individual and community-oriented motivations. *Social Marketing Quarterly, 5*, 34–49.

Urberg, Kathryn A., Shyu, Shiang-Jeou, & Liang, Jersey (1990). Peer influence in adolescent cigarette smoking. *Addictive Behaviors, 15*, 247–255.

Vandell, Deborah L. (2000). Parents, peer groups, and other socializing influences. *Developmental Psychology, 36*, 699–710.

Voydanoff, Patricia, & Donnelly, Brenda W. (1998). Parents' risk and protective factors as predictors of parental well-being and behavior. *Journal of Marriage and the Family, 60*, 344–355.

Wade, Nicholas. (2000, June 27). Now, the hard part: Putting the genome to work. *New York Times*, D1, 4.

Walsh. Mark. (2000, June 14). Court affirms rights of parents to control children's upbringing. *Education Week, 19* (40), 22.

Webb, Eugene J., Campbell, Donald T., Schwartz, Richard D., & Sechrest, Lee. (1972). *Unobtrusive measures: Nonreactive research in the social sciences.* Chicago: Rand McNally.

Werner, Emily E., & Smith, Ruth S. (1992). *Overcoming the odds: High risk children from birth to adulthood.* Ithaca, NY: Cornell University Press.

What grown-ups understand about child development: A national benchmark study. (2000). Washington, DC: Zero to Three.

What teens are saying: Highlights of the 2001 Uhlich Report Card grades. Chicago: Uhlich Children's Home (www.uhlich.org/reportcard).

Williams, Robin M., Jr. (1968a). The concept of norms. In D.L. Sills (Ed.), *International encyclopedia of the social sciences* (Vol. 16, pp. 204–208). New York: Free Press.

Williams, Robin M., Jr. (1968b). The concept of values. In D.L. Sills (Ed.), *International encyclopedia of the social sciences* (Vol. 16, pp. 283–287). New York: Free Press.

Wolfe, Alan. (2000, May 7). The pursuit of autonomy. *New York Times Magazine*, 53–56.

Wood, Wendy. (2001). Attitude change: Persuasion and social influence. *Annual Review of Psychology, 52*, 539–570.

Wood, Wendy, Christensen, P. Niels, Hebl, Michelle R., & Rothgerber, Hank. (1997). Conformity to sex-typed norms, affect, and the self-concept. *Journal of Personality and Social Psychology, 71*, 523–535.

Wuthnow, Robert. (1994). *God and mammon in America.* New York: Free Press.

Young, H. Peyton. (1998). Social norms and economic welfare. *European Economic Review, 42*, 821–830.

Youth and money: Results of the 1999 Youth and Money Survey. (1999). Washington, DC: American Savings Education Council.

Youth involvement. (1998, August 27). *Lutheran Brotherhood Reports: A survey of American beliefs, attitudes, and practices.* Minneapolis: Lutheran Brotherhood.

Zill, Nicholas. (1999). *Setting an example: The health, medical care, and health-related behavior of American parents.* Washington, DC: Child Trends.

About the Author

Peter C. Scales, Ph.D., senior fellow in the Office of the President at Search Institute, is a developmental psychologist widely recognized as a leading authority on adolescent development, family relationships, effective schools, and healthy communities. He directed the national study of adult engagement with children and youth on which this book is based. In addition to more than 250 scientific articles and chapters, Dr. Scales is author or coauthor of more than a dozen books and monographs, including *Developmental Assets: A Synthesis of the Scientific Research on Adolescent Development* (Search Institute), *Great Places to Learn: How Asset-Building Schools Help Students Succeed* (Search Institute), *A Portrait of Young Adolescents in the 1990s* (Search Institute/Center for Early Adolescence), and *The Sexual Adolescent: Communicating with Teenagers About Sex* (Duxbury Press).

Index

United States Census Bureau, 7
United States Supreme Court, 17
Unrelated adults, 14–15, 18–19, 24, 28–33,
    92–93; *see also* Nonparental adults

Values: *see* Social values
Vandell, Deborah L., 23, 25
Violence, 11–12
Volunteerism, 29–30, 50, 50n, 68, 171–174

Well-being, indicators of, 26
Werner, Emily E., 47, 74
White House Conference on Teenagers,
    32
Williams, Robin M., 42
Wolfe, Allan, 67
Wood, Wendy, 59

Women, 150, 154–158
Wuthnow, Robert, 120

Youth
    African American, 11
    at-risk, 7, 10–11, 25, 32
    gender and, 157
    healthy development of, 10, 18, 20–24, 22,
        47–48
    marginalization of, 64
    negative images of, 70–74
    neighborhood influences on, 24
    schooling, 55, 112
    social norms and, 75
    unrelated adults and, 28–33

Zero to Three, 73